cybering democracy

electronic mediations

Katherine Hayles
Mark Poster
Samuel Weber
Series Editors

cybering democracy

Public Space and the Internet   **Diana Saco**

MINNESOTA

Electronic Mediations, Volume 7

University of Minnesota Press   Minneapolis / London

Published by the University of Minnesota Press
111 Third Avenue South, Suite 290
Minneapolis, MN 55401-2520
http://www.upress.umn.edu

Library of Congress Cataloging-in-Publication Data

Saco, Diana.
    Cybering democracy : public space and the Internet / Diana Saco.
        p.   cm. —   (Electronic mediations ; v. 7)
    Includes bibliographical references and index.
    ISBN 0-8166-3540-4 (HC : alk. paper) — ISBN 0-8166-3541-2 (PB : alk. paper)
    1. Internet—Political aspects.   2. Cyberspace—Political aspects.
  3. Internet—Social aspects.   4. Cyberspace—Social aspects.   5. Democracy.
  6. Information society.   7. Public spaces.   8. Body, human.   I. Title.   II. Series.
    HM851 .S23 2002
    303.48'33—dc21

                                                              2002000861

Printed in the United States of America on acid-free paper

The University of Minnesota is an equal-opportunity educator and employer.

12 11 10 09 08 07 06 05 04 03 02   10 9 8 7 6 5 4 3 2 1

To my sister Nikki Saco,
who made this possible in countless ways
beginning with the sage advice that I should get a modem

Contents

Acknowledgments

This book exists because I've had the privilege of knowing some very remarkable people whose intelligence, generosity, and support sustained me through an occasionally difficult process. First, my doctoral advisor and friend Lisa Disch provided encouragement and guidance at each step of this project, which began with a conversation in a coffee shop in Minneapolis where Lisa convinced me that "this cyberspace thing" I had become so interested in was worth pursuing. I could not have written this study without her input and anything else would have been unsatisfying. Second, my colleague, cohort, and friend Mark Laffey read and commented on early drafts of various chapters and sections and helped me through a tough argument on more than one occasion. What Mark provided me with, in the process, was critical perspective, coherence, a sense of purpose, confidence, an abundance of laughter, and the will to get it done. Third, my twin sister and lifelong partner in crime Nikki Saco read through several chapters and reminded me repeatedly what my argument was when I seemed to be getting lost in the details. A paralegal by vocation and a writer at heart, Nikki is one of the smartest people I know and a consummate critic, prodding me always to keep it simple and get to the point. Readers will regret that I didn't take her advice more often.

Many more colleagues and friends helped me formulate the ideas developed here. For stimulating conversations and constructive criticisms on one or more parts of this and related projects, I thank Jennifer Milliken, Jutta Weldes, Ellen Messer-Davidow, Bud Duvall, John Mowitt, Dick Price, Michael Shapiro, Clay Steinman, Tarak Barkawi, Hugh Gusterson, Mike Barnett, Edward Kolodziej, Jonathan Hill, Naeem Inayatoullah,

David Blaney, Ralph Litzinger, Alex Wendt, Himadeep Muppidi, Steve Niva, Shampa Biswas, John Borneman, Pamela Ballinger, Elisabeth Binder, and Joel Grossman. For additional comments and insights (via e-mail) on chapter 1, particularly in connection with his own work on *heterotopia*, I'm extremely grateful to Kevin Hetherington (whom I've never actually met face-to-face). I'd also like to give a special thanks to Mary Dietz, who first taught me about political theory.

The editors at the University of Minnesota Press made the process of turning a four-pound manuscript into a hardbound book painless enough that I might actually consider doing this kind of thing again someday. For their guidance and patience, I'd especially like to thank Richard Morrison, Pieter Martin, and William Murphy (who is no longer with the press but was very helpful in the early stages of the publication process). Copy editor Linda Lincoln did a marvelous job correcting my errors and offering a number of fine suggestions for finalizing the manuscript. I'm also grateful to the editors of the Electronic Mediations series—Mark Poster, Samuel Weber, and Katherine Hayles—whose own works provided me with a great deal of insight and inspiration.

Finally, thanks to the rest of my family and friends—especially Bertha Saco, Ernesto J. Sacoibarra, Darcy Bunce, Cookie Rainey, and Ernie Saco—for giving me the emotional support to complete this project. And a very special thanks to my niece Alexis, who was born shortly before I began this project in earnest. As I babysat her while also writing this study, she proved a constant source of amusing distraction, providing me with a balanced set of priorities and making the process of reading theory almost fun. For her part, Alex learned how to use the Escape key on my computer before she turned two. When I first considered that, I wondered if it had a deeper philosophical meaning that I hadn't yet discovered. I now think it constitutes an apt social commentary for our times and spaces ... and maybe even (at least occasionally) for our bodies.

D.S.
dsaco@gate.net

The Politics of Visibility

On 5 August 1993, convicted murderer Joseph Paul Jernigan was executed by lethal injection in Huntsville, Texas, leaving to scientific research, at his own request, the otherwise healthy corpse of a well-developed, thirty-nine-year-old male who was free from the ravages of disease, age, and trauma. Technicians of the state anatomical board placed Jernigan's body in one and a half gallons of one-percent formalin for temporary preservation and transported it by jet to the dissection lab of the University of Colorado Health Sciences Center. There the remains were scanned by magnetic resonance imaging (MRI) and computerized tomography (CT), frozen, and then CT scanned again, giving the dissection team an anatomical map to refer to later for alignment purposes. Using a carbide-tipped blade, the lab technicians then proceeded to saw through Jernigan's body, cutting it into four sections of approximately the same length—head to a torso, abdomen to a pelvis, thighs to knees, and calves to feet. To secure the forearm-and-hand sections next to the abdominal section and the pairs of leg sections symmetrically to each other, technicians placed corresponding body parts into aluminum molds, filled the molds with a blue gel, and then refroze the contents, producing four ice blocks of the portioned cadaver, each measuring about twenty by twenty by fifteen inches. The bluish cubes were then taken to a grinding area that was enclosed by Plexiglas to avoid debris from the corpse flying everywhere as it was sectioned further. Over the next several months, the quartered and twice-frozen body of Joseph Paul Jernigan was painstakingly sliced, millimeter by millimeter, into 1,871 cross sections. As they sectioned the corpse further, technicians polished and digitally photographed (in twenty-four-bit color) each sliver of Jernigan's body, giving them axial images, at one-millimeter increments, of his organs, tissues, and bones in their exact orientation to each other. By the time the sawing, photographing, and digitizing were complete, the lab crew had compiled a fifteen-gigabyte, anatomical data set of what they felt was a near-perfect male specimen (despite an absent appendix and a missing testicle). In the fall of 1994, as part of the National Library of Medicine's Visible Human Project (VHP), these electronic images of the insides of Joseph Paul Jernigan were posted on the Internet.[1]

For those involved, the VHP has accomplished what it set out to do. By photographing cross sections of a corpse and making the raw images available in electronic form, members of the project created a virtual resource that other medical professionals, both commercial and academic, could use to put together digital human atlases, clinical-diagnostic programs, pharmacological software analyzing the effects of certain drugs, and even supplemental practice programs that could allow medical students to amputate an arm, remove a kidney, or perform a coronary bypass. Their hopes realized, Jernigan has become, according to one commentator, a "medical tool extraordinaire and ultimate guinea pig" (Anthony 1996). The reference to a guinea pig, as much a test subject of the high-school biology lab as of the professional medical lab, highlights the central goal of this project. According to its purveyors, the VHP was meant to distribute knowledge to people both inside and outside the medical profession by giving them the chance to glimpse the inner workings of the human body. In other words, laypeople could now gain access to a type of formerly privileged knowledge. UCLA radiologist Dr. Paul Chesis, who incorporated the VHP images into his virtual anatomy software, summarized his interest in the project in the following manner: "We wanted to democratize this information" (Anthony 1996).

At one time, that claim seemed to me wholly unremarkable: to put anatomical data on computers is to *democratize information*. The conceptual path from the former to the latter was like an instantaneous electrical connection that makes the needle in a battery tester sweep all the way to the right to indicate a full charge and then sweep back home to a place that when our synapses are fired up by our own thoughts we call "understanding" and that when they are fired up by others' words we call "communication." (Something about the subject matter—anatomy on computers—makes this combination of neurological and electrical metaphors seem appropriate.) Were we to trace, however, all the synaptic connections that have to fire off in our brains from one nerve ending to another—all the definitions, articulations, presuppositions, and paradigms of thought—in order for us to make sense out of that statement (to arrive home, as it were), we would find that, in fact, quite a lot of discursive energy is required to get from *computers* to *data* to *information* to *communication* to *democracy*. This study is fundamentally about how those flows of thought are generated and disrupted and, more modestly, about how to generate a few new ones.

The claim that projects like the VHP democratize information rests on several rather pervasive discourses that have helped to pattern and normalize these connections (most of them implicit) between democracy, universal access, communication, informed citizens, scientific knowledge, and the progressive faith that they can all be united through technological innovations like the Internet. Read as such, the VHP draws from and contributes further to a growing literature, in both the popular media and official U.S. government pronouncements, about the democratic potential of computer networking (e.g., Friedland 1996; Browning 1996; Bowen 1996; cf., Wright 1995). On the basis of these apparently self-evident claims, then–Vice President Al Gore, in a 1994 meeting of the International Telecommunications Union in Argentina, lauded the benefits of a "Global Information Infrastructure" (GII) by making the still bolder declaration that computer networking could actually usher in "a new Athenian Age of democracy." The speech is worth quoting at length for the remarkable metaphor Gore engineers, likening citizens to microprocessors and the GII to a form of participatory democracy that could harness the power of all these parallel civic computers:

> [T]he distributed intelligence of the GII will spread participatory democracy.
>
> To illustrate why, I'd like to use an example from computer science. In the past, all computers were huge mainframes with a single processing unit, solving problems in sequence, one by one, each bit of information sent back and forth between the CPU and the vast field of memory surrounding it. Now, we have massively parallel computers with hundreds—or thousands—of tiny self-contained processors distributed throughout the memory field, all interconnected, and together far more powerful and more versatile than even the most sophisticated single processor, because they each solve a tiny piece of the problem simultaneously, and when all the pieces are assembled, the problem is solved.
>
> Similarly, the GII will be an assemblage of local, national, and

regional networks that are not only like parallel computers but in their most advanced state will in fact be a distributed, parallel computer.

In a sense, the GII will be a metaphor for democracy itself. Representative democracy does not work with an all-powerful central government, arrogating all decisions to itself. That is why communism collapsed.

Instead, representative democracy relies on the assumption that the best way for a nation to make its political decisions is for each citizen—the human equivalent of the self-contained processor—to have the power to control his or her own life.

To do that, people must have available the information they need. And be allowed to express their conclusions in free speech and in votes that are combined with those of millions of others. That's what guides the system as a whole.

The GII will not only be a metaphor for a functioning democracy, it will in fact promote the functioning of democracy by greatly enhancing the participation of citizens in decision making. And it will greatly promote the ability of nations to cooperate with each other. I see a new Athenian Age of democracy forged in the fora the GII will create. (1994)

Despite the apparent anachronism, other commentators have made this connection between an ancient political ethos and a seemingly futuristic form of communication. Computer writer Howard Rheingold, for example, argues, if a bit more critically, that "the vision of a citizen-designed, citizen-controlled worldwide communications network is a version of technological utopianism that could be called the vision of 'the electronic agora'" (1993, 14). A term of classical Greek extraction, the Athenian agora was not simply an open space but more fundamentally a public space where the ecclesia, the popular assembly of Athenian citizens, could gather, exchange information, engage each other in debate, and deliberate issues affecting the polis (see Held 1987, 1–35). In this sense, the term links a particular kind of space to certain democratic practices, especially open discussion and deliberation. Those discussions, however, were face-to-face. That is, the spatiality of democracy, in this context, presumed physical bodies gathered together in a physical space, a point that has not been lost on advocates of direct democracy, who have insisted that true democracy can exist only in small polities, built on "human scale" (Sale 1980), where citizens can gather and appear before each other in the flesh without having to travel onerous distances.

If this is the ideal evoked by the notion that computer networks are forging "a new Athenian Age of democracy," our flows of thought require some rather radical rearticulations of space and body for us to settle back into the calm assertion that this notion makes. Discourses about the Internet already evoke (almost relentlessly) different spatial understandings in their ubiquitous references to specific online sites, rooms, and forums, and more generally in terms of an electronic agora, the Electronic Frontier, the Information Superhighway, or quite simply cyberspace. Rather than dismiss Gore's comments as hype and these Internet spatial references as mere metaphors, I want to suggest that we take these explicit references seriously. What interests me here is how the discursive move (the flow of thought) might be made from the ideal of an Athenian agora grounded in physical space and fleshy bodies to one of an electronic agora that is also grounded but in a cyber space and in digital bodies. What makes possible these different inflections of *space, body, visibility, gather, meet, face,* and so forth that are tacitly presupposed in associating cyberspace with Athenian democracy?

Questions like this one cannot be addressed adequately within the limits of current debates about the Internet. Thus far, Internet commentary has tended to fall into two broad camps. In what has been characterized by critics (and even by some sympathizers, like Rheingold) as the "technological utopian" position are those who argue that computer networking is revolutionizing society in positive ways. According to this view, technological advances like the Internet democratize information by simplifying the creation, duplication, storage, and distribution of data. In addition, networking via computers also facilitates communication among a larger number and broader spectrum of individuals, enabling people from different remote locations to associate with each other, to engage in economic transactions and political debates, and, more generally, to make their opinions matter by having their voices heard. In the "technological dystopian" position—also referred to as the neo-Luddite position by its opponents—stand those detractors who claim that computer networking, like other modern technologies, is changing society in decidedly negative ways. Critics argue that the burgeoning flows of data that computers have made possible are serving primarily to numb people with a glut of unnecessary and often inaccurate information. The investments of personal time and money actually needed to go online, moreover, further isolate and disaffect individuals from their communities, create an ever wider gap between the knowledge-rich and the knowledge-poor, and distract people from social problems and collective-action remedies by giving them a false sense of political effectiveness.

To the apologists of high tech, in short, computer networking provides solutions to many of the problems of space, population, access, and participation that confront large societies. To critics, on the other hand, such technologies exaggerate these problems by further alienating people from each other and even from themselves. These arguments raise interesting and important questions about the role of public communication in democracy—how citizens talk to each other, exchange ideas, assess the validity of the information they share, and deliberate different courses of action—and about how new media affect the prospects for this type of communication. Ultimately, however, both sides offer deficient responses to these critical issues. Maintaining that adequate democratic participation does not have to be direct (i.e., a face-to-face encounter), proponents assert that the Internet simply *is* democratic in some way; precisely how this is meant, however, remains vague. By contrast, opponents of technological fixes, who discount anything other than direct participation, argue that the Internet is yet another coercive technology, restructuring our daily lives in often antidemocratic and asocial ways. This position, too, however, is problematic precisely because it denies (and therefore ignores) questions of agency, of how Internet users might appropriate, explore, and realize other, more progressive, uses of this technology.

The fundamental issue underlying these extreme positions is whether an electronically mediated democracy can exist. Are the forms of public communication that are central to the proper functioning of a democratic polity possible under conditions of electronic mediation (and if so, which forms, e.g., Internet but not television?), or must public communication always be unmediated to avoid its distortion, its delimitation, and its control by interested and powerful others? Opponents and proponents of the Internet reach a kind of impasse on this issue.

In this study, I complicate these two positions to move beyond this impasse. I complicate utopian assessments of the Internet by exploring the spatiality of cyberspace, showing how it is produced as a social space and in ways that occasionally (perhaps often) reproduce existing power asymmetries, despite the faith that the Internet is a unique medium of communication that gives us a fresh, unencumbered, nondiscriminatory, and universally accessible way of being and acting in the world. I complicate the dystopian position by showing how far cyberspace has developed, by the agency of its users, as a space for exploration and experimentation, opening to critical analysis the role of the body in communicating our needs and our identities.

Three issues are at stake for me in this inquiry. First, I want to show how our theories of democracy have presupposed "elaborate spatial strategies" (Shapiro 1992, 4). Democracy, in other words, is related to space. We need to begin exploring that relationship to analyze some of the different ways in which democracy has been, is, and can be spatialized. Second, I want to suggest that many of our democratic theories reach a dead end in addressing problems of public communication and collective action because they begin with a rather limited conception of what constitutes spatiality. Space has been too narrowly defined in physical terms: for example, as an area within which bodies move. Third, I want to propose alternative notions of social space to broaden our flows of thought about democracy, particularly in the context of some of our current technologies. If we rethink spatiality, we can begin better to understand how cyberspace becomes a social space and one, more to the point, that is challenging and changing the ways we think and do politics. These flows of thought, I argue, turn on three central concepts, which are the focal point of this study: namely, *space, technology,* and the *body.* The Visible Human Project, as the following introductory analysis suggests, invokes and rearticulates this relational triad in provocative and illuminating ways.

The Virtual Body of the Condemned

In two of his classic works, *The Birth of the Clinic* (1994a) and *Discipline and Punish* (1979), Michel Foucault links the visibility of the body with the unfolding of the modern disciplinary practices of pathology and penology, respectively. In the former, Foucault locates the origin of contemporary medical knowledge—the "anatomo-clinical method"—in the "discursive space of the corpse: the interior revealed" (196). An emergent medical discourse, in short, spatialized the body, reconstituting it as an area to be visually explored.[2] So, when in the late 1700s and early 1800s doctors resolved to "open up a few corpses" (146), they fundamentally redefined the medical gaze. Before this shift, clinical understanding had rested on a superficial examination of observable symptoms in living organisms. Death, by contrast, had constituted the limits of this knowledge—"the great dark threat in which [the doctor's] knowledge and skill were abolished" (146). This notion of death as darkness gave way to the conviction that only through analysis of the internally visible corpse could the invisible workings of life and disease be revealed (159).

In what amounted to a reversal of perspective, then, death had become day and life night. Foucault, in his characteristically taunting fashion, underscores the irony:

> With the coming of the Enlightenment, death, too, was entitled to the clear light of reason, and became for the philosophical mind an object and source of knowledge. . . . A fine transmutation of the corpse had taken place: gloomy respect had condemned it to putrefaction, to the dark work of destruction; in the boldness of the gesture that violated only to reveal, to bring to the light of day, the corpse became the brightest moment in the figures of truth. Knowledge spins where once larva was formed. (125)

In *Discipline and Punish,* the story Foucault tells of the birth of the prison hinges, as well, on the visibility of the body and processes of spatialization: here not with the body *as* space, but rather with the body *in* space. He begins with a graphic retelling of an eighteenth-century incident: the public torture and execution of a condemned regicide named Damiens.[3] Foucault then notes a shift in modern societies from the spectacle of torture as a method of individual punishment and social control to the surveillance of prisoners—notably, through the architectural innovation of Jeremy Bentham's *panopticon.* The panopticon was a prison designed to heighten inmates' sense that they could be constantly and covertly monitored by authorities. The cells were arranged in a circular pattern, several floors high, around a central tower from which an unseen-but-potentially-all-seeing guard could watch any prisoner through the bars of his or her cell. At the same time, the sides of the cells were walled to isolate the prisoners from each other, further limiting their own ability to see and interact with others. For Foucault, the most telling feature of this *pan-optic* design was how it made visibility "a trap" (200). The inmate "is seen, but he does not see; he is the object of information, never a subject in communication" (200). The point is not that the panopticon gave authorities the power to watch all prisoners at all times, which is physically impossible, but rather the way its spatial configuration situated the inmate in that field of vision—that is, as visible at any time but never aware of precisely when he was being watched. The defining feature of panopticism, then, is that it enables a form of seemingly pervasive, covert surveillance that, in turn, fosters in the object of visibility (the prisoner) a form of self-discipline: it engenders, in short, the will to behave because the guards might be watching.[4]

Like the corpse of the recently deceased, then, the body of the condemned underwent a change from being the object of a superficial gaze (the spectacle of torture) to becoming the site of a more penetrating (because internalized) gaze. It became the target of a *technique* of surveillance that—together with other techniques for partitioning space (into individuated grids) and serializing time (into schedules) and regulating movement within these spatial stalls and temporal installments— disciplined the body, instructed it, shaped its activities down to the smallest detail through the imposition of timetables, procedures, drills, and tactics. Here, too, Foucault comments with some irony on the nature of this shift to the more penetrating gaze of panopticism—except here the irony is that we are all, in a sense, *free inmates:*

> Our society is one not of spectacle, but of surveillance; under the surface of images, one invests bodies in depth; behind the great abstraction of exchange, there continues the meticulous, concrete training of useful forces; the circuits of communication are the supports of an accumulation and a centralization of knowledge; the play of signs defines the anchorages of power; it is not that the beautiful totality of the individual is amputated, repressed, altered by our social order, it is rather that the individual is carefully fabricated in it, according to a whole technique of forces and bodies. (217)

Foucault's point is three-pronged. He notes, first, that surveillance is more insidious because more invasive, ubiquitous, and controlling, but he also argues, second, that its techniques produce (fabricate) rather than simply repress the Enlightenment individual. Hence, it is not just social control that is produced here, but also freedom. In fact, control and freedom—like power and resistance—are mutually constituted. Finally, central to these techniques for creating disciplined subjects are "the circuits of communication" with which information ostensibly about us is manufactured, compiled, sold, and distributed. These, then, are the defining features of modern, disciplinary societies: productive techniques of freedom and social control that include, at their base, technologies of communication for the production, reproduction, and dissemination of disciplinary knowledges.

The Visible Human Project invites a reading through the parallax of Foucault's two studies. In both name and practice, it exemplifies and even exaggerates—through "the violence of the dissected corpse" (Foucault 1994a, 159)—the extent to which the body can be opened up to a penetrating anatomo-clinical gaze. At the same time, detailed accounts of the project in the popular press can scarcely avoid some kind of commentary that seeks to justify the clinical dissection of a human being by identifying the body in question as having belonged to a "condemned killer," thereby implying that the violence done to it, much like the torture of Damiens, is a fitting kind of social justice under the circumstances. This is not, of course, a feature of the scientific discourse on the VHP. In fact, none of the documents at the NLM Web site identify the male body of the VHP as Jernigan's, an anonymity that makes sense given the way that the medical discourse inscribes this body as an acceptable stand-in for *any* body—i.e., as normal. The popular imaginary, by contrast, has been much exercised by the fact that the Visible Man was an executed murderer. Reporter Ted Anthony, for example, begins his summary of the project by noting, "Alive, he wasn't much. Joseph Paul Jernigan spent many of his 39 years as drug abuser, alcoholic, robber, killer. . . . But the conclusion of [his] mortal existence sent his body on a most unusual odyssey that has made him into something life couldn't—a productive member of society" (1996). Even David Rothman, in his considerably more sanguine treatment of Jernigan, seems compelled to justify the violence done to his body. He constructs Jernigan as a man who "felt so contrite that he wanted to die," refers to Jernigan's bequest as "The Gift," and notes that even though Jernigan did not know at the time that he would become the Visible Man, he very likely would have been "happy" and "delighted" (1996, 184, 194).

When viewed in light of these biographical accounts, the painfully graphic images of Jernigan's anatomized body seem to signal a return to spectacle—to the practice of setting apart, of making Other, exemplified by the hypervisibility of the multiply dismembered cadaver of a murderer.[5] The irony here, as Foucault might have noted, is that despite these efforts at distancing, what qualified Jernigan for "Visible Manhood" (Rothman 1996, 182) was precisely the fact that he could stand in, as it were, for almost any healthy male. If the images haunt and disturb, perhaps it is because Jernigan's generic male body is made to suffer indignities that indeed any body could, in principle, suffer.[6] It is our own subtle awareness of this possibility that invites us to empathize, to be both amazed and appalled when we hear details about the project: "'Wow,' I thought . . . (And: 'Ew')" (Laskas 1996). This "wow" and this "ew" are honest expressions of the ambiguities that such images, perhaps rightly so, engender in us.[7]

That these images were splattered over the Internet "for all to see" (Anthony 1996) is the most compelling aspect of this story for me. The Internet is part of (indeed magnifies) the violence perpetrated here: not the violence of the scalpel, but of visibility itself.[8] In a sense, Foucault's references to "the violence" to which the dissected corpse is subjected cannot be a violence *for* the corpse any more than chopping is an act of violence for the wood. Inanimate objects, corpses included, cannot feel. To the extent this is so, the violence experienced here is something that a sentient onlooker, through her own feelings of empathy, displaces onto the corpse. It is through this transference that the onlooker, like a Dr. Frankenstein, brings the corpse to life again and imagines *its* pain and humiliation. The violence therefore is not in the cutting, but in the looking. It is in the duplicitous gaze that empathizes as it invades. Placing these images on the Internet opens the body up not just to the distanced inspection of clinical analysis, but to multiple, anonymous, gaping stares, constituting, as Rothman notes, "the ultimate invasion of privacy" (1996, 195).

"The ultimate invasion of privacy": that phrase, too, when I first read it, seemed self-evident. Of course, the account with which I began this introduction—in its painful detail—plays off the horrified sentiment expressed by the notion that corpses can have their privacy invaded, can have violence done to them, can feel pain. But this notion, too, is another one of those flows of thought that the translation of bodies into bits further disrupts. When the body is digitized, it is not just that anatomical information is transferred to a different medium, but rather that data are created (Poster 1990, 94). This conversion is both prosaic and insidious. What started out as flesh and blood becomes just another way of arranging pixels on a computer screen (Waldby 1996b).[9] In the process, the body is materialized through very different normalizing discourses (Butler 1993). No longer the site of an embodied identity with a rich biography, it becomes instead, in this instance, a space of exploration: either serious (when converted into medical programs) or playful (when converted into video games) or most often both, as in the new interactive media category of "edutainment."[10] It is worth noting, in this respect, that one proposed use of the Visible Human data set (Rothman 1996, 173) is to create a computer-game version of Isaac Asimov's sci-fi adventure *Fantastic Voyage,* in which a team of intrepid doctors in a submarine are miniaturized to microscopic size and injected into the body of an ailing scientist to destroy a blood clot in his brain.[11] Digitized images can be integrated into a variety of interactive programs that simulate (rather than simply represent) physical events, conditions, and phenomena, and this incorporation—the materialization of bodies in a different field of discourse (involving integrated circuits on silicon chips rather than bundles of carbon-based molecules)—helps to change our understandings of the body. Simulation parodies the physical in a way that potentially (perhaps often) mocks and disrupts it. As a consequence, meanings and concerns that matter in our fleshy encounters—a patient's pain, a person's death—may become irrelevant in digital simulations.[12]

What status can the physical body retain in a place like cyberspace? In a sense, once identities are projected into cyberspace (as virtual personae) and embodied, if at all, in digital bodies, the physical body can be dispensed with, forgotten. At its most basic level, cyberspace constructs the physical body as *meat* and the physical space it inhabits as "meatspace" (Barlow 1995). Speculative-fiction author William Gibson, who first coined the term *cyberspace* in a lesser known story (1982), conveys this understanding of the human flesh within the first few pages of *Neuromancer* (1984), the novel that made the term famous. Case, the story's protagonist, is described as a former data thief—a one-time "console man . . . [or] cyberspace cowboy"—who, with the benefit of neural implants in his brain, had regularly "jacked into a custom cyberspace deck that projected his disembodied consciousness into the consensual hallucination that was the matrix" (5). Once inside the matrix, he would invade corporate systems and steal valuable data for his employers. One day, however, he made the fateful mistake of stealing from those employers. When the story opens, then, he is no longer able to jack in: the result of a neuro-inhibiting drug injected into him by his former bosses as payback for his betrayal. Gibson describes Case's predicament this way: "For Case, who'd lived for the *bodiless exultation of cyberspace,* it was the Fall. In the bars he'd frequented as a cowboy hotshot, the elite stance involved a certain relaxed contempt for the flesh. *The body was meat.* Case fell into the prison of his own flesh" (6, my emphasis; cf., Heim 1993, 75). Though treated, arguably, with more care than contempt (given its importance as the central object of knowledge for the VHP), Jernigan's flesh, too, has in significant ways become meat: *raw data* for a wide variety of computer programs. As Rothman notes, the light solution of formalin used to preserve Jernigan's body in transport to the dissection lab was intended expressly "to keep his tissue looking nice and bright like prime meat" (1996, 184). Cyberspace exaggerates this sense of the body as meat by offering the casual observer a form of "information" that is out of context. Lacking the anatomo-clinical knowledge to interpret what they see as part of a human body, the uninitiated are more apt to see an image that to them looks remarkably like something one might have picked up at a butcher's shop.

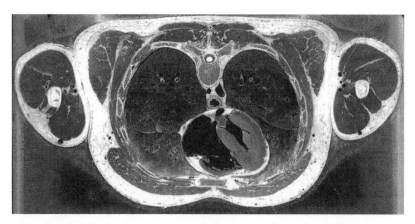

Figure 1. The body as "meat." Reprint of the sample image of a thorax cryosection from the National Library of Medicine's Visible Human Project. Downloaded from and reproduced courtesy of the National Library of Medicine. Retrieved 22 August 2000 from http://www.nlm.nih.gov/research/visible/image/thorax.jpg.

This image, of course, exaggerates the point and intentionally so. I mean it as a ludicrous overstatement—but for that reason, a very vivid illustration—of one of the ways cyberspace redefines the body as abject, as meat. The VHP seems to belie this claim if focus is placed on the great skill and care that the dissection team applied in their handling of Jernigan's body, but consider the point of the project. In digitizing and saving images of this standard male, the creators of the VHP hoped as well to help future researchers dispense with the body, to enable at least some anatomy lessons to proceed without the presence of a body. This conversion of flesh to bits transforms the body into a medium (binary code) that is infinitely reproducible (without cloning), easily stored (without freezers), almost instantaneously available (without transport), and extremely durable (without preservatives).

There are other bodies and spaces, of course, that never make it into cyberspace in even mock digital form. In his analysis "Forsaken Geographies: Cyberspace and the New World 'Other'" (1996), Olu Oguibe describes attending a conference in Guadalajara, Mexico, where a boy of about five, a poor street performer, had entered the hotel lobby where the conference was being held and had been making gestures toward the staff and visitors. Unable to communicate what he wanted, he had been hastened away by one of the hotel staff, who had understood anyway, he later explained, that all the boy had wanted was water. In recounting this incident, Oguibe highlights the following points: "[T]his story . . . is about communication, or the failure of communication. It is also about location and privilege. It is about power and its proclivity for insensitivity. It is about priorities, also." He explains that for many like the boy, cyberspace is not a reality.

My point in reciting this story is not to oversentimentalize bodies in need, though maybe some of that is inevitable and appropriate. Rather, what I want to foreground are the ways in which the cultures that construct cyberspace as a space of bodiless exultation construct the physical body—the body that eats, drinks, sleeps, gets sick, and dies, as Sandy Stone says (Leeson 1996, 114)—as in many respects the abject body, the forgotten body. "Forgetting about the body," Stone points out, "is an old Cartesian trick, one that has unpleasant consequences for those bodies whose speech is silenced by the act of our forgetting; that is to say, those upon whose labor the act of forgetting the body is founded—usually women and minorities" (1993, 113).

Here then are two bodies and two politics of the body. One is digital (the Visible Man); the other is abject (the boy's). One is subjected to the violence of a hypervisibility; the other is relegated to a realm of invisibility. One becomes the splayed public display of the ultimate invasion of privacy; the other is hastily driven out of public view. And both, from the standpoint of cyberspace, are meat.

Space, Technology, and the Body

"Politics," Stone observes, "works through physical bodies" (Leeson 1996, 114). Indeed, as Foucault's own work has shown, relations of power in contemporary societies are manifested in a variety of disciplinary techniques that are organized around the visibility of the body. To the extent this is so, physical presence before others is a rather risky venture. The paradigmatic ideal for a kind of participatory democracy, however, has been the agora: an ostensibly egalitarian physical space where citizens could have a say, in part because they were physically present, there in the flesh. Being seen, making an appearance before fellow citizens, was a necessary (though not sufficient) condition for becoming empowered, for being a political actor.[13] In one respect, Oguibe's story participates in this ideal. The story he tells is fundamentally about how people are disempowered by being excluded from certain spaces, such as cyberspace. Even while he criticizes utopian claims about the democratic potentials of cyberspace, however, he makes the following challenge: "[T]hat we begin to explore with greater seriousness and humanism [the] means of extending the numerous, practical possibilities of this new technology to the greater majority of humanity" (1996). Hence, despite his criticisms, the technology still retains for him a certain emancipatory promise, which is why it needs, in his account, to be democratized, made accessible to others. Foucault reminds us, however, that if invisibility is disempowering, visibility is a trap (1979, 200). Being seen always comes at a price.

The politics of cyberspace, I want to suggest, foreground these ambiguities in salient ways. Whether by enabling a virtual anatomized body that becomes a quasi-medical exploratory space or by enabling computer forums peopled by virtual personae, computer networking creates virtual spaces and bodies and, in the process, dispenses (with) physical spaces and bodies. The latter, furthermore, should be understood in multiple senses: cyberspace creates, administers, distributes, draws from, manages without, and disposes of physical spaces and bodies. Because cyberspace seems a largely nonphysical phenomenon, however, calling it a space—in the context of our more common understanding of space as physical, Euclidean (i.e., three-dimensional) space—may seem no more than a rhetorical analogy. After all, one cannot walk in cyberspace the way that one can, for example, walk in a city.[14] Notwithstanding this difference, I resist the dismissal of cyberspace as no more than a metaphorical fiction. In fact, the term *cyberspace* evokes a stronger, ontological claim that networking really *is* a kind of space, even if it is (almost) entirely a "consensual hallucination" (Gibson 1984, 5). This claim, of course, depends on a different spatiality than is evoked by the notion of physical bodies in physical spaces. Indeed, those of us concerned with understanding the political implications "of the digital era," as William Mitchell asserts, "must begin by retheorizing the body in space" (1995, 28).

In chapter 1, I draw on Henri Lefebvre's (1991) work on the production of social space to show how social spaces are, in fact, not just physical but also mental and lived, i.e., they are composed of perceptual movements, conceptual blueprints, and experiential trajectories. Cyberspace, I argue, is the effect of a similar combination of components. My point is not, however, that cyberspace is exactly like all other social spaces; rather, I argue that it is an *other* space: a heterotopia. Foucault offered, but never fully theorized, the concept of heterotopia as a countersite that challenges the normalized ordering of the spaces to which it relates.[15] Drawing from other recent work on heterotopias (Hetherington 1997), I develop that concept in more detail as a framework for understanding the specific ways in which cyberspace confounds our more conventionally physical spaces.

Still, because cyberspace is not the sort of space in which physical bodies can meet face-to-face,[16] it seems, on this self-evident criterion, to be incompatible with claims about its utopian promise for a new Athenian style of democracy. The linchpin here is space itself and how it has been conceptualized in democratic theory. In chapter 2, I foreground the conceptualizations of space that have plagued theories of democracy, contributing to the construction of "the problem of scale," of the optimum size of a polity beyond which claims to a participatory democracy must be given up as chimera. Focusing on the public-realm theories of Hannah Arendt and Jürgen Habermas, I show how their respective works presupposed more elaborate spatial strategies and a more complex understanding of spatiality—not to mention a more decisive displacement of the body and its needs—than many political theorists have remarked. What emerges from Arendt's and Habermas's theories are concepts of public spaces that in fact are more compatible with the bodiless exultation of cyberspace than they might seem, particularly in light of their relentless critiques of modern technology and the mass media, respectively.

Such criticisms of technology, of course, are not unique to these theorists. Indeed, until quite recently, computers were typically feared as institutional tools that displaced workers, under the rubric of automation, and that reduced individuals to numerical entries on bureaucratic red tape, under the rubric of efficiency. What is remarkable in this context is how computers could come to be seen, since about the early 1980s, as a source of individual empowerment and democratic communication. This puzzle is my point of departure for chapters 3 and 4, where I turn to a more detailed analysis of the spatiality of cyberspace. Drawing from Lefebvre's three-part framework for the study of social spaces (physical, conceptual, and lived), I organize my analysis around a comparable framework for the study of cyberspace: namely, *hardware, software,* and *wetware* (the human element). Chapter 3 focuses on the technological components (hardware and software) to show how innovations in computer technology—from electronic mainframes in the late 1940s, to distributed networks and packet-switching in the late 1960s, to the microprocessor and personal computers in the 1970s and 1980s—contributed, successively, to the production of cyberspace. I conclude chapter 3 with a discussion of Gibson's concept of cyberspace to show how it helped shape a cybercultural community by conceptually locating it. His conceptualization, however, differs significantly from how the term he coined has been taken up by others. These observations provide a segue to chapter 4, where I explore Internet culture in more detail, focusing on how different online practices have helped finally to produce cyberspace as a social space, one that brings together incommensurable phenomena and with heterotopic implications for the more conventionally physical spaces around it. The jumble of institutional and individual linkages and of local and global connections over the Internet, for example, creates contradictory possibilities both positively for international democratic activism and negatively for new forms of covert government surveillance and control. Similarly, the play of embodiment offline (the computer as prosthetic device) and disembodiment online (the computer as electronic screen) creates the conditions both for nondiscriminatory modes of public communication and also for potentially exploitative deceptions, such as those computer cross-dressers who lie about their sex as part of a malicious con.

Of particular significance for notions of democratic citizenship, as I show at the end of chapter 4, is the related mix of visibility/invisibility that computer networking enables. These ambiguities, I argue, have engendered different politics of space evident in competing metaphors to respatialize cyberspace: that is, as Information Superhighway or as Electronic Frontier. In chapter 5, I analyze these metaphorical blueprints as they have shaped the U.S. encryption debate. That debate, I argue, is illustrative of the key issues raised in chapters 3 and 4. It has been characterized, implicitly (and begrudgingly), as a successful instance of electronic activism (Wright 1995), and it also, substantively, concerns the politics of visibility (through surveillance) and invisibility (through encryption) that computers and networking have ambivalently enabled, highlighting, as well, the implications of these politics for state apparatuses of security, for individual liberty, and for democratic empowerment.

In the conclusion, finally, I return explicitly to the three concepts of space, technology, and the body, foregrounding in summary fashion some of the more salient points that can be drawn from the preceding arguments and highlighting implications for democratic theory and practice. I argue that understanding how these three concepts figure into our social and political practices is critical to developing democratic theories that are relevant to our era and our circumstances. Anything less runs the risk of proffering a nostalgic sense of loss for an ideal participatory space that existed, if at all, only for a privileged few. The overriding point of my analysis is that cyberspace, for all its apparent nonmateriality, is a new kind of social space that enables interactions and practices specific to its own physical laws: ones based primarily on electromagnetic forces. This specificity is what must be researched, cataloged, inspected: indeed, made visible.

The electronic domain of computer networking is certainly an other space in relation to the more familiar spaces we embody daily. At a minimum, it is a space devoid of meat—of the body—and cannot therefore be fully inhabited. As that observation suggests, however, cyberspace, despite its challenges, cannot replace physical spaces and bodies; it can at best supplement and perhaps modify them. How cyberspace constitutes spaces and bodies differently is the crux of the matter for understanding its relation to politics, egalitarian or otherwise. That it harbors the potential for both emancipatory and repressive practices is in my view undeniable and should make us not simply ambivalent, but rather enterprising with respect to the former possibility and vigilant in the face of the latter.

chapter 1

Theorizing Spaces

Don't you see?! Thanks to concrete, man can now shape his own destiny! The Stone Age is over!

—Mr. Slate to Fred Flintstone

According to American popular culture, human beings since at least the Stone Age have sought, often through technological achievements, to direct the course of their lives by reshaping the physical spaces around them. Though the quotation above overstates our ability to do that, it nonetheless offers an insight into the close, perhaps mutually causal, connection that exists between space and society. That insight, while not exactly lost on past social theorists, has not received adequate attention. In the last decade, however, we have witnessed what Edward W. Soja welcomes as a "long-delayed reassertion of spatiality in critical thought and practice" (1993, 115). Social theory, in other words, has taken an important spatial turn, provoked in part by the English translation, in 1991, of Henri Lefebvre's *The Production of Space* and other suggestive works by Michel de Certeau (1988) and by Foucault (1979, 1986).[1]

My study participates in this spatial turn in social theory. The central issue of this chapter is whether and how we can characterize the apparently nonphysical, disembodied realm of the virtual as a social space, or whether, on the contrary, a social space presupposes a physical space in the conventional sense, i.e., as a geographic space where bodies can meet in the flesh, where people can have unmediated face-to-face encounters. I argue that something nongeographic in a narrowly physical sense can nonetheless be a space because social space is practiced. It is the product

1

of human social interaction. I begin by describing how space has come to be retheorized—as a produced and mutually constitutive element of society—in recent efforts by radical geographers to integrate space into their social theories. I then turn to a more explicit discussion, following Foucault, of the relationship between discourse and social space and, in particular, of other spaces in which existing spatial discourses seem to be thrown into question. In the final section, I apply these interrelated theories of produced social spaces and other spaces to virtual spaces: that is, to an understanding of the spatiality of cyberspace.

Practicing Space

The reassertion of space in social theory required its retheorization because conventional understandings were inadequate (Soja 1993, 126–30; see also Soja 1989). Critics maintain that social theorists tended to treat spatiality in terms of either physical space (and therefore given) or mental space (and therefore shaped by something else, e.g., language), but seldom as *social* space—that is, as the practical effect of a process that includes physical, mental, and social relations (Lefebvre 1991, 11–12).[2] Soja, for example, identifies the two common ways space has been undertheorized as follows. The first is to treat space as an objective, external environment of material forms, "a physically fixed container or stage on which is played out the making of histories and societal development" (1993, 127). The second mode, conversely, treats space as "internalized and subjective" (128), as an idea or construct of space that makes a difference for what takes place. Hence, whereas the first mode leads to objective descriptions and measurements of architectural designs and geographic territories, the second leads to some form of interpretive account of subjective mental constructs. Soja maintains, however, that in both approaches—space as a container and space as a construct—space becomes "the same fixed, dead, objective world of externalized material forms" (128).

On the face of it, Soja's critique of space as container makes more sense than his critique of space as construct, particularly since the latter appears to be an improvement.[3] Space as container, to be sure, treats space as more or less given and neutral vis-à-vis the social actions that occur in or on that space, which are themselves explained in terms of other causes. As I understand him, however, Soja makes essentially the same criticism of the treatment of space as construct because in that treatment the tendency has been to problematize the meaning of space (the signified) but not the spatial elements themselves (the signifiers).

Space, as a result, is dead in the sense that it is no more than, in my terms, neutral matter to which virtually any signified (any meaning) could in principle be attached, depending, for example, on the particular *cognitive mappings* (Fredric Jameson's concept) with which one is operating (Soja 1993, 128). Hence, treating space only as a social construction, Soja suggests, denies its materiality, in the Marxian sense of something that is both (re)producer and by-product of social relations. Space becomes a kind of fundamentally malleable matter that can be made to mean virtually anything.[4] The result is that what space means, once again, is determined by something other than space itself, typically by some factor with a temporal dynamic. It is this historicism in social theory that Soja and others have targeted.[5]

That undertaking, however, is more complicated than it might, at first, seem. My own initial reaction to the spatial turn in social theory was "What *about* space?" From my standpoint, space seemed so obvious and transparent that I could not imagine social theorists plumbing it for explanatory potential. I have come to understand responses like mine as a product of a learned philosophy of space, one derived from at least three eminent sources. The first of these sources, historically speaking, is Euclid, whose geometry supplied Western thought with a system for analyzing the physical, two- and three-dimensional space of human perception, making it seem as if this were all that space is. The second source is Descartes, whose coordinate system helped codify a sense of space as container, overlaying it with a grid of measurable distances for locating discrete objects at discrete points within space. The third source is Newton, whose concept of *absolute space* dichotomized space from time, associating space with stasis and time with change. In short, Euclidean geometry, Cartesian coordinate systems, and Newtonian physics constitute for many of us our ordinary, everyday philosophy of space. Put another way, they make up the three dimensions of the mental space with which many of us operate.

Based on this tradition, we are taught to think that time is causal, but space is not. To take a rather simplistic example that nevertheless illustrates my point, elementary school courses in history teach us to narrate events in temporal sequence, inviting us to see some magnificent occurrence as the outcome of a particular prior event or some set of preexisting conditions. Hence, temporal predicates—before and after—seem almost indispensable to causal explanations, even when one is dealing with subject areas other than history. Spatial predicates, by contrast—e.g., inside, outside, beyond, alongside—are not only seemingly irrelevant to causal explanation but, more to the point, difficult to fit into our causal language.[6] How often, for example, do we explain some situation as having been caused by some *proximate* condition rather than some prior condition? We may locate an event and even speak of its being *shaped* by something, but we do not typically problematize that metaphorical usage (Smith and Katz 1993). One reason for this may be that our lessons on the subject of space (certainly in our elementary education but often in upper-level education as well) do not teach us to treat the implied spatiality of everyday terms like *location* as something that can explain; location merely describes. Whatever elementary instruction we do receive on the issue of space—usually a physical or political geography course— teaches us primarily how to identify terrains and boundaries. With respect to the relationship between space and society, however, we receive, at best, a cursory sense of spaces and borders as sociopolitical "obstructions" or "external, material constraints" to be overcome, often through technological innovations. Space is simply a thereness to be reckoned with. Against this view, Henri Lefebvre aphoristically asserted that *"(Social) space is a (social) product"* (1991, 26, his emphasis). This insight has had a sizeable impact on the integration of space in social explanation.

In his seminal work (1991), Lefebvre criticizes social theorists for failing to state, let alone explain, the particular space they are talking about when they use spatial terms. This, in fact, was one of his major criticisms of Foucault's early work:

> Conspicuous by its absence from supposedly fundamental epistemological studies is not only the idea of "man" but also that of space—the fact that "space" is mentioned on every page notwithstanding. Thus Michel Foucault can calmly assert that "knowledge *[savoir]* is also the space in which the subject may take up a position and speak of the objects with which he deals in his discourse." Foucault never explains what space it is that he is referring to, nor how it bridges that gap between the theoretical (epistemological) realm and the practical one, between mental and social, between the space of the philosophers and the space of people who deal with material things. (3–4)[7]

Having criticized this lack of specificity and explanation regarding the role of space in social theory, Lefebvre proceeds to develop an analytical framework that almost painstakingly clarifies the space to which he himself is referring. At the same time, the parentheses in his aphorism— "(Social) space is a (social) product"—denote the semisuperfluous nature of the modifier *social* because space, for him, is always the lived space of social practice, which encompasses both the ideational and the material (12, 27).

This reading is suggested by Lefebvre's threefold understanding of spatiality: his "conceptual triad" (33), or more appropriately triads in the plural, since he refers throughout his analysis to three distinct but related triads. First, in describing the task of theory building at hand, he notes that his aim is to create a comprehensive theory that takes into account three different "'fields'" of experience—the physical, the mental, and the social (11). He then recasts these fields of experience in more explicitly spatial terms: spatial practices, representations of space, and representational spaces (33), or what Shields helpfully retranslates as "spaces of representation" (cited in Hetherington 1997, 145, chapter 2, note 3). Lastly, Lefebvre relates each of these three reconceptualized spatial fields to a specific mode of experience: namely, the perceived, the conceived, and the lived (38–41). These somewhat overlapping triads yield an understanding of social space as a "trialectic" involving, first, the perceived realm of physical experience produced and reproduced through spatial practices; second, the conceived realm of mental experience constructed as (dominant) representations of space; and lastly, a lived, "passively experienced" realm of social experience in (dominated) spaces of representation (39).

On the surface, Lefebvre's decision to speak about the physical in terms of practices (rather than simply as containerlike objects) may seem counterintuitive, but that association is, I think, extraordinarily insightful. Drawing from astrophysics, he observes that "physical space has no 'reality' without the energy that is deployed within it" (13). This formulation implies movement since, in physics, energy is mass times velocity. Physical space, then, is produced by (is an effect of) the movement of one physical phenomenon (e.g., an atom, a body, a car, a planet, or, for that matter, a datum) among other physical phenomena. Hence, spatial practice is best understood as the physical field of sociospatial experience activated by (direct and indirect) human energy (movement). And, of course, given Lefebvre's Marxist problematic, this includes work and leisure activities. Spaces are labored and played into existence. This sense of movement surfaces in Lefebvre's description of the spatial practices of neocapitalism as "the *routes* and *networks* which link up the places set aside for work, 'private' life and leisure" (38, my emphasis).

The social space of neocapitalism, however, is not simply given by these physical routes and networks; rather, as Lefebvre points out, the physical is overlaid by (that is, mediated through) the symbolic at the levels of both representations of space and spaces of representation. Of the representations of space, Lefebvre notes that these are the "dominant space in any society" (39). They are, in effect, the coherent and totalizing scientific ideologies of space (blueprints) propounded by urbanists, architects, planners, and social engineers and instantiated in the layout of cities, buildings, streets, bridges, factories, and even so-called private suburban domiciles. It is for this reason that Lefebvre associates the representations of space with the producers of space. In contrast, he locates the users of space with, in his view, the less coherent spaces of representation. These lived spaces, because they are, in part, products of hegemonic representations of space, are "dominated—and hence passively experienced" (39). But Lefebvre rejects the notion that spaces of representation are only ideological effects. Rather, he suggests that space as lived also involves creative appropriations; these are spaces "which the imagination seeks to change and appropriate" (39). Lived space, in this respect, gives itself over to other (that is, nondominant) representations. It is therefore not only the space of passive users, "but also of some artists and perhaps of those, such as a few writers and philosophers, who *describe* and aspire to do no more than describe" (39). In other words, spaces of representation may include quasi-surreal spaces where the point is not so much to give meaningful order, but rather to disrupt, postpone, and even overturn meaning.[8] Lived space, in this respect, is a potential site of resistance. A product of all three of these spatial processes, then, social space is the imbricated effect of (1) perceived material relations that enable certain trajectories, (2) "strategic" conceptualizations that strive to order human movements, and (3) lived practices involving both a passive reproduction of those spatial orders and creative counter-"tactics" that attempt to resist them.[9]

Lefebvre's provocative analysis obviously outlines a shift in the proper object of knowledge for social/spatial theory from, in his terms, "*things in space* to the actual *production of space*" (37, his emphasis). This shift has had two significant implications I want to highlight here. First, it rejects the notion that space is neutral. In contrast, Lefebvre and subsequent theorists have indicated how the spatial itself has been central to the reproduction of particular political-economic relations, even while it has been partially effected by those relations. So, for example, Smith and Katz maintain the following:

> The emergence of capitalist social relations in Europe brought a very specific set of social and political shifts that established absolute space

as the premise of hegemonic social practices. The inauguration of private property as the general basis of the social economy, and the division of the land into privately held and precisely demarcated plots; the juridical assumption of the individual body as the basic social unit; the progressive outward expansion of European hegemony through the conquest, colonization and defence of new territories; the division of global space into mutually exclusive nation-states on the basis of some presumed internal homogeneity of culture (albeit a division brought about with economic motivation and through military force): these and other shifts marked the emerging space-economy of capitalism from the sixteenth century onwards and represented a powerful enactment of absolute space as the geographical basis for social intercourse. (1993, 75)

This passage contributes to my analysis of cyberspace and its possible effects by suggesting how a specific space—in this case, the absolute space drawn from Euclid, Descartes, and Newton, which can be mapped, organized in a grid, and measured, and in which objects can be treated discretely in that they occupy unique locations—undergirds and reproduces a particular social formation (i.e., capitalism). This close connection implies that new spatial orders (or disorders) may well affect the continuance of these very social practices precisely because they are also spatial practices. As it happens, the passage also lists in summary fashion some of the very sociospatial practices that increasingly are being challenged by cyberspace. I address the precise nature of that challenge in later chapters, but it amounts to showing how the particular (seemingly nonphysical and, in a sense, antigeographic) spatial practices involved in computer networking have begun to complicate the notion of private property (especially intellectual property), to frustrate juridical assumptions relating one body to one identity or personality, and to violate the principle of exclusive location, on which the sovereignty of nation-states depends. These challenges reinforce the understanding, advanced in Lefebvre's work, that space is not neutral.

Lefebvre's work, secondly, redefines space not as physically given, but as a set of practical relations of which the physical is certainly an important component, but only one component. It is this insight in particular, if taken to heart, that can move social theory beyond the Stone Age of absolutist conceptions of space. All space, in this respect, is practiced. Michel de Certeau tries to get at the same point with his aphorism *"space is a practiced place"* (1988, 117, his emphasis). While in some senses helpful, however, the distinction he makes between space and place is also suspect. He defines place *(lieu)* as a stable configuration of positions that locates things in their proper positions, or, as he puts it, an instantaneous order that "excludes the possibility of two things being in the same location *(place)*" (117). This definition arguably reproduces the notion of absolute space by another name. As such, de Certeau offers as a general analytical category a space-related term, *place,* that assumes a conventional and specific manifestation of the spatial: for example, one that precludes the possibility of two or more things occupying the same location. Notwithstanding this objection, his distinction does have the advantage of recasting space itself as the more fluid of the two concepts. Space, according to de Certeau, is a dynamic network of pathways, "composed of intersections of mobile elements" and "actuated by the ensemble of movements deployed within it" (117). (This emphasis on movement parallels Lefebvre's understanding of spatial practice.) It seems then that for de Certeau, place is a static order and space, which entails a certain degree of freedom of movement, and is a dynamic instantiation of a particular order. Thus, he continues, the street (ordered by a particular system: urban planning) is a place that "is transformed into a space by walkers" (177). Or similarly, a written text is "a place constituted by a system of signs" but a "space produced" by readers in that the activity of reading activates those signs and conveys a meaning: one, of course, mediated and hence in important ways written (rather than simply read) through the reader's interpretive frame (117). By analogy, computer network sites are *places* ordered by certain imperatives (physical and technological), but the *space* of networking is produced by, for example, the act of surfing the Internet. To the extent that the sites that make up a network are different places around the globe, then, it is no accident that we experience the clicking of hyperlinks on the World Wide Web as a movement from site to site. It is this movement that helps constitute the spatiality of cyberspace.

This is still a very general restatement, following de Certeau, of the first of Lefebvre's triad—spatial practices—vis-à-vis cyberspace. The social, political, and economic character of cyberspace, as Lefebvre's framework further suggests, requires attention to the relations of production and reproduction that inform its spatial practice, the representations of that space that are seeking to order it in particular ways, and the spaces of representation through which cyberspace is lived, and in both orderly and disorderly ways. As Lefebvre himself noted in the 1970s, however, the space of information science and computer technology, of which cyberspace is a recent instantiation, is relatively unknown and perhaps impossible to map: "We know enough in this area to suspect the existence of a space peculiar to information science, but not enough to describe that space, much less to claim close acquaintanceship with it" (1991, 86). Even though over twenty-five years have passed since Lefebvre made that statement, I am not convinced that we necessarily know more about that space, only that we have more of that space to know.

Despite this difficulty, one can detect an urgent need to understand more about cyberspace in popular notions that the Internet is the latest and most transformative moment of a broader "computer revolution." Whether or not one accepts that notion, it is nonetheless clear that networking is having an impact on a wide-ranging set of practices. These include changes in interpersonal communication, sociality, and community (Rheingold 1993; Jones 1995); in courtship and romantic relationships (Ullman 1996) and even in divorce (Quittner 1997); in surveillance and privacy issues (Lyon 1994); in grassroots social movements and campaign politics (Bonchek 1995; Browning 1996; Bowen 1996); in education, literature, authorship, and readership (Barrett 1994; Landow 1992; Spender 1995); in class politics (Kroker and Weinstein 1994); in statecraft (Swett 1995); and most profoundly in potential changes to the construction and presentation of self (Poster 1990; Stone 1996; Turkle 1995). Taken together, these literatures suggest that what is needed is not just any sociospatial theory of cyberspace, but one, more specifically, that can address the relationship between spatiality and social change. This is where Lefebvre's framework falls short.

Lefebvre's notion of social change is far too teleological, assuming, first, that "every society—and hence every mode of production . . . produces a space, its own space" (31), and second, that a new space will arise out of contradictions within the abstract space of the modern, neo-capitalist social formation. So despite the more central role he accords to space in his philosophy, the underlying logic of social development in his analysis—the motor of change, if you will—is still time. The passage of time is what will permit the contradictions within the capitalist space-economy to rise up and effect a new space and hence new possibilities: "[I]t can be shown that abstract space harbours specific contradictions. Such spatial contradictions derive in part from the old contradictions *thrown up by historical time*. . . . Thus, despite—or rather because of—its negativity, abstract space carries within itself the seeds of a new kind of space . . . 'differential space'" (52, my emphasis).

To be sure, Lefebvre offers an impressive and even intimidating historical analysis of sociospatial change, outlining what he maintains was a transition from natural space to absolute space to abstract space. But even assuming that this backward-looking part of his analysis is correct, why accept that its conclusions can be projected onto the future? Such projections assume that history unfolds according to a certain law of development: in Lefebvre's case, one about the inevitable transition from one space-economy to another. This, as I understand it, is historicism. That term, of course, has become a red flag for social theorists, especially those wanting to reprioritize space. My specific problem with historicist explanations is not that they are wrong—who can know that?—but rather that they foreclose attention to other possible factors. Specifically, as Keith and Pile point out, this tendency toward historicism "detracts from the conceptual richness of the notions of the spatial that Lefebvre outlines" (25). One way to plumb the conceptual richness of his notions of space would be to explore the possibility that social change, rather than an effect of *diachronic* developments within one sociospatial formation, may be effected instead by contradictions arising from a *synchronic* relationship among different spaces. Theorizing this synchrony of multiple spaces, however, requires us to cast aside absolute conceptions of space, of an exclusive locality and a monolithic spatial order. Instead, we must think in terms of overlays and intersections of different social spaces.

Let us take the example of the software market, which on the face of it seems very much a part of a capitalist space-economy. Software producers trade in information (computer programs) rather than in more straightforwardly physical commodities. In this respect, their ability to conduct business and make profits depends on intellectual property rights. Some computer users, however, suggest that the notion of *intellectual property* is an oxymoron because, as Stewart Brand notes, "[i]nformation wants to be free" (Barlow 1993c). That claim is not simply about altruistic motives. Rather it is more fundamentally about the assumed nature of soft products: namely, that information, software programs, and digital data in general are nonmaterial, at least in the sense that the form they take, binary currents, is neither visible nor tangible. This apparent nonmateriality, moreover, complicates intellectual property rights in two senses. First, the copyright and patent laws that helped in the past to codify and sustain intellectual property rights have not been based on the protection of ideas per se, but on protecting their expression in some physical medium: books, newspapers, record albums, and so forth. With the advent of digital technology, however, ideas have come to be expressed in the apparently nonmaterial form of binary currents, which can themselves be perfectly stored, reproduced, and transmitted in a wide variety of relatively inexpensive ways (see chapter 3). This complicates the application of existing property laws inasmuch as those laws have "always found definition" in "the physical plane" (Barlow 1993c). Put another way, digital technology confounds the long-standing correspondence that has been established between Western absolute space—as a container of physical objects with "discrete and mutually exclusive locations"— and a concept of private property that until recently referred to "precisely demarcated plots" or some other material and hence assignable phenomenon (Smith and Katz 1993, 75).

The nature of digital data complicates the notion of intellectual property rights in a second, related way. Inasmuch as data can be conveyed in a wide variety of storage units, claims about theft are strained. How, concretely, am I stealing something if I go out and purchase a floppy disk, which I then own, and use it to copy a program someone purchased and has loaded on her home computer, and then upload that program onto my own home computer? I have not broken into a computer store to do that, nor have I taken anything tangible that belonged to someone else. In fact, inasmuch as I have my friend's permission to copy the program she purchased, this feels more like an act of sharing than an act of stealing.[10] Furthermore, if I add to this example the fact that I may not even have to go physically to my friend's house to get the program but can, instead, dial up her computer on my modem and download her program directly into my computer, then it becomes apparent that a different kind of spatial practice with a different spatial ordering is involved here—perhaps, indeed, a spatial ordering in which "information wants to be free." This suggests that we are dealing with an *other* space. These overlays of different spaces (physical and virtual) and the relationships between them are what need to be theorized.

Other Spaces

So far, I have said very little about the place of discourse in the constitution of social space, even though some sense of the discursive is already implied in Lefebvre's discussion of representations of space and symbolic reappropriations in the spaces of representation. As I noted briefly in the introduction, for Foucault a discourse is the quasi-structural regularity that emerges, over time, in the meaning-constitutive symbolic associations (articulations) that people make.[11] These symbolic associations, moreover, are not only linguistic, but also nonlinguistic (Laclau and Mouffe 1987, 82–84): that is, they involve both words and things. In fact, the original French title of Foucault's *The Order of Things* is *Les mots et les choses,* which literally means *words* and *things* (1994b). The things articulated in a given discourse, moreover, may include spatial phenomena—such as the physical walls of a building or a walkway or a stairwell—and, by extension, spatial practices as one aspect of the institutions that Foucault argues are part of a discursive formation, such as the penal system (see especially 1979, 195–228, and 1984). Hence, spatial elements (that is, places and the movements between them that give rise to spaces) can also be, and often are, subject to discursive articulation. In fact, the moment that a location comes to be identified as a specific kind of place or that some notion of a meaningful spatial order arises, a discursive articulation has been made.

I repeat these arguments here because in many critical and even some sympathetic theoretical discussions of Foucauldian discourse, especially in relation to such apparently physical things as space, a number of category mistakes are customarily made. First, it is assumed that words, languages, ideas, or the linguistic are either synonymous with or instances of *the discursive,* and that by contrast things, practices, the physical, the material, and the nonlinguistic are all *nondiscursive.* To say, therefore, that discourses involve both words and things—and indeed subjects and objects and practices, as well—is to reject these facile distinctions. But once this is said, it is assumed that the claim being made is that "discourse is everywhere," and that, consequently, "there is no such thing as the nondiscursive." This counterclaim, too, misrecognizes discourse. It assumes that the discursive process is a totalizing one.

This was certainly not Foucault's argument. On the contrary, his understanding of discourse was that it always involves a process of negation, that it is a system of ordering that depends on excluding something *other,* something unintelligible, deviant, abnormal. In fact, for Foucault, *genealogy,* the name he adopted for his historical analyses of discourses, is fundamentally about revealing the "local, discontinuous, disqualified, illegitimate knowledges" against which emergent disciplinary discourses have defined themselves (from "Two Lectures," 1980, 83). So, for example, in discussing the emergence of the penal system, Foucault noted how that development depended, in part, on a break with other symbolic practices (e.g., drawing and quartering, inquisition, beheading), other devices (pincers, molten lead), and other places (such as the scaffold and the dungeon), as well as other turns of phrases (e.g., "judicial torture"). These are just some of the practices, things, places, and phrases that have come to be excluded from modern penal discourses. Hence, it is wrong to argue that discourse is everywhere for Foucault because, according to the theoretical framework he advanced, any one discourse always depends on a process of negating something that is nonsensical to it: an Other that falls outside a particular discourse's grid of intelligibility and that may even come to disturb that grid, to challenge a given discourse's way of ordering. Such exclusions, of course, may make sense from the standpoint of some other discourse: in the way, for example, that judicial torture, while an apparent oxymoron vis-à-vis most discourses today, can be made intelligible via a historical discourse of sovereign justice. However, this observation does not contradict the main point that no single discourse is totalizing. Nondiscursive elements may remain nondiscursive, or they may come to be articulated as part of a dominant or alternative grid of intelligibility. The point is that something always remains (or more often is pushed) outside the realm of the intelligible relative to any particular discourse.

To summarize these points, then: it is not just that words are discursive and things are not, nor that the whole notion of the nondiscursive is evacuated once we acknowledge that discourses have both linguistic and nonlinguistic elements. Rather, a discourse is a process of articulating words and things that effects meaningful associations among them and, at the same time, excludes other words and things that are characterized generally, from its standpoint, as nonsensical.

It was in the context of describing a kind of nonsensical spatiality that Foucault first proposed the term *heterotopia*, "other spaces" (1994b, xviii). In his preface to *The Order of Things* (xv–xxiv), he applies that term to the incongruous space created by Borges in his description of a Chinese encyclopedia. To Foucault, the categories brought together in this imagined encyclopedia—which divides animals according to a bizarre mix of classifications that include "(a) belonging to the Emperor, (b) embalmed, (c) tame" and others—seem so unrelated that their juxtaposition comes off as absurd, defying all necessarily discursive attempts to make them intelligible. In this respect, the Chinese categories challenge "our" (occidental) taxonomies. Foucault's entire preface is about the experience of reading that passage in Borges, about "the laughter that shattered, as [Foucault] read the passage, all the familiar landmarks of [his] thought—*our* thought, the thought that bears the stamp of our age and our geography" (xv, his emphasis).

Heterotopia is the term Foucault proposes for that "disturbing" space of otherness where mismatched objects appear together. Our familiar discourses fail here because they cannot give order to those objects; they fail inasmuch as heterotopias, as Foucault argues, "make it impossible to name this *and* that" (xviii, his emphasis). Foucault treats the Chinese encyclopedia as exemplary of the "heterotopias . . . found so often in Borges" (xviii). He describes the disturbance in terms of a mismatch between the conceptual space of an idealized China and the actual space of the encyclopedia that becomes another China. Through Borges's ascription, the encyclopedia operates as a metonymic representation of this other China. In the process, two spaces of China are juxtaposed: a "dream-world" China that "in our traditional imagery" represents meticulous and rigid order and another China that is mediated through Borges's wit and becomes the projection, "at the other extremity of the earth we inhabit," of another spatial ordering, of "a culture entirely devoted to the ordering of space, but one that does not distribute the multiplicity of existing things into any of the categories that make it possible for us to name, speak, and think" (xix). One China is produced by Borges's text; the other was the product of Foucault's imagination. Hence, the important point to grasp is that the otherness Foucault describes as heterotopia is not simply given by the nature of the space Borges creates, but rather by the relationship between spaces established in Foucault's act of reading, which, given his occidental frame of reference, incites the confrontation, first registered in laughter, between the two spatial orders to which he alludes.

Shortly after *Les mot et les choses* came out in 1966 (see Foucault 1994b), Foucault provided a more complete description of this relational understanding of heterotopia in a March 1967 lecture presented to a group of architects and published after his death as *"Des espace autres"* ("Of Other Spaces," 1986). There Foucault establishes more explicitly that heterotopias refer to relationships between spaces inasmuch as they "have the curious property of being in relation with all the other sites, but in such a way as to suspect, neutralize, or invert the set of relations that they happen to designate, mirror, or reflect" (24). A heterotopia, then, is a kind of in-between space of contradiction, of contestation: a space that mimics or simulates lived spaces, but that in so doing, calls those spaces we live in into question.

Heterotopias, Foucault explains, are not the same as utopias. The latter are idealized versions of society that have no real existence: they are "fundamentally unreal spaces" (1986, 24), a discursive "consolation" with "no real locality" (1994b, xviii). By contrast, heterotopias are real, existing places that function as "counter-sites" (1986, 24). The mirror, according to Foucault, is an example of both a utopia and a heterotopia:

The mirror is . . . a utopia, since it is a placeless place. In the mirror, I see myself there where I am not, in an unreal, virtual space that opens up behind the surface; I am over there, there where I am not, a sort of shadow that gives my own visibility to myself, that enables me to see myself there where I am absent: such is the utopia of the mirror. But it is also a heterotopia in so far as the mirror does exist in reality, where it exerts a sort of counteraction on the position that I occupy. From the standpoint of the mirror I discover my absence from the place where I am since I see myself over there. Starting from this gaze that is, as it were, directed toward me, from the ground of this virtual space that is on the other side of the glass, I come back toward myself; I begin again to direct my eyes toward myself and to reconstitute myself there where I am. The mirror functions as a heterotopia in this respect: it makes this place that I occupy at the moment when I look at myself in the glass at once absolutely real, connected with all the space that surrounds it, and absolutely unreal, since in order to be perceived it has to pass through this virtual point which is over there. (1986, 24)[12]

It bears emphasizing that the heterotopic effect of the mirror Foucault concentrates on is this confusing sense of being two places at once, a simultaneous here/thereness that calls into question the very notion of being by exerting "a sort of counteraction on the position that I occupy."

Like the passage from Borges then, which required Foucault's act of reading for a heterotopic relationship between spaces to be activated, the mirror becomes another heterotopic passage (a movement) activated this time through an act of looking. In this respect, then, heterotopias, like all spaces, are practiced. Their key mark of distinction, however, is that—like the perfect, ideal spaces of utopias—their constitution exerts a confrontation among the different spaces they juxtapose. But unlike utopias, their starting point is a place (e.g., a text or a mirror) that exists in reality.

Foucault's own brief discussions of the concept of heterotopia— including, in addition to his preface (in 1994b) and the lecture (1986), a brief mention of the term in an interview on the subject of "Space, Knowledge, and Power" (1984)—have in some respects raised more questions than they have answered. Even his own attempt to clarify his notion by listing, in the lecture, a series of actually existing heterotopias has not entirely helped matters. Benjamin Genocchio maintains, for example, that in his more "geographic" treatment of heterotopia in the lecture, Foucault actually contradicted his own more radical use of the term in the earlier preface, where heterotopia seemed to refer more to an imagined spatiality that could only exist in language (Hetherington 1997, 46–51). Indeed, Foucault does say,

> What is impossible is not the propinquity of the things listed, but the very site on which their propinquity would be possible. The animals "(i) frenzied, (j) innumerable, (k) drawn with a very fine camelhair brush"—where could they ever meet, except in the immaterial sound of the voice pronouncing their enumeration, or on the page transcribing it? Where else could they be juxtaposed except in the non-place of language? (1994b, xvi–xvii)

In his lecture, by contrast, Foucault does list a number of actual sites that he labels heterotopias. In addition to the mirror, these other spaces include "crisis heterotopias" like the boarding school (i.e., places for people in a state of crisis, such as adolescents or the elderly, and, at one time, menstruating women) (1986, 24); "heterotopias of deviation" like asylums, prisons, and cemeteries (25); heterotopias of mixed spaces like the theatre, cinema, and garden, or like the traveling space of the ship, which Foucault calls "the heterotopia *par excellence*" (25, 27); heterochronic heterotopias (i.e., places of alternate temporal orderings) like the epoch-spanning space-time of the museum and the ephemeral space-time of the fairgrounds (26); heterotopias of ritual practice like the Muslim hammam or the Scandinavian sauna (26); heterotopias of illusion like the brothel "that exposes every real space . . . as still more illusory" (27); and heterotopias of compensation such as the Puritan and Jesuit colonies of the early modern period that seemed "perfect" and "well arranged" in contrast to the broader social spaces they negated (27).

How should we make sense, then, of the apparent contradiction between the impossible site of the Chinese encyclopedia and the actual sites of the heterotopias listed above? Perhaps the answer is that we are simply dealing with different kinds of sites: one set predominantly linguistic (composed of words) and the other set predominantly nonlinguistic (composed of things). The lecture was presented to a group of architects who were arguably more interested in hearing something about actual sites. We should not find it surprising, then, that Foucault might take a spatial concept that he had been thinking about primarily in relation to language and try applying it to an analysis of places. Perhaps he does contradict himself in the process, as critics charge. Nevertheless, I find it remarkable that his application of the concept of heterotopia to a literary text (1994b) should be regarded as more radical than its application to actual sites (1986), especially given that the explicit point of even the former study in *The Order of Things* (1994b) was to analyze ordering relationships between words and things.

As I understand it, what makes Foucault's earlier treatment of heterotopia more radical is that it proposes a different ontology, where what exists can only exist in language and thereby puts into question our own existence outside of language. Certainly, Foucault argues that the absurdity of Borges's enumeration performs a kind of "vanishing trick" by removing the "table" on which one could imagine bringing all these incommensurate objects together (1994b, xvii). He notes, moreover, that he means "table" in both the physical sense of an actual piece of furniture and also in the classificatory sense of "a *tabula*," with rows and columns and categories for ordering things. Put another way, the Chinese encyclopedia pulls the ground out from under us and leaves us, in a sense, nowhere. Those who object to the application of heterotopia to actual sites seem to be suggesting that no comparable vanishing trick is accomplished with actual sites because they are in a sense like physical tables. This criticism, however, actually makes the mistake of assuming that space is given by the physical table rather than by the relationship between a material form (e.g., a wooden board on four legs) and the tabular grid of intelligibility that orders the items deposited on its surface. Instead of discounting the notion that actual sites can be heterotopias (other spaces), I think the more interesting issue is how they perform this vanishing trick (this ontological questioning) even while they partially depend on the very thing they seem to make disappear (e.g., physical tables). Foucault's suggestion, in the lecture, is that they perform this vanishing trick always in relation to the spaces around them. The key questions to be asked of heterotopias, therefore, are how they relate to the spaces around them and what new practices, identities, and sociospatial relations might be inaugurated in relation to those places of Otherness by virtue of their being set apart. These issues, to be sure, remain implicit in Foucault's work. The task of elaborating more fully the notion of heterotopia as an explanatory concept in social theory has been left to other theorists.

In his recent analysis of heterotopia as a constitutive component of modernity, Kevin Hetherington notes that the concept, partly as a consequence of the spatial turn in social theory, has become fashionable among cultural theorists and geographers, particularly as a way of describing the spatiality of postmodernity (1997, 40–41). Hetherington identifies six different uses of the term, many of them derived from Foucault's

examples in both the preface and the lecture. These include an incongruous site of transgression, an ambivalent site with multiple meanings, a
mysterious site, a site of absolute perfection, a marginal site within a
dominant social space, or a literary site of incongruous elements that
resists discursive articulation (41). Despite their apparent differences,
Hetherington maintains that each of these uses are better understood as
possible effects of heterotopia rather than as exhaustive definitions of
that notion. In contrast, he argues that heterotopias be understood as
"spaces of an alternate ordering" (9, his emphasis).[13]

Hetherington's rejection of two related tendencies in recent sociospatial theory partially motivates this redefinition. One tendency is to
identify modernity as a form of social control, treating it as a thing that is
complete, finished, and discrete. This tendency is most evident, he argues,
in works, ostensibly following Foucault, that point to sites of apparent
control, like the prison, and see them "as total institutions standing as a
metaphor for modernity" (57). In contrast, Hetherington reminds us that
for Foucault freedom and control are always intertwined, even (in fact especially) in panoptic societies. The other related tendency Hetherington
rejects is the treatment of postmodernity, by contrast, as a kind of disorder
against the order that modernity ostensibly represents. Exemplary here are
recent studies of marginality—including, for that matter, Lefebvre's notion of spaces of representation (Hetherington 1997, 24)—that define and
celebrate the marginal as a site of resistance or transgression without also
noting how such sites invariably propose a different type of order. Against
these customary tendencies, Hetherington insists that modernity—and,
by implication, postmodernity (whatever that may be)—should be looked
at "as a social and indeed spatial ordering" (ix). His emphasis on ordering,
rather than order, is meant to convey the sense that what is involved here
is an incomplete process. In addition, this process of ordering is an ambivalent one that vacillates between ideals of freedom and ideals of order,
a vacillation that Hetherington argues lies at the heart of the distinctively
modern idea of *utopia* and that is instantiated spatially as *heterotopia*.

Although Hetherington does not say so explicitly, his focus on heterotopia as a process of alternate ordering is one that can be derived directly
from Foucault's arguments in the preface. Foucault notes that the codes of
order that a particular culture employs are not typically apparent as such
to the members of that culture; rather, they appear simply to be given. At
the other extreme, he continues, a culture's reflexive knowledges, including its sciences and philosophies, explain the general function, law, and
principle of an order, and why *it* was established instead of another. As I

read him, however, Foucault seems to be suggesting that at both extremes, order appears in its secondary state, as an already established unity that is either spontaneously enacted or scientifically and philosophically justified. In this respect, the "already 'encoded' eye," on the one hand, and "reflexive knowledge," on the other, are both blind to order "in its primary state": that is, as a process of ordering (1994b, xxi). Foucault's innovation is in positing a "middle region" where this process is revealed as such:

> [B]etween these two regions, so distant from one another, lies a domain which, even though its role is mainly an intermediary one, is nonetheless fundamental: it is more confused, more obscure, and probably less easy to analyse. It is here that a culture, imperceptibly deviating from the empirical orders prescribed for it by its primary codes, instituting an initial separation from them, causes them to lose their original transparency, relinquishes its immediate and invisible powers, frees itself sufficiently to discover that these orders are perhaps not the only possible ones or the best ones; this culture then finds itself faced with the stark fact that there exists, below the level of its spontaneous orders, things that are in themselves capable of being ordered, that belong to a certain unspoken order; the fact, in short, that order *exists*. (1994b, xx, his emphasis)

It is here, I think, in this middle region, that Foucault implicitly locates heterotopias. Other spaces function as countersites, in other words, precisely because (and to the extent that) they reveal spatial order for what it is: a process of ordering.

What does this mean concretely? Ironically, Foucault has already answered this question. Inasmuch as he lists asylums and prisons among his examples of "heterotopias of deviation" (1986, 25) and that he wrote lengthy studies of each of these (1973 and 1979, respectively), he has been, in a sense, indicating all along how other spaces make processes of ordering manifest. What was the panopticon, after all, if not a place of Otherness where the transparency of former codes of order, like judicial torture, was suspended long enough to discover that some other order was possible? Where what was revealed was precisely the sense that the body was capable of being ordered? And where, as a result, technologies of the body were semiconsciously developed, by fits and starts? It is only because these technologies have come to influence the practices of surveillance in what Foucault refers to as "disciplinary societies" that they now appear to us as totalizing codes of order; but they remain, nonetheless, incomplete processes of ordering.

That is precisely what genealogical analysis as a critical practice is intended to reveal: to indicate, through a juxtaposition of different spatial orders, how every dominant order today is the effect of a more contingent historical process of ordering. Michael Shapiro makes the same point when he notes that "[t]he imaginative function of the critical interpreter is, in Foucault's words, 'to create a space of illusion that exposes every real space, all the sites inside of which human life is partitioned as still more illusory'" (1992, 17). Ironically, the work Shapiro cites here is Foucault's lecture on other spaces (1986), and hence the "space of illusion" he mentions without naming is what Foucault explicitly calls heterotopia (and actually only one kind of heterotopia). But whereas Shapiro seems to want to treat heterotopia primarily as an effect of a kind of critical writing (perhaps like Genocchio), Hetherington (1997) treats heterotopia as the effect of a kind of spatial practice associated with actual sites (more in line, actually, with the bulk of Foucault's work). One of the most salutary features of Hetherington's work, then, is that he makes explicit what tends to remain implicit, even in Foucault's work.

Hetherington follows Foucault in regarding heterotopia as a relationship between spaces, as in effect a middle region or "space-between" (1997, ix) where processes of ordering reveal themselves as such by juxtaposing different spatial orders. In this respect, no space is inherently Other (whatever that might mean), but rather Other always in relation to the spaces it opposes (and that oppose it). It is possible, of course, for something to be characterized as different without that recognition throwing everything into question. This, I think, is what Hetherington tries to address with the distinction between *resemblance* (or metaphor) and *similitude* (or metonymy). To establish the difference of something on the basis of its content presupposes a meaning or standard of sameness and difference—privileged values for those properties—on the basis of which one can then classify a space as different by pointing out the way it does or does not resemble the privileged referent or referents. This, as Hetherington points out following Foucault, is the way metaphor works (42–43). The effect, moreover, is that the disturbing nature of difference is neutralized in a very specific way, namely, by relating something Other to something familiar. In the process, a specific order is maintained. Part of what gives heterotopias their shock value, however, is that no privileged point of reference—no standard of order—is immediately available to give meaning to the incommensurate mix of objects brought together. In this sense, spaces are heterotopic on the basis of the apparent but confusing similarity they establish among those objects by virtue of their co-presence (which is more akin to the way metonymy works): "Things are cast adrift, more or less like one another without any of them being able to claim the privileged status or 'model' for the rest."[14] To be sure, this sense of difference, too, gives rise to efforts at neutralization; but here, because no standard of order is immediately available, ordering itself becomes an issue. Put another way, discursivity is problematized, giving rise to new discourses.[15]

Instead of pinning down meaning by deference to a privileged metaphorical standard, metonymy postpones meaning by setting off a "series of deferrals" among similar objects of equal status (Hetherington 1997, 43). The constant movement implied by this operation of similitude helps to suggest why, for Hetherington, heterotopias constitute what he calls, following Bruno Latour, "obligatory points of passage" (68).[16] The perception of a sense of negation or otherness already implies a passage between two spaces precisely in the sense that a disturbing spatial similarity is established and a comparison is invited. Put more simply: one cannot arrive at a sense of one space as the opposite of (or, for that matter, as like) another space without at some point passing between them. The key focus, then, should be not on the sites themselves but on "what they perform in relation to other sites . . . a new way of ordering through the heterogeneous ways that they represent" (49).

As should be clear from this discussion, Hetherington situates the concept of heterotopia in a broader explanation of sociospatial change. The centerpiece of his explanation is Louis Marin's concept of *utopics*, "a spatial play on the theme of utopia" (1997, 11). In partial contrast to blueprint-like utopian ideals of social order, utopics is meant to convey some of the original fallibility intended by Thomas More when he first coined the word as a pun on the Greek terms *ou-topia* (meaning "no place") and *eu-topia* (meaning "good place" or "perfect place"). Utopia, in this respect, represents *perfection in constant deferral*. Hetherington relates the ambiguity of no-place/good-place implied by that term to the ambivalent drive toward control/freedom that characterizes modernity. As an effect of these ambiguities, then, other spaces are produced or appropriated that, on the basis of some notion of social improvement (the "perfect place" ideal) and in juxtaposition to their surrounding spaces (the "no-place" actuality), propose an alternate ordering. For Hetherington, in short, the utopic and the heterotopic occupy the same space in-between carved out by the modern ambivalences between ideals of control and freedom and related spaces of order and chaos. These ambivalences are Hetherington's point of departure. They represent a kind of Scylla and Charybdis that constitute an obligatory point of passage for us, carving out our modern spaces. As Hetherington seems to suggest, in other words, Odysseus's dilemma is our own.

Obvious parallels can be drawn between Lefebvre's lived spaces (spaces of representation) and the concept of heterotopia as advanced by Foucault and further developed by Hetherington. Clearly, both of these spatial concepts project the sense of a space where meaningful order is disrupted through a quasi-surreal juxtaposition of elements.[17] For Lefebvre, however, that disruption occurs as part of lived space and has the effect simply of resisting the dominant order. Both Hetherington and Foucault, however, theorize this disruption as an effect of a relationship between spaces and, by dint of that, as a more fundamental disruption of ordering itself. Foucault in fact may be read as positing heterotopia as an intermediary space between what Lefebvre has called spaces of representation (the lived), on the one hand, and representations of space (the conceived), on the other: "Thus, in every culture, between the *use* of what one might call the ordering codes [Lefebvre's lived space] and *reflections* upon order itself [Lefebvre's mental space], there is *the pure experience of order* and of its modes of being" (Foucault 1994b, xxi, my emphasis). These arguments suggest something about the way ideas about space are translated into spatial practices, and vice versa. In other words, it is because a culture at times superimposes "another kind of grid," a heterotopia, that neutralizes its "linguistic, perceptual, and practical grids," its dominant spaces (Foucault 1994b, xx)—or as Hetherington puts it, because a particular utopics is spatialized in a heterotopic space—that spatial ideas get translated into spatial practices and that spatial practices, in turn, give rise to new spatial ideas, including new orderings.

While Hetherington's implicit theory of social change is more compelling and open ended than Lefebvre's, however, it is not without its problems for an analysis of cyberspace. Because his focus is on the emergence of modernity, his explanations of these developments always begin with the same "impossible tension" between freedom and control (1997, 51). This is essentially a liberal problematic and certainly pertinent to an age defined by the emergence of the bourgeois liberal subject. However, one would reasonably expect the ambiguities that shape other ages, if one can speak in those terms, to be different ones. For example, one could infer from a reading of Augustine that the ambiguities that shaped the sacred and profane spaces of the Middle Ages very likely involved tensions between this-worldly and other-worldly concerns. By the same token, the virtual spaces generated in the Age of the Internet seem to be confronting us with new kinds of impossible tensions. Approaching these new tensions in terms of the liberal problematic between freedom and control may arrest our understanding of their radicalness. As I indicate in chapter 5, debates over the U.S. government's encryption policy have been set by both sides in the narrow terms of this modernist dilemma, as if the tension between freedom and control were the only significant one; but that debate seems, on my reading, to be an effect of a more fundamental contradiction between the physical and the virtual. It is to this discussion that I now turn.

Virtual Spaces

In the first section of this chapter, I proposed a conception of social space, following Lefebvre, as the product of perceived, conceived, and lived experiences. This alternative, as I noted, directly opposes both the treatment of spatiality as a given, physical container and its treatment as no more than matter that can be molded into any social construct. These considerations identify two extremes I wish to avoid in characterizing cyberspace—e.g., as a naturalized location within which virtual interactions take place (space-as-container) and as nothing more than a "common mental geography"[18] (space-as-construct). In the second section, I tried giving a clearer sense, following Foucault, of the place of discourse in the production of space and, additionally, how disruptions of discursive intelligibility in the juxtaposition of other spaces (heterotopias) might in time give rise to new discourses and, by extension, new spatial practices. In this section, I want to begin suggesting how it is that these spatial theories might be useful in understanding the spatiality of cyberspace.

To give a sense of what is at issue here, my initial description to others of the topic of this study—analyzing the space of cyberspace in relation to democracy—met with two very different reactions. Some responded skeptically by taking it for granted that cyberspace, because it is "only virtual" (read: not physical), is not *really* a space. At the same time, others emphasized the radical implications of viewing cyberspace as a space: namely, that this perspective could foreground for us that *all* space is in a sense virtual because it is discursively constructed. This insight, I was told, calls into question the very distinction between the physical and the virtual. Hence, whereas skeptical critics of my project assumed the distinction between the physical and the virtual and wanted me to address "the problem" of how a nonphysical cyberspace could be considered a "real" space, my more radical commentators urged me to discard the physical/virtual distinction by characterizing all space as discursive construct. Both sets of critics contributed useful insights to my thinking on these issues. Ultimately, however, their respective conclusions were only half right.

The distinction between the physical and the virtual is not one that can be completely abandoned. Doing so would evacuate the notion of cyberspace of what is distinctive about it: namely, its partial nonphysicality or, better, its different kind of physicality. To be sure, the spatiality of cyberspace does, I think, have radical implications, but not simply because it calls the physical/virtual distinction into question. In a sense, its radicalness depends in part on that distinction in that by offering up digital versions of conventionally physical phenomena, it skews practically every idea, every labor, every law, and every human interaction that has been conventionally understood or premised on the physicality of the things thought about, the commodities produced, the objects legislated, and the bodies engaged. The problem is not in retaining a distinction between physical and virtual, but in confusing that distinction with other notions, such as the difference between "real" and "not real."

In computing, the term *virtual* refers to "a simulation of a process or device," where simulation, in turn, means "the process of modeling and representing an activity, environment or system on a computer" (Cotton and Oliver 1994, 208, 182). Hence, *virtual* from a technical standpoint refers to a digital representation of something else, typically something that does or will exist in the physical world. The sense that the virtual refers to something nonphysical arises because binary digits are not perceived in quite the same manner as the "physical" things they simulate. Even this much, of course, assumes that we know what we mean by *physical*. In general, that term has been understood somewhat unproblematically as a reference to any phenomenon: that is, to objects or occurrences that can be perceived by the senses of sight, taste, touch, smell, and hearing. That understanding is evident in Lefebvre's notion of physical space as that field of experience that is perceived. What complicates this cursory understanding, however, is that numerous phenomena have a physical existence that cannot be directly perceived by the human body, though their effects are perceptible: for example, gravity. Add to this the vast regions of physical space that have been opened up to human perception through some technical medium, such as the microscope or the telescope, and one begins to realize that the physical includes much more than what can be perceived directly.

Despite such innovations, however, the inner space of the atom and the outer space of the cosmos are not routinely involved in most people's everyday social experiences. That is, inasmuch as what concerns us here is the physical as a component of social space, the phenomena that matter most are those that are typically involved in people's day-to-day interactions with each other. Conventionally, this has meant that the physical spaces at issue in any analysis of social space have been those phenomenal, perceptible spaces through which human bodies themselves move and interact. Put another way, physical space is typically defined in relation to the human body, i.e., as a space for the body, perceived and occupied by the body, and in many respects directing the movements of the body. Following this, the body has been the implicit locus around which social space has been perceived, conceived, and undoubtedly lived.

In ordinary language use, then, the physical is that which is present to our bodily senses. This conventional understanding of the physical is at the heart of the physical/virtual distinction. The virtual, by extension, is nonphysical only in this conventional sense, as something not open to unmediated perception. I follow these ordinary language uses here, employing the term *virtual* to refer broadly to anything that is in digital form: combinations of binary programming codes and electrical impulses that make up the bulk of the invisible data traversing computer circuits and network routes. These data may include a simulation of something that is conventionally physical (i.e., visible or tangible) and also something that only exists in digital form and is therefore, from a conventional standpoint, only ever "nonphysical."

What then of the skeptical and radical critiques of my topic? Both of these assertions, as I read them, assume, first, that cyberspace is indeed nonphysical. In addition, the skeptical assertion, while not exactly assuming that space is only physical, does nonetheless place undue emphasis on physicality as conventionally understood—i.e., as something that can be touched and seen—as an essential feature of all space. So the second assumption that skeptics make when they argue that cyberspace is not a real space is that all space proper must be fundamentally open to unmediated perception. In other words, they seem to believe that the only real spaces are those we can embody. In the meantime, the radical assertion, by insisting that the inherent discursiveness of all space does away with the physical/virtual distinction, denies that physicality is an important separate component of social space. So a third assumption at work here—this one stemming from radical interpretations of space—is that physicality is irrelevant. At the risk of opening myself up to further criticism from both sides, the responses I offer challenge all three of these assumptions.

First, the Internet, contrary to popular opinion, does have a physical component, namely, the technological objects that compose the inter-networking infrastructure or "backbone" and the data-transfer systems and remote terminal devices that people employ to communicate with each other across that backbone. This physicality can include, among other things, personal computers, monitors, keyboards, pointing devices, microphones, video cameras, modems, network interface cards, servers, routers, switches, telephone lines, coaxial cables, fiber-optic cables, radio towers, communications satellites, and, increasingly, handheld comput-ers and Internet-ready cell phones. In addition, the currents of binary data (as electricity, pulses of light, and microwaves) that flow in and out of these other physical components that make up computer networks are themselves also physical. What makes them a fundamentally different type of physical phenomena, however, is that they involve electromag-netic rather than mechanical forces and hence have different physical properties (see chapter 3). One consequence of this difference is that they cannot be perceived in conventional ways. What we see and hear of these data streams—the hodgepodge of words, images, and sounds on personal computers (PCs)—are the effects of computer *bits* (an acronym for "bi-nary digits") exciting phosphors on a computer screen or activating cir-cuits on a sound card. These bit streams nonetheless have a physicality that cannot be denied, and one, moreover, that requires computers and communications lines for their existence and transmission. Following this, what is chimerical about the Internet is this idea that it lacks a physi-cal presence. The truth is that cyberspace is present to us—that is, to our bodies—by dint of a physical interface, one composed of the tactile, visu-al, and auditory devices just noted. Furthermore, because one needs to be able to work at a computer (literally, to touch a keyboard, see a computer monitor, click a mouse) in order to go online, questions of access to the Internet are by and large also questions about physical proximity, about the proximity of one's own body to the computer at the interface. Indeed, as Olu Oguibe asserts, "[W]ithout this component, without this point of entry, this interface, cyberspace and its myriad promises and excesses, do not exist" (1996).

While these physical components are a condition for the existence of cyberspace, however, it is equally clear that people's sense of it as a promising social space "out there, somewhere" suggests that it cannot be reduced to the physical features just mentioned.[19] In other words, contrary to the second, skeptical assumption that social spaces are fundamentally spaces of, for, and by the body, the bodily interfaces with which we access the Internet are only small parts—and hardly the most fundamental ones—of what makes up the spatiality of cyberspace. That said, however, it would be a mistake to regard these bodily interfaces (conventionally physical in their nature) as irrelevant to what cyberspace is, as radical critics tacitly suggest when they insist that all space is virtual. The experiential interplay and occasional disjuncture between the *bodily hereness* before the screen and the *digital thereness* on the screen make cyberspace a unique kind of social space. Its difference and even dissonance could not be remarked but for the perceptual, conceptual, and living differences between the physical and the virtual.

Perceptually, networking is a spatial practice that requires, in addition to people and computers, the human activity of sending inherently invisible data through networks. It is this movement of bits (rather than of bodies) that constitutes the physical space of networking. This more general spatial practice of networking includes a variety of network systems with different protocols and access rules.[20] In addition to different networks themselves, the spatial practices of networking are shaped as well by the number of different modes of computer-mediated communication (CMC) that computer users employ.[21]

The social space of cyberspace is also constituted conceptually by various spatial discourses about what that networking space is and how it should be ordered. Initially, those discourses were novel, technical ones about resource sharing and using the computer as a communications tool instead of just a computational one. The spatial orders implied in these technical concerns led to the development of particular software programs and hardware innovations that instantiated, at the interface, a particular way of experiencing the spatiality of cyberspace, e.g., as a nonlinear (because randomly accessed), comparatively manipulable, logical workspace on a shared system (see Bolter 1984, 83–85). At the same time, these early technical discourses were themselves part of a broader political discourse of cold war tensions, giving rise to notions and actual blueprints for "robust" command-and-control communications networks (see chapter 3). As access to that space expanded to others outside the defense research community, however, it became subject to different technocultural and political discourses, and hence to different spatial orders. One of the most significant has certainly been the "cyberpunk" discourse of the antiauthoritarian "data cowboy" in cyberspace: a vision vividly in-augurated in the novels of writers like William Gibson and Bruce Sterling. From these fictional origins, the cyberpunk came to be enacted and defined by the activities of "hackers" and "crackers" and others who believed that information wants to be free.[22] These "rebels" quickly devel-oped the technical wherewithal to liberate data from sensitive and pro-prietary computer systems, an activity that became for them a virtue. Such activities, however, are more than just a mark of computer exper-tise. If the act of walking transforms the street into a space, as de Certeau reminds us (1988, 117), then hacking is one of several computer activities that have served further to redefine networking as a kind of space, i.e., to *respatialize* cyberspace according to a particular kind of spatial order, epitomized by references to the "Electronic Frontier," which is in many respects different from the spatiality inaugurated by official references to an "Information Superhighway."

Finally, networking practices and orders (as I show in more detail in chapter 4) are related as well to a variety of lived practices through which the spatiality of cyberspace is culturally experienced. It is here, for ex-ample, that the movement of data across network connections is consti-tuted as a movement of self, evident in references to *going online, surfing,* and the various *welcome-to* "home pages" on the Web that signify an ar-rival somewhere. It is here, too, that regular conferencing in a particular "forum" gives rise to a sense of community, that "flaming" gives rise to in-dignation, and that e-mail "courtships" give rise to actual marriages and divorces. Finally, it is here as well, as part of these practical experiences, that a certain ambiguity arises between the physical and the virtual, a dis-juncture or juxtaposition between ordinary experiences and computer-mediated ones.

It bears emphasizing, first, that no single component of the ones I have just mentioned composes cyberspace to the exclusion of the others; rather, it is the totality and interrelatedness of networking practices, spa-tial discourses, and online/offline experiences and ambiguities that give rise to that (alternative) social space. Second, I put the term *alternative* in parentheses to denote that not everything that happens online is Other; quite the contrary, many networking practices are discursively constitut-ed and intelligible as extensions of spatial practices in the realm of face-to-face encounters. On occasion, however, the ambiguities between fleshy and virtual encounters are foregrounded in ways that make people confront the assumptions, the practices, and the very discourses that underlie their ordinary interactions in the realm of the face-to-face. I have suggested, however, that social space is generally understood as involving, at a minimum, those physical spaces through which human bodies move and interact because it is, after all, human interaction that defines the social. So a key question here is whether and how cyberspace can be regarded as a social space if it does not involve the sorts of physical spaces where people encounter each other in the flesh. In other words, is it possible to have *sociality without faces?*

This phrase can be taken a number of ways. In one sense, I mean it as a tongue-in-cheek (pun intended) play on the conviction that interactions must be unmediated, face-to-face encounters for them to be authentically social. That said, I do not mean to imply at the outset that it is the face more than any other part of the body that matters for giving our encounters with others a certain sociality. Frankly, I consider that an open question. The issue, really, is whether social spaces need to be *embodied,* as some critics maintain. The sense that cyberspace is bodiless is the crux of the problem for those skeptics who resist accepting it as a real social space. I offer the idiom "sociality without faces" as a way of beginning to unravel what precisely is at stake in claims that our social encounters must be embodied. At the same time, *facelessness* also implies anonymity, which is certainly relevant to what many people consider to be a major problem of computer-mediated communication, i.e., that one never knows with *whom* exactly one is having an e-mail exchange. Apropos this, a now well-known cartoon and old (cyber) saw by Peter Steiner shows a canine sitting in front of a computer screen and talking to another four-legged chum sitting nearby. The punch line is in Steiner's famous caption, which succinctly and whimsically captures the faceless nature of the new medium: "On the Internet, nobody knows you're a dog."[23] Such playful turns with the facelessness of cyberspace do occasionally give way to more sinister ones. At a minimum, even people who know each other and are mutually tactful and polite in their face-to-face exchanges will occasionally evince a casually hurtful insensitivity toward each other in their e-mail exchanges. Certainly, the possibility that we act differently toward others when we interact through mediated channels rather than in the flesh does suggest that perhaps the face-to-face matters. How precisely mediated encounters are different, however, and certainly whether and in what sense they are worse remain open questions.

As a preliminary consideration of these issues, it is worth recalling that "mass society," the dreaded object of analysis of Weber, Durkheim, and other sociologists writing at the turn of the twentieth century, was understood as the totality of patterned, semianonymous, and alienated forms of human interactions—of *encounters with strangers*—that had come to characterize modern industrial societies, in marked contrast to the direct forms of interpersonal interactions and associations with familiars that presumably characterized premodern, local communities. No huge conceptual leap is required to move from a notion of sociality among *strange* faces to a notion of sociality *without* faces, particularly once we recognize that even face-to-face encounters with strangers— indeed, all purportedly immediate experiences—are nonetheless discursively mediated the moment some effort is made to understand them (Scott 1992).

This sense that face-to-face encounters are discursively mediated (or "typified") is evident in the work of phenomenologist Alfred Schutz, whose concept of *lifeworld* informs Habermas's theory of communicative-action (Habermas 1987).[24] Although he accords greater significance to fleshy (or "in person") encounters, Schutz argues that the social world is actually an interrelated composite of *immediate* (that is, face-to-face) interactions with others and *mediate* (that is, remote) interactions with others beyond our reach (1967; see also Schutz and Luckmann 1973 and 1989). Schutz's definition of face-to-face encounters is worth quoting at length for the way it clarifies the importance of a shared spatiality (and temporality) in such encounters and the special role it accords the body as the signifier of an inner consciousness (a point that has been challenged recently by critical theorists, as I argue in chapter 4, but which nonetheless conveys what I take to be a common understanding of the importance of the body in our interactions with others):

> I speak of another person as within reach of my direct experience when he shares with me a community of space and a community of time. He shares a community of space with me when he is present in person and I am aware of him as such, and, moreover, when I am aware of him as this person *himself,* this *particular* individual, and of his body as the field upon which play the symptoms of his inner consciousness. He shares a community of time with me when his experience is flowing side by side with mine, when I can at any moment look over and grasp his thoughts as they come into being, in other words, when we are growing older together. Persons thus in reach of each other's direct experience I speak of as being in the "face-to-face" situation. The face-to-face situation presupposes, then, an actual simultaneity with each other of two separate streams of consciousness. . . . We are now adding to it [to the notion of "temporal immediacy"] the

corollary of the spatial immediacy of the Other, in virtue of which his body is present to me as a field of expression for his subjective experiences. (1967, 163)

Schutz maintains that these direct (simultaneous and co-present) encounters with others are important in two ways. First, it is in our early, immediate encounters with others—i.e., in the interpersonal exchanges between a caretaker and a child—that we first acquire language, which becomes the basis for our subsequent social categories or typifications. Second, it is here, too, in our face-to-face encounters, that the other person is fully present to me and I to him in a "We-relationship," as fellow human beings rather than (anonymous) typifications (1967, 164). Hence, even while he regards the social as a necessarily reciprocal relationship between these immediate we-relations and mediate (indirect) interactions that together supply us with the typifications or "stock of knowledge" for understanding all of our social situations (Schutz and Luckmann 1973, 99–100), Schutz nonetheless regards face-to-face encounters as foundational.

His point is not, however, that face-to-face encounters afford us a kind of transparent, nondiscursive apprehension of others; on the contrary, once language is acquired, every person approaches a social situation with a set of preformed categories for understanding the situation she or he is in. These typifications, however, do not remain fixed. Indeed, what is different about the face-to-face encounter is that because others are present before us, we can check and modify our preconceptions. To put it in phenomenological terms: our simultaneous co-presence may make it possible for us to enter each other's "stream of consciousness." We can get clues about each other's dispositions from our bodily appearance and gestures (pursed lips, flared nostrils, agitated breathing). We can engage each other in a mutually reflexive conversation about what we are doing ("Are you picking a fight with me?"). We can mutually direct the unfolding course of action ("This isn't about you; it's about something that happened at work."). We can, in short, partake in an open and reciprocal process whereby we co-produce our situation (e.g., as an effort to blow off steam with a loved one rather than pick a fight with her). The mediate interaction, by contrast, is really a series of semidiscrete actions and counteractions that, because the Other is not present, are each entirely dependent on our discursive categories or typifications for our making sense of them. This point is clearly stated in Schutz's later publications with Thomas Luckmann:

> The Other's consciousness is not graspable in its living forms of appearance but only via the "rigidified" results of his operation, his work. The one acts, the other experiences the results of this action and interprets them in one way or another and then acts in his turn, whereupon the first must interpret the results of this action. (Schutz and Luckmann 1989, 88)[25]

Whatever sense of co-presence *we* derive from these actions and counteractions is only apparent: an "as-if simultaneity" (90).

Clearly, from a phenomenological perspective, the face-to-face encounter remains not simply relevant to sociality but central, constituting an empirical foundation of everyday life—including one's personal identity—by inaugurating our entry into language (into symbolic categories) and providing an interactive context for the development and modification (rather than just the reproduction) of our discourses. On this view, one could imagine a society composed exclusively of face-to-face encounters but not one made up only of mediate "social interactions" (which are really more akin to individual actions and counteractions). Even if we agree with this, however, it remains nonetheless clear that, for Schutz and Luckmann, mediate interactions—forms of sociality without faces—are genuine (albeit, derivative) components of the social world.

Furthermore, and this is a crucial point, Schutz and Luckmann allow that various modes of increasingly remote communications still enable a kind of mutual interaction, even though mediated—i.e., of interactive social exchanges that unfold under the mutual, reciprocal direction of the participants without their physical and temporal co-presence: "Depending on the state of communications technology, the symptoms whereby the Other is apprehended can decrease while the synchronization of the streams of consciousness can still, to a certain extent, be maintained: a conversation face to face but in the dark, a telephone conversation, smoke signals, drum language, televideophone, letters" (1989, 90). We may, in effect, get fewer visual, sensual, or auditory cues about the Other (i.e., of those bodily "symptoms whereby the Other is apprehended") while still deriving or retaining a sense, via our interactive communications technologies, of her consciousness. The fact that Schutz and Luckmann include even smoke signals, drums, and letters in this seems to me astounding inasmuch as these forms of communication are completely devoid of all of the immediate (i.e., perceptible) marks of the Other's body: her face, her voice, her touch. They convey only the barest traces of the rhythms of a person's movements, in, for example, the density and flow of the handwriting in the letter (provided it has not been typed or even computer printed!). What seems crucial here is the possibility of a kind of give-and-take, of *interactivity*. In short, even while Schutz and Luckmann prioritize the face-to-face and consider mediate interactions as, at best, a derivative sociality, they nonetheless allow that some mediated forms of action/counteraction—i.e., those that occur via interactive modes of communication—may approximate the simultaneity and co-presence of the face-to-face encounter.

The implications of this for cyberspace should now be apparent. The issue that motivated my digression into phenomenology was whether one can speak of cyberspace as a social space without there being, as a component of that, a physical space in which human beings could encounter each other in the flesh. The answer, at least as suggested by Schutz and Luckmann, is a qualified "yes": qualified in the sense that they cannot imagine a social world that does not have its roots in face-to-face encounters. That qualification, however, is not really a problem for my considerations here since no one is advocating the complete displacement of the face-to-face, but it does raise a number of interesting questions for democratic theory. Even assuming that human sociality has its foundations in face-to-face encounters, are such encounters necessary to the kinds of open deliberations that participatory democrats advocate? Put another way: does a participatory democratic politics require the production of a space-time in which participants are physically co-present? And if citizens must be present to each other in the flesh, what special role do their bodies play in the performance of democratic politics? Or, alternatively, can certain technologies take the place of the body's presence? How, in short, have space, technology, and the body been theorized in relation to democracy?

chapter 2

Democratic Utopias

Space and democracy correspond in ways that are neither unique nor incidental. This relationship is, in a sense, ordinary in that, as Michael Shapiro observes, "all forms of political theory that are comprehensive and totalizing presume elaborate spatial strategies" (1992, 4). It is also seemingly obligatory in that theories of democracy assume a form of government at least *of* the People (if not also *for* and *by* them) and that has entailed imaginative projections of the spaces through which people collectively engage in their democratic practices. At one extreme, the space of democracy has been imagined in terms of a boundary between state and society, minimally permeated by ballot boxes. At the other extreme, it has been regarded as the space of a self-governing community, constituted wherever citizens regularly meet face-to-face to deliberate public matters.[1] Implicit in most of these spatial strategies has been the sense that physical space—often framed in terms of "size"—constitutes a specific kind of problem for democratic politics.[2] Theorists of *representative* democracy, of course, claim to have solved this problem according to the representative principle of popular sovereignty through the regular vote (e.g., Madison 1988a, 1988b; cf., Barber 1984, 249–51). Notwithstanding their claims, however, this so-called problem has occasionally resurfaced as a set of acute legitimation crises in the form, for example, of the problem of gerrymandered voting districts or, for that matter, as the loss of "social capital" (Putnam 1995), which is fundamentally about the decline of a civility and trust that was engendered in people when they got together face-to-face at social clubs and other voluntary associations.[3] For advocates of *participatory* democracy, by contrast, physical space has been a more chronically salient problem—if not an ineluctable one (Sale 1980; see also Oldenburg 1989)—addressed by explicit reference to "the problem of scale," of the optimum size of a polity beyond which all pretense to a popular government administered by the People must be given up as impractical and delusional.[4]

In addressing these issues, theorists often employ spatial metaphors to construct ideal representations of space (in Lefebvre's sense) or, better, spatial discourses (in a more Foucauldian sense) that advocate a set of spatial practices that, in their view, best realizes the principle of democracy. Though often presented unproblematically, such ideal metaphors actually embody theoretical claims not just about where democracy is located, but also about what it is, what constitutes its proper scope, who gets to practice it, and how it is practiced. Read this way, all democratic theories are utopian cartographies. They propose, in Thomas More's double sense, an ideal nonplace *(eu-/ou-topia)* that does not yet (or does no longer) exist but that can provoke the normative invention of spaces that approach the ideals they project.

In this chapter, I proffer a critical rereading of democratic theories in a way that foregrounds their spatial strategies. I begin by outlining two classic examples of efforts to *scale* democracy, both to surmount the problem of space and to resize democratic societies. The republican doctrine of Madison's *Federalist* No. 10 provides an example of an elitist strategy for spatializing democracy for a mass society, whereas the doctrine of participatory democracy outlined in "The Port Huron Statement" of Students for a Democratic Society (SDS) maps a more egalitarian strategy. As a third alternative, Benjamin Barber's *Strong Democracy* makes a significant contribution to scaling democracy by articulating the problem of space to mechanisms for enhancing civic communication, including the use of electronic media. Despite their differences, however, all of these spatial strategies presuppose a rather fixed set of relationships between physical space and political identity, assuming that democratic politics is always best realized when people can actually meet face-to-face in small settings. Hence, despite Barber's optimism regarding the use of electronic communications technologies to scale democracy, he treats this only as a supplement to a superior kind of interaction enabled when we engage others in the flesh. Physical spaces and bodies are treated with considerably more ambivalence in the public-realm theories of Hannah Arendt and Jürgen Habermas, as I show in the second and third sections of this chapter. Both of these theorists offer up descriptions of social and political spaces that are presented not simply as metaphors, but as quasi-topographical analyses of past spaces intended to provide us with ideal cartographies. In the process, both Arendt and Habermas allude to physical spaces and bodies. Read exclusively in these terms, their work seems to commend an anachronistic conception of face-to-face democracy. Further contributing to this reading is that both theorists speak in terms of a "degeneration" of public, political spaces, due in no small part to technological changes.

The spatial problems that have vexed democratic theory, however, have been perennial because theorists typically misunderstand the nature of space. They tend to treat the space of politics literally as a static, physical container and to treat the citizen as a body that might or might not occupy or have access to that space. In this respect, the corporeal presence of citizens in a shared, physical space has been a key spatial strategy at work in many theories of democracy (a point I foreground in my analysis). What I propose throughout this study, however, is the need to theorize space, technology, the body, and the complex relationships between them. Democratic theory raises the stakes a bit by asking what kind of political agency is effected by particular combinations of these components. By locating allusions to physical spaces and bodies in this kind of inquiry, I foreground that what are at stake in these various utopian cartographies of democracy are questions about the production of various kinds of social spaces (in Lefebvre's sense) and the political identities they help to make possible. Because both spaces and identities are socially produced, what is needed is a much more dynamic conception of how technologies contribute to the construction of new kinds of spaces and identities. Ironically, despite their pessimistic conclusions regarding contemporary technologies, both Arendt and Habermas conceptualize this dynamic in more suggestive ways, providing the basis for a richer understanding of the bodiless seductions of cyberspace.

Scaling Democracy

In American political thought, *Federalist* No. 10 is the classic statement of "the problem of factions" (Held 1987, 61–66), the turmoil that can erupt when citizens motivated by private desires and interests ignore the public good and violate the individual rights of others (principally, property rights). Often less noted by commentators are the spatial practices at work in the defense of an *extended* republic that Madison begins in *Federalist* No. 10 (1988a) and continues in No. 14 (1988b). As a political tract oriented to the politics of its time, *Federalist* No. 10 is, more fundamentally, an argument for why a spatially expansive, federal republic can mitigate this problem of factions better than the smaller state republics preferred by the anti-Federalists and far better, of course, than the considerably smaller "pure Democracy" model, which, significantly, none of the Founding Fathers favored (Madison 1988a, 46).[5] As this suggests, what we today call representative *democracy* was for Madison a *republic* based on the principle of popular sovereignty through representation. The "scheme of representation" he lauded (46) assumes a primary spatial separation between the *center* of government (the official locus of politics) and its administrative sphere.[6] The elected "proper guardians of the public weal" are located in the official assembly sites of government, "at the helm" (1988a, 47, 45). By contrast, the mass of citizens—conceived implicitly as property-owning males[7]—are situated, according to this scheme, in the broader space of administration, exercising their popular sovereignty, minimally, "by regular vote" (45). Their larger numbers in "a greater sphere of country" (46), moreover, best ensure that no single faction will come to power and violate individual rights. In fact, the problem that Madison identifies with a pure democracy is precisely that the closed-in spatial nature of this form of "Government in person" facilitates too much "communication and concert" and hence "nothing to check the inducements to sacrifice the weaker party" to the will of a factious majority (46). In short, various spatial strategies are directly implicated in Madison's argument at each stage. The ownership of land—the typical understanding of "property"—implicitly restricts the domain of citizenship and also gives citizens so-defined a very specific kind of stake in the union, which is itself territorially defined. A larger union territory, moreover, extends the scope of government and multiplies the number and variety of factions, mitigating the possibility that a majority faction might arise. Or if one did arise, the geographic dispersion of citizens in an extended republic, according to Madison, would make it more difficult for the emergent majority faction "to concert and carry into effect schemes of oppression": that is, to meet, communicate, and conspire (46).

This elitist sense that geographic space provides a buffer against factions has been updated for the era of electronic mediation in Robert Wright's 1995 *Time* cover story on "hyperdemocracy."[8] Wright begins by identifying a popular criticism that the "Washington Beltway"—Interstate Highway 495, which surrounds Washington, D.C.—has come to symbolize a "great invisible barrier, impermeable to communication, that separates the nation's capital from the nation," keeping politicians "with an 'inside the Beltway' mentality—out of touch with the needs of the citizenry." Against the multipartisan spectrum of computer optimists—including

Al Gore, Newt Gingrich, and Ross Perot—who maintain that an "electronic town hall" can "break through the Beltway barrier," Wright argues that the new information technologies have made the "nation . . . thoroughly plugged in to Washington—*too* plugged in for its own good." (This is arguably a questionable claim, if not downright obnoxious, in the context of an ostensibly democratic system.) Demonstrating the deleterious effects of too much communication, Wright points out that when congressional deliberations begin drifting away from their interests, Washington lobbyists can now instantaneously muster what appears to be popular reaction, swamping legislators with "a deluge of protest borne by phone, letter or fax." As a consequence, "There is no buffer allowing Representatives to think about what's going on. . . . In the old days you had a few months or weeks, at least a few days. Now you may have a few seconds before the wave hits."[9] The ideal the Founding Fathers sought to realize, Wright laments, "was cool deliberation by elected representatives, *buffered* from the often shifting winds of opinion—*inside-the-Beltway deliberation*" (my emphasis). Madison's sacrosanct legacy, in Wright's remapping, becomes a *Washington-Beltway Democracy,* one that depends (or perhaps depended, once upon a time) on geographic distance as a way of partially isolating public-minded politicians from factious lobbies.[10]

In 1962, Students for a Democratic Society (SDS) completed a document called "The Port Huron Statement," which has come to be viewed as the classic exemplar of an opposing, more direct form of participatory democracy (SDS 1994, 329–74). Among the contemporary problems the statement identifies is that political apathy, too often treated as a subjective disposition, is objectively reinforced by "the actual structural separation of people from power, from relevant knowledge, from pinnacles of decision-making" (336). Implicitly constructing the symbolic Washington Beltway buffer as part of the problem, the SDS argued that politics had become unrepresentative and socially irresponsible, with disenfranchised constituencies, an "enormous lobby force" that distorts "the focus of political attention" away from social problems and public-minded solutions, and a "Remote Control Economy" that excludes the vast majority of individuals from basic decisions affecting their lives (337–38). The result of this structural isolation of people from effective political and economic participation has been "a democracy without publics" (336). For SDS, the solution lay in returning democratic power to these publics, which meant reversing Madison's top-down legacy by empowering the poor and other disenfranchised groups, enabling collective decision making "by public groupings," and providing all individuals with access to knowledge and power so that "private problems" could be expressed and "formulated as general issues" (333). This last point in particular meant practicing a form of local consensus politics for organizing a mass coalition, in direct contrast to the geographically dispersed form of controlled conflict that Madison helped to institute. The spatial assumptions underpinning this reversal are best captured in the title of James Miller's history of SDS: *Democracy Is in the Streets* (1994). Against a disempowering Beltway-buffer politics, the SDS proposed a "participatory democracy" (333) that sought to relocate political power where it properly existed—among the people (universally conceived)—and where, as it turned out, that public power could be its most strikingly visible—among the literally tens of thousands of bodies that gathered throughout the 1960s to march in protests on the sidewalks along Pennsylvania Avenue, i.e., inside the Washington Beltway. This remapping proposed a more localized, noninstitutional, and distributed political space (or better: spaces), where individuals could meet face-to-face, deliberate matters, and arrive at a consensus that would have real consequences at other levels (i.e., at the centers of government). What SDS proffered, in short, was a bottom-up, *in-the-streets* democracy that would begin at the grassroots and "March on Washington."[11]

As these examples suggest, two constitutive dimensions typically underlie ideas about what counts as democracy. One of these dimensions, as I have been suggesting, is geographic: it involves suppositions about the physical scale of politics (large or small) appropriate to the particular definition of democracy being vaunted. The other dimension is ontological: implied, on the one hand, by Madison's emphasis on individuals and their rights and, on the other hand, by SDS's emphasis on consensus, community-building practices, and social responsibilities. That is, in addition to making claims about the physical space of politics, theorists also presuppose some conception of political agency, of the nature of the human beings involved in the political process. These assumptions run from an individualist ontology at one extreme (which presupposes individual agency as the appropriate subunit and emphasizes ethics of liberalism, pluralism, and a rights-based notion of citizenship) to a social ontology at the other extreme (which proffers a collective agency—i.e., the community—as the basic political subunit and places greater normative emphasis on communitarianism, conformism, and a responsibilities-based notion of citizenship).[12] What emerges from these two constitutive dimensions is a theoretical corridor, as it were, within which most scholars locate theories of democracy: between ideals that spatialize elite variants of a representative form of democracy in large-scale societies, at one end, and those that spatialize a more egalitarian notion of direct democracy in local communities, at the other.

The most remarkable feature about this typical way of mapping democratic theories is the presumption that both physical space and political agency are, in a sense, separate but correlated dimensions that are relatively fixed vis-à-vis each other. Physical space (large or small) simply confronts political agents (individual or communal), whose own natures are shaped by whether or not the size of the polity affords them the opportunity to meet face-to-face, i.e., to encounter each other in the flesh. It is in this respect that democratic theories have tended to treat space as a physical container, within which bodies of citizens (in both the individualist and collectivist sense, i.e., the *corporeal* bodies of individual citizens and the *corporate* bodies of communities) conduct their politics.

This is, of course, a rather crude typology (or, better, typography). The points at which one would place particular models of democracy

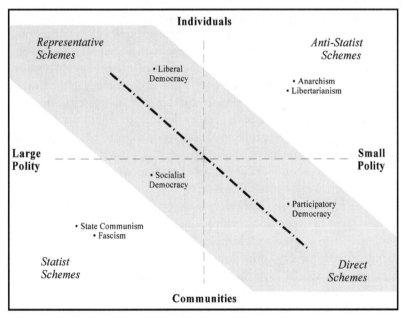

Figure 2. The democratic corridor: a graphic representation of the imaginative limits of democratic theory. Drawing from assumptions about the relationship between scale and agency, political philosophers have theorized ideal and less-than-ideal democratic polities that can be mapped to specific areas within this corridor. These assumptions, in short, have shaped the ways many theorists spatialize democracy.

(e.g., liberal democracy) and models of government types that many theorists consider undemocratic (e.g., the ostensibly anything-goes, anti-statist inclinations of anarchism) are certainly open to debate. However, as a general scheme for showing how common assumptions about size and agency lead theorists to map democratic space, this legend is useful. Of particular significance is the tendency among theorists to locate participatory schemes in the quadrant between the "Small Polity" and "Communities," and the obverse tendency to locate representative schemes in the quadrant between "Large Polity" and "Individuals." Clearly, Madison's doctrine belongs in the latter category (indeed, it helped to create that category), whereas the doctrine of local, face-to-face, consensus politics proffered in "The Port Huron Statement," which helped make the concept of "participatory democracy" famous, belongs in the former category (SDS 1994, 333).[13]

Although they offer opposing (if not exactly extreme) spatial strategies, both of these familiar examples make similar assumptions about democracy and space. "The Port Huron Statement" assumes that a truly participatory democracy must begin at the local, face-to-face level (in the streets). Similarly, despite the contemporary inclination to read Madison's doctrine as a defense of representative democracy, Madison understood himself explicitly to be promoting a republican system of government over and against those "turbulent democracies of ancient Greece" (1988b, 63). To the extent that our contemporary liberal democracy in the United States is based on this unapologetic antidemocratic doctrine, it is not surprising that theorists of participatory democracy regard the attenuated liberal solution to the problem of scale as no solution at all. Indeed, as Benjamin Barber concludes, "The representative principle is not the salvation of democracy under conditions of mass society: it is the surrender of democracy to mass society" (1984, 251).

Barber's study, *Strong Democracy* (1984), offers a unique contribution to the debate between liberals and communitarians in contemporary democratic theory (see, for example, Sandel 1984). According to Barber, liberalism offers a very "thin" conception of democracy (4). Implicit in this term is the spatial sense that the liberal solution of spreading democracy over such a broad expanse has left that notion vacuous: literally insubstantial, like a space devoid of matter. In place of a substantive form of democracy, liberalism has proffered the passive voter (with no corresponding theory of active participation beyond occasional interest-group affiliations), a pluralist politics characterized by the bargaining and negotiating of private interests (with no alternate conception of public goods or common interests), and a representative government that actually invites citizens to give up, by delegating, most of their capacities for self-government (145–47). A radically communitarian orientation, at the other extreme, proffers, according to Barber, a "*unitary democracy*" concerned more with consensus and homogenous will formation than democratic self-expression (148, my emphasis). Barber argues that this position may have been appropriate for the small-scale communities of the past, in which decisions could be settled unanimously because members were more or less homogenous; he acknowledges (with liberals), however, that this ideal is inappropriate "in larger settings" and can turn "malevolent," placing an overriding emphasis on "monism, conformism, and coercive consensualism" through appeals to a "communal will" (149–50). If liberalism is too thin, then, Barber's critique that radical communitarianism offers a unitary democracy suggests that its ideals are, in a sense, too thick, insisting on a singular, substantive notion of the common good and squashing diversity in the process. In this respect, communitarianism tends toward a rather provincial notion of democracy (in the double sense of a delimited space and a narrow vision). Barber's concept of strong democracy, by contrast, is meant to provide, first, a less spatially concentrated and hence less provincial form of communitarian politics by spreading community-building practices and sensibilities across a mass, plural society, in the hopes, secondly, of redressing the vacuousness of the thin, liberal ideal of representative democracy. In the process, Barber makes a rather significant contribution to the problem of scale: he assimilates it explicitly to "the problem of communication" (248).

Barber argues that the size of a polity is actually a relative rather than an absolute measure, shaped in part by sometimes mediated senses of affiliation: "political size . . . is relative both to psychology and to technology" (246). Because a political community is "a human network rooted in communication," the problem of scale can be ameliorated, as liberals suggest, but in ways that are sanguine for a more robust participatory politics than Madisonian Beltway politics has allowed. In this respect, scale is no longer "an insuperable barrier" against democracy (247). Barber places part of his faith in electronic communications. Although typically an instrument of one-way mass communication, television, he argues, can be developed as an interactive "civic medium," contributing to the production of a technologically mediated space for democratic politics. What he proffers is the sense of an open, talk-oriented "electronic town meeting," together with the development of an informational

"Civic Videotex Service," that can complement (rather than replace) local political institutions (274, 278). Wright (1995) notwithstanding, Barber does not suggest that such technologies will help lobbyists plug through the Washington Beltway more decisively; rather, his point is to reempower citizens by connecting them primarily to each other in ways that extend the developmental benefits of civic participation beyond those immediately present and that enable an informed and reactivated citizenry on a large scale. Such technologies, Barber suggests, can conquer space—counteracting not just geographic distances but also psychological and social distances—in the process of enhancing "sympathetic communication" (247).

Despite his participatory convictions, however, Barber's notion of strong democracy has nonetheless seemed to some critics to provide a still-too-thin, plebiscite version of citizen participation: one that reduces civic engagement to registering opinions and votes on a videotex system rather than engaging others in rational debate in a political, public space (see Elshtain 1982; Masciulli 1988). In fact, Barber's suggestions are not quite so radical as his more classically minded critics suggest. Perhaps because his recommendations in the early 1980s predated the significant advances in and popularization of personal computing and networking, his notion of strong democracy actually depends on first securing the possibilities for what he refers to as "*proximate* self-legislation": "strong democratic talk" first and foremost in "neighborhood assemblies" (132, 271, my emphasis). He argues, moreover, that the neighborhood assembly "should have a physical home in the neighborhood" to give it permanence (271). In this respect, Barber insists on the continuing significance of small-scale, physical spaces within which neighbors can meet face-to-face to deliberate local issues. Electronic town meetings, in his view, would have to be both parasitic on these local political spaces (in that electronic town meetings begin as televised versions of neighborhood assemblies) and also supplemental to them (in that electronic town meetings merely—though helpfully—expand the context of local deliberations to those others who cannot be physically present). Hence, having outlined a program for scaling democracy—that is, for surmounting the problem of scale by conceptually and technologically resizing political space—Barber winds up scaling back his theory. Despite his willingness to explore the new spaces opened up by modern media technologies, he returns to old ground, retaining a classical sense of democratic politics that leads him to privilege those physical spaces within which citizens can meet in the flesh. And despite his inclination to assimilate space to communication and psychology, he adheres to a rather literal understanding of local politics and neighborhood assembly, instead of, say, a media-facilitated localized politics and neighborly assembly among people who are not physically co-present.

Barber's retrenchment invites questions about whether, in attempting to spatialize democracy in relation to the extraordinarily large spaces of modern societies, something necessary to strong, participatory democracy is irrevocably lost. Citing Rousseau's communitarian ideal of democracy, Masciulli, for his part, maintains that protechnology theorists like Barber confuse "the mere familiarity and informality that people might experience through telepolitics" with "the kind of *rooted intimacy and transparency*" experienced only in the face-to-face communications that Rousseau considered essential to democracy (1988, 157, my emphasis). Even Barber similarly asserts that "[t]here is little doubt that the electronic town meeting sacrifices intimacy, diminishes the sense of face-to-face confrontation, and increases the dangers of elite manipulation" (274). Neither Barber nor Masciulli, however, actually explains what lies behind this language of "intimacy," nor how, as Masciulli asserts, it is different from "mere familiarity." What they allude to is a vague emotional connection among a group of people, a civic-minded sociality that ostensibly emerges only among those who encounter each other in the flesh. Here I want to return more explicitly to the question posed at the end of the last chapter: that is, whether the ideal of a participatory democracy depends always on a mode of sociality derived only from face-to-face interactions with others; or whether, alternatively, one can derive a participatory democratic politics from a sociality without faces.

Although Barber and Masciulli raise this issue implicitly in their respective claims regarding intimacy, neither of them goes far enough in explaining what is at stake in their similar assertions. Elsewhere in his text, however, Barber does articulate a notion of "affiliation and affection" as a function of strong democracy (186), one that is important to the development of a feeling of "empathy" that "transcends private interests and the antagonisms they breed" (189). It is this affective aspect of strong democratic talk that I take to be at stake in Barber's concerns with intimacy. Because mass politics is a politics among strangers, engaging others in discussion, on Barber's account, stimulates in us a kind of "artificial kinship" with those others (189), one that gives me a stake in democratic talk because through such engagements, I can develop, first, the empathetic sense that "'I am like others' and 'I like others'" and, second, the transformative sense that I am part of a larger *we* (188, 190). The issue

Barber raises is, of course, relevant. How in the context of plural societies and in the face of the strong sense of individuality that liberalism has fostered can individuals develop a stake in solidarity and collective action? In addressing this issue, however, Barber vacillates between a communitarian language of intimacy, empathy, and kinship and a liberal language of individuality. *Intimacy,* in this respect, is an elusive concept and perhaps intentionally so. That is, despite Barber's objections to a unitary form of democracy, the intimacy he lauds comes close to a kind of conformism and consensualism, curbing antagonisms and conflicts by encouraging not just familiarity (getting strangers to know one another), but empathetic assimilation ("I am like others"). Hence, rather than addressing the problem of a politics among strangers, an emphasis on intimacy, when read through Barber's ambivalent discussion of affiliation and affection, actually sidesteps the problem of strangeness by eradicating difference. Rather than a radical reconfiguration of democratic politics, then, strong democracy evinces standard convictions about the relatively stable and necessary relationship between small-scale, physical spaces and communitarian principles of agency; televisions are thrown in merely as a kind of second-order extension of the affiliation, affection, and empathy that ostensibly are rooted in the face-to-face situation (247). In this respect, what Barber proffers as strong democracy is the notion of a media-enhanced (though not produced) space of sympathetic communications.

Hannah Arendt, for her part, remained deeply suspicious of the communitarian emphasis on intimacy, empathy, kinship, and community as the basis for a democratic politics.[14] Intimacy implies not attention to a plurality of different perspectives, but rather the effort to embrace the singular perspective of an Other through a process of empathy. In this view, it poses a threat to the very plurality and difference that characterize modern societies. As we shall see, it was precisely against such threats that Arendt proffered her notion of an at once embodied and bodiless *space of appearance* as her ideal cartography for mapping democracy.

The Human Condition

In her seminal study *The Human Condition* (1958), Hannah Arendt argues that politics proper has been lost in the modern age. Arendt constructs this loss in specifically spatial terms, i.e., as a displacement of one kind of political space by the predominantly apolitical realm of the social, whose ethos is the administration and regulation of the formerly private issues of necessity. Drawing from her own historical understanding of the classical polis of Greek antiquity, Arendt defines politics, by contrast, in terms of an ethos of speech and action in a space of appearance. In the Athenian public realm, which she holds up as a standard, citizens collectively concerned themselves not with bodily necessity—which for the Greeks was "a prepolitical phenomenon" (31)—but rather with debating public matters, giving voice to the plurality of opinions on any one issue, distinguishing themselves as unique individuals by taking a public stand on such issues, and jointly determining the course of their actions as citizens by means of rhetoric and persuasion, rather than by force and violence. In this respect, Arendt's premodern standard of a truly democratic space is closer to the egalitarian pure democracy that Madison and his contemporaries rejected, but it is also a substantive standard at odds with SDS's ideal of a political order where "private problems" can be "formulated as general issues" (SDS 1994, 333).

As will become clear, Arendt's diagnosis of the modern age is based in part on a critique of technology. On the face of it, this makes her theory less open to the possibilities of creating technologically mediated public spaces via computer networks. Because she returns, perhaps more decisively than any other twentieth-century political philosopher, to the classical ideal of the Athenian polis, however, her work seems particularly relevant to the analysis of a technology that has been characterized in precisely those quasi-utopian terms, as forging "a new Athenian Age of democracy" (Gore 1994). Furthermore, despite her critique of technology, Arendt's description of the space of politics as one that necessarily excludes the body and its necessities bears a striking resemblance to discourses of cyberspace that construct it as a bodiless conversational space in opposition to "meatspace," that is, to the space of the physical body. This similarity motivates my exploration of the classical, democratic utopia Arendt outlines in her philosophy.

To some readers, however, characterizing Arendt's political philosophy as democratic and utopian is wrong on both counts. Indeed, her valorization of Athenian politics, based as it was on a slave economy and on the systematic exclusion of women and propertyless males from the public realm, seems elitist and on that account fundamentally antidemocratic.[15] Furthermore, her critique of the modern age as one where the public realm has been displaced by a mass society of atomized individuals concerned only with the preservation of their own lives is arguably more dystopian than utopian. In a sense, however, it is precisely because Arendt seems at times so pessimistic about the possibilities of reinvigorating politics as she understands it that the standard of public deliberation among citizens that she lauds is utopian: albeit, a retrospective utopia rather than a prospective one.[16] Offering less an emancipatory theory of politics than a profoundly cynical assessment of its degeneration, she has left the task of positive theory building to later scholars, who have nonetheless managed to find provocative insights in her efforts to invite us "to think what we are doing" (5).[17]

With respect to the first point—the antidemocratic conditions that her ideal political space ostensibly presupposes—Arendt's idealization of Athenian politics is a defense of its principled commitment to a public space of deliberation rather than of the exclusionary conditions that made it possible for citizens to detach themselves from household concerns. To be sure, in *The Human Condition,* Arendt does merely describe without criticizing the exclusion of women and slaves in Athenian politics.[18] Elsewhere, moreover, she in fact suggests that the inclusion of formerly disenfranchised groups actually contributed to the demise of the political. According to Honig, Arendt, in *On Revolution,* attributes the failures of the French Revolution "to the fact that 'the poor, driven by the needs of their bodies, burst onto the scene' and effectively closed the spaces of politics by making the 'social question' the center of political attention" (1992, 218, with internal quotations from Arendt). This objection to the poor, however, is not directed at some innate inability on their part to engage in politics proper; rather, as Arendt suggests in her explanation of Aristotle's views on slavery, what makes the enslaved (or by analogy, the poor) unfit for politics is that their activities and hence their concerns are totally consumed by necessity, by the bodily needs of survival (84). These exclusions, then, are directed more against issues (base "social" questions, in Arendt's sense) than against specific sets of people (women, laborers, the poor, and so forth).[19]

In fact, Arendt's spatial practices provide the basis for a much more radical critique of the kinds of exclusions that the Founding Fathers instantiated in their citizenship restrictions, in their separation of political from administrative spaces, and in their relegation of politically active representatives to the former and the mass of largely passive citizens to the latter. Rather than regarding private interests as "sown in the nature of man" (Madison 1988a, 44), Arendt suggests that such interests follow from people's structural conditions of existence. Alter those conditions—which would mean, in effect, redistributing wealth and eliminating social hierarchies—and people would necessarily become less driven by the needs of their bodies.[20] They would then be fit for participation in the public realm of politics, where citizens rightfully belong since the particular model of democracy Arendt maps makes no distinction between legislators and voters. Anyone can, in principle, traverse the divide between public and private. In fact, Arendt's chief concern is with addressing the central issue of what it is to be human, and her response is that no one can be fully human who is entirely relegated to the private realm of the household and its activities. Those activities include the bodily labor of "*animal laborans*" or the skilled, manual work of "*homo faber*," activities oriented, respectively, to the animalistic imperatives of survival (unproductive labor) and the human endeavor toward instrumental creativity (productive labor) (84–85). These are the activities and concerns that Arendt wants to keep out of the political realm because they only define what we are, not who we are. Something more is needed to define who we are as human beings distinct from other human beings. Arendt associates this process of self-disclosure with the highest of human activities: speech and action in the public realm (175–81). It is through our words and deeds in the company of others, she argues, that "like a second birth" we disclose who we are and "insert ourselves into the human world" (176). Speech and action in a shared public space, in short, are the activities through which we become most fully human.

Although Arendt never states her principle quite so baldly, it is a variation on the theme that human beings do not live by bread alone, and that they cannot, therefore, be fettered to those private spaces where all labor is oriented toward such unproductive goals. This is, in fact, the basis for a very powerful critique of any political, social, and economic restriction on citizenship: a people's ability to enter a public, political realm of speech and action. Boiled down to these terms, her philosophy, I think, is less objectionable. It amounts to claiming that what defines us as human beings is much more than just animal-like concerns with sustaining life or instrumental uses of the things and people around us (174). More to the point, if maintaining life were all that mattered, such a goal, in Arendt's view, could easily be achieved by a benevolent despot or through some other nonviolent yet also nondemocratic form of government. It could be maintained, significantly, by an administrative society that tends only to our needs as jobholders and consumers and reduces our democratic participation to checking preferences on voting ballots. And this, according to Arendt, is precisely where we are now. The modern age has transformed us into a society of breadwinners— outside the Beltway seats of power—as if we did, indeed, live by bread alone.

What makes a principled critique of this transformation even more pressing for Arendt is her view that technology has brought us to the threshold of a new world:

> The modern age has carried with it a theoretical glorification of labor and has resulted in a factual transformation of the whole of society into a laboring society. The fulfilment of the wish, therefore, like the fulfilment of wishes in fairy tales, comes at a moment when it can only be self-defeating. It is a society of laborers which is about to be liberated from the fetters of labor, and this society does no longer know of those other higher and more meaningful activities for the sake of which this freedom would deserve to be won. . . . What we are confronted with is the prospect of a society of laborers without labor, that is, without the only activity left to them. Surely, nothing could be worse. (4–5)

The liberation Arendt alludes to here is one she describes in more detail later as Marx's seemingly utopian ideal of "the emancipation of man from labor" (130). She warns that the continuing development of "automation" could turn "the utopia of yesterday" into "the reality of tomorrow" (131). These points imply a dynamic relationship between space and identity and the impact technology can have on that connection. If the encroachment of the social realm on the political realm of speech and action has turned us all into laborers (a space-identity dynamic), automation threatens, in turn, a radical transformation of our social space, significantly displacing us as laborers and leaving us wanting for an alternative sense of self and purpose.

Arendt's views on technology have not received nearly as much attention as her notions of politics and the public realm.[21] As the passage cited above illustrates, however, her philosophical critiques were motivated in no small part by her assessment of technological change and its impact on our social and political spaces. Nowhere is the import of technology to Arendt's thoughts about space and identity more apparent than in the prologue to *The Human Condition* (1–6). Arendt begins, curiously enough, with a discussion of space flight: "In 1957, an earth-born object made by man was launched into the universe, where for some weeks it circled the earth according to the same laws of gravitation that swing and keep in motion the celestial bodies—the sun, the moon, and the stars" (1). This artificial, earth-born object temporarily admitted to the "sublime company" of natural, celestial bodies was the Soviet satellite *Sputnik*; its national origins matter less to Arendt, however, than how its launching—an event "second in importance to no other" (1)—was received. She observes, with equal doses of curiosity and alarm, that the immediate response was not pride or awe at human ingenuity but a sense of relief that we had taken "the first 'step toward escape from men's imprisonment to the earth'" (unnamed commentator, cited in Arendt, 1). For Arendt, this comment indicates how *Sputnik* had come to represent for many not just a means of conquering outer space, but of conquering terrestrial space. She deploys *Sputnik* as both symbol and culmination of the desire that has defined and driven the modern age: its "world alienation" (248).

Arendt outlines three historical events as having been catalysts of the modern age: the discovery of America, the Reformation, and the invention of the telescope (148). Of the three, however, she maintains that it was the invention of the telescope, "man's first tentative steps toward the discovery of the universe" (249), that had the most profound and lasting impact. This remarkable claim is fundamentally about positionality and perspective, and, by implication, about space, knowledge, and power. As an instrument for viewing things at a distance, the telescope enabled us to construct not just an abstract (i.e., remote), observational knowledge about the universe but, by turns, an ostensibly abstract, universal knowledge about ourselves. It resituated the mind's eye in the cosmos and turned it back on the Earth, enabling an Archimedean perspective of "disinterested impartiality" from a vantage point that "purports to be detached and disembodied" inasmuch as it is figuratively (and, with *Sputnik*, literally) outside the Earth (Disch 1996, 27).[22] From the telescope to *Sputnik*, Arendt suggests, technology has provoked a reorientation of our way of thinking that is itself premised on a new kind of spatial practice: on taking up a standpoint that is abstracted from our interactions with others in a shared, public space. This shift in spatial position and perspective has a number of significant consequences. First, it implies an intersection between knowledge and power (actually, force) that, on Arendt's reading, lay at the heart of Archimedes' philosophy: drawing from the simple mechanical properties of levers, Archimedes inferred that "our power over things grows in proportion to our distance from them" (Arendt, cited in Disch 1996, 28). What he proposed, then, was a form of abstract knowledge, about things at a distance, that would enable a form of abstract power: the ability to act on bodies at a distance. This "Archimedean ideal of power as leverage," as Disch observes, is at odds with Arendt's notion of "public power" (1996, 48). Power for Arendt—as opposed to individual strength or violent force—is always a shared exercise effected in the process of communicating and acting with others in a common political space (199–207). Power-as-leverage (acting on bodies at a distance) is in this respect inconsistent with Arendt's conceptualization of the public realm and, instead, wholly consistent with her view of the social as a space of administration. The advancements in satellite technology inaugurated by *Sputnik* make this point rather vividly, I think, enabling the transmission of digital reconnaissance images of bodies and buildings in one part of the planet to interested others in another part of the planet. Such Archimedean mechanisms of surveillance, as Arendt might have argued, have displaced acts of personal self-disclosure in the company of others.

Arendt's analysis invites this conclusion. She makes a quite self-conscious and literal connection between the spatial practice of distancing, on the one hand, and abstract knowledge production, on the other. If the invention of the airplane has conquered physical space by shrinking the Earth, she argues, it is important to note that this could be accomplished only by "leaving the surface of the earth altogether": flight, therefore, "is like a symbol for the general phenomenon that any decrease of terrestrial distance can be won only at the price of putting a decisive distance between man and earth, of alienating man from his immediate earthly surroundings" (251). As this suggests, any remapping of our ways of thinking fundamentally alters our social and political relations and our senses of self: with space travel, "we established ourselves as 'universal' beings" (263). In her view, then, the conceit that modern science had "'succeeded in freeing itself from the shackles of spatiality'" was self-deluding: we do not simply conquer space without it also, in turn, conquering us.[23]

This dynamic sense of the relationship between technologically produced spaces and identities leads Arendt to a rather pessimistic diagnosis of the problem of scale. She agrees that size is a problem for the kind of democracy she lauds, favorably citing the ancient Greeks' awareness of "the fact that the *polis,* with its emphasis on action and speech, could survive only if the number of citizens remained restricted" (43). Indeed, she even goes so far as to assert a positive correlation between size and the demise of a political, public realm: "[T]he larger the population in any given body politic, the more likely it will be the social rather than the political that constitutes the public realm" (43). Arguably, certain technologies might have attenuated these threats to the political in the modern broadening of the size and population of cities, but Arendt never even considers this possibility. Focusing on transportation technologies and automation, she addresses only their negative impact on our human condition, including our spatial practices and the Archimedean outlook they have engendered or, alternatively, the mechanistic rhythms of our labor processes that automation has required.

Against technology's implosion of space and time and the world alienation, and even bodily alienation, it has engendered, Arendt seeks to revitalize the political importance of "the close at hand" (251), of our common public realm. Her diagnosis of the modern age, however, offers little hope for this revitalization because, in Arendt's view, machines have become not only part of the human condition, but a more demanding (read: determining) one than the mere adjustments required of our earlier tools:

> [I]f the human condition consists in man's being a conditioned being for whom everything, given or man-made, immediately becomes a condition of his further existence, then man "adjusted" himself to an environment of machines the moment he designed them. They certainly have become as inalienable a condition of our existence as tools and implements were in all previous ages. . . . The case of the machines [however] is entirely different. Unlike the tools of workmanship, which at every given moment in the work process remain the servants of the hand, the machines demand that the laborer serve them, that he adjust the natural rhythm of his body to their mechanical movement. . . . Even the most primitive machine guides the body's labor and eventually replaces it altogether. (147)[24]

On the face of it, this critique seems to dispose Arendt's philosophy decidedly against the possibility that technology could ever be truly liberating. The problem, however, is that as she suggests in this passage, no return to some pretechnological age is likely or even imaginable (with the possible exception of some catastrophic event).[25] The task, then, is to think through our technologies, rather than against them, to consider whether, for example, communications technologies (as Barber suggests but addresses incompletely)—in contrast to Arendt's exclusive focus on transportation, nuclear, and industrial technologies—might open up public spaces for speech and action. Indeed, given her considerable emphasis on speech, it is surprising that Arendt never addresses the role of communications technologies in the modern age. Perhaps this is so because with the possible exception of the telephone, the electronic communications technologies that had been invented at the time of Arendt's writing (radio and television) were already in the process of being developed as broadcast media, with their one-way, few-to-many distributional paradigm. This inattention to communications technologies helps explain why Arendt's public-realm theory is more retrospective than prospective, despite her tacit recognition that there is no going back. Even so, some surprising affinities exist between Arendt's ideal public realm and the bodiless space effected in computer-mediated communications. The two key points of similarity are that despite allusions to the physical in each—i.e., in cyberspace and in Arendt's theory—both realms (so to speak) bear an ambiguous and ambivalent relationship to both physical spaces and physical bodies.

To be sure, Arendt implies the importance of physical spaces and bodies in her comments on "the close at hand" (251) and, relatedly, in her sense that the public realm is composed, at a minimum, of things that appear before all and that therefore can, in principle, be seen and heard by everyone present. These comments imply the physical inasmuch as, unlike thoughts or feelings, only the physical is "close at hand" and capable of being perceived by all those bodies that are physically present. Despite this, Arendt makes clear that this space of appearance cannot be reduced to a physical space: "not Athens, but the Athenians, were the *polis*" (195). This is so because what defines the public realm as such is a collective human activity rather than a given physicality:

> The *polis*, properly speaking, is not the city-state in its physical location; it is the organization of the people as it arises out of acting and speaking together, and its true space lies between people living together for this purpose, no matter where they happen to be. . . . [A]ction and speech create a space between the participants which can find its proper location almost any time and anywhere. (198)

In line with Lefebvre's arguments about the production of all social spaces, the physical, as this passage suggests, is at best a condition of possibility for the emergence of a public realm. It assures us that "everybody is always concerned with the same object" (57–58). Even so, it is unclear what constitutes the sameness of such objects for Arendt since a more decisive factor for the existence of the public realm is that no uniformity of opinion or perspective exists over those objects. In other words, Arendt presupposes the existence of an objective physical world that offers up phenomena for human perception, but she maintains that what we perceive is always, in principle at least, open to multiple interpretations.

A key point of Arendt's philosophy, of course, is that this openness of interpretation is not always allowed to exist in practice. Indeed, for her it is only when and where multiple interpretations are allowed to exist and in fact given voice that we can be said to be in the public. Hence, Arendt premises her notion of the public on the existence of a common world shared by people in the presence of others, but for this world to be truly public in her sense—and not merely social, which she regards in terms of an "unnatural conformism" (58)—people must be gathered together to speak and act their own distinctiveness and hence the plurality of their opinions and perspectives regarding the things and people around them. In a sense, then, Arendt's public realm has an, at best, cursory material form (perceivable objects) but is devoid of any necessary material content. The walls and laws of the polis, for example, do not constitute it; they merely help to sustain (or stabilize) the continual reconstitution of the polis by citizens acting together:

> [T]he political realm rises directly out of acting together, the "sharing of words and deeds." Thus action not only has the most intimate relationship to the public part of the world common to us all, but is the one activity which constitutes it. It is as though the wall of the *polis* and the boundaries of the law were drawn around an already existing public space which, however, without such stabilizing protection could not endure, could not survive the moment of action and speech itself. (198)

The physical space of the polis matters, therefore, primarily to the extent that it helps sustain our speaking and acting before others.

Arendt's notion of the public realm, however, may not be entirely devoid of a necessary material content. An important exception, she suggests, is the physical, co-presence of others: "The only indispensable material factor in the generation of power is the living together of people" (201). In other words, implicit in Arendt's focus on the space of appearance is the conventional sense (assumed in most mappings of participatory democracy, as I indicated earlier) that the body still matters for the constitution of the public because citizens must appear before each other in the flesh. Dietz (1991) gives Arendt's theory this very reading in order to recuperate it for a feminist politics. Deflecting feminist critiques that interpret Arendt as disparaging the female body and women's work by relegating women to the private realm, Dietz maintains that Arendt's public realm does, in fact, contain a "'bodily politics'" (249). What is rejected "is not the presence of the body or a bodily politics but rather a political theory that locates the identity of persons only in a collective, singular, physiology—or in practices tied to the rhythmic cycles of nature" (249). Despite this exclusion, however, Dietz insists that for Arendt our bodies are "integral to our appearance in the public world," or again that action for Arendt is "the collective power of embodied persons made political" (249). Hence, the Arendtean public realm, in this view, requires that the body make a public appearance.

The problem with this argument as a response to feminist critics, however, is that, as Dietz herself admits, the importance of the body is clearly attenuated in Arendt's philosophy: it cannot be the basis for any identity politics, which Arendt would have deplored. Arendt does, in a sense, map a democratic politics of public visibility, but with a very specific sense of what counts as public (plurality rather than commonality) and how that is made visible (i.e., through speech and action). Woven through her arguments, as this suggests, is a modern, liberal concern with the threats to plurality posed by an overriding effort to achieve consensus. It is this that most puts her at odds with the sort of politics outlined by SDS (1994) in its "Port Huron Statement." Despite the best intentions,[26] consensus, for Arendt, tends to devolve into communitarian efforts with building a homogenous community, and that path, she argues, leads to commonality rather than plurality, visceral reaction rather than reasoned debate, demagoguery rather than individuality, and totalitarianism rather than liberty. The challenge lies in revitalizing a visibility politics of individual "whos" rather than an identity politics of categorical "whats" (Arendt 1958, 179). This makes Arendt's bodily politics more ambivalent than Dietz suggests. More to the point, a careful analysis of Arendt's arguments regarding the body and the public realm reveals that little, in fact, rides on whether we appear before others in the flesh.

Though Arendt does not engage in any lengthy explanation of the body in public, one could argue that the body does, in fact, serve as many as three general functions. First, my body—composed as it is of voice and hands and feet and so forth—provides me with the material faculties for speaking and acting. Accordingly, the body matters because it is the very medium through which I speak and act before others. But is this a necessary medium? If these bodily capacities were essential to my political being, no mute or paraplegic, for example, could take part in the public realm. It is clear, however, that "disabled" people are "differently abled," finding other, perhaps technological means for communicating and acting in the company of others. From the standpoint of physical capabilities, then, the necessity of the body for public, political interaction with others is indeterminate and must remain so if we are to avoid excluding others on the basis, simply, of their physical handicaps.

A second possibility, however, is that my body matters because it pro-

vides others with an at least vague sense that they are dealing with someone else, other than themselves, and hence that I am a distinct person.
Here, the body matters as a subject of identification, one that discloses
my distinctiveness inasmuch as my outward appearance is different from
almost everyone else's: my face is mine only and not someone else's. As
Honig points out, however, all bodies for Arendt are essentially the same
in that they have the same basic, biological needs. So, from this standpoint, they are similar in appearance: "If this inside [of the body] were to
appear, we would all look alike" (Arendt, cited in Honig 1992, 219).[27] It is
in this respect that the human body is for Arendt, as Honig puts it, "a
master signifier of necessity, irresistibility, imitability, and the determination of pure process. The body is a univocal instance of complete closure" (1992, 217). Even so, Honig considers Arendt's claim that we all look
exactly the same on the inside as patently "false" if taken literally (233
n. 20). Arendt's point is perhaps better made by reference to the example
of identical twins whose distinctiveness is manifested not by their outward appearances, but by the differences of their actions and statements
in their repeated interactions with others. Put another way, Arendt insists
that the mere presence of my body without action or speech presents me
only as a categorical *what* rather than a distinctive *who*. My personal
identity—in its uniqueness and in contrast to my physical identity—is
disclosed only in the process of my acting and speaking (1958, 179). Hence,
the body cannot be said to matter as the manifest source of my unique
identity in the public realm.

Here, however, the body may be said to serve a third and perhaps decisive function in my interactions with others: namely, to provide a fleshy
reference point to which my words and deeds can be attributed because
others can perceive them as emanating from my body. In other words, the
body can function as an object of identification in an articulatory process:
in the process of attaching identity-disclosing words and deeds to a somebody. Without this somebody as the referent of *my* words and deeds, the
latter might remain anonymous. In this respect, it is the physical co-
presence of others that most assures me that *their* words and deeds become their own and most assures them that *my* words and deeds become
my own. If Arendt's philosophy presupposed such facile attributions,
however, she would surely seem incredibly naive, assuming that people
are always earnest in their statements and actions and also that they act always on their own behalf rather than as someone else's puppet. Arendt
would have no basis, moreover, for theorizing the rise of the social—that
is, as essentially a new kind of public sphere, but apolitical in that people

disclose not their distinct identities, but an "unnatural commonality," evidenced in a pervasive and overriding concern with the preservation of life as the highest good. In short, no simple connection can be made between the self and the body, even when the latter becomes no more than a placeholder for our publicly constituted distinctiveness. Even if that connection could be made, however, it remains unclear whether Arendt's philosophy actually requires the body as a material reference point for our self-disclosing acts; rather, she suggests that a person's name could serve that function of articulating a deed to an identity when she makes the obverse point that "[a]ction without a name, a 'who' attached to it, is meaningless" (180–81).

The only logical conclusions to be drawn from these considerations is that despite Arendt's vague allusions to the body in her notion of appearance, the body in fact serves no essential function in her conception of politics, except, significantly, to foreclose its coming into being.[28] Inasmuch as what counts for Arendt is not the brute fact of our physical identities but the constitution, through speech and action, of our distinct, personal identities, it is impossible to explain why our political acts should be embodied as Dietz maintains. In fact, in the absence of any such explanation (either by Arendt or by Dietz), the requirement that our bodies make a public appearance rests on nothing more than the rather facile sense that the physical co-presence of others is what assures us that our actions are intersubjective. Other (perhaps technical) means surely exist, however, for obtaining the assurance that our words and deeds impact on others, that they, in fact, have an audience even when others are not physically present.

Indeed, as Disch maintains, political action for Arendt is not simply about what occurs "center stage" (i.e., in the physical presence of others), but rather "depends on publicity, which in turn requires being recognized, responded to, and later remembered by others" (1996, 84). Recognition and response imply interactivity, which (as I argued in the previous chapter following Schutz and Luckmann 1989) can be mediated: a conversation face-to-face but in the dark, or even a letter. This is not, of course, Arendt's claim; on the contrary, she always begins with the assumption that people must gather together (implicitly, in the flesh). My point, however, is that nothing follows from this bodily co-presence. The key factors for Arendt are whether actions occur as part of the intangible but nonetheless real "'web' of human relationships" (183) and whether, in the process, they disclose the (albeit incomplete but distinct) identity of the agent in the act (180). If the performance of such actions, for Arendt, must be live, it is more for the sake of the spontaneous and unpredictable give-and-take by which their multiple meanings are disclosed to their audience, indeed *by* their audience. The sense that this disclosure can be mediated is suggested in Arendt's discussion of remembrance, which involves certain intermediaries. Arendt's two principal examples of these intermediaries are the polis and the storyteller:

> The organization of the *polis*, physically secured by the wall around the city and physiognomically guaranteed by its laws—lest the succeeding generations change its identity beyond recognition—is a kind of organized remembrance. It assures the mortal actor that his passing existence and fleeting greatness will never lack the reality that comes from being seen, being heard, and, generally, appearing before an audience of fellow men, *who outside the polis* could attend only the short duration of the performance and therefore needed Homer and "others of his craft" *in order to be presented to those who were not there.* (198, my emphasis)

As this passage suggests, both the polis and the storyteller expand the political space of appearance—the political impact of the actor's words and deeds—by broadening the audience beyond those who are physically and temporally present. "Thus, the task of storytellers," as Disch concludes, "is to make action public by crafting the story of a performance that makes it *visible to a broader audience*" (1996, 85, my emphasis). To be sure, in ancient Greece, storytelling was a live performance, suggesting that the actor's body, at least—as a physical stand-in—was important to this process of making the hero's actions visible to a remote audience. However, this is only an intermediary body, an instrument through which the hero's identity is disclosed to others through the performance of his life story. Here the hero's *story*, rather than his or anyone else's *body*, is what matters for disclosing his political agency, for making his deeds known to others who were not physically present when he performed those deeds.

In the final analysis, Arendt's insistence, sustained throughout her analysis of the human condition, that our bodily needs of survival belong properly to the private realm suggests concretely that if we could be assured of the presence of others—with the spontaneity, interaction, and publicity that this notion implies—without their bodies making an appearance, this bodiless public space would, in fact, be preferred.[29] In such an ideal space, a person's political being would be the effect solely of her distinctive words and deeds, irrespective of the bodily needs and attributes she had in common with others. The Greek solution for creating this political realm, free, at least, of the body's needs (if not of actual physical bodies), was to assign those concerns to a subclass of women and slaves and then exclude them, literally, from the public world of the citizen. If Arendt's retrospective theory of the public realm, from our contemporary standpoint, gives rise to a democratic politics that seems to us unworkable and even unattractive, it is because we no longer view these exclusions as acceptable. This does not, I think, make Arendt's mapping of democratic space simply (or quite as) elitist as is Madison's doctrine. Arendt decries rather than celebrates the establishment of any beltway buffer that separates citizens from the seats of government. Her exclusions of the body and its needs, however, distinguish her philosophy, as well, from an SDS brand of in-the-streets democracy to the extent that the latter is premised on a consensus-oriented identity politics: private interests, in Arendt's view, should remain private. It is this fixing of the barriers between the public and the private and between the political and the social that most seriously limits her philosophy, ruling out efforts to politicize needs in response to the modern structural mechanisms by which categories of people are disempowered.

A second limitation of Arendt's philosophy is her rather overstated technological determinism: her easy conclusion that *Sputnik* and telescopes and machines have launched us into an ineluctable space of their own creation. This conclusion fails to take into account the variety of technologies available and the plurality of ways that people incorporate them into their lives. In the process of making these assertions, however, Arendt proffers a sophisticated understanding of the relationship between technology, space, and identity. She understands (better than Barber, I think) that technologies are not simply tools we can use to conquer space by extending practices initiated in one location across a wider area; rather, technologies are spatial practices themselves that engender new spaces (e.g., a distant, outer space), new knowledges (e.g., Archimedean vantage points), and new identities (e.g., world-alienated selves). Arendt's examples, however, are surely not the only ones produced by contemporary technologies. That some of these new spaces are bodiless, moreover, invites critical reflection of the possibilities they open up for the spatialized politics of public visibility that Arendt's philosophy retrospectively traces, but which she failed adequately to map for a modern world.

The Public Sphere

Among Arendt's most sympathetic critics is Jürgen Habermas, whose theory of the public sphere as a realm of rational-critical debate is inspired by Arendt's communicative notion of power in a public realm of speech and action (see Habermas 1986, 1989, and 1993). Even so, Habermas faults Arendt for wanting to exclude social and economic concerns from the public realm, arguing that her exclusions reveal "the limits of classical theory" (1986, 82). He maintains that one cannot sanitize modern politics of putatively private, socioeconomic concerns insofar as what characterizes modern times as such is precisely the "complementary relationship" that has been established between the state and the economy under the capitalist mode of production (82). The politicization of these kinds of concerns by workers and others is a direct consequence of the way power (or what Arendt calls "force") is exercised by dominant classes under capitalism. To defend such exclusions in the context of contemporary circumstances, he continues, "leads to absurdities," not the least of which is the proffering of "a radical democracy which inhibits its liberating efficacy just at the *boundaries* where political oppression ceases and social repression begins" (83, my emphasis). What Habermas rejects, in this respect, are the borders of the political that Arendt's philosophy maps.

Like Arendt, Habermas's theory is couched in terms that explicitly articulate space to democracy, specifically by constructing the notion of a *bourgeois public sphere*. One key difference, as I have just suggested, is that he expands the bounds of the political to include the (partly economic)[30] realm of *civil society* as a privately organized but publically relevant proto-political space. In his mapping of this new political space, two other significant differences surface. First, the ambivalently corporeal notion of public visibility recedes in importance, displacing the body as a medium for the expression of political agency. Second, the role of media technologies in helping construct a public, political space and a (disembodied) public identity increases in importance. As my terms may already suggest, these two points are related.

According to Habermas, the bourgeois public sphere was the combined product of economic, social, and political transformations that spawned new spaces and redefinitions of publicness. The centralization of political authority under absolutism during the Renaissance period had already generated permanent administrative organs and standing armies, giving political authority a kind of "objective existence"—a state apparatus—"over against the person of the ruler" (1989, 18, 11). By the sixteenth century, *public* had come to refer to the state, and *private* denoted what was excluded from the state apparatus (11). The publicness of political authority, however, was still restricted to the visibility of the king's body as the representative expression of the sovereign power of the realm. This "*publicness* (or *publicity*) *of representation*" in the Renaissance period and up to the eighteenth century, Habermas argues (7), was a holdover of feudal society, within which no distinction between public and private spheres had existed. Representative publicity had constituted itself, therefore, not "as a social realm" but as "something like a status attribute" embodied in the manorial lord and symbolizing a "'higher' power" (7). As in the Athenian polis, then, power became manifest in relation to some form of corporeal public visibility,[31] but in this case it was vested entirely in the visibility of the body of the feudal lord and later the king as the site/sight of an asymmetrical form of power (a higher power).[32]

The embodied display of sovereign power in the restricted space of the monarch's court was addressed to a very select audience of subjects because entrance to this space was limited to those nobles and high-ranking members of the emergent commercial class admitted by sovereign favor, i.e., granted the privilege of an audience with the king.[33] These privileged interactions in the restricted space of the court, in turn, allowed the formation of a "framework of sociability," an "enclave within a society separating itself from the state" (Habermas 1989, 10, 11). As state authority became more "depersonalized"—i.e., transferred from the king's body as the site of representative publicity to a burgeoning state apparatus that included parliamentary institutions and administrative and judicial organs—this enclave came into its own, developing into an equally depersonalized civil society that no longer drew its recognition from political authority and that, in fact, came to define itself, if not exactly over and against, then at least alongside of and against the state, abrogating to itself a separate authority in the form of "public opinion" (19, 25–26).[34]

It is here that the specifically modern, liberal senses of public/private are most clearly distinguishable from the classical, Athenian conception of public/private mapped by Arendt (see also Calhoun 1993, 6–7). Unlike the Athenian public realm (which had no social component), the modern public includes the state (as a depersonalized locus of political authority) and civil society (as an impersonal counterpart to political authority). Furthermore, whereas Arendt, drawing from the Athenian ideal of the household, constructs the private as the realm of necessity, in its modern remapping as that which excludes the state, the private becomes a realm of individual freedom. Indeed, as Habermas argues, it is the locus not just of the economy, but also of the family, in whose bosom the subjectivity of "the privatized individual"—"*bourgeois* and *homme*"—was fully nurtured (1989, 55). What the rise of the social manifested from the standpoint of the bourgeois subject, however, were sets of economic relations that directly impacted on the life-sustaining activities of the private realm but that transcended the individual's capacity to regulate those relations. Put another way, "the social" named those sets of relations that might occasionally require state regulation and were, therefore, publicly relevant to a class of property owners who wanted to oversee, direct, and (where possible) minimize state intrusions into the economic realm (Calhoun 1993, 9). In this respect, society, as Habermas maps it, is *a zone of contact* between the political authority of the state and the personal freedom and life-sustaining activities of individuals in the private realm, and it is this contact zone, according to him, that gave rise to a critically debating public:

> Because, on the one hand, the society now confronting the state clearly separated a private domain from public authority and because, on the other hand, it turned the reproduction of life into something transcending the confines of private domestic authority and becoming a subject of public interest, that *zone* of continuous administrative contact became "critical" also in the sense that it provoked the critical judgment of a public making use of its reason. (1989, 24, my emphasis)

What Habermas understands as this "bourgeois public sphere," then, is this critical sphere "of private people come together as a public" to confront state authorities over the regulation of the social (27). "The medium of this political confrontation," Habermas continues, "was peculiar and without historical precedent: people's public use of their reason" (27). Put another way, this was not an undifferentiated mass of bodies motivated by passions and visceral reactions; it was, rather, a public of educated and informed privatized individuals using their critical faculties to evaluate social relations and administrative policies vis-à-vis their own interests.

The print media, according to Habermas, were central to the development of this critical-debating public in two respects: they contributed to the formation of a particular kind of critical practice, and they helped engender and sustain the identity of "the public." With respect to the first point, Habermas notes that the public sphere emerged first in the world of arts and letters as a critical reading public oriented around a growing number and variety of published books, journals, pamphlets, and the penny presses (29). He locates these reading publics, moreover, in actual sites, namely, in English coffeehouses, French salons, and German table societies. Hence, this literary public sphere in its infancy was composed, at least in part, of physical spaces and bodies. It included, specifically, people gathered together informally in voluntary associations that, according to Habermas, were egalitarian, sociable, and communicative (55). It is worth emphasizing here that what developed out of this combination of printed matter and salon debates was, as Habermas puts it elsewhere, "a relatively dense network of public communication" that, though bourgeois in origin, provided "the training ground for what were to become a future society's norms of political equality" (1993, 423, 424; see also 1989, 29).[35] So even though the content of discussion initially involved only literature and art, this reading public's style of argumentation and debate was, in time, transferred to political discussion. In the case of France, for instance, the Revolution, according to him (1989, 69–70), spurred the politicization of this rationally critical reading public and its institutionalization into a political, public sphere.[36] Habermas's second claim is that the print media did not simply supply topics for debate nor did they simply reflect a public attitude; rather, they helped to constitute their readership, performatively, as a public. Or, as he puts it, when bourgeois men gathered in the coffeehouses and salons to discuss something they had read in newspapers like the *Spectator* or the *Guardian,* "the public that read and debated this sort of thing read and debated about itself" (1989, 43). The modern identity of the public, in this respect, is a mediated construct.[37]

Unlike Arendt, then, Habermas incorporates communications technologies into his theory of the bourgeois public sphere. This is not to suggest, however, that he is completely sanguine about technology—quite the contrary. Like Arendt, he is critical of the instrumentally rational outlook engendered by techno-scientific ideologies (1971). Furthermore, he attributes "the structural transformation of the public sphere"—that is, the specific demise of the bourgeois debating public that is the subject of his major work on the public sphere (1989)—in no small part to "the rise of the electronic mass media, the new relevance of advertising, [and] the increasing fusion of entertainment and information," to the emergence, in short, of mass media institutions with their concentration of production and distribution and the ideological character of their content (1993, 436).[38]

These media transformations (spurred by economic considerations and technological changes) had a variety of significant effects, and some specifically spatial. The development of the media into information markets concerned with maximizing profits meant extending the base of readers beyond educated elites and beyond a single class with relatively homogenous interests, and this in turn entailed, in Habermas's reading, creating information commodities that would appeal to the lowest common denominator, both in terms of prepackaging news to make it more understandable—"serving up the material as a ready-made convenience, patterned and predigested"—and of depoliticizing content by reducing the number of political news stories and editorials (1989, 169). Second, increasing production costs, especially with the newer broadcast media, contributed to the concentration and centralization of media production (186–89). Third, and relatedly, the emergence of broadcast media displaced the kind of *critical distance* that reading, as a process of reception, facilitates: "Radio, film, and television by degrees reduce to a minimum the distance that a reader is forced to maintain toward the printed letter—a distance that required the privacy of the appropriation as much as it made possible the publicity of a rational-critical exchange about what had been read" (170).[39] This last point is crucial: it indicates how, for Habermas, the bourgeois public sphere had constituted itself as a *critical buffer zone* not simply against too much state intervention into the putatively private realm of the economic, but also against an emergent mass media that was constituting itself as the purveyor of public opinion rather than simply its means of expression. What has been lost, Habermas argues, is a critical buffer zone in both of these senses: the degeneration of the bourgeois "culture-debating public" into a "culture-consuming public" (159).

The early print media, together with salon discussions, had constituted, in this respect, a comparatively informal yet stable base on which could flourish the kind of public communication that had helped to both generate and sustain the bourgeois public sphere. With the rise of the mass media and altered forms of reception (the minimization of critical interpretive distance and the production of information for consumption rather than debate), that grounding crumbled. As a consequence, public opinion, too, has become a manufactured form of mass or "nonpublic" opinion (1989, 249). Habermas draws this distinction from C. Wright Mills, noting that for opinion to be *public*, it must (1) involve as many givers of opinion as receivers (i.e., be the product of a many-to-many communications paradigm); (2) be organized to allow immediate response (i.e., be based on a system of open access and two-way communication); (3) be easily translatable into public action, even against public authorities; and (4) remain relatively autonomous from authoritative institutions in its operation. *Mass* opinion, by contrast, is based on a system of communication that (1) significantly limits the number of people giving opinions (i.e., is based on a few-to-many paradigm); (2) is organized in such a way that individuals cannot readily or effectively answer back (i.e., has restricted access and a one-way communication flow); (3) limits the ability to translate opinion into action because channels are regulated by authorities; and (4) is thoroughly penetrated by authoritative institutions and therefore has no (or little) autonomy from them (249). According to Habermas, his analysis reveals that these criteria for what would count as mass (nonpublic) opinion are met by current conditions, confirming the "collapse of the public sphere" (249).

Having diagnosed the contemporary mass-media sphere as a space where social administration had replaced democratic politics, passive consumption had replaced rational-critical debate, and ideological reproduction had replaced the media's role as a channel for the expression of public opinion, Habermas, in his subsequent work, has turned his attention toward outlining an ethic of "communicative action" (1984, 1987), shifting his focus, as Calhoun notes, "from the institutional construction of a public sphere as the basis for democratic will formation to the validity claims universally implicit in all speech" (1993, 31). That is, whereas his earlier work had sought to ground the possibility for democratic communication in an empirical, historical, and institutional account of an actually existing public sphere,[40] his theory of communicative action rests on a transhistorical, quasi-evolutionary notion of communication competence. That prospect seems to me less interesting and more utopian than the kind of ideal-yet-grounded cartography he maps in his earlier work.

Some of Habermas's critics doubt, however, whether "the *idea* of the public sphere" is applicable today except as a rather general "critical yardstick" (Thompson 1990, 119). Thompson, for example, argues that this idea is inapplicable as "a model for institutional reorganization" because the conditions today are completely different:

> Habermas suggests that, while the traditional fora that nurtured the public sphere have long since declined or disappeared, the idea of the public sphere could be reactivated on a different institutional basis. The problem with this suggestion is that the development of technical media has dramatically altered the nature of mass communication and the conditions under which it takes place, so much so that the original idea of the public sphere could not simply be reactivated on a new footing. The media of print have increasingly given way to electronically mediated forms of mass communication, and especially television; and these new media have transformed the very conditions

of interaction, communication and information diffusion in modern societies. The original idea of the public sphere, bound to the medium of print and to conduct of face-to-face interaction in a shared physical locale, cannot be directly applied to the conditions created by the development of new technical media. If we are to make sense of these conditions and of the opportunities afforded by them, we must pay closer attention than Habermas does to the nature of technical media and their impact on social and political life. (119–20)

Thompson's point is actually a restatement of Arendt's general thesis regarding the dynamics of technology and space, i.e., that technologies do not conquer space but rather create new spaces and identities. As such, I regard his general point as essentially correct, but as an assessment of Habermas's philosophy, Thompson's contentions are both right and wrong. They are right inasmuch as Habermas's efforts to construct a transcendental communicative ethic largely ignore analysis of the contemporary conditions that would make that ethic possible, and this despite his obvious understanding that different technologies enable different kinds of spaces and practices. They are wrong inasmuch as Habermas's original idea of the public sphere did not depend as much on physical spaces and bodies as Thompson's summary suggests.

As with Arendt's public-realm theory, the importance of physical spaces and bodies to Habermas's theory of the public sphere is at best tenuous. To be sure, he does argue that a certain kind of conversational, democratic engagement—associational, egalitarian, rational-critical—was effected in the physical space of the coffeehouses and salons he highlights in his historical analysis. As Warner (1993) argues, however, the nature of the conversational practice that emerged from these sites and that Habermas came to characterize as definitive of the bourgeois public sphere was based in no small part on a "rhetoric of *abstract disembodiment*" (385, my emphasis). Warner's analysis focuses on the transition, implicit in Habermas's work, from a bourgeois public subject to a mass subject. He maintains that the public is a moment of apprehension that interpellates us in a different and necessarily self-alienated subject position— i.e., as a "public subject" that is a "nonidentity with ourselves" (377). The process of public-subject formation depends on our negating the particularities of our bodies and, by extension, our personal needs and interests. Warner identifies this notion of the public as a legacy of civic-republican philosophies of virtue that characterize the ideal citizen as one who concerns herself with public matters in a disinterested fashion—

indeed, the similarities between this liberal notion of publicity and Arendt's classically-clad-but-equally-liberal conception of the citizen free of bodily concerns are apparent. Warner proceeds to suggest that this civic value came to be expressed implicitly in the early print media through the practice of publishing articles either anonymously or under a pseudonym: his example is Richard Steele's eighteenth-century writings in the *Spectator* (380–81).

According to Warner, the public persona of the Spectator constituted for Steele "a prosthetic person," a term Warner borrows from Lauren Berlant to convey the sense of an identity "that does not reduce to or express the given body" (381). The adoption of a public persona (or prosthetic) apparently unrelated to an individual's personal and physical identity could, concretely, allow a kind of public voice to emerge.[41] This "public print discourse," according to Warner (1993, 382), could present (that is, constitute) its "public opinion"—and eventually its so-called objective news coverage[42]—as "authoritative" insofar as it could portray itself as detached and disinterested. And the most direct way it could portray this was by presenting itself as anonymous and disembodied: "The anonymity of the discourse was a way of certifying the citizen's disinterested concern for the public good" (385). In effect, a connection between public virtue, validity, and disembodiment was established in that statements could be characterized as true or valid for a public only to the extent that they could be generalized beyond the particular needs and differences of both the writer and his audience. [43] As Warner argues, "[T]he validity of what you say in public bears a negative relation to your person. What you say will carry force not because of who you are but despite who you are. Implicit in this principle is a utopian universality that would allow people to transcend the given realities of their bodies and their status" (382). Hence, an implicitly utopian "principle of negativity"— discernible also in Arendt's philosophy, as I suggested above—became "axiomatic" for the bourgeois public sphere that constituted itself, through a practice of reading and debating, in relation to this disembodied style of public writing (382).

This is not to suggest that face-to-face encounters are completely irrelevant to Habermas's theory. Since the ideal he proffers, however, is based on a confluence of, as Warner calls them, "Utopias of Self-Abstraction" (379)—including a public print discourse of anonymity/objectivity, a republican tradition of civic virtue as disinterestedness, and a liberal distinction between public and private realms, all of which, in turn, inform a bourgeois rhetoric of disembodiment—these observations do raise the question of how precisely the face-to-face matters in his framework. The answer, I think, is that what matters for Habermas's notion of a spatialized democracy is not the physical co-presence of others, but rather the existence of shared social spaces (in Lefebvre's sense) that teach and encourage a kind of communicative exchange that is public in orientation, equally accessible, subject to normative standards of evaluation, and rational-critical. And, in fact, as Habermas has argued more recently, "If there still is to be a realistic application of the idea of the sovereignty of the people to highly complex societies, it must be uncoupled from the concrete understanding of its embodiment in physically present, participating, and jointly deciding members of a collectivity" (1993, 451). What should be looked for instead, he says, citing Claus Offe, are "relations of association," a concept he suggests is vaguely "reminiscent of the 'associational life' that at one time constituted the social stratum of the bourgeois public sphere" (453). But the cardinal criteria for these relations of association, Habermas suggests, are not that they be face to face (though they may include that), but rather that they enable public discussion and that they remain noninstitutional "opinion-forming associations" (454).

Habermas's point, then, in calling attention to the coffeehouses and salons of the eighteenth and nineteenth centuries as exemplary sites for a kind of practiced, democratic engagement was to emphasize that such engagements were situated in a kind of interactive social space; that is, they allowed public (as opposed to mass) communication and opinion formation. Consequently, his spatializing of democracy depends even less than Arendt's on physical spaces and bodies. Whereas Arendt's cartography projects a political space of appearance separate from the private realm of the household and constituted by the corporeal presence of citizens engaged in speech and action (attenuated, as I have said, by Arendt's profound anxieties about the body), Habermas's cartography projects an ideal critical buffer zone situated between the state and the private realm and constituted by private individuals who come together as a public to read about and critically discuss publicly relevant matters. Since the print media were part of this bourgeois public sphere as Habermas conceives it, the latter's spatiality was never simply reducible to the physical movements of human bodies in a shared physical space; rather, information flows, the exchange of arts and letters, and the distribution of news were constitutive and sustaining components of the public sphere. Part of the problem that Habermas identifies when he speaks in terms of its structural transformation is that the public constructed by the mass media began gradually to crowd out those interactive spaces that had sustained critical reflection. What matters, then, is whether a public sphere today can be respatialized in ways that include, once again, noninstitutional and interactive critical buffer zones where people can engage each other in public debate. When one adds to this the notion that this engagement, ideally, depends on a kind of disembodiment, the move from the coffeehouse to the cyber café, as a new, computer-mediated site of public debate, not only makes sense, it actually approximates the utopian ideal of self-abstraction more literally.[44]

None of this is meant to suggest, however, that Habermas's ideal mapping of democracy is not, in its own way, problematic. Like Arendt, Habermas's ideal is based on a topography that, at least initially and in practice (if not in principle), excluded women, propertyless men, and the uneducated. As Benhabib notes, any topography that begins by accepting the public/private split may be deeply problematic for women, who traditionally have been confined to the private realm and have seldom experienced it as a space of personal freedom (1993, 92–93). Furthermore, the related issue of what counts as *disinterested* public discourse—if that is indeed central to Habermas's theory—is equally problematic. As Warner points out, "rhetorics of disincorporation" are easier to manage by those whose subjectivity is already the "unmarked" norm—which, in the context of the bourgeois public sphere (not to mention a few others), means "white, male, literate, and propertied" (1993, 382). The liberal notion of the *unencumbered self* as the ideal participant for a public-oriented debate (quite aside from its mythic independence) is particularly problematic for those whose identities are marked and who may, in fact, be concerned with contesting the conditions of their marked existence by politicizing that issue, i.e., making it a publicly relevant topic for discussion. In contrast to his ideal speech situations and ideal speakers, the criteria that Habermas (1989, 249) draws from Mills regarding what counts as "public" communication seem to me much more fallible, inclusive, and open-ended and hence defensible on the grounds that they outline communications criteria that are ultimately more compatible with the sorts of multiple publics likely to engage in critical debate today.

The Spatial Lament

In the preceding discussion, I showed how a variety of theorists, in spatializing democracy, make the similar assumption that scale is a problem for all participatory forms of democracy, which depend, according to common wisdom, on citizens being able to communicate with each other in the flesh. Barber distances himself from this assumption slightly, though not decisively, by assimilating space to communication and suggesting that the crucial issues are the mode, frequency, and quality of communications between citizens. Arendt and Habermas, for their part, allude to the need for an embodied form of interaction among citizens, but little actually rides on this notion; in fact, they each, as I demonstrated, construct an ideal notion of the unencumbered (i.e., disembodied) liberal self.

It is possible, however, that face-to-face communication does nonetheless offer something important to a participatory democratic politics that mediated communication does not. Garnham, for example, maintains that technological developments in communication, including computer networking, have tended to focus on rights to free expression without attending to "the reciprocal duties inherent in a communicative space that is physically shared" (1993, 367). These include a "duty to listen" and "responsibility for the effects of the actions that result" (368). Despite his normative language, I take his point to be less an ethical one about obligations citizens ought to bear toward each other than a spatio-structural one about the kind of engagement to which citizens are disposed when they must confront each other in the flesh. That is, the so-called duties of attentiveness and responsibility follow conditionally from the fact that those present will, at least occasionally, demand to speak and may, as well, react overtly and spontaneously to some of what I say. Consequently, because others are physically present before me in a conversational space we share, I cannot as easily ignore their demands for my attention nor dissociate myself from the sometimes obvious effects of my statements.

By contrast, a missive, as that term implies, may be sent out, without any comparable conditions of attentiveness and responsibility attaching to the writer, especially in the case of anonymous writing. Indeed, like missiles, missives may be thrown into a public space to do their damage without the sender ever having to confront the effects of his or her actions. These arguments suggest that a constitutive relationship obtains between a mode of communication (speaking versus writing), its spatiality (proximate versus remote), and the kinds of social interactions engendered (responsible versus irresponsible, engaged versus dissociated, or intimate versus impersonal). As a result of these observations, Garnham provides a clearer sense of why mediated communication simply may not do where democratic politics are concerned. The physical absence of others whose mediated messages I may nonetheless receive via some electronic medium may facilitate the development, according to this argument, of a kind of antidemocratic inattention to their demands and contempt for their needs: to give an example, if I prefer not thinking about children starving in what the media construct generically as "some Third World country," I can always dismiss Sally Struthers by turning off the TV.[45] Face-to-face communication, by contrast, might be important to democracy because the possibilities for developing a sense of responsibility toward others tends to be greater, according to Garnham, when others are physically present and hence more difficult to ignore.

In short, two related assumptions lie behind the assertion that face-to-face communication matters for democracy: that a sound, participatory democracy depends on citizens being disposed toward others, both in terms of attentiveness and responsibility, and that citizens are more likely to be disposed toward others when they are repeatedly exposed to them in a shared physical space. I accept the first point, but not the second. In fact, it can be shown empirically that the physical presence of others does not always ensure attentiveness and responsibility toward them. Studies of gender differences in interpersonal contexts, for example, indicate that because of the greater deference typically ceded to male speakers, a woman's statement may often be overlooked or dismissed by others; whereas when a man makes essentially the same point, others are more likely to acknowledge and discuss the issue *he* has raised (see, for example, Spender 1980). Hence, in this instance, proximity may give rise to contempt rather than respect because social cues are more available and thus may allow social prejudices to affect the speech situation. It would follow, then, that if in a written communication the sex of the sender is neither known nor easily discernible (cf., Herring 1993; Spender 1995, 244–47), then a person's written message may not be quite as subject to gender and other kinds of discrimination.

Despite such evidence, critics of modern society and mass communication continue to treat the "loss" of a sociospatial practice—face-to-face civic engagement—as a problem for democracy, maintaining that this kind of close-up interaction with others helped at one time to inculcate people with a democratic disposition toward others, in the minimal (liberal) terms of a faith in collective action and solidarity with strangers, if not in the extreme (communitarian) terms, more strongly, of an intimacy among friends. An example of this lament is Robert Putnam's article, "Bowling Alone: America's Declining Social Capital" (1995). The metaphor of "bowling alone" refers to an actual drop in the number of Americans engaged in league bowling and in other voluntary associations, a decline that Putnam infers from statistics and conveys, in economistic terms, as America's regrettable loss of "social capital," i.e., "features of social organization such as networks, norms, and social trust that facilitate coordination and cooperation for mutual benefit" (67). Focusing on the social context in France, Jean Leca similarly postulates that the "sphere of altruistic participation in voluntary associations" is "the most strategic" because even while such associations are not in themselves political, "they are, nevertheless, 'reservoirs of citizenship'" (1992, 21). It is worth emphasizing, with these examples, that the importance for democracy of face-to-face encounters is not unique to the communitarian position. Indeed, this assumption is evident even in liberal-pluralist arguments that posit the significance of face-to-face contact in voluntary associations as important for helping people develop a habit of civic-mindedness and civility.

In his critique of Putnam (and others who argue in this vein), Michael Shapiro reveals that their "neo-Tocquevillean lament" (1997, ¶48) is itself the effect of a kind of conceptual blindness toward other spaces—or, less politely, of a "unitary" notion of society and "an aggressive non-recognition of the variety of incommensurate social spaces constitutive of the 'society' and the variety of different kinds of political enactment within different social venues" (¶10).[46] His point is that contemporary theorists who rehearse Tocqueville's arguments regarding a close connection between voluntary associations and democracy in America tend as well to reproduce his totalizing gaze and moral geography, imagining the nation as a unitary social space with only one model of civic engagement: "the familiar, white spaces of civic assembly" (¶24). This inherited blindness, in other words, has led some theorists, Habermas included, to speak in terms of one and only one all-encompassing bourgeois public sphere without acknowledging the existence of (or considering the other viable forms of sociality at work in) a proletarian public sphere (Negt and Kluge 1993), a black public sphere (e.g., *Public Culture* 1994; Shapiro 1997), a female public sphere (e.g., Ryan 1993), or multiple publics more generally (Fraser 1993). When Shapiro speaks about different political enactments in different social venues, moreover, he implies that this blindness about spaces of otherness entails a reciprocal blindness about other kinds of democracies: that is, about other modes of interaction, cooperation, participation, communication, and mutual self-governance. Indeed, the stories of political degeneration that Arendt, Habermas, Putnam, and others tell are excessively univocal, proffering an ideal of democratic politics as if all the members of every society practiced democratic politics in only one way. If, however, people's practices are diverse and multiple, then so, too, are the public spaces and democracies they create.

The challenge, then, in scaling democracy for modern societies is not to lament the displacement of face-to-face democratic spaces by ostensibly less democratic, technologically mediated ones. As I hope to have shown in my analysis, the sense of loss evinced in such arguments is itself the effect of imagining only one possible type of public space (conceived largely as physical) with only one type of civic engagement (i.e., face-to-face encounters). If we were to describe, however, what is at stake in the kind of sociality that many political theorists seem to regard as important to democracy, we could define that, minimally, as an interactive form of communication that enables attentiveness and responsibility toward other participants in a shared *social* space, understanding by the emphasis on *social* that such spaces do not reduce to the conventionally physical spaces within which bodies move. The challenge, then, is to discern what new forms of democratic sociality, so defined, are made possible by the newer technologies now available, and one way to start that kind of inquiry is by attending to "the respatializing implications of new technologies" (Shapiro 1997, ¶6).

chapter 3
Hardware and Software

A Techno-Topography of Cyberspace

Computers were feared as purveyors of disempowerment long before they became the stuff of revolutionary hopes and democratic dreams. Prior to the early 1980s, they remained very much a special-interest technology: a high-tech toy for nerds at various research institutes and, what was worse, a powerful tool in the hands of governmental and corporate giants. Where they were felt to have an impact on the lives of normal, everyday folks, this impact was decidedly negative. Under the rubric of automation, workers by the thousands lost their jobs to robotic arms and computer brains in the so-called boom years following World War II. At the same time, the computerization of administrative functions was having an equally profound effect on our senses of self in relation to the state bureaucracies doling out social welfare. "Computers," began the customary complaint, "are reducing us all to numbers."

This unease derived in part from postwar nightmares about a new kind of threat to individualism: the threat of communism. Recent events had revealed the Soviet Union to be far more advanced and powerful than the West had imagined, giving rise to warnings about the monstrous partnership between totalitarianism and technology. Explored to chilling effect in dystopic, futuristic novels such as George Orwell's *1984*, this partnership, it was feared, would lead to a system of centralized social control so irresistible that the dynamic liberal self would be vanquished, leaving behind a soulless, expressionless, and unremarkable drone. Despite their cold war origins, similar anxieties persist even today, as is evident in fictional representations of societies of cybernetic organisms, like the Borg collective of the *Star Trek* universe, destroying the sublime individuality of human beings through their technological processes of assimilation. What is puzzling in this overwhelmingly negative context is how computers could come to be seen, especially within the last decade, as a source of empowerment for the average person.

Two curious circumstances heighten this irony. First, the hardware and software innovations that gave rise to computers and networking, as I show below, actually began as extensions of U.S. national security concerns and defense projects. In that respect, they have had much longer histories as instruments of institutional than of individual power. Second, the term *cyberspace*, which originated in works of speculative fiction, initially referred to an expansive, corporate-dominated, electronic space for the traffic of information. Where individuals had access to that fictional space, it was as self-interested digital mercenaries and data junkies hooked on the full sensory stimulation of jacking into the matrix (see Gibson 1982 and 1984). Both technologically and etymologically, then, little about the origins of cyberspace suggests a social space for democratic empowerment. This puzzle is my point of departure.

In this chapter, I begin providing a more detailed analysis of how cyberspace has come about and why it is often experienced as an *other* space, a heterotopia that challenges our more conventionally physical, social spaces. As described in chapter 1, a heterotopia is an in-between space of contradiction and contestation: one that mimics or simulates lived spaces but that calls those inhabited spaces into question. In contrast to utopias, moreover, I noted that heterotopias are not simply imaginary, conciliatory spaces that make (discursive) sense out of some aspect of our social existence that is otherwise troubling and ambivalent; rather, heterotopias are real, existing places that function as "counter-sites" (Foucault 1986, 24). In this respect, the task before me now is to give a more detailed explanation of how cyberspace is both real and other.

As a real space, cyberspace is amenable to the same kind of analysis that Lefebvre (1991) recommended for the study of social spaces. As he argued, any social space is the product of three components, each of which implies a different type of spatial experience: the perceived realm of physical experience produced and reproduced through spatial practices, the conceived realm of mental experience constructed in and through dominant representations of space, and the lived realm of social experience in everyday spaces of representation. For analytical reasons, the story I tell here and in the next chapter focuses on three components of computer networking that relate suggestively to each part of Lefebvre's triad. These constitutive features of cyberspace are its *hardware*, its *soft-*

ware, and the *wetware* (the human element) that operates its devices and programs.

Hardware, of course, refers to the physical components that make up the technologies involved in computer networking. As I show below, these components help constitute a different kind of physical space, one for the electronic movement of digital information rather than the mechanical movement of matter. Software is vaguely analogous to Lefebvre's representations of space, which are both a kind of conceptual blueprint and a written code in that "[c]onceptions of space tend . . . towards a system of verbal (and therefore intellectually worked out) signs" (1991, 39). Similarly, in the vernacular of both the professional computer programmer and the hacker, to produce software is to "write code." Like the urban blueprints it mimics, programming code maps the *logical space* of data, determining both memory architecture (where data are stored) and user interface (how data are seen), thereby shaping how people experience computer technology by structuring (often through spatial graphics) how we interact (or interface) with computers. The development of the *Graphical User Interface* or *GUI* (pronounced GOO-ee) in operating systems and, by extension, in the applications they support has made computers both more "user friendly" (accessible) and also more conventionally spatial in their imagery. For Internet-related programs, this point is implied in both the visual content and the names of Web browsers like *Netscape* and *Internet Explorer* and in the creation of the *home page.*

Finally, the concept of *wetware,* a common hacker slang for human beings (Cotton and Oliver 1994, 216; *The Jargon File* 2000: "wetware"), refers to the actual users of cyberspace and hence parallels the third component in Lefebvre's framework: the lived experiences of users in the everyday spaces of representation. As I argued in the previous chapter, however, technologies do not simply conquer physical space; rather, as both Arendt and Habermas have indicated in their respective studies, technologies more often help to produce new kinds of spaces and new senses of self. That implies a much more complex dynamic at the interface where human and machine meet. Because human beings do not simply help to produce cyberspace through their online practices but are also in important ways transformed by that space, the human-computer relationship is sufficiently complex that it merits an entire chapter (indeed, entire books have been written on the subject). I therefore devote the next chapter to that discussion, focusing here only on hardware and software considerations. Notwithstanding this separation, I want to emphasize that, like

Lefebvre's triad, hardware, software, and wetware are mutually constitutive elements that together produce the social space of cyberspace.

My argument, however, involves more than simply showing that cyberspace is a social space; rather, my point is that we encounter it as an *other* space in relation to our more familiar embodied spaces: as a heterotopia that juxtaposes objects in often stimulating and sometimes confrontational ways. In this respect, computer technologies (pace Barber) are not simply instrumental tools that can be put to the task of solving the perennial problems of space for large-scale democratic societies, nor are they simply contributors to a new kind of separate space with its own norms, cultures, and practices. Rather, they are communications media that help create environments of *productive confusion,* i.e., spaces of alternate ordering that pose new challenges and new possibilities for our social interactions and, more fundamentally, for our ways of being. The key questions, then, include the following: How does cyberspace relate to the nondigital spaces around it? What, if any, productive confusions are emerging in relation to this space of alternate ordering? What new and possibly challenging practices, identities, and sociospatial relations has it enabled?

The story I tell here unfolds as a kind of chronological topography. Focusing on the technological makeup of cyberspace, I analyze its physical and conceptual production through three successive episodes in hardware and software innovations—electronic computing, computer networking, and the invention of the personal computer (the PC)[1]—and the layers of spatial ambiguities they generated. As a first step, electronic computing gave rise to *bit space:* a composite (or juxtapositioning) of the physical space of hard circuitry (atoms) and the logical space of soft data (bits), whose electromagnetic and symbolic properties have yielded different spatial practices and representations of space than those shaping the more conventional spaces of matter. The development of networking technology helped extend bit space beyond geographical bounds, compressing physical distances through the creation of a weblike *network space* that juxtaposed the *here* and *there,* bringing researchers at remote institutional sites together in a common, virtual workspace. Lastly, with the invention of relatively inexpensive, single-user, "personal" computers, individuals have gained access to a kind of technological power that formerly only institutional users had enjoyed. The extension of these technologies to individuals carved new paths between governmental and corporate institutional spaces and the more personal space of the home, juxtaposing the institutional and the individual in ambivalent ways that have generated other, related ambiguities (e.g., between public and private). It is out of this final intermixing of institutional and individual practices—superimposed on the atom/electron mix of bit space and the here/there mix of network space—that what can minimally be called *cyberspace* finally emerges.

Having discussed the technological basis of cyberspace as a result of innovations in hardware and software (and the productive confusions they have generated), I turn, in the conclusion, to a brief discussion of the cultural origins of the term *cyberspace*: significantly, as a literary construct coined by novelist William Gibson that proffered a rather depressing image of a computerized future where everyone traffics in information and greedy multinational corporations tend to call the shots. Historically speaking, the invention of the term *cyberspace* occurred after the technological innovations of electronic computing, networking, and the PC, but it predated the explosive growth of the Internet and the wide variety of online practices that have come to constitute that space as a particular kind of social space. As such, Gibson's sense of cyberspace provides a particularly provocative segue between a predominantly technological discussion of its production (in this chapter) and a more explicitly cultural one (in the next).[2] Implicitly critical of the partnership between computers and capitalism, Gibson offers a future vision of cyberspace that is clearly at odds with the optimism, autonomy, and sociality implied in contemporary references to "cyberdemocracies" and "electronic town halls." As a conclusion to this chapter, then, his "paranoid" alternative (McRae 1996, 242) suggests where the technology may still lead us. As a preface to the next chapter, it helps heighten the sense that something more is needed to explain the current optimism about cyberspace, i.e., that to understand how it has evolved into a democratically empowering social space, we need as well to consider what people actually do when they turn on their computers, launch their Web browsers, and log onto the Internet.

Electronic Computing: The Development of Bit Space

If, as Lefebvre argues, physical space, as one component of social space, is constituted by movement, then an understanding of the production of any social space must begin with a discussion of the elemental units whose movements give rise to its physical spatiality and, by extension, to the particular set of spatial practices involved in the production of that social space. For the most part, the physicality of hitherto existing social spaces has been shaped, at the most fundamental level, by the movement of atoms. Even the apparently nonmaterial spaces of communication constituted by circulations of meanings have involved the movement of atoms, e.g., in the proximity of human bodies and the sounds conveyed between them in spoken communication or in the production and distribution of books and other reading materials in written communication. Indeed, it was the close connection between ideas and printed matter—established in the era of print culture—that gave practices like book burning their political import and that ultimately helped to shape our currently existing social, legal, and political norms governing intellectual property rights, censorship, export, immigration, brain drains, and so forth. Put another way, the circulation of ideas has most often been regulated by controlling the movement of the atoms—broadsheets, books, and even bodies—through which ideas traditionally have been conveyed (literally, transported from place to place). By contrast, the physicality of cyberspace derives more from the electronic movement of binary digits (or bits) than from the mechanistic movement of books or bodies (that is, atoms).

This characteristic of cyberspace has led writers to speak in terms of a decisive technological shift from atoms to bits (Negroponte 1996) or in terms of the related shift from analog representation to digital simulation (Poster 1990, 94–98; Wark 1993). While helpful for understanding the different kind of spatiality that is cyberspace (a point to which I will return later in this section), computer pundits and critics alike have tended to overstate these distinctions. In fact, bits are not a perfect antonym for atoms since binary information may exist in some material form, and indeed often does inasmuch as digital information is stored in a variety of physical media and devices (memory chips, floppies, hard drives, magnetic tapes, CD-ROMs, and so forth) and exists only as pure electronic information in those moments (measurable in nanoseconds) when it is being processed. The distinction between analog and digital is similarly overstated since a lot of computing actually depends on the continuous conversion of analog signals to digital signals and back again. In fact, this is what a modem (modulator/demodulator) does. Consequently, while these notions are important, if we are to speak in terms of the first decisive historical shift toward the production of cyberspace, that rupture is best characterized in terms of a shift from mechanical to electronic computing.[3]

Exemplary of the institutional origins of computer technologies, the move toward electronic computing occurred in the 1940s at the behest of the U.S. Army's Ordnance Ballistic Research Laboratories. In the midst of

World War II, army officials were concerned with devising faster methods for computing ballistic firing tables to be used by artillery personnel at the front. Speed, not space, was the primary concern here. Most of the calculators then in existence used a series of mechanical relays, which could perform at most some fifty additions per second; computer researchers at the University of Pennsylvania argued that an electronic machine they were designing could, by contrast, add five thousand numbers per second and could therefore calculate ballistics tables in minutes rather than days (Winegrad and Akera 1996). In response to such promising reports, the Army helped subsidize a secret project for the development of the *ENIAC* (the "Electronic Numerator, Integrator, Analyzer, and Computer" or "Calculator"), the first successful, general purpose (i.e., programmable) electronic digital computer (Brader 1994). As most commentators note, the ENIAC was "a grotesque monster" by contemporary standards: a half-million-dollar, thirty-ton, thousand-square-foot colossus with about nineteen thousand vacuum tubes, fifteen hundred relays, and "hundreds of thousands of resistors, capacitors, and inductors [that] consumed almost 200 kilowatts of electrical power" (Weik 1961; see also Brader 1994). Clearly, its bulk and price tag meant that machines like the ENIAC could be built and operated by only a very select group of users: first governments and later large corporations. Ironically, the origins of computing in such monstrous and elite machines, I would argue, give today's computers part of their mystique. Indeed, comparisons between yesterday's mainframes and today's microchips are what make the marketing rhetoric of "putting computing power on your desktop" meaningful, particularly when we are reminded that these technologies emerged first as tools for national security.[4]

Despite national security–motivated concerns with improving speed and efficiency in military computations, the shift to electronic digital computing inaugurated by the ENIAC in 1946 and furthered by other innovations in electronic circuitry—such as the invention of transistors in 1949—has had a number of unexpected spatial consequences. In contrast to mechanical calculators with manually operated relays, electronic computers employ electromagnetic forces to manipulate electrical currents. This is what makes their calculations so speedy, as quick as changing voltages within a circuit (Bolter 1984, 33). But several other significant features follow from the fact that electronic computers work primarily on electrons. From the standpoint of human perception and spatial practices, the processing done by an electronic computer—because "Electricity and magnetism . . . act on bodies at a distance"—is invisible and indirect, conducting calculations that programmers "can neither see nor feel directly" (Bolter 1984, 38).[5] It is worth recalling in this context that in his description of (conventional) physical spaces, Lefebvre assumed a close connection between spatial practices and human perception, i.e., that the spatial practices defining a particular physical space could be perceived. Electronics, by contrast, breach that connection. They enable spatial practices that cannot be directly perceived by the human senses. Indeed, they even redefine the body's relationship to the machine, making possible the development of computers that "would not be like the old mechanical calculators in immediate contact with a human operator but would work from a set of previously coded instructions" (Bolter 1984, 33–34). Remarkably, because the manipulation of electrons is invisible, the designers of the ENIAC added panels of lights to the machine before its public unveiling in 1946 so that reporters could see how quickly the machine worked. From these surreal beginnings in what amounted to a very deliberate, public-relations initiative on the part of the ENIAC's inventors, panels of flashing lights became the symbolic embodiment of computing in the sci-fi movies of the 1950s and 1960s (Winegrad and Akera 1996). This anecdote also indicates how, from very early on, the developers of electronic computing have sought ways to make apparent— that is, to (re)present in some familiar and perceptible way—the strange, invisible workings of the electronic computer.

The representation of the computer's inner workings occurs at the *interface:* the intermediary space where body and machine meet. It is here that computer software—easily changeable codes of instructions— regularly translates the currents coursing through computer hardware (so named because it is the "'hard' to change," material side of computing [Bolter 1984, 52]) into data that can be perceived and interpreted by computer users. Physical devices store units of data in one of the numerous cells arranged geometrically on silicon chips. This physical space, as Bolter points out, "is discrete and limited" and arranged much like a Cartesian grid, with addresses serially assigned to each cell (82, 83). In contrast to computer engineers, however, programmers generally know very little about the physical location of a particular memory address; instead, the articulation that interests them is the datum associated with that address and more often with some arbitrary label for that address. These arbitrary associations between data and addresses are dynamic and nonsequential. In effect, an address is assigned and reassigned (in fractions of a second) to a new datum wherever physical storage or processing space has become available on the hardware components at work. This fundamental feature of electronic computing—namely, *random access*—means that, for all intents and purposes, programmers can rearrange data into a wide variety of logical spaces (computer desktop, graphical windows, directory trees, iconic folders and cabinets, online rooms and forums, and any other virtual structure) irrespective of the physical arrangement and location of that data.

What the ENIAC and other innovations in electronics made possible, in short, was the social production of bit space: a heterotopic combination of atoms and electrons embodied in the physical spaces of hardware circuitry and the logical spaces of software programs. The argument that bit space juxtaposes both atoms and electrons is crucial. Computer enthusiasts have tended to overstate the characteristics of electronic bits in their exaggerated claims about the revolutionary potentials of computers without paying sufficient attention to the materialist point that individuals need access to hardware. Indeed, as Luke argues, "digital flows always require an atomic infrastructure of wires, circuits, transmitters, chips or relays to work" (1997, ¶3). In the meantime, critics have, for their part, overemphasized the materialist dimension and have consequently tended to dismiss computers as anything but an extension of currently existing power relations. My argument is that the social and political implications of computers are more complicated than either of these extreme positions allows. In fact, one of the characteristics that makes computers so challenging is their odd mix of atoms and electrons, which gives bit space its peculiar features: at once imperceptible, indirect, and malleable at the level of electronic bits and perceptible, tactile, and fixed (albeit, upgradeable) at the level of hardware components and the "flickering signifiers" of the interface (Hayles 1993). The juxtaposition of atoms and electrons in the production of bit space leads in turn to a variety of other paradoxes in the way bit space is experienced, that is, as a complex play of both (material) presence and absence and (informational) pattern and randomness (Hayles 1993), as both embodiment and disembodiment (e.g., Hayles 1992), as both visibility and invisibility, as, in general, a confusing mix of the physical and the virtual.

If computer advocates have emphasized the different nature of bits, however, it is because what Timothy Luke calls "physiocentrism"—the privileging of what may be variously described as atoms, bodies, or the physical, broadly speaking—still dominates our ways of thinking about space, technology, and the body, and even (as I indicated in the previous chapter via the notion of a democratic corridor) our ways of scaling democracy:

[P]recybernetic categories of (meta)physics parcel up the world in the tired conventional bundles of Nature/Culture, Humanity/Technology, History/Society, Being/Time. Thus, hardware (computers or telecom networks) and software (code constructs or packaged routines) appear as nothing more than inanimate objects, or "technology," that "humanity" uses as tools. . . . [A]ll inquiries into cybernetic subjectivity must challenge this physiocentrism of humans as "atoms" and invite instead an openness to other realms of mentality/dimensionality/temporality/activity that may be unfolding in hyperrealities as "bits" beyond the physiocentric space. (Luke 1997, ¶8)

If we are to understand these "other realms," then, we need a better understanding of the bit side of that mix of atoms and electrons that I have been referring to as bit space.

A binary digit or bit, as Nicholas Negroponte explains, "has no color, size, or weight" (1996, 14). Rather than matter per se, a bit is information about the current state of something. Any condition that can be expressed in binary terms—on or off, black or white, in or out, and so forth—can be translated (coded) into bits. More complex conditions, moreover, can be coded into strings of bits with exponentially increasing numbers of permutations: 2-bit strings, for example, have 4 permutations, while 8-bit strings (a byte) have 256 permutations (15). Inasmuch as complex information can be digitized—that is, boiled down to a series of such binary terms—a bit may be understood metaphorically as "the smallest atomic element in the DNA of information" (14). To say, then, that cyberspace is fundamentally about bits is to say that it is a largely mathematical, electronic space where information is reduced to numbers, and that, therefore, cyberspace typically functions according to physical laws that are different from those ordering the material world, where information is embodied in books and other atoms.

These differences have occasionally been described by reference to the related shift from analog to digital computing and communication. As I have said, the rupture implied here has tended to be overstated since computing generally involves the perpetual conversion of analog to digital to analog, and so forth. Still, the fact that information today can be digitized, at least part of the time, does have a number of significant implications, and this makes the differences between analog and digital worth noting. An analog device creates a continuous reproduction of some phenomenon by duplicating its physical properties through an analogous medium. In the case of photography, for example, the amount of emulsion chemically deposited on a two-dimensional film negative corresponds directly to the amount of light bouncing off the original objects photographed in three-dimensional space (Wark 1993). By contrast, a digital device simulates a continuous phenomenon (like singing or lighting) by creating digital *samples:* discrete frequencies or points of light converted into measures of voltage taken at particular intervals and then translated into bits of information (Negroponte 1996, 14). The measures are absolute rather than relative: on or off, black or white. What gives such discrete measures the illusion of continuous variation is that the samples are spaced sufficiently close together to be perceived by the human ear or eye as a flowing melody or a variably shaded object.

A number of important characteristics of bit space follow from the creation of informational bits that simulate audio and visual phenomena. First, because the measures are absolute, bits may be perfectly reproduced without the loss or degradation of data. When the measures are relative (continuously variable), as is the case with analog devices, the process of rendering a duplicate or representation is subject to fluctuations: mechanical, electrical, and even interpretive. The children's game of Telephone is a classic example of how messages degrade in an analog chain of communication.[6] In the language of information theory, the problem revealed in this example is that analog communication is extremely vulnerable to "noise." When measures are absolute, however, noise is considerably reduced: a binary switch (as opposed to, say, an analog dimmer) is either on or off, but not both and not somewhere in between. Variation is possible, but it is the effect of a series of closely spaced absolutes, just as interspersing tiny black and white dots on a paper will, when viewed from a certain distance, give the appearance of shades of gray. The point is that if one knows, with the help of a gridlike pattern (a program), exactly which points (bits) are black (1) and which are white (0), one can perfectly reproduce another person's pointillistic creation. Programs, moreover, can be automated to make redundant backups of particular files. Similarly, the electronic documents at one location can be "mirrored" (copied bit for bit) at a number of other locations called "mirror sites." In contrast to the limited resource that is geographic space, therefore, these electronic characteristics make bit space, in a sense, self-replicating and seemingly limitless: "a peculiar kind of real estate which expands with development" (Barlow 1992).[7]

Second, once information is coded into bits, it can be processed in a wide variety of ways to recreate some preexisting phenomenon or, significantly, to create something totally new. A digital (re)production, in other words, is always a coded simulation of something that may or may not exist "IRL" ("in real life"); an analog reproduction, by contrast, is always a representation of some preexisting physical phenomenon. In this respect, an analog always privileges the "referent space" that precedes it and to which it corresponds, whereas digital simulations "need no such precedent in physical space" (Wark 1993).[8] This feature helps to set bit space apart from physical space, allowing it to have a separate and semi-autonomous existence.

Third, because digital reproductions are serially discrete rather than continuous, they can be more easily manipulated. A single point in a grid can be randomly accessed and modified without affecting the surrounding points or in ways that instantaneously adjust the surrounding points, if one so chooses. This has two further implications. First, while methods exist for distinguishing an analog "fake" of some original, a digital image can be "retouched" at the level of the initial, underlying binary code so that no detection of change may be possible at the level of the perceptible image on the screen. Similarly, a deleted word in an electronic text, unlike a white-out in a typewritten manuscript, leaves no apparent trace of itself. Second, because one is dealing with discrete bits, it is possible to juxtapose sometimes incommensurate objects in the same virtual space: for example, by inserting a variety of strange, new images into a preexisting background scene.

These two technical possibilities—undetectable alterations and variable juxtapositionings—have been exploited extensively by advertisers and filmmakers through the development of *computer-generated imaging* (or CGI) techniques. Using CGI, advertisers have been able to resurrect long-dead film stars to hawk their products (e.g., Fred Astaire dancing with a Dirt Devil vacuum cleaner), and filmmakers have been able to construct a photorealistic white whale breaking the ocean surface (in the 1998 TV version of *Moby Dick*), to superimpose actors on a frozen sea (in the 1997 film *The Winter Guest*), and to create mercurial androids that can transform into a variety of humans and objects (in the 1991 film *Terminator 2*). The latter was accomplished through the CGI processing technique of *morphing*, which makes it possible to depict one face metamorphosing into another—graphically alluding to the plasticity of identity—and to show slow-motion, splashing droplets transforming magically into a group of ballet dancers (as in a 2000 installment of the "No Limits" ad campaign for the Showtime cable network)—suggesting subtle parallels between hydrodynamics and the fluid motions of a pirouette. Such techniques, in short, have effectively created a heterotopic space in which a variety of anachronistic or incommensurable objects can be placed together and in which identities seem to have become infinitely variable (a point I explore more fully in the next chapter).

As the preceding discussion has indicated, electronic computing helped create bit space for stand-alone units. Because bit space is partly composed of atoms, however, linking computers to each other through the copper wires and other material components of the telephone infrastructure (as I show in the next section) helped extend bit space into a network space encompassing different geographic locations. This next innovation contributed further to the production of cyberspace.

Internet: The Growth of Network Space

The origins of the Internet, like the ENIAC before it, lie in a set of institutional concerns and national security motives on the part of political officials and defense researchers, this time in the context of the cold war. In October 1957, the Soviet Union launched *Sputnik,* the first in a series of artificial satellites intended to explore outer space. At the same time that this unprecedented event was helping Hannah Arendt crystallize her understanding of the human condition, *Sputnik* was proving an embarrassment to President Dwight D. Eisenhower and his cadre of national security experts, who had dismissed communiqués about the pending Soviet launch as mere propaganda. Their immediate reaction was not the warm glow of wonder at human ingenuity, but a cold war shock that the USSR had become technologically advanced enough to put a satellite into orbit. Determined to avoid future "technological surprises," the administration established, in the following year, a new Department of Defense (DoD) research and development section called the Advanced Research Projects Agency (Norberg and O'Neill 1992, 33). ARPA was intended to fund technological ventures too risky for industry and, more specifically, to provide a forum for defense research on command-and-control issues, hence, its original name, "The Command and Control Program" (Norberg and O'Neill 1992, 1 n. 1). The agency itself was later renamed the Defense Advanced Research Projects Agency (DARPA) to emphasize further its national security mandate. Networking research fell under the auspices of a branch of DARPA called the Information Processing Techniques Office (IPTO).[9]

DARPA research into computerized communications networks began in earnest in the late 1960s and resulted in a new network design.[10] This innovation in network design merits attention since it was partially implemented in the physical layout of the Internet. The following origin story, moreover, has become part of Internet lore as the basis for some of the more exaggerated claims made today about the resilience of cyberspace to centralized control. It is therefore a story worth retelling as a partial explanation for some of those claims.

Communications networks in the early 1960s (principally telephone networks) were hierarchical in their design: remote nodes wired to each other through central switching stations that controlled routing functions for the entire network. The "centralized" network architecture, for example, had a star-shaped design, with the links rayed out from one central switching station (or router) to each of the several remote sites around it; and the "decentralized" system, relatedly, was more of a constellation, a cluster of star-shaped subnetworks linked to each other through their central routers (Baran 1990a, 195). In the event of an emergency— a natural disaster or an "enemy attack" (Baran 1990b, 15)—damage to a central switching station could bring down a large portion of the network, if indeed not all of it. The trick therefore was to remove the points of vulnerability: the central switching stations. If a node were directly attached not just to one switching station but to several other nodes simultaneously, then damage to one of those points in the network would not result in a serious breakdown in communications. In theory, a message could still get to its destination via another node. This could work, however, only if each node were capable of functioning autonomously: that is, if each node could make its own smart decision about how to route a message through the network.

This reasoning resulted in two related innovations: a *distributed* network architecture and the *packet-switching* technology required for routing messages through other nodes to their final destinations. In contrast to the starlike design of centralized systems, distributed networks would be based on a weblike design. Each computer node would be linked redundantly to several other neighboring nodes, each of which could function independently both as a message router and a final destination point (Baran 1990a, 195). This autonomous routing was to be facilitated by yet another innovation, later dubbed *packet-switching*. With packet-switching, messages would be segmented into smaller blocks combined with delivery information (an address). These "packets" in turn would be transmitted through the weblike network in any direction and then reassembled as the readable message once all packets reached their final destination (Baran 1990b, 19; Haring 1994, 464). Since adding more redundant links would provide nodes with extra options for routing packets, expanding the network could, in principle, further enhance

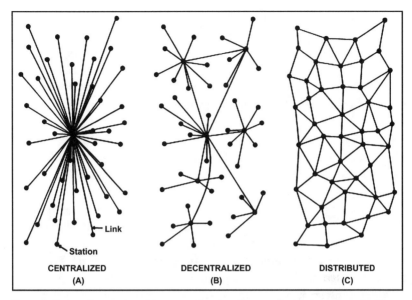

Figure 3. Types of network architectures. Reprinted by permission from RAND, *On Distributed Networks,* Paul Baran (Santa Monica, Calif.: RAND, 1964); copyright RAND 1964. From volume 1, retrieved 22 August 2000 from the RAND Web site at http://www.rand. org/publications/RM/RM3420/RM3420.chapter1.html.

its overall reliability and performance. In short, packet-switching technology combined with a distributed network architecture provided the conceptual framework for a very "robust" communications network (Baran 1990a, 195).

In contrast to RAND's more security-oriented initiative, the researchers at DARPA/IPTO were not as directly motivated by cold war concerns to create a survivable network. Instead, they became interested in computer networking as a way to facilitate communication and resource sharing among defense researchers at different, geographically distant sites (Roberts 1989). Given their mandate, however, they were constrained to develop technologies that addressed national security issues and that could eventually be transferred to the military to assist it in its command-and-control operations. With these goals in mind, DARPA/IPTO researchers put distributive networking concepts to work in 1969 in a prototype network called ARPAnet.

Initially, the ARPAnet was connected to nodes at only four research institutions, but it expanded steadily, with twenty-four nodes connected by 1972 (Norberg and O'Neill 1992, 60). Networking expanded further in

1974 with the development of a suite of protocols for inter-networking, that is, for communicating across networks with different protocols (McKenzie and Walden 1991, 362).[11] The resulting *Transmission Control Protocol* and *Internet Protocol* (TCP/IP), as they were called, became standards in 1981. Over the next fourteen months, ARPAnet nodes were switched over to the new suite of protocols. By 1983, the Internet was in place.

To foreground the spatial assumptions underpinning these early developments, the reconceptualized network design that became the basis for the Internet's physical infrastructure was motivated in no small part by the conviction that military personnel and defense researchers faced a communications environment that was either hostile (the implicit RAND perspective) or, at least, inefficient (the DARPA/IPTO perspective). For both, in other words, the problem consisted in being mired in a context in which communication was vulnerable to geography. From the RAND standpoint (Baran 1964 and 1990b), the destruction of a switching station in one location, under the older centralized and decentralized network designs, would have had a rippling effect throughout the network area that a damaged router served. The point was to ensure that no matter what disaster befell part of the physical infrastructure of a network at one or more actual sites, message bits might nonetheless persevere, finding other nodes to route through until they reached their final destination. From the DARPA/IPTO standpoint, the point was to digitize data and make it available to other researchers on the same "galactic network," conceived implicitly as a kind of universally accessible research space for the transfer and sharing of bits of knowledge, irrespective of the actual physical distances separating researchers.[12] In short, the flow of bits through a weblike network helped to weaken the link between communication and geography, making the former more protected from problems in the latter.[13]

As this brief history indicates, the R and D conducted at DARPA/IPTO proceeded largely by design. But what we know today as the Internet—with its newsgroups, e-mail capabilities, and tens of thousands of networks connected around the globe—is the product of a number of unexpected and unintended consequences. As Alexander McKenzie and David Walden have observed, "Perhaps the biggest surprise of early ARPAnet use was the enthusiastic (even zealous) adoption of electronic mail as the primary medium for scientific and management communication in the DARPA research community, both intersite and intrasite" (1991, 357). This form of relatively immediate and inexpensive communication became so popular that researchers outside defense began demanding access. Academic interest in network communication led the National Science Foundation, in 1986, to create its own network (NSFnet). Operating according to a principle of "universal educational access," the NSF's funding activities helped extend Internet access to college faculty and students in nondefense areas (Krol 1994, 13). In a short while, the NSFnet took over the ARPAnet's role as the backbone of the Internet. The transfer of networking technology to the nondefense community arguably reached its apex in 1990 when the ARPAnet, the defense-funded network that had started it all, ceased to exist (Zakon 2000). And in what was perhaps the next inevitable transfer (in the context of a liberal society), the NSF began sharing backbone services with private companies in 1994 and completely ceded its Internet backbone function to them in 1995 (Miller 1996, 46; Tony Rutkowski, in Ubois 1995).

The Internet's origin story typically stops here, at about 1994. What matters most for computer civil libertarians who recite this history is that at its inception, the Internet was hardwired with a set of technological features—redundant links, autonomous routing, standardized protocols, compatibility—that made it (physically) resilient, anarchic, expansive, and as a consequence comparatively secure from localized threats. In the long run, the lack of centralized control built into the ARPAnet did open networking up to innovative, unexpected, and unintended uses, especially as individuals outside the defense community began demanding and getting access (McKenzie and Walden 1991; Cooke and Lehrer 1993).[14] From a technological determinist perspective, the capacity of bits to move freely throughout this type of network enabled the emergence of unrestrained online activities. It is to these structural properties of *distributed* networking and their apparent consequences that computer civil libertarians have alluded when they claim that today's Internet is "headless and self-organizing" (Barlow 1994b).

However, as it has evolved through three phases of growth—from the days when the ARPAnet constituted the Internet backbone (1969–90) to the second phase of growth under the NSFnet backbone (1986–95) and into the current phase dominated by multiple commercial backbone services (1994 to the present)—the Internet has become a far more complex, multitiered system of networks and protocols.[15] The flat, weblike topography conceptualized in Baran's distributed network and more or less realized in the layout of the Internet in its infancy has mutated into a network of networks that better resembles a three-dimensional, hierarchical system.[16] The commercialization of the Internet is directly responsible for this change in its topography. As the number and variety of Internet access companies proliferated in the second half of the 1990s and incompatibility issues surfaced, so did the need for a structured form of network access across the different types of backbone services (Rybaczyk 1998, 26–27).

Today, millions of users connect to hundreds of thousands of networks through thousands of different Internet Service Providers (ISPs). Regional and local ISPs, which have limited geographic "points of presence" (PoPs) and focus primarily on the end-user market (targeted for individual subscribers who prefer the cheaper low-bandwidth, shared-access connections), constitute the lower tiers or levels of the Internet-access hierarchy. Because of their limited facilities, these smaller ISPs, in turn, are dependent on Network Service Providers (NSPs) for their interconnectivity. NSPs are actually larger regional or national tier-1 ISPs with sufficient connection facilities—PoPs in several major cities—to qualify as "backbone" or "transit" providers for smaller ISPs to connect to each other. With the proliferation of backbone providers from only one in the days of the ARPAnet and the NSFnet to the approximately forty-five backbone services currently in operation worldwide, the need arose as well for Internet exchange (IX) points—also referred to as Network Access Points (NAPs) and Metropolitan Area Exchanges (MAEs)—to interconnect these different backbone providers. At the time the NSF ceded backbone functions, it had four sponsored NAPs in place, managed by major regional phone companies, to provide this exchange function for the new commercial backbones. They included Pacific Bell's "PacBell NAP" in San Francisco, the Ameritech-operated "Chicago NAP," the "Sprint NAP" or "New York NAP" located not in New York but in Pennsauken, New Jersey, and the Metropolitan Fiber System (MFS)–operated "MAE-East" NAP (for "Metropolitan Area Ethernet-East" but later changed to "Metropolitan Area Exchange-East") in Washington, D.C. (Rybaczyk 1998, 192). These four IXs have since been joined by over one hundred and fifty other "public" exchange points worldwide.[17] In addition, an undisclosed number of "private Internet exchange points" (Rybaczyk 1998, 193)—also called Private or Peer Network Access Points (PNAPs) (Botsford 1999, slide 22)—have begun to emerge. PNAPs are the result of closed, bilateral negotiations between typically large ISPs that have a lot of traffic between them and want to avoid having to send their data upstream to the public NAPs to access each other. Clearly, the largest ISPs are thoroughly linked, benefiting from several public peering agreements and often dozens of private ones, as well (see Gareiss 1999, table 3).[18]

So if the architecture of the Internet continues to resemble a distributed network design, it does so primarily at this upper level, where the NAPs and tier-1 ISPs (the backbone providers) do business. As Peter Rybaczyk (1998, 21) notes, this networking infrastructure has, in a sense, come full circle, returning to a *decentralized* form of circuit switching (in Baran's sense, 1990a, 195), where second- and third-tier ISPs must rely on backbone providers and centralized exchange points to link to each other. It will be recalled that Baran's criticism of networks dependent on central switches was that they are more vulnerable because nodes at lower levels could be cut off from service if and when a central switch goes down. What characterizes the "New Internet" (Botsford 1999, slide 9) as "new," in short, is the complex hierarchical restructuring that has occurred in the wake of backbone commercialization and the consequent return to dependence on central exchange points.

Even with its reliance on NAPs, however, the New Internet is still less vulnerable than this return to a form of hierarchical circuit switching implies. Many redundant connections are built into the Internet at the lower levels, as well. Local and regional ISPs may arrange Internet connectivity by subscribing to more than one backbone service, and they can also subscribe directly to one or more NAPs. These redundancies create subsidiary weblike connections, making the Internet's architecture still more complex. Although he doesn't use the language of a return to a more distributed topography, Rybaczyk does speculate that just as the four ARPAnet nodes of the first computer network have proliferated into millions of nodes over the last thirty years, it is conceivable that the number of Internet exchange points may, themselves, be in the millions in another thirty years (1998, 193).

The proliferation of exchange points (public and private) has been motivated by one inefficient feature of the newer, NAP-dependent Internet architecture: namely, that bits destined for a server across town may have to be routed first to nodes across country. In effect, any traffic between two different ISPs with no private "peering" (reciprocal traffic exchange) agreements between them may have to take this sort of circuitous route, traveling upstream to a public IX before arriving at its destination. To give a concrete example, in November 2000, I had a dial-up Internet account with an ISP (CyberGate) that began as a local operation here in South Florida, with offices and servers originally in Deerfield Beach and later headquartered in Fort Lauderdale. I also had Internet access through a few other services, including an ADSL account with Telocity, a residential-market, broadband, national ISP headquartered in

Cupertino, California.[19] When I accessed the CyberGate home page on one of the company's servers in Fort Lauderdale using my CyberGate dial-up account from my home in the adjoining city of Dania Beach and only 15.2 miles from CyberGate's headquarters on Commercial Boulevard, the packets were routed through local servers and made an average of just six "hops."[20] By contrast, when I connected to CyberGate using my Telocity account, the packets had to go upstream in search of an exchange and took about seventeen hops in the process, including several cross-country excursions. In fact, traceroutes I ran showed that the packets left my home in South Florida and were routed through servers in Dallas and Atlanta before returning to South Florida. Needless to say, this was a rather roundabout way to communicate across town.

All else being equal, Internet access is faster when packets have to take fewer hops and particularly when they are able to bypass public IXs, which can become congested. For this reason, end users typically benefit when their ISPs have a number of private peering agreements with other ISPs. In general, however, users remain unaware of all the places through which their data streams are routed. Cyberspace travel, as Rybaczyk notes, is as rich as physical travel but more hidden: "You experience the destination, but you miss the trip" (1998, 9). This is so because networking, for the most part, exists in a different space-time: one where bits can travel hundreds of miles in milliseconds just so they can end up less than twenty miles from where they started.

The development of networking has not simply contributed further to distinguishing bit space from physiocentric space. Rather, it has expanded the challenges that electronic space poses for conventionally physical spaces. Where bit space jumbled atoms and electrons, network space ambivalently combined the "here" of one researcher with the "there" of another, bringing them together in the same heterotopic space of a "galactic network." This paradoxical pairing of here and there is what has contributed to the sense that cyberspace is a borderless space, one that confuses other traditional demarcations: between, for example, national and international, local and global, domestic and foreign, intra- and inter-, near and far. As a consequence of its mix of here/there linkages, cyberspace has raised a number of vexing jurisdictional issues both within the United States and across different states internationally (see, for example, Branscomb 1994).[21]

In addition, its mix of here and there, as I show in the next chapter, has been crucial for the development of senses of sociality among individuals at different geographic locations, both institutional and private.

The expansion of networking into the private sector, however, required yet another crucial development: the invention of personal computers, which extended bit space, finally, beyond institutional and corporate network sites and into the putatively private and personal space of the home.

From Technocratic Mainframes to Democratic PCs: Wiring Cyberspace

As the ENIAC's massive specifications may have already suggested, the first electronic computers were anything but personal.[22] They were imposing and intimidating machines—a collection of bulky and environmentally sensitive vacuum tubes—the more complicated of which filled entire rooms and required several operators. Their sophistication (by then-current standards) and the complexity of their operation also made them exceedingly expensive. Despite all this, they were barely more than high-powered calculators designed initially for military computations concerning ballistics, cryptology (i.e., making and breaking coded messages), and defense research, and in due course employed at other government agencies, large corporations, and universities for a variety of statistical studies and data processing, including record keeping, billing, and marketing or academic research (Lubar 1993, 311–53; Jennings 1990, 26–51). Until the late 1970s, in short, computing remained largely an institutional practice. Too costly and esoteric for the average person and still relegated to performing number-crunching functions of a kind typically useful only to those who could exercise some degree of social control, the technocratic mainframe had a limited though steadily increasing appeal: according to one report, the number of mainframe computers in the United States jumped from 10 in 1951 to 75,000 in 1970 (Lubar 1993, 318).

While clearly a growth industry, the impressiveness of the market for mainframes pales in comparison to the astounding popularity of personal computers, for which a market had to be created beyond the niche of computer hobbyists in Silicon Valley (*Triumph of the Nerds* 1996). Indeed, its popularity led *Time* magazine to select the PC as the "Machine of the Year" (in lieu of a Man or Woman of the Year) for 1982, citing national sales figures of 724,000 in 1980, 1.4 million in 1981, and an estimated 2.8 million units for 1982 (Friedrich 1983). While a large share of these figures referred to the sale of office computers, the sale of PCs for home use in the first half of the 1990s increased steadily by about 20 percent each year (Pike 1997). By 1997, over 37 million U.S. households (approximately 37 percent) had PCs quietly processing bits (U.S. Census Bureau 1997b). According to another report, that figure rose to 49 percent of U.S.

households by December 1998 and was expected to reach 65 percent by the end of 2003 (internet.com 1999c).[23]

From a technical standpoint, the hardware innovation that made the PC possible was the invention of the microprocessor in 1971, which replaced vacuum tubes with circuitry on wafer-sized silicon chips and eventually helped to put computers on people's desktops, in their laps, and even in their pockets (Cotton and Oliver 1994, 132). Improvements to this innovation, of course, have continued apace, resulting in "a wonder of economics," an unusual commodity that has tended to become more powerful yet less expensive with each generation (Kane 1997).[24] In addition, its advanced capabilities, including multimedia capabilities, make today's average home computer considerably more functional than the sophisticated calculators and glorified typewriters of the past. In fact, the first PC, the Altair 8800, introduced in 1975, was little more than a box full of circuit boards and toggle switches with no discernible function, no keyboard or monitor, and no ports for connecting such interface devices. These deficiencies mattered little in a context where computer enthusiasts yearned for an alternative to institutional computing and the limited access to mainframes that it offered the average individual. Furthermore, the hobbyists in Silicon Valley and elsewhere who purchased the Altair, according to Cringely's portrayal of them, were ecstatic about the prospects of inventing uses for it and keen to share information and solutions with each other in what amounted to an extension of the communal ethic of the "California counterculture," which contributed significantly to the revolutionary development of personal computing (*Triumph of the Nerds* 1996). Hence, in marked contrast to the national security origins of electronic computing and networking, the innovations that resulted in Computer Power to the People (to pun a famous slogan from the 1960s) were piecemeal, distributed, and grassroots: technologies developed not by credentialed defense researchers at government installations, but by clever teenaged nerds working out of suburban garages.

The extension of computing power to individuals depended not just on making the technology cheaper and hence more materially accessible, but also on making it "user friendly" and hence more intellectually accessible. Originally, the operation of computers and networks required users to learn complex programming languages like Unix, which limited users to those who had the enthusiasm and time to learn these languages. Quicker and higher capacity circuitry and more sophisticated programming, however, enabled the creation of graphical user interfaces (GUIs) with easier-to-operate, point-and-click capabilities.

In 1989, Tim Berners-Lee combined the random-access nature of bit space with the point-and-click facility of GUIs to propose the development of a "global hypertext space" that he called "the World Wide Web" (1998). What most people know today as the Internet is actually this graphical subset, also known as the Web: a growing amalgam of hypertext files stored at sites with IP addresses[25] and transmitted among a vast internetwork of computers at different locations using some version of the original TCP/IP suite of protocols invented by Vinton Cerf and Robert Kahn. Berners-Lee explicitly had in mind an open, easily accessible space for distributing knowledge, a space where virtually any document, no matter who contributed it, would be as accessible as any other. As he explains, "The dream behind the Web is of a common information space in which we communicate by sharing information. Its universality is essential: the fact that a hypertext link can point to anything, be it personal, local or global, be it draft or highly polished" (1998).

By its very nature, hyperlinking is counterlinear and counterhierarchical. I prefer these terms over *non*linear and *non*hierarchical because mechanisms do exist for enforcing the linear reading trajectory and hierarchical organization of the Web content on sites. The commercialization of the World Wide Web—conveyed in the neologism *e-commerce* and exemplified by the emergence of Amazon.com and eBay—has required the development of interactive, dynamic Web designs to enable users to search inventories, place orders, and make payments over secured servers. That process is linear and structured, employing client-server network principles and Common Gateway Interface (CGI) programming to create a real-time interaction between the commercial Web server and the online shopper's browser (the "client"). When the transaction is initiated, the Web server creates a dynamic set of links with tokens and time stamps embedded in them. As the user clicks on those dynamic links, her client-browser sends this embedded token and time stamp information back to the server. If the user fails to click on those dynamic links in a particular order and within a specified time frame, the links become stale, which is why online shoppers are sometimes forced to reload a page to refresh it. Of course, CGI has uses beyond e-commerce. With sufficient expertise and the authority to store scripts on the Web server hosting his or her site, any Web author can use CGI programming to shape how and by whom his or her site is accessed.

The bulk of the Web, however, is still composed of plain hypertext files, which can be accessed randomly through hyperlinks to the URLs for those files. It is in this respect that hyperlinking resists (i.e., counters) linear and hierarchical forms of organization (see Landow 1992). A simple hypertext page littered with hyperlinks is counterlinear insofar as its author cannot predetermine the path that each visitor will take in accessing the various pages linked. Some visitors may choose to read through the full content of the current page and click on hyperlinks later, and then only on some links. Others may ignore the hyperlinks altogether. Still others may read each hyperlink as it occurs, completely interrupting the flow of the page with which they started and to which they may never return. Linking to simple hypertext pages is also counterhierarchical in that one can link to other sites in ways that ignore the organizational structures of those sites. One can, for example, "deep link" to embedded pages: linking to a plain hypertext page several levels into a site's hierarchical structure instead of linking to a site through its home page, in deference to the way that site is organized by its owners.[26] Deep linking is the exercise of the computer principle of random access applied to the world of hypertext. That, after all, was part of Berners-Lee's initial point: to make it easy for people to access anything in hypertext machine language (HTML) by giving them a point of entry as simple as a clickable link.

The development of hypertext coupled with the graphical interface has helped to make the experience of navigating the Internet at once spatially familiar, like walking the city, and slightly fantastic, like pressing buttons that activate secret doors and hidden passages. This process of exploration, however, is not simply *like* pressing buttons unto whole new vistas. Because the mouse, or some other pointing device, becomes a virtual extension of a person's physical hand, one actually *does* press buttons. This is part of the embodied experience of operating computers. The physical action of clicking the mouse and the resulting, software-generated rearrangement of pixels the user perceives on the computer screen is, of course, electronically mediated: that is, a mouse click initiates a chain of events that amounts to the jiggling of various electrons in the hardware circuitry. But because this electronic processing cannot be seen and often causes an almost immediate change (measurable in nanoseconds) in what one does see finally on the monitor, this mediation is typically transparent.[27] This often invisible mediation, moreover, has perceptible spatial consequences, presenting users with new "windows" for their work spaces, transporting Web "surfers" to different hyperlinked "sites," and even thrusting gamers into whole new "worlds."

It is worth noting, in this respect, that what was true of first-generation electronic computers is even more so for PCs. Bits can be reconfigured in a variety of dimensions, providing spatial perceptions and experiences different from the actual, physical location and configuration of data: a location that now, with the advent of networking, might and often does extend beyond the geographic bounds of any one computer. The graphic creation of new spaces is obvious with gaming examples, like Myst and Riven, that present gamers with imaginative and visually stunning landscapes to explore. In fact, the graphics are so self-evidently spatial in their constructions that step-by-step cheat sheets for these types of puzzle games are called "walk-throughs," and they describe in detail "where" the gamer has to go and how to solve the part of the puzzle she encounters "there." Similar and more "pedestrian" examples (pun intended) of computer spaces are evident on a number of Web sites. Using a picture file and fairly simple "image map" codes, these sites offer a graphical interface with hyperlinked areas that the Internet user can click on to link to other pages and even other sites. One of the most obviously spatial examples of these is a site that was originally called Planet Oasis, a "3-D 'Internet city'" with clickable buildings linking to other sites that "provides users with an easy and enjoyable tool to explore the World Wide Web" ("Planet Oasis Fact Sheet" 1997). The site subsequently changed its name to "MySpace Online." This renaming emphasizes the individually manipulable character of Web browsing (i.e., its "interactivity" and "user-friendliness") while also foregrounding the spatiality of that experience. The connection between spatial graphics and the desire to increase Internet access to nontechnical users is suggested in the way the original designers of this site described the point of their citylike graphical interface: "The Internet can be a confusing and intimidating place, so we wanted to bring the best the 'Net has to offer in such a way that is understandable, entertaining and enriching to users" (Tom O'Rourke, in Ark Interface 1996).

The rise of home computing through the developments of so-called personal computers and user-friendly interfaces is significant in three interrelated ways. It alludes to the spatial practices made possible by the invention and popularity of PCs and PC software. It relates directly to the issue of individual access. And it begins suggesting the kind of shift in computing power being lauded under the rubric *personal* computer. From the standpoint of spatial practices, the development of the PC relocated the computer from institutional sites (both governmental and corporate) to the quintessential domain of the individual: the home.[28] Clearly, this has meant that (some) individuals now have access to a kind of computing power formerly enjoyed only by government agencies and large corporations. But the implications of this expanded space for the movement of bits are more than just this broader distribution of computing power.

Figure 4. The MySpace Online home page. Copyright 1999, The Pixel Company. Original publisher, Ark Interface, II, 1996. Reprinted with permission from The Pixel Company. Downloaded 15 April 1999 from http://www.myspaceonline.com.

The movement of bits across institutional and individual domains provided the final technological basis for the production of what we can begin, legitimately, to characterize as cyberspace. Leaving aside for the moment the online practices that contribute to its production, cyberspace is, minimally, the culmination of the technological achievements of electronic computing (which yielded the odd mix of atoms and electrons that is bit space), computer networking (which brought here and there together in the heterotopia of network space), and finally personal computing (and the space it has opened up for mixing together institutional and individual online practices). As with the ambiguities of bit space and network space before it, moreover, the productive confusion of institutional and individual in the heterotopic space of cyberspace has led to other significant paradoxes. It has made networking at once impersonal and personal, mass mediated and popular, governmental and grassroots, corporate and individual, serious and playful. It has given rise to temporal ambiguities (heterochronia) between past and present in the mix of archived data and real-time exchanges. And perhaps most significantly, it has thrown public and private together in the same space, blurring that traditional liberal distinction and thereby raising still more vexing issues, such as whether individuals have a right to privacy on public networks and if so how much. While pundits laud the Internet for the gigabytes of public information it provides the average person, it also makes personal information open to public scrutiny: "The cables that bring information into our homes today are technically capable of bringing information out of our homes, instantly transmitted to interested others" (Rheingold 1993, 15).

Finally, diversifying access across a greater and more heterogeneous number of individual users has also, by extension, increased the variety of practices that take place online. This, in turn, has broadened the very space of cyberspace inasmuch as what people do online (in addition to the hardware and software they employ in the process) has helped to produce, and continues to produce, that social space. Indeed, the history of that space, as with any social space, is the history of the societies and cultures that have produced it and that have, in turn, been changed by it. I discuss that cultural history extensively in the following chapter; as I show next, however, that history began with the invention of a place name.

Gibsonian Cyberspace: Back to the Future?

In the preceding sections, I foregrounded the hardware and software features of computer technologies to indicate some of their implications for the production of cyberspace, postponing, as a promissory note, discussion of the users of cyberspace and the social practices by which they have realized and experienced some of the potentials outlined above. Innovating a technology, however, is itself a social practice and one very much embedded in particular cultures, as my allusions above to ballistics tables, cold war politics, research agendas, and a California counterculture already suggest. Computer innovators were products of these cultures, and they engaged in spatializing practices that were meant, at least initially, as extensions of the more conventional (and equally produced) social spaces that defined them as university academics, RAND and DARPA researchers, and Silicon Valley nerds. At the same time that they were soldering circuits, conceptualizing schematics, and coding logical addresses, however, these inventors were using their own technologies to share resources and ideas, send e-mail messages, and create listservers, increasingly on topics that had nothing to do with their professional or scholastic mandates. Through these communication practices, they began, by turns, to spatialize their own technologies further: by inhabiting them as the virtual subcultures they were becoming. Significantly, one of the first topics they defined themselves around was science fiction: "The first large list, the first to foster its own culture, ARPAnet veterans recall, was SF-LOVERS, a list of ARPA researchers who wanted to participate in public discussions about science fiction" (Rheingold 1993, 77). In a way reminiscent of Arendt's polis and even more so of Habermas's culture-debating public, these regular and reciprocal instances of shared, electronic "speaking and acting" helped to constitute e-mail lists as a kind of online forum where participants could meet and discuss issues.

Despite the virtual spaces they had started producing for themselves, however, these programmers, researchers, and computer engineers remained, as Sandy Stone describes them, fairly "scattered" and disconnected throughout the 1970s, engaged in diverse computer-related activities at several corporate and governmental sites, in Silicon Valley, and in other "electronic industrial ghettos" (1993, 98, 95). And then, in the early 1980s, novelist William Gibson coined a term—for a futuristic computer space he had been writing about—that unintentionally captured the imaginary of these disparate innovators and, on Stone's account, crystallized them into a "new community." "In a single stroke," she continues, "Gibson's powerful vision provided for them the imaginal public sphere and refigured discursive community that established the grounding for the possibility of a new kind of social interaction" (1993, 95). This declaration, with its vaguely Habermasean tones, misstates, I think, the significance of Gibson's construct, which is far less sociable and far more dystopic than the phrase "public sphere" implies.[29] Still, the remarkable popularity of Gibson's term among computer veterans does support Stone's claim, elsewhere, that his work "was for many of them a signal announcing their existence to a larger audience, and simultaneously naming their subculture for themselves in a spectacular and definitive manner" (1996, 33). This less ambitious claim has the virtue of reminding us that social space is never simply physical nor simply given, but is also a good deal conceptual and always, in principle, open to provocative rearticulations. This is what Gibson offered.

The term *cyberspace* was invented by Gibson in 1982 in a lesser known short story called "Burning Chrome," which includes a passing reference to a "matrix simulator" called the "Cyberspace Seven."[30] He expanded on the concept more famously in his 1984 novel *Neuromancer*, where he memorably describes cyberspace as a "consensual hallucination. . . . A graphic representation of data abstracted from the banks of every computer in the human system" (51). What made him regard this hallucination in explicitly spatial terms, Gibson explained later, was his observation of teenagers playing video games at an arcade in Vancouver:

Their posture seemed to indicate that they really, sincerely believed there was something behind the screen. . . . I took that home and tried to come up with a name for it. I literally did sit down at a typewriter one night and go, "Dataspace? Noooo. Infospace? Boring. Cyberspace? Hmmm. It's got sibilance. It sounds interesting." What did it mean? I had no clue. It was like an empty chocolate cup awaiting the whipped cream. (Gibson, in Johnson 1995)

As this suggests, cyberspace, for Gibson, was initially little more than an empty signifier, albeit one with "a nice buzz to it . . . something that an advertising man might [have] thought up, and when I got it I knew that it was slick and essentially hollow and that I'd have to fill it up with meaning" (Gibson, in Woolley 1992, 122).

Two points are worth noting here about Gibson's own efforts to fill the term up with meaning. First, by referring to a kind of space and then deliberately leaving it ill-defined, he actually managed to convey something that resonated with the way users were coming to experience computer networking: the strong sense of a vast, nonphysical, and still largely unknown space created at least partially by the machine. Second, the term had a critical impetus (less often remarked by enthusiasts). It was meant to suggest, as Gibson himself notes elsewhere, "the point at which media [flow] together and surround us. It's the ultimate extension of the exclusion of daily life. With cyberspace as I describe it you can literally wrap yourself in media and not have to see what's really going on around you" (in Woolley 1992, 122; interpolation in Woolley). Gibson intended his stories as works of "critical fiction" that prognosticated a terribly dismal future spawned from the marriage of information technologies, possessive individualism, and profit-worshiping capitalist multinationals (Cotton and Oliver 1994, 53). His explicitly political aim was to incite readers to question Reagan-era policies, to think critically about the consequences of deregulation, including the deregulation of mass-media corporations that profit from making people's lives more technologically mediated: "What I tried to do was give people a future that is the world of the Reagan '80s carried five steps forward and the volume turned up 20 clicks" (Gibson, in Kim 1994).[31]

Coined at about the same time that Internet protocols were being implemented and years before the Web's explosive growth, Gibson's cyberspace was the prefigured endpoint of where television, video, and computers might logically lead us. What he imagined was a network space of multidimensional data that users "jacked into" (Gibson 1984, 5) by placing

electronic probes directly into their brains, providing a neural stimulation that encompassed the full human sensorium: a "total immersion" of
the senses (Woolley 1992, 122).[32] Some writers have likened this sense of
a total sensory immersion to Marshall McLuhan's (1964) concept of the
global village. For McLuhan, modern communication technologies, principally television, have the effect of electrically shrinking the world, making the globe "no more than a village," and in that respect establishing a
different relationship between bodies and spaces than our previous technologies had done:

> After three thousand years of explosion, by means of fragmentary and
> mechanical technologies, the Western world is imploding. During the
> mechanical ages we had extended our bodies in space. Today, after
> more than a century of electric technology, we have extended our cen-
> tral nervous system itself in a global embrace, abolishing both space
> and time as far as our planet is concerned. (McLuhan, in Woolley 1992,
> 123–24).[33]

Absent any qualification, McLuhan's description seems to treat space
and time, much like Barber does, as problems that "electric technology"
has overcome. These optimistic assumptions underlie the way some
computer enthusiasts have adopted the "global village" label without
further explanation or commentary. The Electronic Frontier Foundation, for example, has an "EFF Global Village Archive" for articles on
Internet connectivity in other countries.[34] While not entirely misap-
plied, these implicitly positive associations between the global village
and cyberspace ignore that Gibson actually inverts such facile appropriations of McLuhan's concept, teasing out the unsavory consequences of
this implosion of (physical) space and (real) time.

Gibson's self-described (in Cotton and Oliver 1994, 53) "critical, pessimistic, left-wing" critique of hypermediation resonates with Habermas's
own analysis of the mass media and the need for a critical public sphere
as a stopgap—or, as I have said, a critical buffer zone—against the mass
media. However, where Habermas places his faith in the reinvention of
an ethic of communication articulated to an emancipatory, democratic
politics, Gibson places his faith, such as it is, in the rebellious activities of
the lone cyberpunk. *Cyberpunk* refers both to a literary genre and to the
streetwise and tech-smart antiheroes that are exemplary of that genre:
digital mercenaries, like Case in *Neuromancer* (Gibson 1984), who can
turn a profit on their technical know-how. Gibson's allusions to the electronic alterations of body and space that computers and networking now

(or will soon) enable are, as Cotton and Oliver note, two of the three perennial themes of the cyberpunk literature: "the technological invasion of body and mind" and "the dislocation of time and space through the action of electronic global networks and the machinations of multinational corporations" (52). To this, they add a third theme that relates directly to noninstitutional and even counter-hegemonic uses of technology: "Above all, cyberpunk explores and celebrates the eclectic use and misuse of the products of high technology on 'the Street'—the place where hi-tech meets pop underground—and extrapolates from that into possible futures" (52). This last theme, in particular, seized the social imaginaries of early hackers, who (as I show in the next chapter) saw themselves in similar terms, as urban heroes appropriating the high technologies of institutions and putting them in the hands of individuals (a "street" philosophy, metaphorically speaking, that vaguely echos SDS).[35]

Gibson's term helped to crystallize many early and subsequent computer users into a community by, in effect, conceptually resituating them. Despite this, the cyberspace of his imagination, in truth, has yet to be invented. The current, still largely text-based and partly ad-free Internet is at best a precursor to his all-encompassing, sensual, capitalist, data environment for the traffic of information commodities. With further advances in VR technology, however, and the increasing commercialization of the Internet, we do seem to be tending toward the future Gibson predicted: toward the production, that is, of a "National Information Infrastructure" and a "Global Information Infrastructure"—Al Gore's vision (1994)—that, despite the best intentions, will likely be dominated by a new "virtual class" (Kroker and Weinstein 1994). The Internet, whose creation and initial growth was funded with public monies and supported on the networking backbone provided by the NSF, developed as a kind of public work guided by a principle of universal access. Those principles arguably changed once private, for-profit companies took over the backbone service.[36] Added to this privatization has been a trend toward media consolidation through the deregulatory telecom reforms enacted by the U.S. government in 1996.[37] The issues directly relating to democratic concerns with public communication or, minimally, with individual access to public information are how to define and ensure universal service, maintain content diversity, and, as Steven Miller puts it (1996, 217), reserve "noncommercial space" on the National Information Infrastructure in this burgeoning context of information commodification, privatized service, and oligopolistic control.

Ironically, just as his predictions have become more prescient than ever, the popular press and computer pundits alike seem to be settling on more bland, if not rosy, metaphorical rearticulations of the ambivalent term Gibson coined. Nowadays, *cyberspace* sooner evokes images of electronic town halls and virtual shopping malls than of irreverent console cowboys jacking into a corporate-controlled matrix. The term, however, is still to a large extent vague, connoting the general sense of an institutional/individual network space for the movement of bits. This is the reason I have couched my analysis in terms of the study of cyberspace: indeed, it is this generic sense of the term that I mean throughout my analysis. The technological innovations I have emphasized in the bulk of this chapter provide at most a sketch of the perceptual and conceptual spatiality of networking, leaving aside the many ways in which it may be experienced in practice. Technology, in this respect, is a set of latent potentials. My point has been that cyberspace is still something that, as Gibson put it, has to be filled up with meaning.

Different efforts are currently underway to do just that, partially through the practices that users engage in when they go online. As can be expected, however, different users practice (and hence, further spatialize) networking in different ways. In the next chapter, I turn to an analysis of some of these users (the wetware) as the third component in the production of cyberspace. Focusing on three general sets of practices in which they have engaged, I show how this mix of practices has generated other productive confusions, particularly in terms of our senses of self and the problematic relationship between identity and the body that the bodiless exultation of cyberspace has made more acute.

chapter 4

Wetware

An Ethno-Topography of Cyberspace

In cyberspeak, computer users are often referred to as *wetware*—the organic, carbon-based component in the otherwise silicon and binary world of computing. Other common synonyms for the human element in computing include *liveware* and, of course, *meatware* (recalling the discussion in the introduction). Since water makes up between 50 and 90 percent of the weight of living organisms, the adjective *wet* is another fitting modifier for humans, the principal living organism involved in the production of cyberspace (references to "mouses" and "bugs" notwithstanding). It is also a particularly salient symbol for humans in an age when fears about the exchange of bodily fluids haunt the popular imaginary. In this context, the term also connotes a thing that is contaminated and messy, in contrast to the dry, solid, pristine, and hopefully virus-free precision of computer machinery and programs.[1] At the same time, the suffix -*ware*, by recalling the other, more common computer terms *hardware* and *software,* draws humans, by association, into the wired matrix of computers and networking, recognizing, if ambivalently, that human practices are an unavoidable third force in the production of cyberspace. Finally, even while the term implies an opposition between sloppy atoms and crisp electrons, it provides a vivid reminder that computer users are embodied beings, even if their online practices seem, at times, to disembody them. This reminder provokes questions about how going online may be experienced in the flesh and how such experiences are, in turn, transforming our senses of place and identity, even as we use these technologies in apparently instrumental ways.

At the beginning of the previous chapter, I argued that little in the institutional and national security origins of networking technology and in the dystopic underpinnings of the initial coinage of its name could suggest how cyberspace has come to be produced as a social space for democratic empowerment. The expansion of networking capabilities to individuals through the invention of the PC clearly provides a partial explanation, but this tells us only a little about the potential of the technology. Here, I provide a more complete response to the puzzle posed in chapter 3 by showing how some of the technological potentials described there have been realized in practice by computer users. As in the previous chapter, the discussion is sometimes historical and principally concerned with showing how online practices have further contributed to the production of cyberspace as a distinct countersite. While the technology, as I argued, has enabled productive confusions (and related paradoxes) between atoms and electrons, here and there, and the institutional and the individual, it is in the varied practices of users that these ambiguities find political expression, constituting cyberspace as, at once and ambivalently, disciplinary and anarchic, dossier-like and anonymous, (inter)personal and impersonal, sociable and yet faceless. Indeed, one of the central questions motivating this chapter is how people can build up what I have rather cryptically designated a sociality without faces, by which I have meant (picking up on the redefinition I offered at the end of chapter 2) a sense of attentiveness and responsibility toward other persons whom one may never encounter face-to-face.

In recent years, social theorists have begun suggesting ways in which technological advances in communication, as medium theorists like Marshall McLuhan would say, create new environments for the formation of new social interactions and new ways of being. Benedict Anderson (1983), for example, argues that the rise of the print media helped groups of people—bound by territory or circumstance—to establish a unified language and construct a space in which they could imagine themselves as a nation, in communion with anonymous others presumed to be sharing the same space simultaneously. What was novel about this argument was its suggestion that the imaginative projection of a shared space-time, rather than proximity (face-to-face encounters in local villages), could suffice for establishing social and even communal bonds between people who would never meet. Following this line of argument, we should not be surprised to find new languages, new types of social interactions, and indeed new identities becoming possible as a consequence of computer technologies, their cultural appropriations, and their own unique, emergent "technocultures" (Penley and Ross 1991). A small but growing literature has begun analyzing this issue of the complex identity implications of computing and virtual interactions. Bolter's reworking of "Turing's man" (1984), Turkle's "second self" (1984), Poster's "mode of information" (1990), Bukatman's "terminal identity" (1993), Lyon's "surveillance society" (1994), Kroker and Weinstein's "data trash" (1994), and Stone's computer-as-"prosthesis" metaphor (1996), not to mention Haraway's irrepressible "cyborgs" (1989), are just a few of the ways that scholars are addressing—according to different tropes, theoretical concepts, and disciplinary frameworks—how it is that computer-mediated communication (CMC) is (re)shaping our social worlds and creating new senses of self.[2]

What I draw from these works, collectively, is the sense that what makes cyberspace so challenging (in my terms, heterotopic) is the co-existence of many incongruous types of online practices and the different identity-effects they enable. To show this, I focus, in this chapter, on three broad sets of practices. I begin with a discussion of government and corporate users, focusing primarily on their practices of surveillance and the different senses of identity (or better, identification) that data processing requires. I then turn to an analysis of the first individual users of computers and the hacker ethic that inspired their irreverent practices, noting, in particular, the politics of concealed identity (or better, anonymity) they have promoted. Finally, I consider the expansion of computer use to a wider variety of nontechnical individuals and the virtual personae and, in some instances, virtual communities they have helped to create. As I will show, each of these types of practices has contributed, in competing ways, to the construction, growth, and further development of cyberspace as a distinct countersite that challenges many of the "precybernetic," "physiocentric" categories according to which we have understood our spaces, our technologies, our bodies, and by implication, our selves (Luke 1997, ¶8).

For some observers, the crux of the challenge that cyberspace poses is in offering a spatiality that excludes the body. I address this issue at some length in the final section, considering the implications of disembodiment for our notions of political agency and citizenship. Ultimately, however, I argue that the three sets of online practices discussed here—digital surveillance, hacking, and computer conferencing—have identity-effects that bear more complex and uncertain relationships to the embodied individuals assumed to exist somewhere in the offline world. Computer surveillance, after all, depends on relating data to identifiable and locatable individuals, while the most successful hacks leave no traces.

It is this coincidence of embodying and disembodying practices that makes the experience of cyberspace that much more indeterminate and that, in turn, gives rise to competing political efforts to make cyberspace more safe (a topic to which I turn in the next chapter). As this suggests, the issue for me is not which of these identity constructs relates to democratic politics in the truest sense (whatever that might mean), but rather what different kinds of socially lived spaces, types of politics, and forms of power are enabled by their (co-)production.

From Guard Towers to Tower Systems: Tracking the Data-Image

As the histories of the ENIAC and the ARPAnet recounted in the previous chapter demonstrate, among the earliest users of electronic computers were governments, specifically, defense workers and contracted researchers with national security mandates. While initially interested in exploiting electronic power for computational purposes, their R and D quickly expanded to a variety of communications uses (as in the network projects conducted at DARPA) and eventually to the use of computers in communications intelligence—i.e., for surveillance and countersurveillance. Despite the ideological implication that a state's national security is about protecting its own citizens from the actions of foreign states and their citizens, governments quickly turned computer surveillance practices, sometimes illicitly, against their own citizens. The U.S. National Security Agency (NSA), for example, conducted illegal surveillance of American citizens in at least two of its covert, message interception programs: Operation Shamrock and Operation Minaret (Bamford 1983, 302–55). The computerization of the communications channels from which the NSA culled messages facilitated these operations. In 1963, for example, RCA Global, one of the NSA's message suppliers for Operation Shamrock, informed the agency that it would be transferring over to a new computerized telegraph system that would record messages on magnetic tapes (312). By the time the new system was operational in 1964, the NSA had developed the "Harvest" computer, which, as Bamford describes it, "could be programmed to 'kick out' any telegram containing a certain word, phrase, name, location, sender or addressee, or any combination. It might be a name from a watch list, any message containing the word *demonstration,* or any cable to or from the Israeli UN delegation" (313). Despite the pastoral imagery implied by its name, the Harvest computer was designed to reap information from ostensibly private messages, including those of American citizens, that had been illegally obtained: that is, without demonstrated probable cause and legal warrants and in violation of the NSA charter as a spy agency intended only for *foreign* intelligence gathering. Supercomputer use for making and breaking code is now a standard at the NSA ("Open Sesame" 1994).

Computerized surveillance by governments and eventually by corporations has led some observers to associate computers with Foucault's panopticon (e.g., Rheingold 1993, 15). As Mark Poster notes, however, surveillance in an era of computerized databases no longer requires that observer and observed share the same proximate location. The jumble of atoms with electrons, here with there, and the institutional with the individual in the heterotopic space of computer networking has enabled a more pervasive kind of surveillance, which Poster describes as a "Super-panopticon, a system of surveillance without walls, windows, towers or guards" (1990, 91, 93). This description, however, somewhat overstates the case, making it appear that surveillance in the Age of Information lacks any specific spatial limitation: indeed, that it occurs everywhere and hence nowhere in particular. In actuality (and as Poster is well aware) networked databases do have an identifiable spatiality, one suggested by the notion that users must *input* data and that they implement various actions on the basis of data *output*. Part of what is different about the Superpanopticon is that the physical spaces of the prison and other disciplinary institutions have been annexed (literally, *wired*) to the more expansive electronic spaces of binary digits.[3] More to the point, this electronic expansion of disciplinary discourses and practices has transformed the character of observation and even of the objects themselves.

Paralleling the architectural structure of networking, surveillance has become spatially decentralized and distributed, in contrast to its former centralization: for example, in the guard tower of Bentham's traditional panopticon. With digitization and electronic networks, "organizations that are both geographically and functionally remote" can now share (more often, buy and sell) data about individuals (Lyon 1994, 84). David Lyon offers the following example:

> [A] bizarre case concerns an America[n] business, Farrell's Ice Cream Parlour, which sold the name-list of those claiming free sundaes on their birthdays to a marketing firm. Soon after, the ice-cream eaters were surprised to find draft registration warnings in their mail! The marketing company had sold their details to Selective Service System, who had in turn sold them to the Department of Defense. (10)

Actually, it is not entirely clear from this description that these organizations were electronically linked via some network; what the example does illustrate very forcefully, however, is how seemingly innocuous information in one database (the names, presumably of young men, celebrating their coming of age with free ice cream) becomes grist for a wide variety of binary mills whose databases can and do serve more serious purposes with more profound consequences. The point is that once information is digitized and stored on one database, it can be converted and merged with many other databases.[4] Linking these databases together in one galactic network (like the Web) in turn simplifies and extends the possibilities for sharing data, thereby multiplying the sources and stores of digital information.

Lyon's example also shows how people voluntarily participate, if rather unwittingly, in the process by which personal data enters a global circuit of information. Put another way, the sources for this kind of data monitoring are often the targets of surveillance themselves. It is a seemingly benign, indirect, and "participatory surveillance" (Poster 1990, 68) that people voluntarily enable whenever they fill out a warranty card or buy something on credit. In these respects, decentralization and participation—more often positive factors associated with democracy—have, in this instance, replaced a centralized and geographically limited form of surveillance with the more cost-effective and pervasive, because distributed, practice of "dataveillance" (Clarke, in Lyon 1994, 47).

As the foregoing discussion suggests, computer technologies together with the distributed practices of surveillance they enable have normalized a form of social-control-through-individual-participation, which was, of course, Foucault's point in his analysis of disciplinary society (1979). This trend toward a participatory form of social control lies at the heart of what Foucault dubs *governmentality* (1991): the development, in the last two centuries, of an art of government (indeed, a way of doing and thinking government, viz., govern-*mentality*) that has as its chief problematic a concern with the management of populations. That Foucault regards this as a "consequence of the problem of choices of government" (1991, 102) and as a transformation that began in the eighteenth century, not coincidentally the time of the bourgeois revolutions in France and America, suggests a connection between governmentality and democratic forms of politics. He implies, in other words, that coterminous with the rise of modern notions of democratic self-rule (which in its representative strains is also fundamentally about being able to choose how one will be ruled by others) was the development of techniques and apparatuses for a new type of power: a covert, enabling, diffuse, consensual, normalizing, and micromanaged form of power that targets the new datum of the population. The (perhaps unwelcome) conclusion to be drawn from Foucault's observations is that, at least for him, democracy is not simply self-determination, synonymous with a kind of freedom from power; rather, it is concomitantly a form of self-discipline. It solicits our participation in and acquiescence to a different and in many respects more invasive, because more productive, form of power: power that invades by inviting. Foucault's own genealogies suggest that the democratic traditions Western societies have inherited (or rather, constructed) have all depended on parallel developments of what he calls the "apparatuses of security," the mechanisms by which a *population* is managed at the same time that a *polity* is made (1991, 87). Computers, too, are apparatuses of security, not simply in the facile sense that they were bred in the bellies of government defense agencies (though that in itself should give us pause), but in the less conspicuous and more seductive way that they have become *personal*: indeed, that they have become a very normal part of many peoples' everyday lives.

Such normalizations have helped to change who we are in the process of modifying what we do and where we do it. What Kenneth Laudon calls the "data-image"—a digital dossier, based on selective information— is one such innovation (Lyon 1994, 84). The shift from the mechanical to the electronic computer, as I have said, unleashed electromagnetic forces—of acting on bodies at a distance—that make it possible to set computers to work "without direct human intervention" (Bolter 1984, 55). Similarly, the digitization of credit applications, for example, automates processing according to predetermined algorithms. From the standpoint of efficiency, this eliminates the need for time-consuming, inconsistent, and sometimes venal human decision making, but it also, by extension, removes the opportunity for a qualitative, context-specific determination of a person's creditworthiness. Binary conditions are recorded; personal circumstances are not. It is for these reasons that Poster insists that digitization—even though it ostensibly preserves data by reducing noise—actually constitutes a "*loss* of data" (1990, 94, Poster's emphasis). It necessarily entails the reduction of information to the binary logic imposed by the "impoverished, limited language" of zeros and ones (95). Computerized surveillance requires categorization: that is, a lexicon (or, more properly, a discourse) for recording, quantifying, ordering, and tracking individuals' attitudes, tastes, behaviors, affiliations, and statuses. In the process, people are classified and cataloged by types as established by officials, experts, and corporate interests. The resulting data that are inputted and stored in computer databases are the products of these typifications: not the complex narratives, experiences, and details that make up who we are, but bits of information collected according to someone else's interpretive scheme. Biographically rich, conflicted, am-bivalent, cultural selves—indeed, our noisy, analog identities—are re-duced to the digitally sampled composites that become, in a very thin sense, "our" data-images. Selective, discrete, and unambiguous bits of in-formation yield these sharply defined profiles of individuals that are col-lected in the network-integrated databanks of businesses and govern-ment agencies around the world. From the standpoint of dataveillance, these digital profiles become who we are.

Such descriptions provide a compelling case for reading the comput-er, from an Arendtean perspective, as an Archimedean mechanism of surveillance: one that enables a form of power-as-leverage because it acts on bodies at a distance, extrapolating a data-image from the embodied, analog identities of individuals. This is certainly where Poster winds up: with "the uncomfortable discovery that the population participates in its own self-constitution as subjects of the normalizing gaze of the Super-panopticon," and the sure knowledge that databases foster "the multipli-cation of the individual, the constitution of an additional self, one that may be acted upon to the detriment of the 'real' self without that 'real' self ever being aware of what is happening" (97–98).[5] These are impor-tant insights, to be sure, helping us see the big picture by revealing the contours of a new system of symbolic exchange that Poster calls, with a nod to Marx, the "mode of information" (6). But left at this, the Super-panopticon becomes an apparatus of complete closure, one to which we inevitably and unwittingly acquiesce. This conclusion, however, is not entirely consistent with the Foucauldian theories from which Poster draws, which posit a more enabling, contingent, and open form of power as always embodying its own immanent forms of resistance.

Or perhaps the problem is that Poster follows Foucault too closely. Foucault, after all, never said very much about those forms of resistance or under what conditions they might erupt. His studies, as Norman Fairclough points out, focused on the formation of disciplinary discours-es and their constitution of subjects and objects without attending very much to people's actual practices, i.e., to "real instances of people doing or saying or writing things" (1991, 57).[6] If we attend to practices, however, possibilities open up for understanding how computers enable the more productive and incomplete form of power Foucault theorizes, and not simply the Archimedean form of power-as-leverage that Arendt attrib-utes to advanced technologies (which becomes, in view of the nuances of practice, a facile technological determinism).

In fact, Poster's claim that people remain unaware of Superpanoptic surveillance is correct by degrees rather than absolutely. Filling out surveys (a preliminary of data inputting) or reviewing a credit report on oneself (a data-image output) can make an individual acutely aware that she is contributing to a process of surveillance, and aware, too, of how that process works. The complaint that we are being reduced to numbers is, as I have suggested, a common expression of how we experience the depersonalizing effects of the bureaucratic reduction of our identities to bits of computer data. This salient disturbance, however—registered at the level of individual identity—is a heterotopic effect. It is engendered (sometimes) when we are confronted by a survey form or a credit report whose precisely delimited categories we experience in ways that contradict, often jarringly, our noisy self-understandings. Such data entry and output forms can become, in this respect, "obligatory points of passage" (Hetherington 1997, 68) between the binary realm of digital information and the bodily realm of analog existence. They are a heterotopic in-between (an interface) that brings together, by comparing them, a data-image and an analog identity, unsettling the *grounds* (in an explicitly spatial sense) on which either or both of those are constructed. This is by no means inevitable, of course. Given the number of forms some of us may complete in the course of a year (let alone a lifetime), we may become quite adept at extrapolating information about ourselves to fill out such forms. It is this degree of indifferent competence that I think best fits Poster's sense of Superpanopticon.

On occasion, however, we may come across a category or question that forces us to stop and think (how annoying!): indeed, to consider what we are about in relation to that box we are asked to check that is supposed to reveal something about us. On occasion, too, this site of confrontation may become a site of contestation, a point at which we may begin to question some particular ground. And this can go either way. We may question our own senses of self in relation to survey categories, e.g., "This form lists *Hispanic* as a *Race* category. Does that mean I'm not a white person?" Or we may come to question the categories themselves and respond in ways that enact a subtle form of resistance:

Sex:	Frequently
Marital Status:	Satisfied
Race:	Lemon Meringue
Religion:	Old-Dog-with-New-Tricks

Whether such examples evoke shattering laughter or not, they do at least shake up a few familiar landmarks of our thought (Foucault 1994b, xv).[7]

Computer technologies, of course, did not invent these categories, but they have made possible the sorts of programmatic algorithms by which such landmarks of thought are used, routinely, to reconfigure conventional social spaces: concretely, by contributing to calculations affecting, for example, financial resource allocations (corporate, national, and international), the reshaping of voting districts, the construction of highways and dams, a variety of redlining decisions by which lenders and investors exclude "high-risk/low-return" areas (typically ghettos populated by low-income minorities) or, more positively, by providing information with which government agencies can monitor and enforce "civil rights in areas such as housing, mortgage lending, educational opportunities, employment, and voting" (U.S. Census Bureau 1997a). Everything from individual decisions about where to live to World Bank economic restructuring plans are routinely decided on the basis of computerized survey results. It is in these various respects that such surveys matter and why they may, therefore, become sites of contestation. What bears emphasizing here, however, is how such contestations are enabled, first, by the kind of confrontation between competing discursive orders that such surveys—as a kind of interface between institutional binary algorithms and individual analog experiences—make possible. These confrontations help to reveal the processes of ordering on which institutional algorithms and individual experiences, respectively, are based. As I said, such heterotopic effects may work in either direction or perhaps in both. The reevaluation of racial and ethnic categories is just one example of the kinds of politics such confrontations can spark.

Computer technologies and related techniques for data manipulation may have been developed initially by the state for security purposes and then extended to a variety of corporate and governmental institutions for administrative and investment calculations, marketing, research, and so forth. Before long, however, other computer users emerged, with different agendas, intent on exploring and developing the potentials latent in digital technology for personalized and perhaps also counter-hegemonic ends. It is to their story that I now turn.

Byte Me! Hackers and Other Strangers

On 2 November 1988 a Cornell graduate student by the name of Robert Morris Jr. introduced a program onto the Internet that temporarily crippled the system, causing approximately six thousand computers to crash. Although disrupting the network was not Morris's intent—in fact, the problem was caused by a flaw in his program—the incident created quite a stir, raising concerns about the vulnerability of the Internet to hacker invasions.[8] The notorious "Internet Worm," as it has come to be called, is now part of Internet lore (Zakon 2000; Sterling 1993, 86). Incidents like the Worm—or more to the point, the way the incident has been cited as evidentiary proof that computer viruses pose a social menace—have made state and corporate security experts generally leery of hackers, even to the point of blaming them for crashes that were later discovered to have been caused by software glitches.[9] Until his arrest in February 1995, the notorious deeds of computer outlaw Kevin Mitnick further helped to confirm fears about the hacker threat (Garfinkel 1995).

For many observers, the faceless nature of electronic space has partially contributed to these and other questionable online practices. Because our bits rather than our bodies travel in cyberspace, people can, and often do, adopt online user IDs and pseudonyms that mask their identities. Such anonymity, of course, is not guaranteed when network managers can trace modem calls and match Internet addresses to the accounts of identifiable individuals. And, in fact, digital surveillance depends on this ability to establish links between a computerized dossier and the individual to whom it ostensibly pertains. Some computer users, however, have learned more sophisticated techniques for concealing their identities. Call tracing can be thwarted through a variety of *phreaking* (telephone fraud) techniques. Internet Protocol (IP) addresses can be faked by "IP spoofing," which, as Garfinkel puts it with a remarkable flair for anthropomorphizing machines, allows "an attacking computer [to] masquerade as another" (1995). And, of course, accounts can be masked through the use of anonymous remailers.[10]

This anonymity and the relative lack of authority built into distributed networks has meant that laws and social norms from "the real world" seem far more flexible and, in some instances, inapplicable in cyberspace. Some critics take the argument further, however. Pointing to (often exaggerated) instances of hacking, e-mail harassments, cyberstalking, and, above all, child pornography, they maintain that the faceless nature of electronic space actually encourages a variety of illicit online practices. Philip Terzian, for example, characterizes the Internet as a "global sewer," arguing, in barely veiled elitist overtones, that "if you consider the distinguishing features of the Internet—no rules, secrecy, mass access, anonymity—you have the ingredients for the lowest common standards" (1996). As this suggests, for some observers, electronic anonymity—like the myth of Gyges's ring that makes the wearer invisible—leads inexorably to immoral and even illegal behavior.[11]

If census forms and credit reports can incite one kind of heterotopic disturbance registered at the level of individual identity, then electronic anonymity constitutes another kind of heterotopic disturbance, this one registered at the level of institutional identity. Governments are becoming particularly vexed by the problem of electronic anonymity, especially as regards the whole enterprise of law enforcement, whose reason for being is precisely to ensure social order through the management of the population.[12] The capacity to monitor, as I have already suggested, has been the sine qua non of that enterprise. To be sure, devices like telephone wiretaps, security cameras, bugs, trackers, parabolic microphones, and now database systems, together with practices like patrolling a beat, conducting surveillance of suspects, doing undercover work, fingerprinting, and monitoring the activities of prisoners and ex-convicts are standard, day-to-day features of law enforcement. Similarly, spying on known terrorist organizations and on enemy governments (and even on friendly governments) are mainstays of intelligence work. Taken together, these sets of devices and practices have become so commonplace in the art of government that they have helped to naturalize the conviction that governments should be able to monitor literally anyone in order to safeguard state and society. In sum, whether spatialized centrally according to Bentham's blueprint or distributively by a web of security apparatuses that include networked databases, Surveillance has been the perennial ground for those Twin Pillars of Society we call National Security and Public Safety. The effect of electronic anonymity, however, especially through the added veil of encryption (maintaining the secrecy of communications by converting messages into codes that, in theory, only their intended recipients can decipher) challenges that very ground. This is one way that cyberspace can become heterotopic for institutional actors as well, disrupting a few foundations and, less obviously but also evidently, stirring up a subtle crisis of identity. Witness the following metaphorical scenario, proffered by FBI official Jim Kallstrom, explaining the dangers posed by strong encryption programs:

> O.K., someone kidnaps one of your kids and they are holding your kid in this fortress up in the Bronx. Now, we have probable cause that your child is inside this fortress. We have a search warrant. But for some reason, we cannot get in there. They made it out of some new metal, or something, right? Nothing'll cut it, right? And there are guys in there, *laughing* at us. That's what the basis of this issue really is— we've got a situation now where a technology has become so sophisticated that the whole notion of a legal process is at stake here! (Levy 1994, 48)

Given the discursive effort being exerted here to construct encryption as a threat (to kids, no less), it remains clear that, whether or not the situation is as dire as this suggests, electronic anonymity is shaking up a few landmarks from the state's perspective, too.[13]

The often anonymous character of online interactions, however, is open to another interpretation. Precisely because we live in a context wherein surveillance has become ubiquitous (if not exactly as insuperable as Poster suggests), anonymity can become a viable and even advisable form of resistance. That is, from a political standpoint, techniques for ensuring electronic anonymity may be seen as direct responses to institutional digital surveillance. So, for example, Andrew Ross argues that "in a society whose techno-political infrastructure depends increasingly upon greater surveillance and where foreign wars are seen through the lens of laser-guided smart bombs, cybernetic activism necessarily relies on a much more *covert politics of identity,* since access to closed systems requires discretion and dissimulation" (1991, 120, my emphasis). Furthermore, even on the open system of the Internet—inasmuch as it, too, as Pentagon analyst Charles Swett has observed in telling tones, is an abundant source for a kind of "strategic reconnaissance 'by modem'" (1995)— anonymity makes political dissension safer. Indeed, as I argued in chapter 2, anonymity and pseudonymity have a long and respectable tradition in American politics. Even Madison and his cohorts availed themselves of aliases when they penned *The Federalist Papers,* though perhaps more for reasons having to do with constructing a public voice through the emergent print media than with ensuring their personal safety.

In a similar vein, electronic *pseudonymity*—anonymity through the adoption of an alias—can have the parallel effect of constructing a kind of public voice even as it protects personal identity. Writing about anonymous remailing systems, Steven Levy, for example, notes: "Ideally, if someone chooses a pseudonym in one of these systems, no one else can send mail under that name. This allows for the possibility of *a true digital persona—an 'identity' permanently disembodied from one's physical being"* (1993, 8, my emphasis). As this description suggests, the true digital persona is obviously not the same as the data-image constructed out of digital surveillance practices. For the data-image to operate as a means of surveillance and control, digital records must be articulated to the embodied individual they are meant to represent, often through the use of a name or a social security number. This articulation, moreover, is completely determined by those interested others who compile, merge, and assess the significance of data, even while the targets of surveillance may contribute some of that data.

The *true digital persona,* by contrast, exploits the bodiless character of electronic space, allowing one to create one's own alternative identity: indeed, a nonidentity vis-à-vis the embodied individual who constructs it inasmuch as the digital persona need bear no resemblance to one's embodied self. Because online encounters are not face-to-face, none of the usual physical traits and the cultural meanings attached to those traits (e.g., gender, race, affluence) need come into play in our online practices unless we choose to identify ourselves in those terms. It is for this reason that people are able to adopt online personae that are different from who they are in the offline world. From this perspective, offline identities can remain entirely private; only the virtual persona is open to public scrutiny. This, too, helps constitute cyberspace as a different kind of social space: one for the exploration and development of new and different senses of self. The (partially) nonphysical properties of electronic space, the custom of using pseudonyms, and other, more exceptional techniques for concealing one's embodied identity, taken together, all help to make identity more fluid in cyberspace and bodiless anonymity a potential feature of many online practices.

As countless commentators, both critics and pundits, have noted, a computer underground has constituted itself in relation to this exploratory social space.[14] Perhaps at one time, the term *underground* referred to an actual place; in reference to a subculture, however, it has come to mean a group engaged in some sort of counter-hegemonic (sometimes illicit) activism through concealed identity, a concealment that is only metaphorically related to a hiding place. That is, a countercultural underground is more often ontology (a way of being) than topography (a place of being). In the case of the computer underground, however, the term is a little of both. Poster has noted how, in the development of computer science as a disciplinary practice, the computer functioned as a stable identity referent: "[W]hat keeps us together," computer scientist Maurice Wilkes maintains, "is not some abstraction . . . but the actual hardware that we work with every day" (Poster 1990, 147). The computer underground, which includes both hardware and software hackers, similarly constitutes itself in relation to the machine and, more importantly, to the electronic space it helps constitute. Put another way, a computer underground can exist inasmuch as cyberspace, as a space for bits rather than bodies, can be made a kind of hiding place: one where authority-wary, suspicious, and otherwise vulnerable offline identities can remain anonymous. It is in this context that "hackers"—operating under a variety of suggestive pseudonyms, including "Phiber Optik" and "R.U. Sirius"—have constituted themselves as a counterculture.[15]

Etymologically, a *hack* job, in its original quotidian sense, meant something that was done quickly and just well enough to perform some task adequately. In keeping with the oppositional attitude of the computer underground, this negative sense was inverted and came to mean "[a]n incredibly good, and perhaps very time-consuming, piece of work that produces exactly what is needed" (*The Jargon File* 2000: "hack"). Hackers are first and foremost computer experts: technophiles who painstakingly create programs and learn network systems often just for the fun and challenge of the process. That they break into proprietary systems at all has, in general, less to do with malicious intent than with a desire to test their own abilities, to see whether they can break into a system and whether they can do so without getting caught. In fact, a successful hack, apropos the connection between hacking and anonymity, leaves no trace of itself: "[C]ontrary to their media image, hackers avoid deliberately destroying data or otherwise damaging the system. Doing so would conflict with their instrumental goal of blending in with the average user to conceal their presence and prevent the deletion of the account" (Meyer and Thomas 1990). That is the trick that requires skill, which in turn contributes to the formation of a subculture based on technical merit: "Hackers consider themselves something of an elite (a meritocracy based on ability), though one to which new members are gladly welcome. There is thus a certain ego satisfaction to be had in identifying yourself as a hacker (but if you claim to be one and are not, you'll quickly be labeled *bogus*)" (*The Jargon File* 2000: "hacker").

A second important motive behind hacking is the conviction that individuals, and not just institutions, should have access to computing power. In fact, one of the central, original tenets of "the Hacker Ethic," according to Steven Levy, was the belief that "[a]ccess to computers should be unlimited and total" (cited in Brand 1995). In addition, hackers maintain, relatedly, that "[a]ll information should be free," that "[c]omputers can change your life for the better," and that one should "[m]istrust authority—promote decentralization" (Levy, in Brand 1995). If computers were initially institutional tools of surveillance, then these early tenets conveyed the alternative sensibility that computers could empower individuals as well. This conviction inspired early hackers to devise several hardware and software innovations that, in a sense, actually did help to democratize computing and networking. To the extent, then, that we can speak at all about cyberspace as a democratic space, computer hackers were, in a strange way, the Founding Fathers.

The first generation of hackers, in the 1960s and early 1970s, learned their avocation as students in computer science departments, which afforded them access to university mainframes. Because they predated the PC and the Internet, these early hackers were forced to access computers from the institutional sites in which they were located; through various techniques, however, they managed to transform "mainframes into virtual personal computers" (Brand 1995), employing them for individual rather than institutional ends. Indeed, as '60s radical Stewart Brand has observed, while "[m]ost of our generation scorned computers as the embodiment of centralized control . . . a tiny contingent—later called 'hackers'—embraced computers and set about transforming them into tools of liberation" (1995).[16]

The second and third generations of hackers, in the late 1970s and early 1980s, continued this transformation by inventing the PC and the software that runs on it, thereby extending computing power to non-academic and even nontechnical individuals (Brand 1995) and becoming billionaires in the process (*The Triumph of the Nerds* 1996). For Brand, the "tens of thousands of netheads" who have created bulletin board services, the Usenet newsgroup system, and the bulk of the Internet more generally constitute a "fourth generation of revolutionaries" who still abide by "the Hacker Ethic." As his statistics indicate, of course, the average Internet user is too young (about thirty years old) to have been part of the '60s generation. Brand contends, nonetheless, that the distributional ethic that gave rise to the computer revolution, the PC, and "the global digital epidemic known as the Internet" has its roots in the countercultural '60s: "We owe it all to the hippies" (1995).

To be sure, several parallels can be drawn between the 1960s hippie counterculture and the 1990s computer counterculture, including their shared anti-authoritarianism, their anticentralist views, and their ambivalent mix of individualism (Do Your Own Thing) and communitarianism (Power to the People). Despite Brand's well-intentioned homage, however, these parallels invite other, less sympathetic ones. After all, the '60s hippie was also typically constructed as someone who desired an escape from physical reality through the use of hallucinogenic drugs, like LSD, which afforded a kind of somatic escape to an alternate psychic reality, a reality that has been depicted with the same brash display of psychedelic color and stylistic excess that is used today to symbolize cyberculture (exemplified, ad nauseam, by *Wired* magazine). Similarly, cyberpunks, as Gibson reminds us, seek the "bodiless exultation of cyberspace," an alternate reality experienced through the medium of electronic space. As I have said, today's cyberspace still falls technologically short of the total sensory immersion Gibson's characters experience when they jack

into a cyberspace deck. Still, the hacker experience of "writing code"—
sometimes for thirty or more straight hours, as Microsoft founder Bill
Gates has fondly described his early days in the business (see *The Triumph
of the Nerds* 1996)—can, in its own way, induce a kind of somatic escape.
This sense of escape, however, masks a certain ageist conceit: in fact, code
writers have tended to be young men and hence probably healthy (if a bit
pale). In that respect, they could afford more than most to forget the
body. And apparently they often did, as they sat for long stretches in front
of their monitors, pausing occasionally to ingest stale pizza and flat cola,
showering infrequently, and remaining otherwise transfixed by a steady
stream of luminescent pixels in the alphanumeric world of code.

Because of their all-consuming fascination with the virtual, however,
hackers contributed materially and culturally to the expansion and growth
of cyberspace, opening it up to other users. Some of these newcomers, as
I show next, have turned the hacker politics of concealment into a kind of
ordinary social practice for the exploration of alternative identities and
new kinds of virtual relations.

Toward "Virtual Communities" . . . and Their Discontents

If digital surveillance and hacking are stories, respectively, centering on
institutionally employed electrical engineers and computer scientists, on
the one hand, and idiosyncratic, code-writing rebels, on the other, virtual
communities are primarily about average people with middling computer skills who just like to chat online. Their relative lack of expertise has
often made them the targets of online "flame wars" (electronic verbal
abuses) launched by hackers and other early denizens of cyberspace. Indeed, while much of the Hacker Ethic concerned the laudable effort to
empower individuals, it is also the case that many hackers, in practice,
have tended to display an often hurtful and unforgiving contempt for
nontechnical latecomers: the "clueless newbies" of the Internet.[17] These
newbies, however, are the most relevant for any analysis of the democratic possibilities of cyberspace inasmuch as their online communicative
practices contribute the most toward the production of an electronic
space for social interaction.

This is not to trivialize the contributions institutional actors have
made toward building the technological infrastructure on which cyberspace partially depends nor the contributions various generations of
hackers have made toward expanding access to those infrastructures.
Rather, my point is that the electronic spaces constituted by digital surveillance, on the one hand, and hacking, on the other, are in some respects

more limited than is evoked by the concept of cyberspace as a social space. In the case of state and corporate digital surveillance, the thrust has been the creation of an expanded space for social control through the medium of data manipulation (see Stone 1993, 99). The key interaction here is between some database program (an algorithm set to work on the machine) and the data (about us) it manipulates.[18] In the case of hacking, the point is to create an exploratory digital space for its own sake: a space primarily for establishing a relationship between human (hacker) and machine (computer system), and only secondarily among humans (other hackers), whose common bond, anyway, is this desire to interact with the machine. When online practices turn toward communication, however, electronic spaces become social spaces in the fullest sense, i.e., spaces of interaction among people.

These interactive practices have been varied. Electronic mail (or e-mail) was one of the first and most (unexpectedly) popular forms of interaction that networking technology made possible. Principally a one-to-one mode of communication, e-mail was easily amended to a form of group communication with the addition of listservers, electronic mailing-list systems that automatically distribute messages posted by any one member to all the others on the list. (As I noted in the previous chapter, the first Net cultures, made up of sci-fi aficionados, were constituted through such group mailings.) Whereas this system distributes messages to users (or rather, to the network sites where their accounts are located), most other forms of online interaction—the vast array of computer conferencing services—store messages at particular sites from which users can retrieve those messages (i.e., much like a bulletin board in the offline world). Electronic bulletin board services (BBSs) were an early form of posting service that worked in this way, allowing users dial-in access to the server, where they could review various categories of interest and then upload (post) and download (retrieve) a variety of text, graphic, sound, and program files ordered according to those categories and sub-categories. Many of the "forums" on commercial subscriber services, like CompuServe, America Online (AOL), and Prodigy, also work this way.[19]

Perhaps the most famous venue for online discussions, however, is the Usenet system: a public message-posting system organized by user-defined categories. Initially a Unix-based user network invented in 1979 by graduate students at Duke and the University of North Carolina, Usenet developed alongside the Internet and eventually became part of it (see PBS 1996; Bumgarner 1995; Rheingold 1993, 117–31). It is now home to over twenty-five thousand newsgroups worldwide, semiorganized into hierarchical topic categories—on everything from alt.startrek.klingon to talk.politics.theory—and constituting, as one source puts it, "the town square of the Internet; a place where millions of people gather to debate, preach, get information or just leave a group message for people who share their interests" (PBS 1996).

Finally, in addition to the asynchronous exchanges possible through listservers and newsgroups, users can also have real-time (simultaneous) exchanges through a variety of quasi-conversational services, including Internet Relay Chat (IRC), two-person "Instant Messaging" (IM) on AOL, and the more public "chat rooms" available on AOL and other commercial network services, and the many text-based "virtual worlds" of MUDs and their derivatives.[20] The latter are particularly significant. Minor differences aside, all MUDs are basically real-time interactive, multiuser, programmed environments arrayed as a set of "rooms" that a user's character (virtual persona) can explore and within which one's character can interact with other users' characters. Furthermore, because mudding typically involves users in role play, encouraging them to develop one or more complex and richly textured characters, it has enabled online users to experiment with different realities, alternate identities, and new experiences based on how other characters treat and react to their personae. The experiences can become so rich that "real life"—or "RL," in the acronym-peppered newspeak of cyberspace—can begin to lose its pride of place, its privilege, in relation to the alternate realities MUDs make possible. Put another way, mudding can have ontological and epistemological consequences, helping to foreground the variety of ways in which real life, too, is a construct: "RL is just one more window, and it's not usually my best one" (a mudder, cited in Turkle 1995, 13).[21]

Despite differences among these various online practices, many analysts agree that sustained computer-mediated communication (CMC) can, over time, lead participants in a particular MUD environment or in an online discussion forum to develop social bonds with others in the same virtual space.[22] Howard Rheingold (1993) offers the phrase *virtual community* to describe the form of computer-mediated communion that has formed, for example, among members of the California-based computer-conferencing service known as the WELL. In contrast to the private (person-to-person) messaging of an e-mail, conferencing services like the WELL are a form of public CMC. No one who has access to a particular forum, BBS, or newsgroup is, in principle, excluded from reading others' notes nor from posting their own messages (provided they abide by community standards). As a consequence, these particular services facilitate discussion among several participants. By extension, *"virtual communities,"* according to Rheingold, "are social aggregations that emerge from the Net when enough people carry on those public discussions long enough, with sufficient human feeling, to form webs of personal relationships in cyberspace" (1993, 5).

Two points are relevant to an understanding of the community spirit described here. First, unlike Benedict Anderson's (1983) notion of "imagined" communities (which emerged, according to his analysis, from the impersonal, one-way, few-to-many paradigm of the mass media), a virtual community stems from the kind of interpersonal, two-way, many-to-many form of communication that distributed computer networking has enabled. In other words, CMC meets C. Wright Mills's criteria for public communication, as outlined in chapter 2. Consequently, instead of imaginatively projecting a sense of community onto anonymous others in a mass-mediated context, online participants can actually *co-produce* a sense of intimacy by getting to know each other through the personae they project on the Net. Unless participants arrange to meet each other in person, these others may remain faceless (in the mundane sense that one may never know what other participants look like), but they do not therefore remain nameless (anonymous). It is in this respect that what I refer to as a sociality without faces becomes possible. Or as Sandy Stone offers more ambiguously but more provocatively, computer conferencing creates "incontrovertibly social spaces in which people still meet face-to-face, but under new definitions of 'meet' and 'face'" (1993, 85).

Which leads me to my second point: the sense of community that participants have described develops in part out of the different production of spatiality that computer technologies permit. What enables Rheingold, for example, to derive a feeling of community (and even "security") is that the virtual space he shares with others is one in which physical distances between here and there are dissolved, creating an Other space in which, as he puts it, "real people" are available "around the clock" (1993, 17). It is in this sense that online practices are experienced in terms of a certain spatial and temporal presentness: they make others spatially present before us (through their projected digital personae) and temporally present with us.[23] It bears emphasizing, however, that this effected spatiality is the product both of the hardware and software innovations discussed in the last chapter and of the cultural practices alluded to here: put another way, the technology supplies only the potential for this different spatiality, but one could not experience the socially lived space of the WELL that Rheingold describes unless other people actually went online and participated.

Given the apparently disembodied nature of online practices, however, cyberspace raises complex questions about identity. In fact, the assumption that an embodied individual lies behind the virtual personae we may encounter online is more problematic than we might at first imagine. In the early 1990s, Allucquère Rosanne Stone (aka Sandy Stone) wrote an essay on cyberspace and identity that she wryly entitled, "Will the Real Body Please Stand Up? Boundary Stories about Virtual Cultures" (1993). For Stone, the conviction, held by many computer enthusiasts, that "going online" means "leaving the body behind" provoked a number of questions about the relationship between identity and the body. As she explained later, our (precybernetic) senses of identity in the offline world have been based on certain fundamental assumptions about the meaning of one's *true* identity and the sense that this identity is always constituted in relation to one and the same physical body: "[T]he societal imperative with which we have been raised is that there is one primary persona, or 'true identity,' and that in the off-line world—the 'real world'—this persona is firmly attached to a single physical body, by which our existence as a social being is authorized and in which it is grounded" (1996, 73). Cyberspace forces us to break faith with such assumptions because "On the nets . . . *warranting*, or grounding a persona in a physical body, is meaningless" (1993, 84).

Typically our physical aspects cannot be perceived by others when we go online.[24] This general feature of cyberspace has enabled a number of sometimes exploratory, sometimes exploitative experiments with alternate identities. A particularly common version of this is "computer cross-dressing," that is, pretending to be someone of the opposite sex (Stone 1993, 84). In her analysis of one discovered incident of computer cross-dressing, Stone outlines the broader identity implications of virtual personae (1993; 1996, 65–81). She centers her analysis around the story of "Julie," a member in the early 1980s of one of CompuServe's CB channels (a chat room named after citizens' band radio), who described "herself" early on as "a totally disabled, single older woman":

On the net, Julie's disability was invisible and irrelevant. Her standard greeting was a big, expansive "HI!!!!!!" Her heart was as big as her greeting, and in the intimate electronic companionships that can develop during on-line conferencing between people who may never physically meet, Julie's women friends shared their deepest troubles, and she offered them advice—advice that changed their lives. (1993, 82–83)

Several years after "Julie" first appeared on the conference, one of her admirers, who wanted to meet her in person, tracked her down and discovered that "Julie" was really a middle-aged male psychiatrist. According to Stone,

[t]he news reverberated through the net. Reactions varied from humorous resignation to blind rage. Most deeply affected were the women who had shared their innermost feelings with Julie. "I felt raped," one said. "I felt that my deepest secrets had been violated." Several went so far as to repudiate the genuine gains they had made in their personal and emotional lives. They felt those gains were predicated on deceit and trickery. (1993, 83)

In her later and more nuanced discussion of this incident, Stone supplies additional details: explaining that the women who felt most betrayed by Julie formed a support group; that some experienced her unmasking mournfully as a kind of death; that "Sanford Lewin" (Stone's pseudonym for the psychiatrist who invented Julie) tried as himself, and largely in vain, to strike up friendships with friends of Julie's both before and after the ruse was discovered; and that, ultimately, the perpetrator's "Sanford persona" fell short of his "Julie persona" (1996, 77–80).

In one sense, this story suggests the ease with which one can lie in an environment where objects and identities are simulated, foregrounding old problems of trust, responsibility, and accountability (Stone 1996, 87), not to mention new ways of exploiting gender differences. In fact, this incident has been retold so often (with slight differences in names and details) that, as Sherry Turkle tells us (1995, 228), it "has taken on near-legendary status" as an exemplary account of "Deception" in cyberspace (Turkle's section title). Similarly, Howard Rheingold describes it as "a cautionary tale for all who venture into virtual communities" (1993, 164), and Hank Bromley emphatically presents it as a warning that "sexism" flourishes in network communications as well, concluding that (obligatory allusions to "significant benefits" notwithstanding) "participation in CMC carries hazards for women" (1997). Most of these accounts note that the story first appeared in an October 1985 *Ms.* magazine article called "The Strange Case of the Electronic Lover," written by Lindsy Van Gelder, who was a participant on the CompuServe forum where "Joan" (aka "Julie," in Stone's version) surfaced and who, therefore, was one of the women fooled by "her" (Rheingold 1993, 164; Bromley 1997). Van Gelder's title refers to the fact that in her account the male psychiatrist had used his female persona, as a friend introducing another friend, to procure real-life dates for himself (reported in Turkle 1995, 229). Particularly in light of this additional detail, the temptation in many retellings of this story (especially, Bromley 1997) is to view incidents like this one as indications that computer networks are male-dominated (statistically true), male-biased (depends on what one means by "male" here), and particularly detrimental to women (well, maybe).[25] That temptation also resonates with what one of the women quoted in Van Gelder's article concluded: "[A]lthough I think this medium is a wonderful medium, it's a dangerous one, and it poses more danger to women than men. Men in this society are more predisposed to pulling these kinds of con games, and women are predisposed to giving people the benefit of the doubt" (cited in Rheingold 1993, 165).[26] Stone acknowledges that gender differences in comportment and social expectations may exist (1996, 193 n. 6) but sidesteps these concerns to draw more profound implications from her telling of the Julie story.[27]

One ironic lesson in this for Lewin (and for the rest of us), Stone suggests, was the realization that in the online world, the Julie persona had as much—in fact, more—presence than the Sanford persona (1996, 79). This is an effect of the "limited bandwidth mode of the net" as opposed to the "wide-bandwidth mode of physicality": that is, in physiocentric space, an apprehensible form is available, "a single physical body to look at," to which can be articulated, according to our cultural assumptions, one true identity (79). Inasmuch as no such body is perceivable in the bit space of cyberspace, our so-called true and made-up personae have equal presence, and, what is more, they have enough presence for other online participants to respond to each persona differently, as if it were a totally separate person (79). This presence helps explain how people who never physically meet can develop the sense of a shared social space in their online interactions with others.

More to the point, however, Lewin's failure (with all but a few of Julie's former friends) to strike up the same kind of friendship as himself throws one aspect of identity into relief and turns another completely on its head. It reveals, first, the extent to which identities are shaped interpersonally and according to social conventions. Hence, because identities are social, what we presume to be the same "inner person" cannot simply will others to treat him the same way across different outward manifestations (in this case, different virtual personae), i.e., Lewin could not make people treat him the same way they had treated Julie.[28] What was ironic, however, about Lewin's deception was that, for a time at least, he was able to pull it off, even to the point of acting in ways as Julie that he could not manage as himself: that is, Lewin became Julie (Stone 1996, 76). Julie's success is, in this respect, as instructive as Sanford's failure. Perhaps the lesson for us, Stone suggests, is not just that cyberspace foregrounds that identity and appearance are always, already embedded in cultural significations and expectations, but rather that cyberspace, secondly, presents a more fundamental challenge to the whole notion of an inner person, of a singular, unitary, and true identity. In cyberspace (if not also elsewhere), our multiple outward manifestations *are* our identities, which, for Stone, provokes the suspicion that perhaps all identity is like the old proverb that the earth sits on the back of a turtle that sits on the back of another that sits on the back of another so that "it's turtles all the way down": following this, she asks, "Is it personae all the way down?" (81).[29]

The fact that others treat us in particular ways because of our appearance is not, of course, an astounding revelation. Indeed, we are aware of this when we self-consciously select professional-looking attire for a business interview and formal clothes for a fancy party. That realization, however, becomes more acute in cyberspace. What the story puts into relief, in other words, are the various ways that "the body," as Judith Butler has argued (1990; 1993), is already imbricated in meaningful sociopolitical matrixes or orders (of gender, heterosexuality, age, race, body shape, physical ability, and health). These discursive orders are what differentiate bodies anatomically, constituting their specific materiality (Butler 1993, 2): some as male and others as female, some young and others old, some white and others black, some thin and others fat, and in the process establishing some differences as normal and better (e.g., the male in most gendered contexts), some normal but weaker (e.g., the female in most gendered contexts), and some, finally, as deviant (e.g., the whole disruptive set of people who are androgynous, transgender, or hermaphroditic). This process of inscribing some bodily features as culturally meaningful differences effectively produces what Stone, following Butler, refers to as the "culturally intelligible body" (1996, 40).

This does not mean that the bundles of atoms we call bodies do not exist outside of discourse; rather, the point is that those amorphous bundles become meaningful cultural signifiers only through discourse. In fact, rather than dispensing with those bundles of atoms, discursive orders of gender and race and so forth actually *incorporate* them. Such differences, in short, are not derived from physical bodies; rather, they are performatively reproduced (cited) through a variety of embodied practices that effect those bodies (Butler 1993, 12–16).[30] What these repetitive citations mean for our physical encounters with others in the offline world is that those encounters are already partially scripted for us—in a sense, prefigured—even before we begin to interact, to speak and engage with others. Put simply, in the offline world, our appearances precede us.

This productive constraint in our face-to-face interactions with others suggests why "identity-shift" is so commonplace in MUDs and other online interactions (Cherny 1995).[31] It helps explain, that is, why someone like Lewin might feel freed up to become someone else in the online world, where we write our own appearances (albeit, within already culturally informed interpretive frames). Part of Stone's point is that cyberspace enables the exploration of different personae by virtue of the fact that it constitutes a different relationship between bodies and selves than the one-body/one-self paradigm, namely, the prospect of "[m]any persons outside a single body" (1996, 86).

It is worth noting in this respect that both Foucault's various analyses of disciplinarity and Butler's study of drag as a (potentially) subversive act—perhaps because they are concerned with developing an analytical framework for studying the coming into being, the genealogy, of the body—are still focused on practices (of subject formation) that take place in and on (rather than outside) that biological substrate we call the human body. So, for example, Butler, in her analysis of drag in the offline world, argues that the parodying of gender (the copying of what is assumed to be the original and natural embodiment of the feminine or the masculine) foregrounds that gender itself is a performative construct, "a parody of the *idea* of the natural and the original" (1990, 31). As I understand it, the crux of her argument is in the necessity of repetition. Gender does not simply exist; it has to be constantly reproduced to keep it going, which opens up the possibility of its "derailment" (1994, 67). Even the sexed body is, according to this view, a construct: the effect of a (now partially medicalized) sex/gender system that makes anatomical distinctions socially significant, and an effect, moreover, that has become increasingly malleable with the advent of cosmetic surgery and hormone therapy. Despite this recognition that the sexed body is a culturally legible effect, however, it is still important to Butler's analysis that drag is an embodied practice inasmuch as part of what makes it possible for the performance to unsettle gender norms is the apparent mismatch between anatomy and gender: "The performance of drag plays upon the distinction between the anatomy of the performer and the gender that is being performed"

(1990, 137). The excessive and deficient embodiment of the gender norm in drag performances is what potentially makes them "Subversive *Bodily Acts*" (Butler's chapter title 1990, 79–141, my emphasis).

In this respect, Butler, Foucault, and others writing in the same vein—while they provide the theoretical impetus for challenging the naturalism of the one-body/one-self construct (and the essentialist assumptions that follow from that)—still conceive power and resistance in terms of *visibility*: specifically the visibility of bodies in shared physical spaces, a point Foucault showed with almost excessive clarity through the arresting image of the panopticon. Of course, this is one of Foucault's most insightful contributions to the study of modern forms of power and helps explain why his work has made such a splash on both sides of the Atlantic. While Foucault focused on the biopower by which docile bodies are produced, Butler turned her attention toward bodily acts of resistance (i.e., embodied practices that disrupt the normative production of the body); in both of their works, however, a perceptible material substrate has provided the mechanism by which—through the articulation of inscribing and incorporating practices (Hayles 1992, 156)—discursive norms have made the body visible. Put another way, both have been concerned with *a politics of visibility in an analog world.* Their works, of course, foreground bodily visibility as a naturalized effect of power and resistance, but what they emphasize less, and the point that I want to highlight here, is how the discursive practices they analyze depend on a material substrate as the site at which power and resistance operate: specifically by materializing bodies in particular ways.[32]

I highlight this issue not as a critique, but rather as an observation that foregrounds some key issues raised by the invisibility of physical bodies in cyberspace. That is, in relation to CMC, practices of incorporation amount, for example, to the way the mouse becomes an extension of the hand or the speed and accuracy with which one types. Succinctly, the successful production of the normative cyborg body requires the incorporation of computer devices as *seamless extensions* of the embodied individual. This is what enables the creation of what William Mitchell calls (in McLuhanesque overtones) the "bodynet" (1995, 28). The cyborg, he explains (25–44), has television for eyes, telephony for ears, actuators for muscles, telemanipulators for hands, and artificial intelligence for brains, which together constitute, as Mitchell puts it, a quite different sense of *being there:* and precisely, one might add, by redefining both *being* and *there.* What counts as embodied excess and deficiency in relation to this kind of cyborgean incorporation? Clearly, such failures have been redefined in this context. They have become largely matters of technical expertise, mediated by the interface, and made evident to others (occasionally) as, for example, an excess of style—IN THE WAY THAT USING CAPITAL LETTERS IN NEWSGROUP AND E-MAIL MESSAGES IS INTERPRETED AS SHOUTING—or as a deficiency of machine skills—in the way that typos manifest a failure to meld seamlessly with the technology by disclosing *the imperfct humn*[33] behind the perfect machine. These are obviously not the kinds of failures of embodiment that have mattered for normative constructions of the body (although they are perhaps emergent codes by which veteran cyborgs could remark that the wetware behind the hardware is not embodying the machine very well). My point in all this is that computer-related incorporating practices take place primarily in the individuated spaces before the screen, rather than in the shared social spaces online. Given the narrow bandwidth, only a subset of incorporating practices (and not the typical ones we think of) become apparent in cyberspace. As a consequence, inscribing practices take priority (which is why correct spelling, punctuation, and grammar can take on an elevated significance that makes elementary-school English teachers cry with joy).

What these descriptions of cyborg practices of incorporation throw into relief are the heterotopic effects that cyberspace can have in relation to those normalizing discourses that have depended, for their operations, on physical spaces and physical bodies. At issue, then, are the consequences of these disruptions for those landmarks of thought involved in our politics of visibility in the analog world. If embodied individuals have been the perceptible locus for operations of power and resistance, and making "the body" visible has been the sine qua non of normalizing processes (as Foucault and Butler show), what happens to analog politics in a context where embodiment is no longer evident in customary ways, where "bodies" are made "visible" only incidentally, if at all, and primarily through practices of inscription (writing), with some very different practices of cyborg incorporation thrown into the mix?

If You Have No "Body," Can You Take a Stand?

The question I pose here is, of course, ironic. Bodies *are* made visible in cyberspace. Jernigan's body (discussed in the introduction) is one kind of example: the normalized effect, as I have suggested, of the confluence of medical and carceral discourses and digital technology. The sharply profiled data-image (discussed in the first section, above) is another example, one effected by a combination of policing discourses (in the

broader sense of population management) and computerized surveillance techniques. But in posing the question implicitly in relation to political agency—i.e., with reference to "taking a stand"—I am asking if,
how, and to what extent contemporary constructions of citizenship have
depended on conventional understandings of body and space: concretely, on the visibility of embodied individuals in physical spaces. Although
Stone never explicitly raises this question, she makes a number of provocative (though underexplored) comments about contemporary constructions of "the fiduciary subject" and "the socially [or "politically"]
apprehensible citizen" that suggest why this question is particularly relevant today (1996, 39–41, 79). Drawing implicitly on Foucault's work, she
observes that our inherited mechanisms of social order, abetted by improvements in physical and symbolic systems of measurement (e.g., cartography and psychology—Stone's examples), have depended on forms
of "spatial accountability—that is, knowing where the subject under the
law was":

> Accountability traditionally referred to the physical body and most vis-
> ibly took the form of laws that fixed the physical body within a juridical
> field whose fiduciary characteristics were precisely determined—the
> census, the introduction of street addresses, passports, telephone
> numbers—the invention and deployment of documentations of citi-
> zenship in all their forms, which is to say, fine-tuning surveillance and
> control in the interests of producing a more "stable," manageable citi-
> zen. The subtext of this activity is an elaboration and amplification of
> spaciality [sic] and presence—a hypertrophy of the perception of
> where. . . . Implicit in this elaboration of the concepts of spatiality and
> presence is the development of the fiduciary subject, that is, a political,
> epistemological, and biological unit that is not only measurable and
> quantifiable but also understood in an essential way as being in place.
> (1996, 90, Stone's emphasis)

The documentations cited in this passage provide the "warranting" links
by which placeable physical bodies can be tied to particular identities. It is
through such links, moreover, that "the political apparatus of government," as Stone puts it, is able to produce the collection of physical and
discursive elements she variously terms the "socially" or "politically apprehensible citizen" (40–41, 79). Stone alludes to the multiple meanings
of this felicitous phrase but never fully unpacks it (194 n. 9). To explain
why my question about bodies and political stands is not a trivial one,
however, I want to explore her meaning in more detail.

Although the body has tended to be ignored in recent theories of citizenship (e.g., Beiner 1995; cf., Young 1995), its centrality to contemporary citizenship is self-evident when we consider the chain of articulations (self to body to space) by which this politically apprehensible citizen is produced. The one-person/one-vote rule that orders voting procedures, for example, legally instantiates the first coupling between self and body in the production of political agency, i.e., the presumption that political agency is embodied in one discernible biological unit. The "metaphysics of presence" underpinning this notion of embodied agency is what privileges the body as the apprehensible and fiduciary site of agency—i.e., the visible stand-in—for the assumed yet invisible true site of agency—the invisible seat of consciousness variously described as the *soul* or the *self.* This is Stone's point when she notes: "[A] (living) body implies the presence within the body of a socially articulated self that is the true site of agency. It is this coupling, rather than the presence of the body alone, that privileges the body as the site of political authentication and political action" (1996, 91). The second coupling (body to space) is instantiated in terms of a legal articulation that binds certain bodies to certain spaces: specifically citizens' bodies to the physically demarcated states to which they belong. That is, if we accept the axiom that "[a] citizen cannot properly be conceived independently of her insertion in a political community" (Mouffe 1992, 4), then an important corollary to this claim is that the paradigmatic political community in modern politics remains the territorial nation-state. Put another way, "Any theory of citizenship," as Bryan Turner asserts, "must also produce a theory of the state," and this will continue to be the case certainly as long as the state continues to be the "political instrument" through which people press their claims for economic, social, and political rights and entitlements (1992, 38; see also Turner 1997). This reminder alludes to a connection between a physical space (of the state) and a physical body (of the citizen)—a connection implied, though often unacknowledged, in the modern construct of *national citizenship.*[34]

Citizenship is itself a historical production effected, in part, by changes in the territorial arrangements by which groups of people with differential power (i.e., classes) have gained access to scarce resources, the most basic of which include food and shelter and whatever else the body needs to survive. So, for example, Engin Isin argues that it was with the rise of a new warrior class in ancient Greece and the emergence of the city as the locus of capital formation—a regulatory market site (e.g., the agora)—that citizenship first emerged (1997, 119). Similarly, he argues, the development of national markets in the modern period helped establish the nation-state as the relevant space for the exercise of citizenship, initially extended to a property-owning bourgeois class and then universalized to natural-born and naturalized residents as the working class, various minorities, and women pressed for access (127–28). These historical relationships between citizen and city-state and later between citizen and nation-state illustrate, first, that citizenship has been "a territorial institution" (119).

As an expression of the historical competition between classes for, among other things, scarce economic resources—which relate, minimally, to physical survival—citizenship has been, secondly, a partially embodied institution, establishing a set of bodily obligations and reciprocal rights and benefits between the citizen and the state. These obligations include, for example, the indirect embodiment of labor in the taxes citizens must pay and the more direct way citizens may be required to press their bodies into military service and even die for their countries. In return, the citizen body obtains rights of self-determination (e.g., certain freedoms of speech, assembly, and movement) and may receive, as well, various welfare and security benefits that directly address the needs and well-being of the body (e.g., social security benefits or the bodily safety implied, at least in principle, in the notion of national security).[35]

The important point to note here is how these civil obligations and rights are established through the multiple and reiterated processes by which bodies are situated in spaces. This process seems almost a fetish in U.S. voter registration applications, to offer one obvious example. To determine a voter's district and polling place (both physical locations, of course), a voter must either give her street address or, remarkably, draw a map of where she lives if she resides in a rural area with no street number: for this purpose, the application includes a small, blank map of an intersection and asks the voter to fill in the names of the nearest crossroads, to draw an "X" to show where she lives relative to those crossroads, and also to note the location and name of any significant landmarks.[36] In most cases, citizens must then physically go to their designated polling places to cast their votes.[37] This is not, of course, to suggest that voting is the only (or even the most significant) way citizens can participate, though in practice this is the extent to which many citizens actually do participate. As this example illustrates, however, what enables citizens to exercise their political agency in even this small way is that series of articulations of self-to-body-to-space by which the politically apprehensible citizen is produced.

As should now be clear, *apprehensible* in this context means capable of being both understood as a legally warranted political actor (because situated in a grid of intelligibility that links agency to body) and also arrested (inasmuch as that grid also locates particular bodies in particular places). This double meaning is central to understanding how it is that citizens are at once empowered and managed.

We are now in a position to understand the full import of the question that motivated this digression. Our legal statuses as citizens and, more generally, our sociocultural identities (of gender, sexuality, race, age, health) all depend on particular orders of meaning that articulate certain identities to certain types of bodies. As I noted earlier in my discussion of Butler's analysis of drag parody, the mismatch between the gender performance and the (also discursively materialized) sexed body forces one kind of disruption to the discursive order of gender, but within the realm of a politics of visibility. What Stone's boundary story about Julie/Sanford suggests, however, is that virtual personae invoke some of the same performative norms (of sex and gender, for example) but without what has been the central mechanism through which many of our normalizing discourses operate: through visible and direct forms of embodiment. They are citations, in this respect, that mock the norm by making the physical body unreadable (except indirectly as the imperfect human disclosed, for example, through typos!). This is one other sense in which cyberspace can become heterotopic in relation to physiocentric spaces: this time, by confounding normalizing articulations between one identity and one body, situated in physical space. What was disrupted, fundamentally, by the disclosure of Sanford in the boundary story Stone tells was the normal order by which Julie's online friends linked that feminized persona online to a female body offline. That order was revealed to be a process of ordering.

As Stone reminds us, cyberspace permits the constitution and even the proliferation of self, but only ever "a self which moves in a spatiality from which the [physical] body is excluded" (1996, 92, my interpolation). What I have tried to show is how this condition can produce a variety of heterotopic effects for individuals, for institutions, and for communities. The data-image, of course, depends on an articulation between a digital dossier and an embodied identity. In this respect, it is more akin to a virtual profile of Stone's fiduciary subject, with a set of identifying data (e.g., names, social security numbers, phone numbers, addresses) that attempt to link other data to an individual who is not physically present but is nonetheless locatable. Despite this, such sharp profiles are extremely impoverished in relation to our noisy, analog identities. Hence, the confrontation between, say, a credit report (with its fundamentally quantitative ontology) and an embodied self (with its fundamentally qualitative ontology) can produce a heterotopic effect registered at the level of individual identity: "I'm nothing but a bunch of numbers to them." The true digital persona, by contrast, disconnects such locating links, adopting an (in theory) untraceable alias or pseudonym and leaving anonymous whatever embodied identity (or identities) might lie behind it. This breach, as I have shown, disrupts the order of law and order, which has been grounded, precisely, in processes of surveillance: of making populations manageable by making bodies visible. Finally, the virtual personae of computer conferences and MUDs—as the full disclosure in the Julie incident revealed—bear an uncertain relationship to the embodied persons that (may) construct them, and in fact potentially disrupt, by citing, those normalizing discourses that presuppose a unitary relationship between one identity and one body, a presupposition that has depended on visible practices of incorporation that cyberspace excludes.[38]

Because computer users are also embodied beings (at least part of the time), however, embodied experiences in the offline world can and do intrude into cyberspace. This helps better to explain the kinds of reactions some of Julie's friends had when they discovered Sanford. In this respect, Stone is wrong, I think, to suggest that women are more likely to react negatively to online deceptions like the Julie incident because their social expectations are different (Stone 1996, 193 n. 6). What are different are (some) women's social experiences in other social spaces, in those embodied spaces where they may often be reminded of their sexual objectification, their reproductive organs, and their second-class status. The desire to escape the body is not just a bourgeois, white, male fantasy. Why should it be? Those are the bodies, after all, that are unmarked, that are the norm (Warner 1993, 383). Perhaps the conceit is not in young, white, middle-class hackers being able to forget the body, but in assuming that a woman who, for example, has been sexually objectified in the offline world can forget *her* body when confronted by online forms of sexual harassment; or that an African American man can forget his body when confronted with hate e-mails from white supremacists; or, for that matter, that a skinny, pimply-faced, teenaged boy can forget even his body when confronted by a litany of acne jokes on a newsgroup. (It cuts all ways.) These are not arguments for online censorship (and even less a plea for a touchy-feely, be-kind-to-others Netiquette); my point, rather, is that the line between our disembodied selves online and our embodied selves offline may be more porous than we think (see especially Dibbell 1993a). If the bodiless exultation of cyberspace is what makes identity shifts possible, then an important corollary to this is that identity shifts have a funny tendency to keep shifting.

None of this, of course, answers the question I posed in the beginning of this section: if you have no body, can you take a stand? The quick answer, of course, is yes. But that is a trivial response to what is essentially a trick question, in two respects. It is a trick question, first, because cyberspace, as I have said from the beginning, does produce bodies, an entire assortment of digitized bodies, in fact: Jernigan, Julie, even Sanford. The senses in which cyberspace is bodiless, then, are attenuated. The claim is really about the physical body and practices of embodiment, which, while unreadable and nonapparent on the screen, are nonetheless there, before the screen, and do intrude occasionally in our online practices. My ironic query is a trick question, second, because several precedents do exist for a kind of disembodied politics. In chapter 2, for example, I noted Arendt's deep ambivalence about the body, whose exclusion is what defines her politics of public visibility, even while that politics partially depends on citizens gathering together, in the flesh, in a shared space of appearance. I also noted how Habermas displaces the body even more, focusing instead on a disembodied form of publicity (through the media) and on a notion of public opinion whose formation derives only incidentally from the face-to-face encounters of people in informal, public meeting places. I also pointed to the long tradition of political pamphlets and editorials in our early print media that were written under symbolic pseudonyms and that helped give rise to a kind of disembodied (universal) public political discourse. As critics remind us, however, this universalism—which also underpins modern concepts of the ideal citizen, as Iris Marion Young (1995) shows—has historically depended on excluding particular kinds of bodies, principally women and minorities.[39]

I have posed this ironic question about the body and taking a stand, nonetheless, to foreground and unpack what it presupposes—in effect, to show that inclusion comes at a cost. The construction of citizenship depends on producing apprehensible bodies—bodies taking a stand always in relation to a specific locality—which is the mechanism by which citizens are not just empowered but also managed. The flip side of this issue, of course, is who benefits from a politics of concealment, from remaining invisible and hence outside the apparatuses of power. This other issue, perhaps inevitably, has become a politically salient one in relation to cyberspace: evident, as I show next, in the U.S. encryption debate.

chapter 5

Hacking Cyberspace

As I argued in the previous chapter, following Foucault, apparatuses of security are one of the conditions of possibility for democracy as it has come to be practiced in the modern era, enabling the production of what Sandy Stone has called "the politically apprehensible citizen" (1996, 79). My topographies also revealed, however, that the physical, conceptual, and experiential spatiality that is cyberspace complicates such political apprehensions; not simply by making embodied individuals "invisible" on the Internet (a notion that, in fact, oversimplifies the issue), but rather by confounding the wider array of familiar distinctions—e.g., presence/absence, body/persona, offline/online—through which we have tended to understand what we see and what we do not see, who we are, where we are, and the communities to which we belong. These observations relate directly to questions about cyberspace as a condition of possibility for the exercise of certain kinds of political practices. In other words, they address the Internet as a *space of politics*.

Foucault's notion of governmentality suggests, second, that democracy should be studied as the effect of particular discourses of power. But what happens when his notion of heterotopia is thrown into this kind of analysis? It is worth recalling that for Foucault, a heterotopia is a kind of nonsensical space, a space-between where discourses fail because it metonymically names "this *and* that" without privileging either or definitively separating them (1994b, xviii). The point, of course, is that under particular conditions, other spaces may be produced that make our apparatuses of security insecure, i.e., that disrupt our democratic orders. By now, I trust it should be clear why I think cyberspace—inasmuch as its production and reproduction have enabled a variety of unsettling ambiguities—is heterotopic in relation to physiocentric space. If heterotopias are metonymic, however, then one way of attenuating the threats they pose is through a kind of metaphorical (re)ordering of spaces that privileges one (the familiar) over the other (the unfamiliar), reestablishing order by reinstating the norm. What this means, in effect, is that the Internet is not simply a *space of politics,* but a disturbing countersite that generates, in turn, a *politics of space.*

The U.S. encryption debate is a particularly illustrative focal point for this sort of analysis. A significant part of that debate has taken place online, which relates to questions about the sorts of spaces that internetworking makes possible for debate and deliberation by an informed, democratic public. In other words, to the extent that the Internet has become a site for staging this public debate about encryption, it has been produced as a space of politics. At the same time, encryption is a new kind of political problem made possible by the development of personal computing, the Internet, and related developments in cryptography (creating codes) and cryptanalysis (breaking codes).[1] Encryption refers to the technical capacity to conceal one's electronic documents and even one's identity by scrambling messages. As such, it directly concerns the conditions of possibility for anonymity, personal security, and political dissension in the context of the pervasive visibility engendered by state and corporate (and even individual) mechanisms for surveillance and control. This is one sense in which encryption draws attention to a politics of space: specifically, of the radical implications of a bodiless space and the challenges it poses to different kinds of political actors. To be more precise, the encryption debate throws into relief tensions between national security concerns, on the one hand, and personal security concerns, on the other. These tensions, in turn, have given rise to competing blueprints for how cyberspace should be further developed. I focus on two such blueprints: the Information Superhighway and the Electronic Frontier. My argument is that the encryption debate can be understood as a competition between these ostensibly contradictory visions for restructuring cyberspace, i.e., as competing efforts to "hack" cyberspace, discover its inner workings, and develop it in ways that make it safer for particular kinds of political agents. These blueprints, in short, highlight a second way in which encryption issues precipitate a politics of space, in this sense, by inciting differing prescriptive spatial politics as rejoinders to the more radical challenges of cyberspace. That these blueprints occasionally have been defended by making appeals to democracy will be a central focus of my analysis. My purpose is to provide a critical evaluation of the notions of *cyberspace* and *democracy* that underpin these efforts to reinstate order with the advent of computer-mediated communications.

In the first section, I lay out the stakes involved in the U.S. encryption debate and foreground how the spatiality of the Internet has, itself, become an issue. The section begins with a brief anecdote of what Sandy Stone might have called another boundary story about virtual cultures (1993): one, in fact, oriented around the diminishing significance of boundaries and the challenges that poses for those still dependent on them. Having illustrated some of the issues at stake, I conclude the introductory section by describing the players on both sides of the encryption debate, noting how they have helped produce the Internet not just as an object of contention, but also as an important venue in which that contest has played itself out. In the second section, I provide a detailed analysis of the debate itself, outlining the different concerns and policies that are being advanced. I argue that despite their apparent differences, both sides actually draw from a broader liberal discourse, which defines for them a much more limited and overlapping set of concerns. In the third section, I evaluate the ostensibly competing metaphorical blueprints that underlie the debate: blueprints that are vying for dominance in cyberspace, ironically, by proposing ways to reconfigure it. Rather than offering viable alternative visions, however, these metaphorical representations of space evoke thin commitments to issues of universal access, participation, accountability, and responsibility, i.e., to those very issues that for many theorists constitute a more participatory form of democracy. What they offer, instead, are blueprints for reconfiguring cyberspace in ways that abet a new form of information capitalism served, on the one hand, by the restructuring of cyberspace as a superhighway for the distribution of information commodities and, on the other hand, by the free-market spirit that underlies efforts to ensure that cyberspace remains an anarchic frontier. In this respect, these metaphorical blueprints ultimately converge. In the final section, I foreground the implications of Internet-related politics of space for conventional social spaces.

Crypto Politics

In the context of U.S. encryption policies, *crypto politics* alludes to the debates that those policies have engendered. *Crypto* in this respect is simply shorthand for *cryptography*, i.e., for the sort of writing in code (and whatever possibilities may or may not exist for third-party decoding) that is the focal point of policy debates about encryption. The prefix it-self, however, simply means hidden or secret. In this other respect, crypto politics may be taken to refer to a kind of unseen, covert politics. That sense, too, is relevant here since what is at issue in this analysis are the political debates and practices that become possible in a social space where physical bodies tend, for the most part, to remain invisible, implying a marked contrast to the politics of visibility that, as I showed in the previous chapter, has preoccupied both mainstream and alternative political theorists. What becomes visible when people and entities go online are the virtual personae they project there. To run with the theatrical metaphor implied by the notion of persona: in this two-part introductory section, I tell a story (about boundaries) and present the relevant players and their setting (i.e., describe the space of politics).

The Strange Case of a Code Exporter

In June 1991, cryptographer Philip Zimmermann completed a program called Pretty Good Privacy (PGP), a hard-to-crack encryption program that increases computer security by scrambling people's messages. To distribute the program to as many potential users as possible, he made it public domain software and gave it to friends to post on computer bulletin board services (BBSs) throughout the United States. One of these friends then redistributed the program by posting it to Usenet news-groups, in effect, uploading PGP onto domestic computers linked to the Internet (Levy 1994, 60). Because telephone connections cross borders, however, the Internet is not just a national computer network but a global one. Hence, "within hours" after his software was posted on the Internet, "people were downloading it all over the country and beyond" (Levy 1993, 4). Ironically, Internet access to PGP by "foreigners" brought Zimmermann under a federal grand jury investigation in 1993. U.S. attorneys argued that the availability of this type of program on the Internet was a violation of export restrictions on the distribution of arms (Levy 1994, 60; Hoffman 1996).

The International Traffic in Arms Regulations (ITAR) restricts the export of military equipment to "foreign persons" (ITAR 1992). Under the general "munitions" list that was in effect in the early 1990s, ITAR designated "cryptographic devices and software (encoding and decoding)" as "Auxiliary Military Equipment" subject to these restrictions. In alleging that Zimmermann might have violated ITAR, federal investigators were treating the cross-border, electronic distribution of PGP as a national security issue, specifically as a case involving the illegal export of arms

(Rose 1993; Archibald 1994). This raises two central questions. First, how could cryptographic technology come to be considered a type of military weapon important for maintaining national security? On one level, the question seems self-evident. Certainly, no state relishes having its own sensitive communications open to the scrutiny of its enemies, nor being excluded from the communications of others whom it would deem threatening. For its part, the U.S. government has long noted the strategic importance of cryptology (Bamford 1983) and has restricted the export of encryption technology since at least the mid-1970s (Schwartau 1994, 150). In the past, however, this technology consisted of costly, defense-contracted devices and programs operating on bulky mainframes for the protection of government data and national electronic banking systems. What was unusual about the Zimmermann case was that the ostensibly exported item was not an expensive military-industrial tool intended for government use; it was a homegrown, public-domain program for personal computers intended specifically to protect the electronic privacy of "ordinary people and grassroots political organizations" (Zimmermann 1994a). What was also new here was the attempt to apply ITAR to the Internet. This raises the second question: what constitutes *export* when someone transfers an item not by physically taking it across state borders but by posting it on the Internet? According to Zimmermann's attorney, Phil Dubois, "Borders are pretty meaningless with the current information networks" (Schofield 1994).

Borders are not meaningless to states, however. The sovereignty of states depends on a configuration of global space along geopolitical lines, with each state exercising sole authority over its allotment. National security, by extension, has rested on the notion that each state can and must protect its sovereign space by regulating the flow of goods and persons across its borders. Unfortunately for states, the network space of bits confounds "here" and "there" and related dichotomies of inside/outside, local/global, and domestic/international in ways that make borders, if not exactly meaningless, then at least harder to establish. In this respect, cyberspace challenges our conventional ways of thinking about sovereign space and national security. At a minimum, it has allowed a form of distribution that bypasses customs checkpoints, calling into question the state's capacity to regulate the flow of a different kind of strategic item (digital information) through a new distributional channel (global networks). Zimmermann's case was an initial response. It was also only the tip of the iceberg. State officials and security experts have given a much broader sense of the new stakes here, for them, by making dire pronouncements about "Information Warfare" and "Cyberwar" (Schwartau 1994; Waller 1995).

ITAR was but one way the U.S. government tried to curb the availability, abroad, of a technology that undermines its capacity to survey. A second way was to provide an alternate cryptographic technology, for both domestic use and export, that facilitates surveillance. To that end, the Clinton administration and government agencies like the National Security Agency (NSA) and the Federal Bureau of Investigation (FBI) began, in the early 1990s, to press for the adoption of a government encryption standard based on some type of *key-recovery* system, which would allow law enforcement agents, when necessary and with proper warrants, to decode encrypted messages by obtaining backdoor decryption keys from a duly appointed custodian. The initial proposal, announced in February 1994 (White House 1994b), was for government adoption of the Clipper chip: a telephone encryption device with a built-in wiretap mechanism. By trying to make Clipper a standard, the U.S. government sought to normalize its use for telephone security, develop a similar standard for computer security, and crowd out nonwiretappable alternatives in the process. Despite government efforts, however, domestic software companies and civil liberties groups rejected Clipper and continue to resist the adoption of any key-recovery standard, arguing, respectively, that it weakens the competitiveness of U.S. products in the international market and that it violates the individual privacy rights of citizens here at home. This broader debate about encryption—which began with both the Zimmermann federal investigation in 1993 and the Clipper chip proposal in 1994—provokes important questions about security, privacy, and the prospects for democratic practice in a place like cyberspace, where one is both more and less visible.

A Space of Politics: Staging the Debate

On what can be characterized as the pro-key-recovery (and anti-PGP) side of the U.S. encryption debate are several government officials and appointees. These have included President Clinton, Vice President Gore, Vice Admiral John M. McConnell (director of the NSA, 1992–96), Louis Freeh (director of the FBI, 1993–2001), James Kallstrom (assistant director in charge of the FBI New York office until 1997), and Lynn McNulty (associate director for computer security at NIST[2] until April 1995). Other vocal supporters of Clipper and key-recovery systems, more generally, have included Stewart A. Baker, one-time chief counsel for the NSA, and Dorothy Denning, computer science professor at Georgetown University.[3] Key-recovery opponents (who, by contrast, support strong, non-governmental encryption programs like PGP) have included a number of computer civil liberties groups. Foremost among these is the Electronic Frontier Foundation (EFF), as well as Computer Professionals for Social Responsibility (CPSR), the Electronic Privacy Information Center (EPIC), the Center for Democracy and Technology (CDT), and the *Cypherpunks*, a loose confederation of cryptographers and computer professionals.[4] One of the most vocal and prolific individuals opposing Clipper has been EFF cofounder John Perry Barlow, a former Grateful Dead lyricist and Wyoming cattle rancher turned "computer telecommunications devotee" and self-styled "techno-crank" (Sterling 1993, 233).[5] Other notable opponents include Mitch Kapor (EFF cofounder and also founder of the Lotus Development Corporation), cyberculture journalists Steven Levy and Bruce Sterling (better known for his cyberpunk novels), John Gilmore (another founding member of the EFF and one of the pioneers at Sun Microsystems), Jerry Berman (initially of the EFF and subsequently founder of CDT), EFF chief counsel Michael Godwin, and cryptographers Whitfield Diffie (co-inventor of split-key cryptography, which I explain later) and of course Phil Zimmermann (of PGP fame). These organizations and individuals have been joined by a variety of commercial interests, particularly U.S. software companies. The latter argue that export restrictions have required them to make weaker encryption products for the international market, where they consistently lose out to the stronger products their foreign competitors, unhampered by similar export restrictions, have been able to sell.[6]

Given the players involved, the U.S. encryption debate has taken place through a variety of interconnected venues that include White House press statements and fact sheets, congressional hearings, newspaper and magazine articles and interviews, televised news segments, and expert presentations and debates at computer-industry conferences. Computer-industry magazines have also carried several articles on the encryption debate, typically from the standpoint of key-recovery opponents: exemplary of these is *Wired* magazine, one of the premiere journals of the cybercultural community.[7] Significantly, many of these offline articles and proceedings have been reproduced in electronic form and made available in a number of sites on the Internet. In addition, digital essays, articles in electronic journals, and e-mail postings on newsgroups and listservers have circulated on the Internet as part of a concerted online campaign both to inform people about cyberspace-related policy issues, like encryption, and to bring them onboard, as it were, on one or the other side of relevant policy debates. In the process, this variety of electronic posts and reprints has helped produce the Internet itself as a unique kind of space for the staging of the encryption debate, a space that entails different modes of representation and a different semiotics of appearance.

The players described above are obviously quite diverse, including institutions and individuals, public and private interests, officials and nonofficials, and experts and laypeople. As such, they have very different political, economic, social, and technical power bases at their disposal in the offline world. The virtual personae they project in the bit space of the Internet, however, are still predominantly text-based: pixelated words flickering on a screen, unaccompanied by bodies, buildings, three-piece suits, Secret Service entourages, pocket protectors, beards, ponytails, or any of the other culturally corpulent markers that one may find either impressive and intimidating or unimpressive and dismissible. The advent of the World Wide Web and the move toward more graphical interfaces and larger bandwidth connections have, of course, added other dimensions to how personae are projected online. In particular, both individuals and institutions can now use images of themselves (e.g., of their bodies or their associated buildings) to project a persona online. Such images in turn can simulate, by graphically representing, some of the physical markers associated with a face-to-face encounter. From the standpoint of the end user, however, one identifying image may be just as impressive as another given that they are all restricted to the same monitor dimensions and screen resolutions.[8]

Screen resolutions and monitor sizes establish a limiting condition on electronic communication. As a consequence of this mediation, the representation of self on the Web may draw from but is not reducible to the representation of self in everyday life. Because "being there" is constituted by pixelated words and images on a computer monitor, the experience is subject to a different measure—screen scale rather than human scale—with different meanings attached. Hence, characteristics (like physical size) that create one impression (e.g., of importance or power) in the physical plane may become irrelevant in cyberspace, where other factors become more prominent. So, for example, on the Internet, the White House (home of the head of state of the fourth-largest country in the world, with an area of 9.1 million square kilometers) is a 28 kilobyte *.jpg graphic file measuring only 610 x 172 pixels and occupying less than one-fourth of the 800 x 600 screen resolution employed by most Web users.[9] By contrast, the more impressive dynamic image map for the Vatican

City (the geographically smallest state, with an area of only 0.3 square kilometers) is made up of 29 *.jpg graphic files totaling 85 kilobytes in size and yielding a composite image that measures 640 x 480, occupying over half of the screen area available to computers set for 800 x 600 resolution.[10] Since browser toolbars, status bars, and scroll bars occupy portions of the available screen area, a user visiting the Vatican City site with a computer set to a 640 x 480 resolution would have to scroll to get the full effect of the image map. Having to scroll to view a very large image can sometimes give a user the sense of being visually overwhelmed by an image. This is one sense in which the Web employs a different kind of semiotics of appearance. In this context, the relative physical sizes of site owners become less significant than the sizes, complexity, and aesthetic design of their representational images. As a consequence, small countries, home businesses, and even individuals can appear just as large and impressive as the biggest countries, corporations, and institutions.

Disparities in the financial and technical resources at one's disposal are certainly more relevant. At present, however, most Web pages are designed with the same basic layout (text and hyperlinks and some combination of banners, logos, pictures, buttons, backgrounds, and image maps).[11] Awareness of the resource limitations of end-user computers may help account for the pervasiveness of this basic Web layout. Even expert and well-funded Web designers need to be careful about adding too many bells and whistles—video and audio multimedia components that hog bandwidth and resources—if they hope to make their Web pages accessible to the majority of their potential visitors. In short, Web pages tend to look pretty much the same regardless of the amount of capital and prestige enjoyed by the owners behind them. This apparent leveling effect is one of the features of networking to which computer proponents point when they claim that cyberspace has democratic potential.[12] Because states, corporations, and individuals use essentially the same technology (HTML editors, graphics programs, CGI forms, Java applets, and so forth) to post on the Internet, one home page can look just as professional, elegant, and polished as another. The process of converting bodies and buildings to the narrow bandwidth of bit space gives an individual or a small business potentially as much Web presence as a national government or a multinational corporation.

The point is particularly apparent on the EFF's electronic archives of cyberspace-related documents. The EFF began archiving documents before the World Wide Web was adequately established. Like many other early online sites, it used a Unix-based system and file transfer protocols

(FTP) to make electronic transcripts of key documents available to others to increase public awareness of online issues. In the early 1990s, Web browsers like Mosaic, Netscape, and Internet Explorer were not yet popular, but most online users did have simple text editors and FTP capabilities. This meant that they could FTP anonymously (i.e., without having an established user ID and password) to the EFF site, switch to the site's public directory *(/pub)*, review the variety of topic-specific subdirectories at the site (e.g., */Clipper*), download (copy locally) the plain text files available, and view these document files on any text editor or word-processing program. Even though Web browsers are now much more widely available, the EFF has not converted its archived text files into Web (HTML) format (the format that allows hyperlinking, variable fonts and colors, and the use of images, image-maps, and even video and sound in today's Web pages). As a consequence of its use of simple text files, the EFF's archives extend the leveling effect of the Internet, randomly intermingling White House press releases with alt.privacy newsgroup postings, all of which look much the same: simple texts with nonproportional fonts and no logos or images. Furthermore, because Web browsers can read simple text files as well as HTML files, the increasing availability of browsers has made the EFF's archived text files even more accessible, combining their cross-platform (plain text) readability with the easy to use point-and-click interface of Web programs like Netscape and Internet Explorer. In other words, regardless of their sources, the documents archived at EFF all tend to look the same.

Archiving these documents on EFF's own site rather than hyperlinking to them at other sites has two additional effects. First, it mitigates the subtle hierarchy that might come into play if the documents were located at sites with different domain-name suffixes. This, of course, only makes a difference for visitors who pay attention to domain names and have prejudices that inform how they interpret Web content from different types of sources, i.e., the greater deference they might give to a Web page from a U.S. government site (*.gov) over one from a U.S. commercial site (which typically ends with a *.com suffix).[13] Second, archiving allows the collection in one forum of a debate that has spanned years, thereby circumventing the otherwise ephemeral nature of newsgroup postings and even Web pages, which can change quickly, move from site to site, or disappear from the Web altogether: a result of adjustments in people's personal accounts or institutional affiliations. Because the EFF stores these otherwise ephemeral postings, anyone with access to the Internet can link to the EFF site, as I have done, and in effect relive the debate, perhaps even years later, following developments in the Clipper initiative and in Zimmermann's case as they unfolded.[14] This is another respect in which the technical features of networking and data storage, coupled with archiving and retrieving practices, help to produce cyberspace as a social space and one, in this instance, for the staging of a political debate. Finally, it is worth noting that the Net effect, as it were, of these archiving practices may bear little connection to the intentions of the participants involved. When then-NSA director John McConnell, for example, gave testimony before the Senate Judiciary Committee's Technology and the Law Subcommittee in support of the Clinton administration's Clipper initiative (as he did on 3 May 1994), he arguably had no intention (nor perhaps even an expectation) of becoming a participant in an online debate on the government's encryption policies and the NSA's (to some, questionable) role in that policy. But having archived his testimony on its Web site, the EFF has helped to construct him as a virtual participant—and what is more, a seemingly equal participant—in that debate.[15]

At one time hidden and unknown to most people, the NSA today is a more visible presence and has even launched its own "public service" Web site, describing itself on its home page title banner as "Providing and Protecting Vital Information through Cryptology."[16] Since this function involves breaking into the encrypted communications of others, one may find it ironic that the NSA posts a "Privacy and Security Notice" advising visitors of the ostensibly limited scope of information that is collected from their servers whenever they access the NSA site. The agency correctly points out that the statistical information gathered, concerning visitors' IP addresses and requested files, is typical data for Web site management: to help maintain connectivity and discover access errors, such as "dead links" (hypertext links to files that no longer exist on the host server). Beyond this, the NSA claims that "[n]o other user-identifying information is collected."[17]

The appearance of privacy statements on Web sites, which has practically become a standard on government, institutional, and commercial home pages, is itself an effect of the encryption debate and related concerns with how computer technologies may be used covertly to gather information about an individual's Internet usage, from which interested others could extrapolate more personal information about an individual's identity, tastes, activities, and so forth. Whether or not most users are mollified by such disclaimers is an open question, but the fact that the NSA site includes it confirms the agency's awareness that digital privacy has become a salient concern, very likely as a result of the public awareness efforts of online computer civil liberties groups, like the EFF. Posting the standard privacy notice also indicates the agency's willingness to pay at least lip service to these issues. In this respect, too, the NSA's Web site has the look and feel of many others, even to the point of making disclaimers that in a sense contradict (and perhaps intentionally downplay) the NSA's fundamental identity as a spy agency.

The apparent (if limited) leveling effect that Web technologies and practices engender is arguably part of the ideological allure of cyberspace. It interpellates us as virtual personae among other seemingly sui generis virtual personae, inviting us to forget the body, including the very powerful corporate and political bodies behind those other personae projected online. Put another way, the presentation of the digital self in cyberspace is the effect of technological capabilities and practices that are largely the same for all participants. As Joel Schalit observes sardonically, "The liberal doctrine of social equality has never been so aesthetic. Equal home pages have become the same thing as equal wages" (1996). Although overstating the case, Schalit is right to mock any doctrine implying that the ability to have a good looking home page is all the equality people need. Certainly, social equality online is not the same as social equality offline and may bear even less resemblance to economic and political equality in the offline world. However, dismissing social equality in cyberspace as irrelevant to struggles in meatspace is just as shortsighted as assuming it is sufficient.

Internet technology, if not leveling, has at least reduced one important power gap: the power of mass communication. Because they have such a wide reach, the mass media have been central to the processes through which issues have been politicized and made the topic of public debate in modern times. In liberal societies, however, most media organizations are privately owned and controlled. The number of suppliers of print and broadcast media, moreover, has been restricted by high production costs and, in the case of the latter, by the fixed number of broadcast channels (the limited radio frequency spectrum) available for transmission, which is why government agencies like the Federal Communications Commission (FCC) have been established. These conditions have structured the mass media according to a few-to-many distributional paradigm, where only a small number of organizations are producers of news and the vast majority of individuals are relegated to the role of consumers. The flow of broadcast communication, moreover, is one-way, from transmitters to receivers, with only indirect feedback loops, in contrast to the two-way communication flows of face-to-face, telephone, and computer-mediated communication.[18] As a consequence of the one-way, oligarchical structure of mass media, issues for public consumption have been subject to interested mediation by a select few. Corporate interests and complex organizational structures have helped to shape what is seen by the public and how it is seen. (These, it may be recalled, are some of the features that Habermas, following Mills, outlines for distinguishing "mass" from "public" communications, as I showed in chapter 2.)

By contrast, the interactive and weblike pattern of network communication facilitates, as its proponents contend, a many-to-many form of communication. Anyone who can read a particular newsgroup or chatroom message can, in most cases, post to that group or chat.[19] In both the asynchronous forum of newsgroups and the real-time forum of chat rooms, the producers and consumers of Internet content are the same, a circumstance that has unsettled traditional power asymmetries in the area of mass communication. As Howard Rheingold has said, "When any desktop in the world can become an electronic printing press, town hall, audio-video broadcaster, old power structures based on control by a few people over broadcast media that influence many people are going to change radically" (1995). One of the most unsettling aspects—for media corporations, publishers, software companies, and indeed any owner of intellectual property—has been the ease with which copyrighted materials can be duplicated and distributed by others on the Internet without compensation (royalties) to the copyright holder. For governments, the challenge has been the ease with which, for example, troublesome programmers have been able to circumvent export restrictions (Zimmermann's case) or pornographic materials have entered their jurisdictions in violation of local obscenity laws (see Godwin 1993; Twomey 1996; Berlin 1996; Lucyga 1996; Matzkin 1996), or the way dissidents, such as students in China or Zapatistas in Mexico, have been able to circumvent state control of the media by posting on the Internet (Cooke and Lehrer 1993; Langfield 1995). What has been unsettling, in short, is the way the Internet distributes to all its users a modicum of the power of publicity, of making things public.

This is not to say that posting something on the Internet automatically makes others aware of it. For this, too, however, Web technologies and practices have surfaced to help posters publicize their new sites and surfers find those sites. First and foremost, search engines such as HotBot and Alta Vista actively comb through and index available Web content and then provide users with searchable databases that link to sites matching their search queries. Individuals posting new sites on the Internet can also submit their Web site addresses to these search engines. In addition, new, noncommercial sites of a particular content can be advertised on topic-related newsgroups.[20] New sites may also be submitted for membership to any of a variety of "Web rings," a banner hyperlink system whereby sites of similar content (for example, *Xena: Warrior Princess* fan sites) are randomly or sequentially linked to one another. Finally, virtually every Web site includes hyperlinks to other Web sites, typically as a service to the Web community, to share information and sometimes to commend those other sites. New sites with content that attracts attention can be publicized by "word of mouth" through the "Links" pages of already established sites. This user-to-user, "word of mouth" mode of publicizing through hyperlinks provides yet another expression of the potentially *public* (as opposed to *mass*) character of communication over the World Wide Web. Perhaps this is what is most exciting (and threatening) about the Internet: that more than any other new medium, it constitutes a form of communication where the nature of the content, more so than the wealth and privilege of the producer, can determine the size of one's audience. The claim is not, of course, that the Web is universally accessible, but rather that compared to the broadcast media, the costs of entry are far less and the opportunities to participate are far greater.

Even economically deprived and politically subjugated individuals have been able to share their views with multiple others and to participate with them in ongoing discussions. According to Harry Cleaver's "Zapatistas in Cyberspace" Web site, "The international circulation through the Net of the struggles of the Zapatistas in Chiapas, Mexico, has become one of the most successful examples of the use of computer communications by grassroots social movements" (1996b). Cleaver's page proceeds to list an impressive array of Zapatista-related analyses (including strategic studies by RAND), conferences, newsgroups, and Web sites on the Internet. The page is well worth a visit if for no other reason than to see the graphic of "Subcommander Marcos as cyberpunk with DoD infowar images in distant background."[21] One U.S. Web site devoted to the EZLN has a counter indicating that my visit on 19 April 1998 was the 288,504th time the site had been accessed since 6 October 1996: a respectable tally, even taking into account multiple visits by the same users.[22]

Notwithstanding this positive evidence that the EZLN's message is circulating widely on the Web, however, the very idea of "Zapatistas in Cyberspace" is, in a sense, surreal (by definition, an incongruous mix of objects). The political content of the Zapatista movement is a critique of neoliberal policies in Mexico, a reaction to the ways global economic forces (pan-capitalism) have historically and more recently in Chiapas led to the slaughter and dislocation of indigenous peoples. This critique, however, takes place in what is one of the core conditions of possibility for global capitalism: electronic networks, which enable the transnational flow of capital (see Castells 1996; Weatherford 1997). That in itself is not incongruous, of course. Revolutionary tactics have always depended, at least in part, on subjugated groups appropriating state apparatuses and turning them against the state. As I have just argued, however, one of the ways that electronic technologies have a leveling effect is by partially masking class differences and geographic locations, and this, in turn, may dull the point that the Zapatista movement is about international class struggle. In this respect, the political thrust of the signifier "Zapatistas in Cyberspace" becomes, I think, considerably less powerful than the images of class struggle conjured by the signifier "Zapatistas in Chiapas." The spatial referent in the latter has historical and political connotations that the former image lacks. The effort to reveal to an international community that living "south of the border" has dire political and economic consequences is a discursive effort that needs geographic markers. That point seems clear to "Marcos" himself. In one of his political tracts ("Subcommander Marcos" 1992), he conjures the imagery of *"el Sureste"* ("the Southeast")—a reference to the region of Mexico in which Chiapas is located—in order to describe what it means to live specifically there. By contrast, "Zapatistas in Cyberspace" conjures an image of digital uprootedness in the guise of "freedom of movement." It is a floating signifier more consistent with the dictates of liquid capital (another floating signifier) and the libertarian, Electronic Frontierism of the cyberpunk than with the reality of *la lucha,* the struggle against movement, against capital flight, against the dislocation and impoverishment that the flow of capital out of Chiapas has wrought.

Ricardo Dominguez alludes to a similar discomfort in what I read as a sardonic and extremely acute send-up of what it would be like if Oliver Stone made a film of the EZLN's electronic rebellion. Entitled *Zapatistas: The Recombinant Movie* (1996), Dominguez's "script" includes a key character called "Virus," who halfway through the movie asks: "Can the hallucinogenic-State be resisted hallucinogenically? Is electronic activism a mirroring of State-logic as a tool for developing better counter-insurgency networks?"

I take Dominguez's ironic questions seriously not because I believe cyberspace simply is a better counter-insurgency network, but because the questions he poses relate directly to the realm of the possible in cyberspace, to the sorts of political challenges that can be given voice through a medium like electronic networking. They suggest, in other words, that to the issues of access and accountability must be added questions about effectiveness: in this instance, the effectiveness of challenging international capitalist practices through the very medium that most makes those practices possible. These questions, in short, remind us of the close (constitutive) connections that exist between space and politics, inviting us to ask whether or not there are limits to the struggles that can be made visible in a place like cyberspace.

The following discussion of the U.S. encryption debate explores these issues from the standpoint of a "successful" online campaign by privacy advocates. In treating this as a successful campaign, however, I do not mean to suggest that the tension between national security and personal security that is at the core of this debate has been resolved in favor of the latter. That tension, rather, is a chronic one, with successes and failures measured episodically, which is why I focus on a specific time frame. It is a tension, moreover, that is subject to perceived changes in the political climate.

The episode I investigate predates the September 11, 2001, attacks on the World Trade Center and the Pentagon, an event that is having far-reaching effects on state security policies in the United States and elsewhere. Allegations that the hijackers who perpetrated these attacks may have used the Internet to execute their plans (see Holland et al., 2001) have brought encryption and privacy issues to the forefront, with renewed force on the government's side. According to *Washington Technology* staff writer Nick Wakeman, "Talk of threats to important infrastructures, such as buildings and transportation, communications, power and information technology systems, will no longer be seen as hype" (2001). That it was seen largely as hype during the 1990s is certainly evident in the following analysis. Abstract references to terrorists seemed more of a rhetorical move on the part of government officials seeking public support for unpopular encryption policies that threatened to compromise individual privacy for the sake of maintaining the state's surveillance capabilities in the name of national security and public safety. What these attacks have helped to do, however, is make such references less abstract. American citizens can now associate a name and a face with references to "terrorist threats" and are more attentive when intelligence and security experts warn that "terrorist groups are winning the cyberspace battle" (Piller and Wilson 2001).

Despite the heightened sense of anxiety and urgency that these attacks provoked, however, their relevance for Internet policies is not an objective fact but rather the effect of how these events are being articulated (discursively linked) to these policies. Indeed, even Attorney General John Ashcroft has admitted that the Internet-related counterterrorist measures the Bush administration is seeking in the wake of the September 11 attacks would not have prevented those attacks and cannot safeguard us against all future terrorist attacks (Davies 2001). Given that admission, it is arguably not the attacks themselves that have prompted a sharp debate on the scope of surveillance law (Coyle 2001), but the Bush administration's reaction to those attacks, specifically in calling for a broadening of surveillance capabilities and promoting legislation that expands those capabilities, under a suitably rousing title: the Patriot Act. The new laws, however, are not as broad in scope as the government has wanted, owing in large part to criticisms and concerns leveled by civil libertarians (see Espo 2001; Olsen 2001).

Clearly, the encryption debate that began in the early 1990s is not over. While the events of September 11 have heightened the need for greater surveillance and security in some venues (like domestic flights), they have also strengthened people's resolve that these events not be allowed to alter our way of life. Because the policies currently under consideration will have profound and far-reaching effects—more so than the initial attacks that provoked them—it bears emphasizing that this way of life has been premised, in principle at least, on commitments to both individual liberty and democratic self-rule. As I show next, however, the encryption debate in its initial phase was animated more by liberal concerns than by democratic ones. Since terrorism is fundamentally about coercion—about using fear and violence to determine someone else's actions—our acute sense of threat specifically to our right to self-determination may provide an opening for broadening the scope of political discourse on matters like encryption, enriching the terms of debate beyond the surveillance and privacy concerns and focusing our attention, instead, on the conditions needed for democratic self-rule.

Decoding the Crypto-War: 1991–96

One of the most significant features about the encryption debate is the way it has been constructed as a "crypto-war"[23] between, on the one hand, state and law enforcement officials and security experts concerned with national security and public safety and, on the other hand, computer civil liberties groups and individuals principally interested in promoting personal security, with privacy as their focal point (Levy 1994). The government's efforts to establish a wiretappable encryption standard through devices like the Clipper chip contributed to the animus in this debate. In the following sections, I describe the different forms of encryption favored by each side and the rather narrow discursive terrain that shapes their politics.

A Shared Terrain: Renegotiations of the Public/Private Split

The Clipper chip was actually a microchip for scrambling phone conversations rather than computer messages. Even though it was designed for telephone communications, however, several computer groups began opposing the measure almost immediately after the standard was announced (White House 1994b) because they feared that the underlying technology would inevitably be applied to computers as well and with consequences reaching far beyond government communications. They did have a point. According to one source (Levy 1994, 50), the NSA had already developed a Clipper-like chip, called Capstone, for use in computers.

Based on the initial Clipper design, activation of the chip to garble conversations would simultaneously transmit a signal identifying the chip in use. This signaling device—called the "Law Enforcement Access Field" (Levy 1994, 50), in line with the law-and-order discourse helping to justify Clipper policy—would direct authorities to the corresponding wiretap key needed to decode these conversations. The wiretap key was, in fact, two keys that, according to the original Clipper proposal, were to be split by the chip's manufacturer and placed in escrow at two separate government agencies (U.S. Department of Justice 1994). Would-be wiretappers would then have to obtain warrants to retrieve the keys from both escrow agents before they could decode Clipper-encrypted messages. This feature, according to advocates, was intended to minimize the risk of illegal and covert wiretaps even by authorities. As Stuart Baker describes, "The key escrow system is a lot like the system used to protect nuclear launch codes (two-person requirement). It's going to be very hard to compromise, because many people and systems must be compromised to get the keys" ("Center Stage," 1994). The chip, in this respect, could protect individual privacy by allowing people to scramble their phone calls and also by requiring even legal authorities to obtain wiretap keys through authorized channels. At the same time, advocates contended, Clipper's key-recovery mechanism would aid national security and public safety by maintaining the government's capacity to survey.

Clipper's opponents were not easily swayed by pleas to national security. Instead of the breachable so-called privacy (from everyone but the government) that key-recovery programs offer, opponents have favored the "Pretty Good Privacy" that Zimmermann's program promises and, by all accounts, delivers. PGP is a *split-key* encryption program: a message encoded with one key can be decoded only by using its corresponding partner. The user selects one of these keys as her private key to which only she has access and designates the remaining key as the public key to be distributed to others (hence the more popular name, *public-key* cryptography). Anyone then wanting to send a coded message uses the intended recipient's public key for encrypting. At that point, only the recipient can decipher the message because only she possesses the corresponding private key needed to decode the message; even the sender cannot decode it. This split-key system simply requires that people have access to each others' public keys. (Coincidentally, the Internet facilitates the broad distribution of public keys.) In contrast to key-recovery systems, then, public-key cryptosystems are, in fact, more private. Decoding keys are neither shared with senders nor held in escrow by third parties (e.g., government agencies). This last feature has been the decisive one for those most concerned with national security and law enforcement. They have opposed all cryptosystems without key-recovery mechanisms, arguing that "[w]idespread use of non-escrowed encryption could irretrievably damage our ability to encourage the use of key escrow encryption, putting at risk law enforcement effectiveness and critical foreign intelligence activities" (McConnell 1994).

The most remarkable feature of these ostensibly competing visions is the way both presuppose essentially the same spatial strategies. This is evident in the very names given to each of these technologies and the underlying, broader discourse from which they both draw. The public key cryptosystems (like PGP) rest on the liberal public/private dichotomy, reproducing the assumption that the private is the domain of individual freedom. In fact, the split in these split-key schemes occurs precisely along this public/private divide: for personal security reasons, individuals must take care to share with the public only what pertains to it (i.e., only the public keys). This general mistrust of the public extends to a mistrust of the government. Indeed, freedom-from-government is a standard of classical liberal discourse. An escrow agent, on the other hand, is, by definition, a trusted and neutral third party who acts as custodian of a valuable item that is the object of arbitration or negotiation involving two interested parties. Government key-escrow cryptosystems, by extension, draw on another liberal assumption: the pluralist notion that the state can arbitrate between competing interests. In this instance, the two interested parties are the private person (which includes both individual people and private corporations) and the public (an abstract, collective identity reduced to a set of assumed shared interests in public goods, like safety). The state, in turn, is the neutral arbiter who can mediate their competing interests, protecting private persons (where appropriate) from public scrutiny and protecting the public from certain kinds of individuals (e.g., criminals and terrorists).

What these competing visions offer, however, are rather bankrupt notions of the public that follow directly from an overriding concern with security. Both national and personal security are constructed, implicitly, in terms of a *freedom from* certain kinds of hazards. This focus tends to overshadow considerations of the conditions for enabling the positive liberty *(freedom to)* more directly related to democratic concerns with empowerment, public communication, access, and participation.[24] Indeed, negative liberty treats "freedom and power as antonyms" (Barber 1984, 35), and it does so, significantly, by spatially separating them. Freedom is located in the private realm and power (implicitly, power over) is situated in the public realm, within which the state, as Benjamin Barber points out, becomes the chief culprit, according to this view: "If physical constraint and external coercion are the principal adversaries of freedom, then the state, as the principal locus of physical coercion, becomes freedom's most implacable enemy" (35).

In characterizing the state as a coercive public force, Clipper opponents recapitulated these spatialized distinctions between freedom and power. Inasmuch as the point of strong (nonwiretappable) encryption has been to create a separate, protected, noninstitutional space for communications between people, this view, in one respect, gestures toward Habermas's sense of an informal public sphere of private people come together as a public (a point to which I return below). The articulation between democratic communication and strong encryption, however, was made by Clipper opponents more often as an afterthought, secondary to their cardinal concern with privacy rights. So while their commentary evinces a sense of "the public" in references to the "public key" distributed to others, that referent is not entirely synonymous with the collective, democratic subject of "the People"; rather, it refers to a plurality of private individuals whose chief concern is the exercise of their personal freedoms through privacy. Significantly, the kind of communication that split-key cryptography fosters is not really public, in the sense of an open form of communication, but rather private, in the sense of an interpersonal form of communication among an exclusive set of people who know each other's public keys. It is, in short, communication that is meant to stay private, i.e., unreadable by anyone other than intended recipients. Very little room exists in this stark separation of public and private for a notion of public communication by which the People can be empowered. Put another way: this has not been a communications scheme intended to produce a critical, proto-political social space for a type of debate that anyone, in principle, could enter. For this reason, efforts thus far to construct encryption as enabling a kind of democratic communication have tended to ring hollow.

Clipper advocates, for their part, reproduced these spatial distinctions between freedom and power. They attributed the power of the state, however, not to its intrinsic coercive force, but to its mandate as the product of a consensus by which private individuals collectively (as "the public") have established the state as a referee and a benign protector. This liberal state, then, has been given the role of arbitrating between competing interests and of safeguarding the conditions needed for individuals to pursue their interests in the private realm without (that is, free from) certain dangers. This understanding of the state, of course, completely evacuates the notion of the public as a necessary countervailing force against state coercion. Consequently, this pluralist variant of liberalism, too, leaves little room for a form of public communication that might, as Habermas suggested, take the form of a critical buffer zone against the state. And here that possibility was foreclosed in two respects: first, because the focus was, again, on encryption—that is, on securing the privacy of communications—and, second, because the provisions outlined in the Clipper proposal for safeguarding even this private space from institutional intrusion, i.e., from state surveillance, were themselves minimal: the requirement of obtaining legal warrants, a requirement whose enforcement depends entirely on the proper behavior of law enforcers and state agencies.[25]

These preliminary observations suggest that the focus on privacy at the core of the encryption debate actually makes this debate a bad case for analyzing the relationships between cyberspace and democracy. This case is extremely instructive, however, for precisely that reason: because it politicized an issue that (1) foregrounds the state's policing role as one that fundamentally entails *managing the population,* even (if not especially) in the context of a liberal-democratic society; (2) highlights the ways in which liberal concerns with privacy rights can overshadow democratic concerns with *public communication;* and (3) raises key questions about who stands to gain the most from the politics of *invisibility* that encryption makes possible. These are the ways that the content of the debate matters, but the context of the debate, too, is instructive for analyzing the democratic potentials of the Internet: specifically, in the way that part of that debate unfolded online and helped produce the Internet as a critical social space for politicizing this issue, for mustering support, for creating a public opinion on the issue, and for fostering a form of electronic activism that, as far as I can tell, has made a difference (at least provisionally). Even Robert Wright—who, as I pointed out in chapter 2, has been critical of the hyperdemocracy the Internet makes possible—observes that "[t]he circulation of an anti-Clipper petition turned into a kind of impromptu online civil-liberties demonstration, boosting the number of signatures from 40 to 47,500" (1995).[26]

The politicization of this issue is, of course, a matter of discourse, of how it is constructed and made meaningful in a politically relevant way. As I have suggested, both sides in this debate articulated (linked) encryption to liberal assumptions; they disagreed, however, about which aspects of liberalism, in their respective views, should be accentuated.

Border Patrols on the Information Superhighway

In the pro-Clipper discourse, the government's need to assume a mediating role in light of information technologies is highlighted:

> Despite its benefits, new communications technology can . . . frustrate lawful government electronic surveillance. Sophisticated encryption can have this effect in the United States. When exported abroad, it can be used to thwart foreign intelligence activities critical to our national interests. In the past, it has been possible to preserve a government capability to conduct electronic surveillance in furtherance of legitimate law enforcement and national security interests, while at the same time protecting the privacy and civil liberties of all citizens. As encryption technology improves, doing so will require new, innovative approaches. (White House 1994a)

Despite the close connection between surveillance and security in this discourse, the U.S. government has not (as yet) mandated the use of key-escrow cryptosystems outside the government, nor has it outlawed the use of stronger alternatives by citizens. Officials have vowed, as well, that comparable key-escrow standards for computer use also "would be voluntary" (McCandlish 1994).[27]

The state's own liberal discourse partially accounts for this constraint. The voluntary status of Clipper helped reinforce the liberal assumption that private entities (both individual and corporate) can and should be able to make choices. By making Clipper a choice, moreover, the liberal state could appear more neutral on the issue of surveillance than it might otherwise seem if it made key escrow compulsory. Besides protecting individual rights, however, the state must also promote national security and public safety. Therefore, it cannot remain completely neutral on the issue of surveillance. Hence, Clipper could not be presented as just any choice but as the *right* choice: a point connoted in repeated claims that Clipper would have struck a "balance between protection of communications privacy and protection of society" (U.S. Department of Justice 1994). To advocates, this balance was "reasonable" in that the proposed policy could "reflect all of society's values, not just the single-minded pursuit of total privacy" (Baker 1994, 3). Encryption, after all, is "a double-edged sword": "It can be used to protect law-abiding citizens, and it can also be used to shield criminal activities, and also activities that could affect the security of this country" (Lynn McNulty, in "Open Sesame" 1994). The bottom line, for Clipper advocates, was that a compromise of some sort would have to be struck: "There is a trade-off between individual privacy and society's safety from crime. Our society needs to decide where to draw the line" (unnamed "government official" in Markoff 1993).

"Where to draw the line" is a particularly telling phrase since what is precisely at stake here is how changes in technological capabilities—the development of the PC and of encryption software for use on PCs, which together have enabled the distribution of strong cryptographic capabilities to individuals—have created impenetrable fortresses that law enforcement agencies cannot break through (Levy 1994, 48). Drawing the line, in this context, is about reconfiguring the technology in such a way that the barriers around the private realm remain sufficiently porous for the liberal state to continue being able to perform its policing function, here commended not in Foucault's sense of managing the population, but in the more benign, liberal guise through which that function is normalized, legitimated, and made palatable, i.e., to protect and serve. That function entails establishing a wiretappable encryption standard that allows the state always to have access to information about individuals, about who said what and where, ostensibly so it can track suspicious characters across barriers that the state otherwise respects, i.e., those around private communications.

Because the proposed reconfiguration threatened to violate individuals' privacy, the state's normalizing discourse involved articulating the threat of strong encryption to a set of familiar threats that law-abiding citizens recognize as sufficiently dangerous to justify (occasional and authorized) state intrusions: "If encryption technology is made freely available world-wide, it would no doubt be used extensively by *terrorists, drug dealers,* and other *criminals* to harm Americans both in the U.S. and abroad" (White House 1994b, my emphasis). On this view, the doors to our private communications need to remain slightly ajar to the state so that it can come in when necessary and apprehend the culprits endangering us. The connections between criminals and the need for state wiretaps were brought closer to home in a graphic way by Dorothy Denning in her defense of the Clipper initiative. "Wiretaps," she argued, "have been essential for preventing and solving many serious crimes and terrorist activities":

> [W]iretaps were used to help solve a case that involved plans by a Chicago gang from shooting down a commercial airliner. There have been 2 cases where they helped save the lives of kids who were going to be kidnapped for the making of a snuff murder film. They helped solve a case where a man's house was going to be bombed. I could go on. ("The Denning-Barlow Clipper Chip Debate" 1994)

Denning's remarkable economy of words merits comment. In a few short sentences, she manages to link the need for lawful surveillance with a list of the kinds of heinous crimes and enemies most feared by people. These named threats include gangs; deliberate plane crashes; the kidnapping, sexual assault, and murder of children (in the reference to "snuff films," with the redundant addition of the term "murder," apparently for effect); and seemingly arbitrary bombings ("a man's house"). Drawing on what has become a commonplace of law-and-order discourse, Denning deploys a number of implicitly familial, suburban, and urban references (e.g., to children, houses, and gangs) that further frame these crimes as the worst kinds: urban nightmares that haunt the less and less remote suburban idyll, threatening the peace, sanctity, and safety of the family.[28] According to this discourse, criminals habitually invade private domains to violate our families. As part of the consensual mandate we citizens have given the state, moreover, we recognize that law enforcement agents and other state actors will sometimes have to come into our homes to nab the bad guys. That our families are not safe from such threats even in our private domains (e.g., "a man's house") helps by association to justify giving the state the authority and the technological wherewithal to monitor other private domains, specifically, private communications. The potential risk to our loved ones from strong encryption alternatives, according to Denning and others, is simply too great to ignore: "[O]ne of the earliest users of PGP was a high-tech pedophile in Santa Clara, California" (Baker 1994, 2).

References to high-tech pedophiles construct a new kind of enemy for the Information Age: computer-literate criminals who can use certain technologies, like PGP, to conceal their illicit activities. These high-tech assailants are the "constitutive outside" (Mouffe 1991, 78) of the collective identity constructed in this discourse. By contrast, the relevant "we" here are ordinary, law-abiding citizens who have nothing to hide and hence nothing to fear from wiretappable encryption standards like Clipper, and who, indeed, as family-victims and potential targets of these crimes, have everything to gain from the state's maintaining its capacity to survey. This collective We— "*Our society*," which we are reminded, "needs to decide where to draw the line" (cited in Markoff 1993, my emphasis)—is by turns constructed as one big family over which the state maintains necessary guardianship against outsiders. In this respect, part of what further normalizes the blurring of the boundaries around the private realm is this construction of the social, a realm between the political realm of the state and the private realm of the individual, which collectively redraws lines, in favor of state surveillance, precisely because it is, according to this discourse, one big family with common enemies. The similarities between this notion of the social and Arendt's critical description of it are too obvious to ignore: she maintains, "society always demands that its members act as though they were members of one enormous family which has only one opinion and one interest" (1958, 39). What this similarity implies is precisely an effort, on the part of the pro-Clipper discourse, to depoliticize key-escrow encryption: in fact, to normalize its necessity in order to pave the way for its adoption as a standard.

Within this family discourse, by extension, Clipper opponents—who were wrong, but who could not exactly be demonized given their concern with the shared liberal value of privacy—were infantilized, a construction that would help dismiss their views as naive. Their opposition to lawful surveillance has been characterized, for example, as "the long-delayed revenge of people who couldn't go to Woodstock because they had too much trig homework. It reflects a wide—and kind of endearing—streak of romantic high-tech anarchism that crops up throughout the computer world" (Baker 1994, 1). The image of Woodstock associates Clipper opponents with the antiestablishment ethic of the hippie counterculture: when articulated to the notion of "trig homework," it effectively constructs them as the nerds of the sixties generation.[29] The further reference to the "romantic high-tech anarchism" of the computer world accomplishes two things. First, it associates the opposition with disorder and even unruliness.[30] Second, it relies on an old standard of defense discourse: namely, the construction of domestic opponents of national security policies as Idealists, in contrast to the Political Realism of most security experts (see Cohn 1987). Hence, much like their Woodstock forebears, Clipper opponents could be dismissed as a bunch of unruly and idealistic kids who, though endearing, disrespect (parental) authority and, being naive, fail to assess what is good for our common social family.

Within this discursive framework, Clipper advocates presented themselves as being on "our" side in two senses. They explicitly supported measures that would enhance national security and public safety, and they also claimed to be sympathetic to concerns for protecting privacy: "None of us likes the idea of government intruding willy-nilly on communications that are meant to be private" (Baker 1994, 1). Even the NSA, according to this discourse, understands people's need for cryptography and supports its domestic use: the NSA "has no role in limiting the power of cryptographic schemes used by the public within the U.S. We have always been in favor of the use of information security technologies by U.S. Businesses to protect their proprietary information" (Michael S. Conn, in Abernathy 1992).[31] In response to commercial opposition to the government's encryption policy, the NSA has argued that export regulations do not prohibit companies and individuals from exporting cryptography; the law simply requires would-be international distributors to submit their products to an "export review process"(Conn, cited in Abernathy 1992).

Where Zimmermann apparently fell afoul of ITAR was in not submitting PGP to this review process. It is here that the state's efforts to respatialize the Internet according to familiar metaphors become starkly apparent: according to one unnamed government source, Zimmermann is "playing at this stuff, and when it has real consequences, he wants to deny it. How far do you think you'd get arguing you didn't cause the export of nuclear technology if you sold it in an international airport departure lounge?" (Schwartz 1995). Like Baker's references to trig homework, this remarkable statement begins by infantilizing Zimmermann, who is "playing at this stuff" and is then unwilling to take responsibility. It then constructs cryptography not merely as auxiliary munitions (the former ITAR definition), but as an object that is as sensitive and dangerous as nuclear technology. Restricting the "export" of cryptography, therefore, is as vital to national security as restricting the export of weapons of mass destruction. Because PGP was placed on the Internet, finally, the statement concludes by constructing the Internet, self-evidently, as "an international airport departure lounge." This parallel, of course, works to normalize, first, the state's conviction that posting on the Internet is a form of export; by implication, Internet users should be held accountable for what they post (read: export). Second, just as people take for granted the need for airport security on international flights, which are commonly targeted by terrorists and smugglers (undoubtedly on domestic flights, as well, in the wake of the September 11, 2001, hijacked plane crashes into the World Trade Center and the Pentagon), so, too, should they take for granted the need for security on the Internet, given that it simply is, according to this argument, a space for international traffic. This metaphor is not, in this respect, simply a kind of rhetoric; rather, it is a conceptual blueprint (in Lefebvre's sense, a representation of space) for reconfiguring the Internet and computer technologies more generally in ways that will make it obvious, indeed normal, for states to monitor and regulate the flow of information in cyberspace.

While it partially acknowledges the Internet's blurring of traditional borders, the metaphor of "the international airport departure lounge" quickly elides this ambiguity in favor of the easy conclusion that the Internet is always, at least, a preinternational space: data placed there *will* go abroad. Such articulations serve to respatialize cyberspace in ways intended to make it safer for states. Once cyberspace is reconfigured in the familiar terms of the domestic/international divide, it can be made to fit the "moral geography" of the modern nation-state system (Shapiro 1994). This mapping justifies the extension into cyberspace of current norms governing the export of tangible items across geopolitical borders. According to this analogy, then, the transfer of sensitive data on the Internet simply *is* a type of export: it should therefore be regulated. Once the analogy is made, common sense dictates this imperative, opening the way for the projection of existing laws into cyberspace. Hence, the issues raised by Zimmermann's case, according to the U.S. attorney who led the investigation, were "What—if any—policing is to be done on the 'Net? Are we going to throw up our hands and say 'There's no accountability. It's too big to enforce?'" (William Keane, in Schwartz 1995).

These discursive efforts to assimilate the Internet to norms governing geopolitical borders and domestic laws take for granted, of course, that international borders, export regulations, and even states are all self-evident, necessary, and given. These objects, however, are themselves the products of normalizing discourses. As discursive constructs, moreover, they have constantly to be reproduced, just as the ontology of gender and sex, as Judith Butler notes (1994, 33), is not given by a natural body, but rather is effected performatively through, essentially, a speech act: a statement that produces what it names (see Austin 1975). The Declaration of Independence, as Derrida has argued, was itself a performative that produced, by naming, the United States of America, the American People, and even their Representatives: all cited in the Declaration as if they were preexisting objects but which clearly did not exist before the act of enunciation—the declaration—that named them (Petrey 1990, 159–65). This was, of course, a founding moment, one that brought the United States into existence and that was legally established as fact by the U.S. Constitution, which was ratified in 1788 and implemented in 1789. It may be argued, however, that since 1789, at least, the U.S. state and its citizens have existed as given objects and that every subsequent invocation of "the United States of America" is simply a reference to the "original" created by the Declaration. *Is it?* Briefly, in 1789, the extended republic that Madison helped to found was composed of only twelve contiguous states (Rhode Island abstaining from the union until 1790); was based in part on a slave economy; had no Washington, D.C.; had no political parties; had no Bill of Rights (which were not amended to the Constitution until 1791); and had only a limited franchise that excluded women, men without property, and, of course, nonwhites. Which aspects of *this* original are invoked today by the performative "the United States of America"? Someone may well respond, "the principles!" Is it really necessary to point out, however, the extent to which those original principles have been modified since 1789? So much so, in fact, that "democracy," a concept abhorred by the Founding Fathers as "spectacles of turbulence and contention" (Madison 1988a, 46), has since become, in the elegant words of David Held, "a touchstone for good" (1993, 262)? In fact, the promotion of democracy to the status of normative ideal has been so great that President Clinton, in a proclamation commemorating Greek Independence Day and declaring a "National Day of Celebration of Greek and American Democracy," could state the following with unabashed conviction and certitude: "Greek ideology had a profound effect on our Founding Fathers, who molded the American form of government based upon the principles of Greek democracy" (1997). The first part of the statement is accurate enough, but the profound effect that Greek ideology had on our Founding Fathers was exactly the opposite of what Clinton implies. Madison, in particular, was horrified at the prospects of recreating the ancient Greek system of pure democracy. Clinton, however, is not unique in rewriting what was at stake in the founding of "American Democracy." He can rewrite the founding moment because it doesn't exist outside of the narratives that constitute it. "The United States of America" is a performative (re)produced in reference to an "original" that is itself a normalized construct. As Butler reminds us, moreover, every citation of a presumed original "implies the possibility of that structure's derailment" (1994, 36).[32]

What interests me here is the extent to which the normalized construct of the territorial state is being derailed (or at least shaken up a bit) by the productive confusions of here/there, visibility/invisibility, domestic/international, and public/private that the heterotopic space of cyberspace engenders. State efforts to remap the Internet according to familiar cartographies imply this confrontation of spaces. In the process, however, the state itself is being modified: *cited* differently. These changes are evident in the way state actors have begun redefining the state's policing function. Although *policing* typically refers to a domestic activity in which states engage, state security analysts have noted that "[i]n cyberspace, the boundaries between nations and private-sector organizations are porous, rendering distinctions between war and crime, and between public and private interests, less meaningful" (RAND 1996). This heterotopic ambiguity has generated efforts to recast the concept of policing as an international concern, i.e., as a collective security issue that requires the coordinated efforts of all states (Nadelmann 1993). This message can be read as a central point of Clinton's 1995 speech commemorating the fiftieth anniversary of the United Nations. Arguing that "[t]he emergence of the information and technology age has brought us all closer together," Clinton warned that this new closeness broadens the impact of hitherto domestic dangers: "Trouble on the far end of town soon becomes a plague on everyone's house" (1995). He thus called on fellow UN members to join the United States "in negotiating and endorsing a declaration on international crime and citizens' safety." Among the initiatives he outlined, moreover, was the need to form "an effective police force partnership" to fight international crime, drug trafficking, terrorism, and the spread of weapons of mass destruction. Significantly, the spatiality of information technologies—a spatiality that, as Clinton puts it, "has brought us all closer together"—has given rise to this collective security discourse and its calls for extending and coordinating the policing function of states.

This expanded discourse, finally, has permitted state officials to try trumping domestic concerns by pleading national security concerns, as is evident in the following anecdote of a conversation nonstarter that Clipper opponent John Perry Barlow had with Vice President Al Gore aboard Air Force II: "What [Gore] has apparently been thinking about very hard is cryptography. When I started to open this line of discussion he went all blank and said, 'We have national security interests at stake.' End of discussion" (Barlow 1994c). Of course, this was not the end of discussion. As the preceding analysis indicates, Clipper advocates engaged in a great deal of discursive labor to bring collective identities into being (law-abiding citizens, our society, and even an international police force partnership), to name common enemies (high-tech criminals and terrorists), and to justify the adoption of controversial encryption policies (key escrow as a balanced safeguard against our new threats). In the process, they endeavored to respatialize cyberspace according to familiar spaces (e.g., an international airport departure lounge), the better to warrant the application of export restrictions to Internet posts and to justify the state's occasional intrusions (through devices like Clipper) into the private communications of individual suspects. These efforts were resisted by Clipper opponents; although, significantly, their arguments presupposed some of the same liberal spatial strategies, as I show next.

Code Warriors on the Electronic Frontier

Early opponents of Clipper argued that the problems associated with encryption policies are far more complex than just the legal and technical matters of administration, accountability, and enforcement. Even while the Internet is accessible to foreign persons, it is also a domestic space for public conversations among U.S. citizens and for private transactions between them. Because the latter are valued and protected in the United States, policing the Internet raises some vexing normative and constitutional issues. Despite occasional allusions to public conversational spaces, however, the paramount concern for Clipper opponents was the issue of privacy and its relationship to First Amendment guarantees of free speech and freedom of association, to Fourth Amendment protections against illegal and arbitrary search and seizure, and to Fifth Amendment provisions against self-incrimination (Barlow 1993a).

In addressing these other issues, Clipper opponents presupposed the liberal public/private distinction, proceeding to emphasize the dangers posed to privacy by the Internet's blurring of this traditional divide. They noted that even ostensibly private transactions have become more public, because more visible, in cyberspace. Computers have so thoroughly penetrated most spheres of life (particularly, but not exclusively, in advanced societies) that cyberspace overlaps with, and indeed is part of, the space of the physical world. The danger, according to this view, lies in the way a fully digitized society links physical space and cyberspace (e.g., through the data-image), making it possible for interested others to track a person's activities in the physical world:

> Our transactions and conversations are now more easily traced by the digital trails we leave behind. By following the electronic links we make, one can piece together a depressingly detailed profile of who we are: Our health records, phone bills, credit histories, arrest records, and electronic mail all connect our actions and expressions to our physical selves. (Levy 1993, 8)

Strong cryptography "presents the possibility of severing these links" between the virtual and the physical (Levy 1993, 8). By concealing our transactions and identities behind digital code, cryptography creates the conditions for greater personal security and indeed greater freedom in a fully digitized society, ensuring that no matter how many databanks one's virtual self traverses, each person is password protected. Clearly, password-protected identity—i.e., anonymity—is a direct response to the way cyberspace mixes together physical and virtual, individual and institutional, and public and private. It proposes to sever these links essentially by respatializing privacy for this new digital environment: encrypted anonymity, in this respect, is specifically designed to safeguard personal freedoms by casting a new kind of liberal wall, of bits rather than bricks, between individuals' virtual practices and the state's computerized surveillance practices.

Like its counterpart, the anti-Clipper discourse of the EFF and other computer civil liberties groups attempted to effect changes in the way people think about security. In the process, both discourses reproduced the liberal spatial strategy of constructing a private realm as the locus of individual freedom, and both then proceeded to note the threats posed to this sanctuary-from-power by certain invaders. For Clipper opponents, however, the chief culprit was and remains the coercive state, whose ability to invade the private has been dangerously enhanced by computer surveillance technologies. Drawing from the cultural image of Big Brother—the omnipotent and omnipresent symbol of government surveillance in George Orwell's dystopic novel *1984*—they argued that the Clipper chip was a device "with Big Brother inside" ("What You Can Do" 1994). Learning about strong cryptography, relatedly, could "keep Big Brother from peeking in your keyhole" ("Publisher's Note," in *Keep*

Out 1994). The government, as this imagery suggests, is untrustworthy: *it,* and not criminals and terrorists, is the common enemy in this other discourse. The very existence of secret spy agencies like the NSA—aka "No Such Agency" (Bamford 1983, 357)—has helped to contribute to this lack of trust. Against attempts to present the agency as expert in cryptology and therefore best qualified to secure the privacy of citizens, opponents countered with warnings implying that the agency's expertise in spying is sufficient cause for concern: "You don't want to buy a set of car keys from a guy who specializes in stealing cars" (Marc Rotenberg, cited in Levy 1994, 70), nor would you want to trust a "Peeping Tom" with your "window blinds" (Barlow 1992). References to key holes and windows served as further reminders that pedophiles and gangs are not the only— nor necessarily the worst—threats to the suburban illusion of safety; even government can, in insidious ways, violate the private sanctity of home and family.

Unlike the pro-Clipper discourse—which addressed itself most often to an abstract, collective We (as in appeals to "our society")—the anti-Clipper discourse addressed itself most often to "you." This difference relates as well to the competing priorities of each discourse. The former privileged national security and public safety—concerns affecting abstract collectivities. For the latter, however, the key issue was the threat to individual privacy that key escrow and surveillance more generally engender. In other words, opponents were concerned with issues that affected concrete individuals as individuals: me and you. Furthermore, while they accepted, and even championed, the classical liberal distinction between public and private, they rejected the liberal-pluralist notion that government can neutrally arbitrate between public and private security concerns. The point, of course, was to counter state efforts to depoliticize encryption by interpellating individuals through a form of direct address: *you* need to become aware of this encryption issue because it is "Big Government versus Your Privacy" (Aleshire 1994).

For opponents, Clipper was only the beginning of how Big Government would erode the privacy of individuals: "[T]here seems to be a relentless trend here towards reduction of personal liberties, in the name of practical goals like fighting crime" ("Publisher's Note," in *Keep Out* 1994). Such pleas to personal liberties would have made no sense without a shared cultural background in which liberal principles mattered. Zimmermann, himself, assumed this cultural background when he declared metaphorically that "[p]rivacy is as apple-pie as the Constitution" (1994b). He implicitly rejected the notion that only criminals and terrorists have an interest in securing their communications from prying eyes: "Perhaps you think your E-mail is legitimate enough that encryption is unwarranted. If you really are a law-abiding citizen with nothing to hide, then why don't you always send your paper mail on postcards?" (1994b). His point was that even law-abiding citizens with legitimate privacy concerns often prefer using envelopes. By analogy, they may want to (and perhaps should) protect their electronic correspondence by using encryption, the virtual equivalent of envelopes. Zimmermann's analogy, of course, differed significantly from the government's treatment of encryption as arms (or even as auxiliary munitions), and this clearly underscored their different security concerns. More to the point, however, these analogies helped to make different courses of action plausible and even imperative. Government regulation of munitions, especially those likened to weapons of mass destruction, seems sensible; whereas the notion that governments might need to regulate the use of envelopes is absurd by almost every stretch of the imagination.

Characterizing encryption as a kind of envelope, however, ignored the concerns that Clipper advocates articulated; for if the treatment of encryption as a weapon seemed exaggerated, the treatment of it as an envelope trivialized some basic differences between envelopes and strong cryptography. Nothing in the physical or technical makeup of envelopes prevents authorities with proper warrants from opening them; not so with strong encryption. To heighten the sense of the stakes involved, however, some Clipper opponents connected the protection of privacy to the promotion of democracy, which, as I have said, is an unambiguously positive buzzword in the current political climate. Democracy, they argued, depends on citizens having the right and the ability to assemble in order to affect the course of government. According to Clipper opponents, however, citizens could truly exercise this freedom without fear of reprisals only when they could secure their communications from government surveillance:

> There are communications that the government has *no right* to hear—and which private citizens have every right to exclude specifically from government detection. Two examples: first, citizens have the right to conspire (electronically, if they choose) to reform government, because they believe it does not work. Second, they can conspire to remove specific individuals from government, for such reasons, among others, that the government official is believed to be abusing his or her position (e.g., in obtaining illegal wiretaps . . .). If these two kinds

of communication cannot be kept from the government under *all* circumstances—through private encryption means, if necessary—then we do not have a democracy. (White 1994)

Reiterating these claims about the democratic and even grassroots political advantages of strong cryptography, Zimmermann himself highlighted PGP's use "by human rights activists, environmental activists, religious activists, gay activists, and anyone else needing protection from the powerful" (1994a). Strong cryptography, in this view, could protect the privacy and rights especially of "targeted individuals" (Levy 1993, 5). By contrast, weak (that is, wiretappable) cryptography like Clipper would threaten democracy and dissident activism in the United States and, if adopted for export, would hamper democratic movements around the world. Opponents, accordingly, constructed Clipper advocates as antidemocratic and, in some respects, anti-American because they promoted the spread of a technology that would arm governments that were enemies of the United States:

> [P]eople like Saddam Hussein are gonna be using it to round up democratic activists and national minorities. You're going to strengthen the hand of despotism around the world, and then you're going to have to deal with the hordes of state-supported truck bombers these rogue governments are sending our way after annihilating their own internal opposition by using your tools. (Sterling 1994, 72)

The strong claim made in these various statements is that democracy simply does not exist wherever governments have the technical wherewithal to monitor any and every conversation. This concern is even more acute in cyberspace because "in a place like Cyberspace where everyone is generally 'visible,' no truly private [read: secret] 'assembly' can take place without some technical means of hiding the participants" (Barlow 1993a).

As the scare quotes in this phrase suggest, finally, cyberspace has redefined the notions of *visibility* and *assembly,* creating a space where people can gather together through the medium of their bits rather than their bodies. The vaguely determinist point of this claim is that electronic bits can be linked to physical bodies (implicitly, through the surveillance techniques by which data-images are constructed). The voluntarist imperative of the statement is that the technical means of hiding people are also available, and *we* need to employ them. What makes this politics of concealment imperative, according to the claims cited above, is that democracy requires secret assembly. This argument clearly assimilates democracy to privacy, which directly contradicts at least Arendt's and Habermas's respective notions that democracy is first and foremost a public matter. The concept of secret assembly in relation to democracy—that is, of a closed debate to which only a few citizens have access—is not without precedent, however. It is marginally consistent with the Madisonian style of inside-the-Beltway politics that I outlined in chapter 2. It is also consistent with Lyon's point that "the *salon* at the time of the French Revolution . . . was a meeting place in a private home where dissidents could convene without fear of police spies. . . . Yet the discussion concerned 'public' matters; indeed 'the public' in its modern sense was born in places like these" (1994, 183). Even Habermas, finally, outlines connections between secret assembly and some of the public spheres he describes, such as the freemason lodges and the German table societies of the 1700s. Referring to these public spheres, he states:

> The decisive element was not so much the political equality of the members but their exclusiveness in relation to the political realm of absolutism as such: social equality was possible at first only as an equality outside the state. The coming together of private people into a public was therefore anticipated in secret, as a public sphere still existing largely behind closed doors. (1989, 35)

His point, in short, is about a rational, public form of communication that "itself needed to be protected from becoming public because it was a threat to any and all relations of domination" (1989, 35).

What I want to highlight about these arguments regarding the need for secret assembly is the kind of politics they advocate. In the case of a Beltway politics, a closed debate underwrites an elite form of democracy where civic power is delegated to a select few, ostensibly enlightened statesmen. This view is clearly at odds with the more participatory form of democracy lauded by Students for a Democratic Society (SDS), among others. In the case of secret meetings among dissidents and freemasons, it is a politics of concealment in a context of political oppression.[33] This, I think, is the strongest claim for the democratic (or perhaps, more correctly, the emancipatory) potential of encryption. The production of knowledge about human rights violations, environmental issues, and other important concerns has been central to the collaborative efforts of social movements, both domestically and transnationally (see, for example, Bonchek 1995). Where governments control the lines of communication, Internet access coupled with strong encryption can make this activism less risky.[34] In marked contrast to state restrictions on encryption exports, moreover, the export of Western surveillance technologies is unrestrained, "providing invaluable support," as one organization has put it, "to military and totalitarian authorities throughout the world" in their efforts "to track the activities of dissidents, human rights activists, journalists, student leaders, minorities, trade union leaders, and political opponents," with often "fatal" results (Privacy International 1995). In this context, efforts by Zimmermann and others to create and distribute a powerful form of encryption for individuals and oppressed minorities are laudable—perhaps even imperative.

That said, however, it seems to me clear, first, that an emancipatory politics may be, in Habermas's suggestive phrase, "*anticipated* in secret" (1989, 35, my emphasis), but it certainly cannot remain there if it is to be efficacious. Second, the whole notion of a secret assembly implies a certain privilege for those admitted to deliberations. Over time, that kind of habit of concealment can lead, I think, to a form of vanguardism rather than egalitarianism, and hence to another version of elite politics. These observations imply conditional limits on the extent to which secret assemblies can be said to be democratic; at the very least, it should be noted that secrecy is incompatible with participatory forms of democracy.

Finally, however, the sense that people may want to gather and discuss political issues in a private space outside the purview of the state does imply a revolutionary motive of some kind, i.e., deliberations regarding some kind of political action against the state (or some other coercive authority). This, after all, is the kind of talk that would have to be protected inasmuch as it is, as Habermas puts it, "a threat to any and all relations of domination" (1989, 35). Considering the matter in these terms has the virtue of suggesting why it is that states (even liberal-democratic ones) might regard encrypted communications over the Internet as a threat.

Hyperdemocratic Success?

Given its technical features (its distributed, semiautonomous, and globally interconnected nature) and some of the kinds of politics it facilitates (e.g., dissension and revolutionary actions veiled by encryption), cyberspace clearly can pose a challenge to state authority, particularly insofar as it proposes an alternate ordering, a politics of invisibility that fundamentally challenges the state's policing functions. One possible response is political repression: that is, if states are openly willing to adopt access restrictions and censorship policies, they may possess options for controlling local Internet use. In January 1996, for example, the State Council of China approved policies requiring citizens to register for Internet access and adopting measures for funneling all incoming international transmissions through state-run gateways (Sullivan 1996). Such measures would undoubtedly help states to censor their citizens' access to perhaps most international postings. What this suggests, however, is that states, in their efforts to reassert their authority over cyberspace, may stand a better chance of doing so by regulating online debate rather than by entering it.[35] Content regulation, however, poses a serious challenge for self-styled liberal democracies, which define themselves in terms of universal access, rule by the people, and the free flow of information in an open political process that includes dialogue, debate, and deliberation among citizens and between constituents and their representatives. To avoid a crisis of legitimation, liberal states must, at a minimum, seek the consent of computer users for their computer-related policies. And it is here that state security concerns may be circumscribed by the personal security concerns of citizens.

Three subsequent developments in U.S. encryption policy support this conclusion. First, given the strong domestic opposition to Clipper, the Clinton administration, in April 1995, established a joint defense-civilian board "pledged to accommodate a mix of commercial and federal methods for protecting electronic transactions," a move that some observers characterized as a White House retreat on the Clipper mandate (Constance 1995). Since the administration continued supporting a key-escrow standard, that conclusion seemed premature to critics (Maize 1995a). Still, in response to privacy concerns about Big Government holding the keys, the administration did at least drop its initial plan to appoint state agencies as the escrow agents, proposing instead a "commercial escrow" standard that would accept private companies in this role ("Clipper II" 1995). And in an effort to make key-escrow policies more palatable to software exporters, the administration, in May 1996, circulated preliminary plans for what opponents called a "Clipper III" proposal, whereby the state would trade export privileges to software companies in exchange for their agreeing to escrow wiretap keys for their encryption products (Rodger 1996). Opponents rejected these "sons of Clipper" on the principle that any key-escrow system would violate privacy rights and undermine foreign sales, but by attempting to offer compromises, the U.S. state was clearly, at this point, beginning to show its willingness (or perhaps its need, for reasons of maintaining legitimacy) to address opponents' concerns.

Second, in January 1996, after more than two years of investigation, the Justice Department dropped its case against Philip Zimmermann

(U.S. Department of Justice 1996). Officials gave no explanation, but according to one observer, the government wanted to avoid "the public relations nightmare" that Zimmermann's indictment would have caused (Simson Garfinkel, in "Author Won't Be Prosecuted" 1996). This, too, suggests that the liberal state's power over cyberspace may be circumscribed. Certainly, the U.S. government's attempts to construct Zimmermann—a one-time peace activist—as an "international arms dealer" under ITAR rang false to critics of the administration's encryption policy.

Third, perhaps in partial recognition of these failures, Clinton, on 15 November 1996, signed Executive Order No. 13026 calling for the transfer of nonmilitary encryption products from the United States Munitions List (USML), administered by the State Department under ITAR, to the Commerce Control List (CCL), administered by the Commerce Department under the Export Administration Regulations (EAR) ("Executive Order," in White House 1996a). To help implement this transfer, ITAR was amended, in December 1996, to remove from the USML "all cryptographic items except those specifically designed, developed, configured, adapted, or modified for military applications" (U.S. Department of State 1996; see also ITAR 1997). As a result, commercial encryption products have been reclassified from "munitions" to a new category of controlled "Encryption Item" (EI) under the CCL. The administration characterized this transfer as a "liberalization" of export restrictions (White House 1996b), a term meant primarily to connote civil liberties. The comment, however, should also be read in classical economic terms, i.e., as a softening of export restrictions for the sake of a freer market for the international sales of American cryptographic products. Indeed, as Clinton outlined in the memorandum accompanying the order, his decision was spurred in part "because of the importance to U.S. economic interests of the market for encryption products" (White House 1996a).

None of this is to suggest that encryption technology is no longer restricted for national security reasons. On the contrary, the changes removed one weakness of the cold war regulatory regime—the implausible treatment of encryption as "arms"—while shoring up other weaknesses created by the absence of any explicit legislation regarding the Internet. In particular, the modified regulations reinforced the administration's commitment to national security and public safety concerns by establishing an interagency board that permits the Departments of State, Defense, Energy, and Justice, and the Arms Control and Disarmament Agency to review export license applications submitted to the Department of Commerce. In addition, the order explicitly redefines encryption software "technology" (which might be open to First Amendment safeguards for the free flow of information) as a "product" subject to greater scrutiny and export control given its "functional capacity" ("Executive Order," in White House 1996a): that is, given the facility with which source codes (programming algorithms) in electronic form can be converted into working encryption programs. Furthermore, the accompanying memorandum directs that the final regulations to be issued in accordance with the new policy must establish that the electronic posting of encryption software on BBSs and Internet sites "will constitute an export of encryption . . . unless the party making the software available takes precautions adequate to prevent the unauthorized transfer of such code outside the United States" (in White House 1996a). Thus, while the Zimmermann case was dropped, the export regulations instituted in 1996 have provided an explicit legal basis for prosecuting similar cases in the future. Finally, while the Clinton administration slightly backed off its insistence on a key-escrow system, the order reasserted the U.S. state's concern with establishing at least "a key recovery management infrastructure," by which is meant some mechanism (key-escrow or a viable alternative) that will ensure intelligence and law-enforcement access to the plain-text version of encrypted communications. In tandem with this last directive, the administration also named a new "Special Envoy for Cryptography," Ambassador David L. Aaron, charged with the task of coordinating efforts with other national governments "to promote the growth of international electronic commerce and robust, secure global communications in a manner that protects the public safety and national security" (White House 1996b). As critics attest, these last two features in particular make the 1996 regulatory modifications simply a newer version of the same old policy program: a point critics have made by dubbing the policy "Clipper 3.1.1" (see Center for Democracy and Technology 2000).

From the standpoint of the preceding analysis, certainly the most significant feature of the 1996 transfer of jurisdiction over encryption exports from the State Department to the Commerce Department is the decision to stop designating commercial encryption products as defense articles on the USML. Perhaps because old habits are hard to change, however, the memorandum stipulates that if export controls under the new statute prove to be inadequate, the president will retain final authority to determine whether certain products will be "designated or redesignated as defense articles" under ITAR (in White House 1996a). Notwithstanding this last provision, the move toward classifying commercial encryption products as export-controlled "commodities" rather than "munitions" does recapitulate the state's concern with redefining national security for cyberspace, and in a manner that is structurally consistent with the (economic) liberalization of the Internet. Furthermore, this reclassification articulates national security policy in a way that is discursively more plausible to the variety of computer users who have a stake in this technology and in how it is developed further. In this respect, it demonstrates the liberal state's increasing need, in the current context, to take personal security concerns into account in the process of articulating its own concerns.

The extent to which online activism by computer civil liberties organizations contributed to these outcomes is uncertain. It seems clear, however, that the Internet provided a forum for politicizing this issue by extending the debate outside the Washington Beltway and beyond the enclaves of cryptography experts, who may have understood the threats to privacy posed by ITAR and Clipper but might not otherwise have had an outlet for warning people about those consequences and rallying support against these technology policies. The mass media, of course, continue to play the dominant, agenda-setting role in society, as Habermas laments. Even here, however, the Internet may be helping more and varied sources outside the typical arenas of political, economic, and cultural power and influence (e.g., Washington, New York, and Hollywood) contribute to that process. A 1994 article by the Freedom Forum praising an early "cyberscribe" remarks that "more reporters mine computer networks for sources, ideas and data" (Freedom Forum 1994a).[36] According to the same article, when *Time* associate editor Philip Elmer-Dewitt needed information about the Clipper chip, he went to cyberspace: "[I]t turns out that every cryptographer in the world is on Internet. . . . You can get stuff straight from the horse's mouth" (Freedom Forum 1994a). Part of Habermas's indictment of the mass media has been the extent to which it has wrested the formation of "public opinion" from the hands of the culture-debating public—"private people come together as a public" (Habermas 1989, 27)—that is ostensibly its source. As these changes in news-gathering practices suggest, however, private people coming together as a public *on the Internet* may once again figure in the production, and not just consumption, of public opinion.

The Politics of Space: A Tale of Two Similes

The nature of cyberspace and the numerous online practices it has enabled clearly have raised concerns, on the one hand, for the state and its policing agencies and, on the other, for privacy-loving individuals and political dissidents. The encryption debate performatively (re)cites the threats posed for these different subjects. The possibility that individuals could use strong encryption to engage in criminal and terrorist activities has been linked discursively to the state's need for a key-recovery encryption standard. Less remarked, of course, is the threat posed to states by dissidents and revolutionaries who might use unbreakable encryption programs like PGP as a countersurveillance technique to thwart counter-revolutionary measures by oppressive regimes. Meanwhile, unprotected public communications across networks and proposed intrusions, through escrowed wiretap keys, into weakly encrypted private communications have made individuals feel more generally visible and hence vulnerable to threats from a Big Brother–like form of state surveillance. These are just some of the ways that the mix of atoms and bits, here and there, and institution and individual in cyberspace have generated salient ambiguities that have, in turn, given rise to competing politics of space.

Part of what generates these disturbances is that networking technologies and online practices metonymically combine, in the same heterotopic space, things that do not normally go together and without privileging either. So, for example, our senses of here and there—or, for that matter, of domestic and international—are equally valid in cyberspace, complicating our conventional understandings of where we are by introducing new and ambivalent senses of *where* and *we* and even *are*. Instead of associating equal terms through a process of similitude, metaphors signify by establishing a relation of resemblance between something uncertain and something familiar (as I argued in chapter 1). Following this, we should not be surprised to find that efforts to alleviate the ambiguities of cyberspace have involved metaphors for redescribing this relatively new, unsettling space. Indeed, Internet-related metaphors have been contrived, mixed, extended, and repeated ad nauseam. Rather than neutral descriptions, of course, different spatial metaphors provide different prescriptive ways of imagining what cyberspace is and how, if at all, it might be brought under control. They attempt to recast the unfamiliar by associating it with a known, conventional spatiality, which in turn compels (by normalizing) particular courses of action. My analysis of the encryption debate in the previous section highlights some of these spatial strategies. In this section, I want to pull back and evaluate the metaphorical blueprints that underwrite these strategies.

The Information Superhighway

By far one of the most hackneyed metaphors of the 1990s was the *Information Superhighway*, which had other half-lives as "information highway," "infobahn," and "I-way," and also generated a number of spin-offs, including "on-ramps," "traffic jams," "toll booths," and (my personal favorite) "roadkill on the Information Superhighway." According to most accounts (cf., Freedom Forum 1994b), the metaphor was coined by Vice President Al Gore and partly inspired by the work of his father, a U.S. senator who was involved in the construction of the national highway system. This origin story put a personal touch on what Zoe Druick describes as an older and well-worn utopian narrative of "progress and salvation through technology and transportation" (1995).

Given our contemporary understandings of superhighways—their construction, function, and associated costs, for example—a metaphor like the Information Superhighway can perform a great deal of discursive labor with little effort. By association, the metaphor implicitly outlines a role for the government in initiating the building of the rudimentary *National Information Infrastructure* (NII), the Clinton administration's less flashy name for the I-way.[37] The metaphor also warrants, to varying degrees, the government's adopting a regulatory role over the Superhighway (e.g., by establishing traffic laws and perhaps also Checkpoint Charlies). Private corporations, too, can serve a role, according to this metaphor: specifically, as contractors, cobuilders, and, by extension, future access providers.[38] In addition, this metaphor helps to characterize the nature of access as free access to information, but it also leaves open the possibility of future toll payments for information commodities. Finally, to the extent that highways connote rapid movement, typically of lone commuters in their cars rushing to and from work, the Superhighway metaphor also conveys an understanding of the sort of traffic to be facilitated: namely, individual and instrumental access to information (in contrast to, say, "virtual community," which connotes the sense of settling down in a shared space in relation to which the participants develop a sense of belonging). By subtly individuating Internet users, the Superhighway metaphor downplays the sense of the collective, democratic practices the Internet might also foster.[39] It is worth exploring, then, what lies behind this Superhighway.

While the backbone of the Internet is increasingly dominated by fiber optics, individual online access—the metaphorical "on-ramps and off-ramps" to the Information Superhighway—is still dependent on "the last mile" of unshielded twisted-pair (UTP) copper wire between the local telephone company central office (CO) and the location of the terminal equipment: the PC at the end user's home or office. A key section of the Internet's physical layout, therefore, is wired together through the plain old telephone service (POTS) and therefore shares some of that system's shortcomings.[40] Despite this, one of the key advantages of using the existing telephone infrastructure to deliver Internet service is that the phone system reaches almost everyone, at least in the United States. Perhaps because they share the same infrastructure, moreover, computer-mediated communication through the Internet is like telephone communication in other important respects. The telephone, as Robert Adrian reminds us, is "the only generally available, unprogrammed, participatory, personal and interactive communications medium—aside from face-to-face contact" (1995). In the language of information theory, telephone users are both senders and receivers: we produce what we consume. Consequently, the commodity we pay for when we use the telephone and similarly the Internet is the provision of service, the monthly rates we pay to be able to get and receive phone calls and e-mail; the content itself, however, is something we create when we have a phone conversation or send an e-mail message. From the standpoint of commercial concerns with making profits, Adrian argues, this kind of service is a limited commodity with a narrow potential for growth, especially in saturated markets. The obvious solution for telecommunications companies (telecoms) is to provide content as well as service. This content could include on-demand video rentals, televised sporting events and music concerts, interactive video games, online shopping, and other forms of "infotainment": in other words, the kinds of content produced not by individuals engaged in forms of interpersonal communication, but by media organizations and corporations engaged in the production of mass cultural products.

Current analog phone lines with standard modem hookups, however, can transmit only a limited amount of information: about 56 kbps (kilobits per second) without data compression, which is sufficient for voice, facsimile, and low-speed data transmissions (like e-mail and newsgroup messaging) but insufficient for the 1.2 mbps (megabits per second) needed for high-fidelity music transmissions and the 45 mbps transmission rate needed for video (Negroponte 1996, 16).[41] As this suggests, the Internet is at best a rudimentary precursor of the Information Superhighway envisioned by the Clinton administration, the NIIAC, and the pack of regional phone companies, long-distance services, and cable TV companies chomping at the bit to win "the Race for Content" by being the ones to build the infobahn (Dennis 1994). What they have in mind is a form of media convergence—"collaboration among print, broadcast and computer media" (Freedom Forum 1994a)—over a vast network combining existing electronic pathways into the home (e.g., POTS and coaxial cable) with progressive upgrades to high-speed, high-capacity data cables: for example, fiber optics, which, according to Nicholas Negroponte, can transmit "1,000 billion bits per second" on a fiber "the size of a human hair" (1996, 23). Put another way, the NII vision is fundamentally about building broader bandwidth paths *into* (though not necessarily *out of*) people's homes so that the service providers of the infobahn will be able to start delivering (and charging for) content.

The introduction of Asymmetric Digital Subscriber Lines (ADSL) illustrates how Internet connectivity can be developed in a way that recuperates older mass media paradigms for the newer medium of computerized networks. Regular voice communication and conventional modem transmissions over a telephone line use only a small amount of the low-frequency area available over the twisted-pair copper wires coming into our homes. ADSL connectivity takes advantage of the large, unused portion of bandwidth (the higher frequencies) already available on the existing POTS system to deliver digital signals. This has several advantages from the standpoint of the end user. First, since voice and data traffic are split and assigned to different frequencies traveling over the same wire, one can receive calls and surf the Internet simultaneously without requiring a second phone line. Second, ADSL does not require a dial-out to connect to the Internet: with the exception of server outages, it is an "always-on" link. Third, because of the broader bandwidth allocation to data—in contrast to the small spectrum available for voice and analog modem transmissions—the *throughput* (or data transfer rate) can be significantly faster with ADSL than with standard modems. However, what makes ADSL "asymmetric" is that a larger amount of bandwidth is available for data flows *into* the home (240 kHz to a maximum of 1.5 mHz of "downstream" traffic) than for data flows going *out* of the home (25–160 kHz of "upstream" traffic) (see Franklin 2000, 3). The downstream traffic actually varies depending on line conditions and distance from the CO. In fact, ADSL is a distance-sensitive technology, i.e., the service deteriorates the farther users are from the phone company CO and is completely unavailable to users who are too far away. Despite this variance, downstream throughputs are typically about eight to ten times faster than upstream throughputs, which is not surprising since the available bandwidth is as much as 9.3 times greater for data streams coming into the home. Clearly, this type of technology assumes a communications network in which most end users are high-bandwidth consumers and low-bandwidth producers.

ADSL, of course, is too slow and unreliable to deliver video data streams into the home, but the technology is a precursor of precisely the way in which one vision (of a weblike, distributed network facilitating two-way, symmetrical flows of *public* communication) is being displaced by another (of a more complex, hierarchical, and partially centralized network facilitating the asymmetrical flows of *mass* communication). This is the infobahn being hawked as the better and faster Internet of tomorrow.[42] The paradigm at work here is not primarily one for facilitating public communication over a distributed network conceived as a public utility; rather it is a paradigm of information retrieval over a consolidated and metered network designed explicitly as a pay-per-use system. This paradigm (as I noted in the previous chapter) is the same one at work in the data manipulation techniques that enable forms of computerized surveillance. This is one sense in which the government's stand on encryption dovetails with its NII initiative.

Wiretappable encryption (the standard proposed by the government and law enforcement officials) involves making certain that individuals are always potentially visible to interested others: as bits of information (e.g., the data-image). Similarly, the kinds of two-way electronic paths that telephone and cable companies are in the process of paving into people's homes are making those individuals more visible to their service providers than one-way media flows have tended to allow. At the same time that individuals will be retrieving information commodities from the Information Superhighway, the corporations serving up those commodities will be in a better position to monitor what individuals watch, what they consume, the dates and times they use media services, and even how many television sets they have (which can come in handy for those cable companies that want to be able to assess surcharges for additional sets). Part of what makes this kind of information valuable to media services is that audiences themselves are a commodity that broadcast companies can sell to advertisers. In general, however, media services do not have a stake in being able to monitor the personal content (voice and computer messages) that individuals produce themselves and post through an interactive service. What they care about monitoring are the types of information commodities that people consume as a gauge of their tastes and a means of assessing consumption rates on a pay-per-use service.

Governments, on the other hand, do have a stake in monitoring the content of people's communications over digital networks insofar as this type of surveillance facilitates the state's policing function. In a liberal society, however, where information services and hardware manufacturing plants (including computers and digital telephones) are privately owned rather than state-run, this concern makes governments dependent on telecoms and hardware industries to develop technologies and standards that enable this kind of information retrieval. In the meantime, industry is dependent on government for the passage of legislation that interferes as little as possible with its prime directive: turning a profit. This interest, as I suggested earlier, has tended to put software, hardware, and telecom industries at odds with the government's encryption policy wherever encryption commodities themselves have been concerned. Despite these differences, however, the U.S. government and industry leaders (remarkably, with the help of the EFF) have managed occasionally to work out compromises even on this tendentious issue: notably, with the 1994 passage of the Communications Assistance for Law Enforcement Act (formerly "the Digital Telephony Bill," aka "the wiretap bill"), which requires phone and cable companies developing digital telecommunications equipment to ensure (somehow) that communications over this equipment can be wiretapped.[43]

Despite differences of opinion on specific issues, both governments and corporations have an interest in being able to monitor what individuals do (respectively, as citizens and as consumers). The restructuring of the Internet that has been lauded under the rubric of the Information Superhighway facilitates such monitoring. Asymmetric, two-way channels are a dual-use technology that efficiently meets both government and business interests in this area. They offer governments and businesses access to individuals in the guise of offering individuals access to government and corporate information commodities. Commercial content providers win by gaining large-bandwidth, downstream channels through which they can sell media content to consumers and also by gaining access to consumer preferences through upstream channels that have more than enough bandwidth to deliver back information about consumer choices. Governments, too, can win both as broadband producers of government "information services" and as narrowband consumers of the data that trickle upstream from people's homes: data that can be used simply to gauge voter preferences and also as a systematic form of covert surveillance. Whether this is explicitly what pundits have had in mind when they have tried to sell individuals on the concept of the "Information Superhighway" is an open question. My point is that both the metaphor and the spatial blueprints proffered in its name are consistent with the functional needs of mass-media consumerism, corporate market analysis, the state's policing function, and the liberal ideology of freedom of choice.

The Electronic Frontier

Computer civil libertarians view their online activism as countermeasures against state efforts "to establish imperial control over cyberspace" (Barlow 1994b). Against such efforts, they maintain that its lack of formal, governmental control is precisely what makes cyberspace so positive: "a perfect breeding ground for both outlaws and new ideas about liberty" (Barlow 1990). Despite these images, however, some individuals admit that cyberspace has at times been a bit too unruly: "Sovereignty over this new world is . . . not well defined. Large institutions already lay claim to large fiefdoms, but most of the actual natives are solitary and independent, sometimes to the point of sociopathy" (Kapor and Barlow 1990). Early on therefore, in 1990, Mitch Kapor and John Perry Barlow, along with other computer entrepreneurs, set out to civilize cyberspace by establishing the Electronic Frontier Foundation (EFF 1990b).[44] Members of the EFF at that time seemed reluctant to embrace the total anarchy and anonymity that the Cypherpunks endorse. As Barlow himself has argued elsewhere, "[T]o the extent that utterly unbridled liberty seems to favor the reptile in us, a little government is not such a bad thing" (1993b). At the same time, however, the EFF viewed actions like "Operation Sundevil" as the beginning of government efforts to curb the freedoms that an unregulated cyberspace had made possible.[45] Before government precedents could be established, the EFF proposed its own civilizing mission:

> [E]xamination of the issues surrounding . . . government actions [like Operation Sundevil] revealed that we were dealing with the symptoms of a much larger malady, the collision between Society and Cyberspace. We have concluded that a cure can lie only in bringing civilization to Cyberspace. Unless a successful effort is made to render that harsh and mysterious terrain suitable for ordinary inhabit[ant]s, friction between the two worlds will worsen. (Kapor and Barlow 1990; see also EFF 1990a)

As references to the government's hacker crackdowns suggest, an important aspect of this friction between society and cyberspace was the incidence of computer break-ins into the proprietary networks of corporations, such as the 1989 theft of a portion of one of Apple Computer's software programs (Sterling 1993, 220–21). While such apparent violations of intellectual property rights seldom resulted in company profit losses, they did constitute, at least, a symbolic nose-thumbing by hackers against corporate security efforts. Members of the EFF often noted that these threats were exaggerated by both government officials and the mainstream media, who persistently misunderstood the underground hacker ethic. The EFF recognized, however, that it was precisely such exaggerations and misrepresentations that were spawning repressive government countermeasures. In the dialectical process by which the media shape social practices, moreover, actual hackers themselves—typically adolescent, white, middle-class males—further contributed to these exaggerations by adopting the infamous bad-boy posturing associated with them in the media (Barlow 1990).

And so, confronted on one side by insolent hackers intent on violating social norms by engaging in the "time-honored adolescent sport of trespassing" (Barlow 1990) and on the other side by government forces willing to trample civil liberties in order to crack down on the hacker threat, the EFF set itself the task of civilizing cyberspace. Encouraging both individual and corporate computer users to protect themselves (e.g., by using widely available encryption programs) and to respect online norms (at least against malicious break-ins) could serve two ends. Self-protection and self-restraint might forestall the need for police-state actions, thereby safeguarding civil liberties, and could also curb fraudulent incursions into proprietary systems, thereby reinforcing some social norms that can be applied in the online world as well (see Barlow 1993c).

From the standpoint of this discourse, however, most individuals have been conditioned according to social norms, rules, and expectations that simply do not apply to a frontier characterized explicitly as anarchic and individualistic, and which is, for these reasons, the last bastion of liberty. Society knows little and understands less about the Electronic Frontier. What is interesting to note, then, about this mission to bring civilization to cyberspace—here characterized as an Electronic Frontier—is that this strategy has involved both reconfiguring cyberspace (a little) and reconfiguring society (a lot). Society must be reshaped, too, precisely so that none of the best frontier features of the former (its openness, anarchy, and freedom) will be sacrificed. Reconfiguring society, according to the EFF mission, entails educating people about the opportunities and challenges posed by cyberspace, providing them with clearer ethical guides and legal frameworks and, more fundamentally, with information about how to use the technology: because to secure for "the many the possibility of citizenship in Cyberspace," everyone must be "comfortable and pro-

ficient with digital technology" (Kapor and Barlow 1990). The point, as
this suggests, is to change society by making individual users better cyborgs, who (as I said in the previous chapter) incorporate the machine
seamlessly. This mission, second, involves reshaping the austere look and
feel of the terrain—to make it less "harsh and mysterious" at the point
where human and machine meet—by creating software that provides
navigational guideposts, compatible protocols, and graphic interfaces
that make it easier to travel through the digital terrain. The image-map
on the *MySpace Online* home page is only one of the more literal transla-
tions of this effort to make cyberspace more user friendly by spatializing it
in familiar ways (see Figure 4 in chapter 3). User-friendliness, of course, is
not just about simplifying computer use; it is also about diversifying access. Initially, networking required users to learn complex operating systems like Unix, which restricted access to those willing and able to learn
the command language. This restriction also meant that early Internet
users were relatively homogenous, which helped give rise to the hacker
subculture. But with the Web's simpler method for hyperlinking to sites,
"you don't have to be a Unix hacker to use the Internet anymore—you
just point and click" (Tony Rutkowski, cited in Ubois 1995, 62). Ironically,
the effect of these technical efforts to respatialize cyberspace in more user-
friendly ways has led to more friction, given the greater heterogeneity
among today's Internet users. As the frontier metaphor insists, however,
the problems with cyberspace are largely superficial interface issues: little
in this blueprint is meant to change the Internet's (a)social configuration,
its (a)political (dis)order, its (negative) liberty.[46]

Despite this liberal focus on freedom from coercive state control and
society's norms, however, the frontier metaphor is, I think, symptomatic
of a deeper longing for a more *positive* kind of individual liberty: it
evinces what Cathy Schwichtenberg, in a different context, has called "a
romanticized notion of male freedom of movement within a public domain" (1986, 63 n. 8).[47] The freedom to strut across the urban landscape,
to ride the open trail, to sail the ocean blue—these freedoms are alluring.
But they have been increasingly more difficult to sustain with the rise of
proprietary fences and national borders in our physiocentric spaces. What
the advent of cyberspace has enabled, above all else, is freedom of movement in the guise of "surfing the Net." Cyberspace liberates individuals
from the confines of apartment walls, office cubicles, and state borders
precisely by presenting users with a seemingly boundless frontier space,
enabling the freedom of movement to travel, within seconds, to sites
across the country or, for that matter, across the world. No one has ever

needed a passport in cyberspace, only an access account, the virtual equivalent of a birth certificate. What strong cryptography contributes to this characteristically Western mythology is the freedom to move throughout cyberspace in total anonymity, without the fear of being tracked.

If I am right in regarding freedom of movement as a central feature of cyberspace, then it is not too surprising that the government regulations currently under consideration have met with such resistance. Wire-tappable technology like Clipper or some other brand of key-recovery encryption would allow "Big Government" to track people wherever they go, foreclosing one kind of possibility: the ability to travel incognito. Nor is it surprising, relatedly, that the government, for its part, is seeking ways to restrict this freedom of movement. Hacking, as Barlow (1990) has suggested, is akin to "trespassing." The metaphor conveys the stakes on both sides. The irony is that if strong encryption became the norm, proprietary fences (in the form of code blockades) would go up all over cyberspace, making it impossible for even hackers to roam about the Electronic Frontier as easily as they have in the past.[48] For all practical purposes, the Electronic Frontier would no longer exist.

Hyper-Liberal Convergence

Despite the sense of anarchy it implies, the Electronic Frontier metaphor, as I have suggested, is as prescriptive as the government's Information Superhighway metaphor. In fact, the sense that the Internet will determine its own course is belied by the very online Action Alerts and activist efforts in which computer civil liberties groups have engaged: that is, if the Internet were truly as self-determining as some regulation opponents maintain, why would they have to engage in any effort to keep the government at bay? In this respect, the metaphor serves more as a prescriptive norm: another utopian cartography, this time for cyberspace, of a freedom from government and from repressive (or simply annoying) social norms that the frontier outlaws of the American West ostensibly enjoyed (Barlow 1994a). By analogy, this anarchy and the individual liberties it sustains should be safeguarded in the Electronic Frontier as well. The metaphor, in short, underwrites the imperative that government should be kept out of cyberspace so its inhabitants can shape their own virtual destinies.

A point seldom acknowledged in the EFF's discourse, however, is that the Electronic Frontier, like its nineteenth-century predecessor, is vulnerable to more than just state efforts to respatialize it according to a normalizing blueprint. If freedom and anarchy reigned in the frontier of the American West—at least in the social imaginaries of those who projected their hopes there—they did not remain part of its fate for long. As Harry Cleaver observes, the very adventurers who sought escape from the hardships of urban industrial centers brought existing social frameworks with them, in particular, notions about private ownership (1996a). The projection of property rights into frontier space transformed it into the "cutting edge of capitalist civilization," not its antithesis (1996a). The free and enterprising spirit of the frontier was perfectly compatible with the free enterprise spirit of liberal capitalism. The irony is that the very endeavor to sally forth and settle the frontier is what signaled its demise. Whether the Electronic Frontier will meet a similar fate is still an open question. To be sure, the earliest denizens of cyberspace—students, academics, researchers, and educated dropouts—have resisted the commercialization of the Internet: most notably, the arrival of companies willing to violate online norms by advertising on the Internet, especially by sending unsolicited mass e-mailings (Elmer-Dewitt 1994). Even cyberspace veterans, however, are incapable of fully controlling who will gain access to the Internet or how these others will "Work the Web."[49]

Rapid changes are taking place not just as a result of businesses going online but also as a result of how businesses are affecting the ways individuals go online. In 1996, the architects of the Information Superhighway moved further toward finalizing the blueprints for its construction with the passage of the Telecommunications Act (hereafter the Telecom Act), which updated telecom legislation that had been in effect since 1934: "outdated laws, designed for a time when there was one phone company, three TV networks, no such thing as a personal computer" (Clinton 1996). The bulk of the provisions enacted in the Telecom Act further deregulate the very cable, telephone, and long-distance companies that are making a bid to build the Information Superhighway (Stranahan 1996). As a result of some of these provisions, particularly those relaxing restrictions on cross-ownership, telecom corporations that are already large can further diversify their services, consolidate their power, and buy up or elbow out smaller competitors. These so-called deregulatory measures, combined with the privatization of the Internet, constitute a form of re-regulation (Barbrook 1996), following the frontier pattern of what Cleaver refers to as the "thoroughly modern version of enclosure . . . the expropriation of businesses by businesses" (1996a). The aggressive spirit driving these trends is exemplified by a new breed of telecom CEO: what Wired magazine itself has lauded as the "Infobahn Warrior" (Kline 1994).[50]

The rebellious business culture praised by such depictions is perfectly consistent with the image of an anarchic frontier space, i.e., minimal government control, which is precisely what deregulation entails. Rather than opposite visions, then, the paths outlined by the metaphors of the Information Superhighway and the Electronic Frontier tend to converge toward classical liberalism on a new course: namely, toward a form of "information capitalism" (White 1995, 23).

This is not to suggest that the EFF and others are wrong to invoke the frontier metaphor, especially if, as is evident in their discourse, it evokes resistance to repressive regulations by a Big Brother–like state. But given the focus on privacy, little in the current debate, on either side, reflects comparable concerns with the ways that profit-driven blueprints (and not just national security interests) are literally restructuring networking pipelines and reshaping cyberspace in ways that foreclose opportunities for open access, diversified content, and public communication. The commercialization of the Internet backbone, as I noted in chapter 3, fundamentally altered the Internet's infrastructure. The EFF's vision of an anarchic, nonhierarchical frontier space is more consistent with the architecture of the earlier ARPAnet (the origin story) than with the structure of the "New Internet" that surfaced in the wake of the backbone changes circa 1995 and the deregulatory measures instituted with the Telecom Act in 1996. What has emerged, in the words of Robin Gareiss (1999), is an "Old Boys' Network," in which top-level ISPs enter into private peering arrangements with each other, but snub smaller ISPs. The latter, as a consequence, are forced to send the bulk of their traffic upstream to the congested public NAPs, leading critic Jonathan Angel to conclude, "While the Internet may be a public thoroughfare of sorts, some users are walking on dirty pavement, while others are taking taxis or chauffeur-driven limos" (2000, 5). That hardly describes a "level" playing field.

For its part, the EFF's assessment of the Telecom Act (1996b) criticizes only the censorship provisions and its negative consequences to civil liberties without commenting at all on the potential negative effects to universal access that so-called deregulation also may engender (see Barbrook 1996; Benton Foundation 1996). This omission is unsurprising since elsewhere both of the EFF's cofounders—in a manner consistent with what critics have identified as the hippie/yuppy mix of their "Californian ideology" (Barbrook and Cameron 1995)—have applauded deregulation precisely on the classical liberal argument that "[c]ompetition does more to keep firms honest than a roomful of regulators" (Kapor 1993; see also

Barlow 1994c). Perhaps a virulent spread of deregulation from the Internet to other arenas is precisely what Barlow had in mind when he declared: "Mitch [Kapor] and I had always talked about the job of [the] EFF as civilizing the Electronic Frontier. I think that our job, and your job, increasingly, is going to be frontierizing civilization" (Barlow 1994c).

This telling phrase has not been subject to the same level of critical reflection as the state's security discourse and its threat to privacy. The hyperliberalism that the term "frontierizing" evokes, however, poses other valid security concerns: for example, problems of tax evasion and welfare funding if financial transactions become totally anonymous. Advocates of encryption have defended anonymity with the argument that it protects privacy and (incidentally) advances democracy through secret assemblies. Though seldom remarked, however, a politics of concealment has other consequences that would radically reconfigure society even more, including the possibility that strong encryption could lead to total anonymity in monetary transfers. As it is, most major monetary transfers today are electronic (see Weatherford 1997). Given the power that liquid capital already possesses in the digital banks of the global economy—a power that facilitates capital flight, tax shelters and evasions, money laundering, and so forth—this scenario would have a decidedly upward redistributive effect. Crippling the state's social welfare functions, of course, would affect not just the "information have-nots" (a remarkable phrase that already presupposes the very information-as-commodity structure it normalizes); rather, anyone benefiting from public works (which is, frankly, everyone) would be deprived of necessary resources. Evidence exists that government officials have been concerned about these dangers as well: "According to some scenarios, encryption would make it very difficult to collect tax revenues or even cause the dissolution of the state.... So you can understand why some people on the Hill and in the Administration are concerned" (Mike Nelson, cited in Munro 1994).

Some Clipper opponents, for their part, dismiss these concerns as "unmitigated balderdash" (Whitfield Diffie, cited in Munro 1994). They maintain that the government has several revenue-collecting methods that would remain largely unaffected by total encryption, including salary deductions and sales taxes. It is doubtful, however, that the lower- and middle-income workers and consumers most affected by these forms of taxation would find much solace in this rejoinder. In the encryption debate of the 1990s, however, such concerns were barely audible amid cloying reminders of the threats posed by "high-tech pedophiles and cyber terrorists," on the one hand, or by "Big Brother invading your Privacy," on the other.

On the government side, the connections between democracy, the Information Superhighway metaphor, and the Telecom Act were suggested by Clinton in his speech at the bill's signing. After thanking those involved in formulating and passing the bill through Congress, Clinton invoked Thomas Jefferson's "legacy" that "democracy depends upon the free flow of information" (Clinton 1996). What he articulated as barriers to this free flow of information, however, were not economic deprivations, but rather "the barriers of time and space," which he suggested had now been "broken" by "American innovations and communications," i.e., by our technology. This utopian narrative of technological progress ran through Clinton's remarks like a superhighway. He associated the Telecom Act he was about to sign with the Interstate Highway Act that Eisenhower had signed back in 1957. Turning to Al Gore—whom he described as "the father" of the Telecom Act and the coiner of "the Information Superhighway" metaphor—Clinton then asked if he could borrow the commemorative pen that Eisenhower had given Gore's father, who had been present at the signing of the Highway Act and had spearheaded its passage. After ceremoniously signing the new Telecom Act with that historic pen, Clinton proceeded to sign an electronic version of the bill with a computer stylus so that, once done, the bill could be sent "into cyberspace"— evidently to drive home the point that the act he was signing symbolized a midway point in the road to progress from interstate highways to the Information Superhighway.

Notwithstanding Clinton's efforts to associate the technological promise of the reforms he was enacting with the democratic ideals embodied in the notion of the free flow of information, the actual bill fails to outline criteria for assessing and protecting *public communication*. While it does characterize the Internet as a "forum for a true diversity of political discourse," no policy is evident that explicitly declares Congress's intent to preserve that aspect of networking (U.S. Senate 1996, §230(a)(3)). As for access, the bill pays only lip service to universal service principles. According to the Benton Foundation (a policy-research organization concerned with the role of new media in promoting democracy and the public interest), the reforms called for in the Telecom Act leave several funding and definitional issues of access unvetted and will likely exclude advanced telecom services from universal service plans, deeming them nonessential. In addition, the report points out that the final bill as compared to an earlier version omitted stronger language for determining which services "are essential for Americans to participate effectively in the economic, academic, medical, and democratic processes of the Nation" (Benton Foundation 1996). This language, according to the report, would have permitted a "broader interpretation" of what count as "essential" services that would need to be provided universally. Remarkably, neither the term "democracy" nor its derivatives made it anywhere into the final language of the Telecom Act, and this despite Clinton's vaunting the act as a "truly revolutionary" piece of legislation that "enables the age of possibility in America to expand to include more Americans" (Clinton 1996).

Hacking Society

The ambiguities raised by cyberspace, as I have shown here, have given rise to a particularly salient politics of space: efforts to respatialize cyberspace according to ostensibly competing blueprints. My focal point has been the U.S. encryption debate of the 1990s precisely because cryptography is an issue that directly addresses one of the central ambiguities of cyberspace: its mix of visibility and invisibility. By way of conclusion, I offer three observations.

First, the encryption debate, substantively, indicates how characteristically liberal concerns (privacy, profit, minimal government) can overshadow democratic ones (publicity, universal access, empowerment). Perhaps that overshadowing is inevitable, however, with an issue like encryption. As Chuck Hammill, a self-styled libertarian, warned in an early statement supporting public-key cryptography:

> When those who sup at the public trough outnumber (and thus outvote) those whose taxes must replenish the trough, then what possible choice has a democracy but to perpetuate and expand the taking from the few for the unearned benefit of the many? Go down to the nearest "welfare" office, find just two people on the dole ... and recognize that between them they form a voting bloc that can forever outvote you on the question of who owns your life—and the fruits of your life's labor.
>
> So essentially those who love liberty need an "edge" of some sort if we're ultimately going to prevail.[51]

Significantly, the edge for which this commentator argues—strong encryption—is an edge *against* democracy, here defined as the powerful "voting bloc" constituted by people on the dole, which threatens liberty (and, indeed, "your life—and the fruits of your life's labor"). Needless to say, this construct—their democracy versus your liberty—was not a salient part of the anti-Clipper discourse. It nonetheless remains one possible effect of total anonymity, i.e., of a digital privacy barrier encircling not just individuals' communications and identities, but also their economic transactions. When I first read this quote a few years back, I was a little horrified by the politics it advocated; today I read it as a reminder of the tensions that persist between liberty and democracy. I present it here now as an indication of how much work is involved in making words and things fit together.

Second, although the content of the encryption debate concerned civil liberties, particularly the protection of privacy, its extension into cyberspace gave these issues a kind of visibility (publicity) that arguably made a difference, implying, as Robert Wright bemoans, the success of hyperdemocracy (1995). I am encouraged by this success insofar as it implies how the Internet helps individuals (and not just governments and media corporations) have more of a say about what becomes public and what issues get politicized. Still, that prospect is Janus-faced. In addition to making some things more visible, cyberspace also makes other things invisible. It facilitates a crypto politics (in a more general sense) precisely by masking those corpulent cultural signifiers that are usually available to us in the broader bandwidth of our face-to-face encounters with others. In this respect, if cyberspace achieves a leveling effect, it does so not by making online participants equal in any significant sense, but by masking their differences, i.e., it levels by masking classes, institutions, corporations, and individuals. What one gets on screen, then, is an issue shorn of the bankrolls, affiliations, and agendas that underwrite it. In a sense, this is also true of much of what we read and see via the mass media, but there we have had the dubious benefit of having news anchors, professional correspondents, expert analysts, and spin doctors distill issues for us and draw out a narrow set of implications. This distillation, however, is of course no less interested and masking. Ultimately, the challenge for us in our readings of both online issues and mass-mediated ones is to go behind the issue, to decrypt, as it were, the hidden politics and figure out, as best we can, who is behind it and what interests are served. If cyberspace, as I think it might, makes us more acutely aware that some things remain invisible, we may come to approach what we read online with a healthy skepticism: with a hermeneutics of suspicion that will encourage us to take personal responsibility not just for what we say, but also for interpreting more carefully what others say and unmasking their hidden agendas.

Finally, and most importantly, what this analysis has foregrounded is that the divide, as Barlow and Kapor once put it, between Cyberspace and Society is, in fact, a chimera. Nowhere is this more evident than in the sense that the blueprints I had begun to analyze as metaphorical prescriptions for reconfiguring the online world became, on closer inspection, prescriptions for changing the offline world (RL, as mudders would say). Barlow himself admitted as much with the inelegant but revealing phrase "frontierizing civilization." Perhaps because computers today are so thoroughly wired into society, changes in cyberspace have repercussions for the physiocentric social spaces of which the virtual is already a part. Hacking cyberspace, in this respect, is ultimately about hacking society. Is it any wonder, then, that we are finding the points of passage so disordering?

Cybertopia and the Demos

Liberalism is a world of walls, and each creates a new liberty.

Michael Walzer

Spatial strategies are not incidental to politics. Indeed, creating safe havens through the erection of protective walls (beltways, the private realm, encryption fortresses) behind which the liberal individual can exercise his (occasionally also her) freedom has constituted a kind of fetish in liberal-democratic thought, in some instances overriding other concerns of arguably a more democratic nature. In direct, participatory forms of democracy, by contrast, walls have tended to be viewed as a kind of barrier separating privilege from deprivation. The thrust of this alternative philosophy, therefore, has been to break down all exclusionary walls in order to construct open political spaces (the street, the agora, the public sphere) to which all citizens can have access.

What seems evident is that computer networking, for better and for worse, has become part of this process of producing social spaces. Even so, however, its technical features and cybercultural pursuits situate it slightly askew of our more conventional social spaces, producing it as a heterotopic space that mixes together contradictory conditions. We are both more visible and less visible in cyberspace. We are in a public space that further isolates us from face-to-face encounters with others, and we are in a self-designed private space of privilege that can bring us closer together as virtual communities. We can develop social relations and even bonds of friendship with others halfway across the world and yet never know what our next-door neighbor looks like. We can participate in our own surveillance and control and also become adventurers in a space of seemingly unbridled liberty. These contradictory possibilities, I have argued, have helped to generate the kinds of productive ambiguities associated with cyberspace. They also make it more difficult to draw any general conclusions about where we are headed. Ultimately, however, that has not been the point of my analysis. I am more excited by the questions cyberspace raises: how its existence challenges our ways of thinking about democratic politics, how it disrupts various flows of thought, how its productive confusions can be made enlightening. What I would like to do here, therefore, is highlight some of those disruptions and what they imply for democratic theorizing, particularly as it relates to the three core concepts that have animated this analysis: namely, space, technology, and the body.

The Spatial Turn

Despite their avid use of spatial metaphors in conceptualizing different kinds of democratic practices, political theorists, as I argued in chapter 2, have tended to conceptualize space in physiocentric terms: as a natural, given, physical container within which physical bodies move. This framework, I suggested, is what has contributed to the construction of size (territory and population) as a limiting condition in democratic theory: the perennial problem of scale. This fetish about size creates a kind of conceptual impasse, generally committing theorists to a single position somewhere along the "democratic corridor" I described in chapter 2 (see Figure 2). The common premise is that participation by citizens is a face-to-face affair. Consequently, citizen participation is most active in a small-scale community and, of necessity, least active in a large-scale society, where the business of administering government is, therefore, best left to elected representatives.

If, however, we understand, following Lefebvre, that social spaces are socially produced, then different ways of conceptualizing *participatory* spaces become possible. Barber's sense that political community is grounded in a space of communication (1984, 246–48) contributes to this understanding, although he winds up, yet again, privileging face-to-face encounters in neighborhood assemblies as the font of an illusive intimacy and social bond that ostensibly are necessary qualities for the exercise of civic virtue. I am not suggesting we eschew the search for the source, quality, and even the meaning of "civic virtue," but part of what I find problematic about this enterprise is that it often leads theorists to make a number of normative claims about the kinds of relationships in which people should invest themselves for the sake of a "return" to a more enriching, because participatory, democratic idyll (Shulman 1983). Lamenting the so-called loss of small, associational spaces and then proposing some sort of (ultimately utopian) return to them is a fruitless endeavor. Instead of dictating where people should situate themselves in order to become more civic minded, something of the ethnographic spirit of "following the natives" (to put it indelicately) is needed in democratic political theory. As the foregoing analysis indicates, political theorists should perhaps begin by rethinking their conception of space. Social spaces are not simply physical; they are also produced by how we imagine them and by how we inhabit them. The analysis of hardware and software in chapter 3 suggests that we need, as well, to broaden our understandings of the physical. Our studies should include not just spatial practices engendered by the movements of atoms and bodies, but also those involving the movements of electrons and bits, which include transnational data transmissions, speedy movements, perfect copies, invisible electrical flows, and indirect effects. Having rethought what counts as a social space, theorists might then do well to explore those currently existing social spaces where different kinds of people are every day constructing sometimes new frameworks of sociality (some face-to-face, some not).[1]

One additional consequence of the sense that social spaces are socially produced is that such spaces tend to proliferate. If, then, democratic politics are always closely linked to the social spaces through which they occur, then it may be a little shortsighted for theorists to advocate one kind of democratic practice as the best or truest form of democracy. What we may find, in fact, is that we have been, all along, practicing a kind of mixed democracy: a combination of participatory democracy in some social spaces (not necessarily small, local, face-to-face spaces) and of representative democracy in other social spaces (again, not necessarily large, national, impersonal spaces). This implies a less unitary sense of public, political space: indeed, what it calls for is a sense of "a multiplicity of publics" and the need to "theorize the relations among them" (Fraser 1993, 136–37).[2] Looking at the ways in which electronic networking spaces overlie and become part of our conventional social spaces may help us to theorize these relations among multiple publics. As the concept of heterotopia ultimately foregrounds, social spaces cannot really be studied in isolation from each other (assuming even that one can carefully delineate their boundaries). Rather, more is learned about political practices and possibilities by analyzing the ways social spaces impact on each other.

In particular, the concept of heterotopia suggests ways in which a spatial theory of social change might be developed. My analysis gestures toward that. It offers a view of cyberspace as a space of "an alternate ordering" (Hetherington 1997, 9), where, because different spatial practices, concepts, and uses are at work than in conventionally physical spaces, that comparison or juxtaposition between physical and virtual can provide, in Foucault's words, "a pure experience of order" (1994b, xxi). It can bring to awareness the process of ordering itself, calling into question what might have seemed fairly "concrete" assumptions about the orders of physical space. Like Rod Serling's *Twilight Zone* (arguably another kind of heterotopic space), the productive ambiguities of cyberspace have "submitted for your consideration" a number of core concepts in political and social theory, including the very meanings of *participation,* of *face-to-face,* of *here* and *there,* and even of *self.* I am not suggesting, as have some observers (both critics and pundits), that cyberspace has created a state of chaos for everything we used to hold dear. Rather, as Hetherington suggests, a heterotopia provides new instances of both freedom and order. We may find ourselves "free" from some of the dictates of the movement of atoms (e.g., bodiless), but the flow of electrons in cyberspace follows certain orders as well, and it is the nature and impact of this different ordering that must be researched more fully.

Technical Specifications

The spatialized divisions I identified in chapter 2 (between representative and participatory forms of democracy), perhaps not surprisingly, have also tended to inform respective attitudes toward technologies. Advocates of the representative scheme have tended to be not simply more sanguine about technological progress but, in fact, purveyors of utopian narratives of progress, hyping technologies as a way to conquer space and bring people closer together. Advocates of direct democracy, by contrast, have tended to be skeptical, even dystopic, about technologies, precisely to the extent that technical changes alter the character of communities and personal identities—indeed, redefine who we are, as Arendt argued.[3] A major problem with both of these extreme positions is that they tend to operate with unitary conceptions of *technology,* failing to specify, first, differences between various kinds of technologies (e.g., automation, transportation, communication); second, different modes within a general type (e.g., broadcast communications technologies as opposed to interpersonal communications technologies); and, third, different practices within a specified mode of technology (e.g., e-mail as opposed to computer conferencing). The problem, then, is partly one of failing to specify what one means by technology. Arendt, as I argued in chapter 2, exemplifies this failure.

A second general tendency is the failure to recognize the more complex relationships that obtain between technologies and cultures. So, for example, technological utopians tend to regard technologies as completely neutral (that is, apolitical) in the sense that human beings instrumentally direct the uses to which technologies are put; whereas technological dystopians, by contrast, tend to treat technologies as completely autonomous and deterministic, reshaping our lives in ways beyond our control.[4] What the preceding chapters suggest, however—particularly when read through Foucault's notion of governmentality—is that these divisions are perhaps no accident. Inasmuch as some technologies have abetted governments in their function of managing the population, it is not at all surprising to find advocates of what amount to more elite forms of democracy presenting technologies as neutral and depoliticizing their adoption. The result is a technocratic stance that constructs technological issues as best left to the experts. Similarly, the dystopic position may be understood as an effect of how technologies have been depoliticized and adopted without people having any (or much) input into the decision-making process. What are determined here, however, are not the deleterious consequences of "technology" (univocally articulated), but rather the disempowering effects of a technocratic policy process. This is one reason I have found efforts to politicize encryption policy via the Internet an encouraging prospect, even though the way that issue has been politicized—as a privacy issue—rides roughshod over arguably more democratic concerns (as I indicated in the previous chapter). The point is that technologies cannot be treated as the neutral fix for democracy, nor, for that matter, as the deterministic ruination of democracy; rather, they should be seen as issues that need to be themselves democratized precisely by politicizing them, by making their adoption, more self-consciously, a topic of public, political debate (Sclove 1995, 8).

For critics like Richard Sclove, however, this process of politicizing technology policy takes, as its starting point, a conception of what constitutes the best form of democracy, and for him that means a participatory form of democracy that still finds its civic-minded basis in local, face-to-face encounters. That spatial strategy as a precondition of democratizing technology, however, already forecloses certain prospects. Rather than taking one notion of democracy as the starting point, however, it seems to me that politicizing technology may have the more fruitful effect of politicizing democracy itself: that is, of opening up for public discussion precisely what it is that we mean by democracy and why we think some forms are better than others. I find that prospect, ultimately, more democratic because more diverse, more fallible, and more open to possibilities.

The immediate implication of all this for democratic theorizing is, of course, the need to pay closer attention to technological policies and the "crypto" (i.e., hidden) politics that underlie them. "Policy" is in many respects the language of the state. It is the discourse through which state officials, to the extent that they do so at all, put technology on the political agenda. Hence, if theorists want to engage with and affect those agendas, they must connect theory to policy in order to enable that engagement. It is through such processes of disarticulation and rearticulation—e.g., relinking encryption from privacy concerns to public communication concerns or rearticulating the Telecom Act from censorship or efficiency issues to questions concerning democratic politics and universal access—that the ideal cartographies that theorists propose can lead to the production of new social spaces and, in the process, disrupt or derail the normalizing state discourses by which antidemocratic technologies are depoliticized, adopted, and implemented.

Embodied Power: The Return of the Repressed

Finally, the preceding analysis has raised some vexing questions about the body's relevance to democratic theory and notions of citizenship. On the one hand, Iris Marion Young shows that "[a]n ideal of universal citizenship has driven the emancipatory momentum of modern political life" and that this universality is self-contradictory, implying at once an inclusive expansion of citizenship rights to all adults based on an overriding principle of equality, which principle nonetheless depends on the systematic exclusion of all particularities and differences among citizens (1995, 175). In excluding the body, therefore, ideals of citizenship have, by implication, excluded those Others (women, minorities, and children) whose identities are defined in relation to their bodies and to their bodily needs. Despite these exclusions, however, the vexing question of citizenship identified in a recent anthology—"what binds citizens together into a shared political community" (Beiner 1995, 3)—is still explicitly understood by the contributors to that volume as the problem of a "*national* citizenship [that] is being simultaneously undermined by not only globalizing pressures but also localizing pressures" (3, my emphasis). Citizenship, as I showed in chapter 4, depends on a legally articulated connection—"a process of warranting" (Stone 1996, 40–41)—between human bodies and state territories: a link that is central to the construction of the "politically apprehensible citizen" (Stone 1996, 79). In this respect, the problematics of citizenship as defined by leading political theorists have depended on covert assumptions about physical bodies in physical spaces. Put another way, the body has been the persistent yet unacknowledged underbelly of citizenship.

The comparative absence of discussions of the body in theories of citizenship (Young being one notable exception) is particularly remarkable in light of the arguments set forth by Foucault (e.g., 1979, 1991, 1994a) and by contemporary feminist and other social theorists (e.g., Spelman 1982; Sawicki 1991; Butler 1993; Bourdieu 1990; Turner 1984; Schatzki and Natter 1996) who have shown in various ways how it is that politics works on, in, with, and through the physical body (Sandy Stone, in Leeson 1996, 114). Collectively these studies indicate that the materialization of the body has been the mechanism by which citizens are both recognized (giving them a voice) and managed (making them docile). The body, in this respect, has been the fleshy requisite for certain forms of political agency. Notwithstanding this, I have shown that, in fact, some political theorists (notably Arendt and even Habermas) eschew the "emphatically physical body" (Moruzzi 1990, 97). And, in a sense, that exclusion, I have argued, suggests strong affinities between, on the one hand, the ideal democratic cartographies proffered by these theorists and, on the other hand, "the bodiless exultation of cyberspace" (Gibson 1984, 6). One conclusion to be drawn from these affinities, as I have suggested (half seriously), is that cyberspace is the ideal public space. This is not a conclusion I would want to dismiss entirely, for one simple reason: inasmuch as bodily signifiers (e.g., of race and gender) have been the basis for systematically excluding people from political debate or for dismissing what they do say when they gain minimal access to a face-to-face forum for debate, excluding bodies can mitigate against at least some prejudicial conduct in our conversations with others.

Another conclusion, however, is to highlight the ways in which the egalitarian nature of Athenian democracy was itself a kind of fiction given its basis in an insuperable sociopolitical division that systematically excluded women and slaves and, in fact, relied on their labor in the household so that "citizens" (Athenian males) could engage in politics in the public realm (Saxonhouse 1991). This would lead to the conclusion that if cyberspace is like ancient Athens, then perhaps it, too, is based on similar systematic exclusions. That notion puts a very different spin on Al Gore's suggestion that information technologies (specifically, the GII) can forge "a new Athenian Age of democracy" (1994), the very suggestion

I deployed in my introduction to launch this analysis. Brook and Boal make exactly this kind of critical reading of Gore's speech:

> Gore's reference to Athenian democracy is significant, but, like almost everything else in the speech, it requires translation. Athens was an imperialist slave society, with democratic rights enjoyed only by a privileged few. . . . Machines mediating between citizen and ruling institution would in no way enhance individual freedom; instead, the scheme would further naturalize the force of law, regulation, procedure, and other codes of conduct while further depoliticizing the administration of society. (1995, xiii)

This critique of Gore's allusions to Athenian democracy matters for thinking about whether cyberspace depends on similar exclusions (see Oguibe 1996). However, the assumption here is that mediation of any kind necessarily abets the state's administrative power while simultaneously diminishing democratic participation, which precisely begs the question of what role is served by face-to-face encounters, here between citizens and ruling institutions. In fact, face-to-face encounters between citizens and politicians "inside the Beltway," as it were, may run the risk of eroding the critical distance that Habermas, for one, has suggested is important for the construction of a noninstitutional form of critical debate. How precisely that distance is eradicated is a more complex issue than I can address adequately here, but evidence exists that citizens confronted with the institutional machinery of Washington power politics can be intimated by and interpellated into its bargaining-and-negotiation decision-making paradigm.[5] For my part, claims about the importance of face-to-face interactions for a democratic politics are underspecified and inconclusive. The effort to address this issue here, however, has raised for me some interesting observations that I would like to highlight in these last few pages, specifically with respect to the implications of a politics of concealment (the ability to act on bodies at a distance through a form of disembodied projection) and a politics of public appearance (the power of display, of embodied acts).

I have suggested that a defense of anonymity can be read out of Habermas's theory of the public sphere, particularly with respect to the construction of a universalized public voice, in the early print media, through the projection of disembodied public personae like the Spectator. But one can also detect in this strategy a liberal concern with individual safety. The public persona of the Spectator, for example, allowed the person Richard Steele to conceal his identity. Drawing from Lauren

Berlant's work, Michael Warner makes the strong claim that this charade actually provided "an intimate subjective benefit" for Steele, shielding him from the possible repercussions his words might incite: the Spectator persona protected Steele's own body by constructing a "public, prosthetic body" that could act as "a kind of prophylaxis against violation" (1993, 381). This claim acknowledges that taking a public stand can sometimes be a dangerous undertaking. Indeed, Arendt herself maintains that to take a public stand on an issue is to stick one's neck out, sometimes literally. Leaving the household means leaving behind one's primary concern with self-preservation in favor of pursuing some glorious deed or enterprise, no matter how risky. This is perhaps why in ancient Athens, as Arendt explains, *courage* "became the political virtue par excellence" (1958, 36). If the venture were life-threatening, however, Arendt gives the impression that this was because leaving the household originally meant, implicitly, entering battle or some other enterprise involving physically dangerous travel. She does not suggest that other citizens, whose opinions I might publically oppose, could pose a direct physical threat to me. Nor could they pose an indirect one by threatening my livelihood since Arendt's Athens is devoid of class politics.

What I am attempting to highlight here is that the courage Arendt lauded among ancient citizens—the courage necessary to make oneself visible, to expose oneself to danger by taking a public stand—was perhaps not as extensive in ancient Athens as the courage of visibility needed for a modern citizen to take a public stand. Not only are differences more likely in contemporary plural societies, but the instruments of retribution—handguns, automatic rifles, bombs, and so forth—are both more immediate and more decisive. It is worth noting, with respect to the modern exaggeration of the association between visibility and danger, that the origins of the liberal tradition of the secret ballot box is one Bryan Turner associates, in the case of Britain, with the nineteenth-century broadening of the franchise to the working class and associated efforts to institutionalize the political right to vote (1992, 35–36). Concealing how one voted, in this instance, was a means of taking a political stand without endangering one's life or one's livelihood. Electoral reformers understood that the uncoerced votes of socially and economically vulnerable individuals could be better ensured if powerful groups were less able to monitor how those individuals voted. Hence, alongside the civic-republican concern with revitalizing citizenship by creating *open* spaces of discourse must be added the liberal concern with creating *safe* spaces for the exercise of politics. This, I think, is part of what underlies Habermas's notion of a noninstitutional critical buffer zone free from the manipulation and control of a coercive state machinery.

The disembodied expression of one's will, therefore, has had ambiguous consequences. While, on the one hand, it has helped to effect the liberal ideal of a universal subject, thereby silencing the needs that stem from being different, it has, on the other hand, forwarded our practical concern with being safe, and not just in the modest sense of procuring a private space where individual freedoms can flourish, but rather in the stronger sense of producing safe, public spaces through which subjugated groups can declare their needs without risking their lives. This concern could go a long way toward explaining the appeal of a bodiless cyberspace. Concretely, the technologically mediated public space produced through the Internet might provide the basis for a politics that is safer for citizens, a form of participation that does not require one to put one's life on the line because one cannot put one's body online.[6]

Sue-Ellen Case, for her part, defends the importance of the "visibility politics" of collective action as if the centrality and efficacy of becoming visible by bursting en masse into conventionally physical public spaces were self-evident (1996, 2). The success of TV programs like *The X-Files* and other conspiracy stories attests, however, to a deep and abiding popular suspicion that a substantial degree of power, pace Case and others, may be exercised by those who remain behind the scenes. Indeed, Foucault's various arguments about modern disciplinary societies speak to a new form of hidden (because capillary) power that targets the visible body. Against, at least, this form of disciplinary power—which, like the prison guard, sees without being seen—anonymity rather than visibility may constitute a more viable form of resistance. Put simply, anonymity makes it harder for one to become a target.

Ultimately, however, concealment seems to be a liberal strategy that is somewhat at odds with the ways participatory democracy has been defined, notably by SDS, as a kind of collective politics of visibility in the streets. I want to close this analysis with an observation about what I take to be a liberal anxiety about this kind of embodied collective power. One particularly symbolic event in recent history will illustrate my point: the dismantling of the Berlin Wall in November 1989. The characteristic reading of this event is that it revealed, more clearly and more profoundly than any other event in recent history, that "the People" could still be a powerful political force, bursting on the scene and retaking control of their lives from an oppressive regime. What strikes me the most about this event, however, is not that it *has* this one meaning, but rather that it so thoroughly interpellated individuals from virtually all points along the political spectrum in its revolutionary euphoria: so much so that the wall's dismantling typically gives rise to this single narrative.

Underneath this euphoria, however, one can detect the strains of a deep and abiding fear of the People when they gather en masse and in the flesh in open, physical spaces (the squares and streets) and declare their embodied power: notably, by tearing down walls. Theorists are schizophrenic about this embodied mass power. On the one hand, they celebrate the ability of the People to express their will in collective action. On the other hand, they fear the degeneration of that collective will into a kind of mob rule. Seyla Benhabib betrays this anxiety (for both herself and for Habermas, I think) in her review for *The Nation* of a set of essays Habermas wrote in the early 1990s regarding German reunification and the mistakes to be avoided. She notes:

> During November 1989, as East German crowds in Leipzig marched through the streets, quite unsure about where their actions would lead, they shifted their chant from *Wir sind das Volk* (we are the people) to *Wir sind ein Volk* (we are one people). This simple change signaled an unstable oscillation: Whereas the concept of "the people" anchored the protesters' demands in the history of democratic uprisings against tyranny, oppression, inequality and domination, the slogan "we are one people" echoed with fantasies of national union and purity, of the exclusion of those who are different and of foreigners. (1997)

Benhabib's remarks fundamentally encapsulate for me what I take to be at the heart of pluralist fears about the masses: namely, that the People as a (literal) embodiment of the collective, democratic power of individuals come together as a public can transform too readily into *one* People as the embodiment of a majoritarian totalitarianism (here linked historically to fears about a revival of the German nationalism that gave rise to Auschwitz and related horrors). Cast in these terms, Benhabib's warning is an important one, inviting us to think about other barriers and the dangers of crossing them. A politics embodied by "the masses" and made visible when they burst on the scene expressing their will is, by its nature, univocal. A subtle but important line is crossed, however, when a cry that began as an effort to give voice to a previously subjugated knowledge grows into a roar that drowns out other voices. This reminder suggests that in addition to theorizing how politics works on the body, we must also think very hard about how we embody our politics and, more importantly, to what end.

The fears that provoke the classically liberal concern with embodied power, however, are less laudable. What is more typically at stake in the ideal of the unencumbered self is a privileged self free from the stark demands not just of his own body, but of the bodies of subjugated others. The embodied power of collective action, in this respect, is better understood as the effect of exclusion and disempowerment. It is an effort to politicize an issue and make it visible (by taking it to the streets) when the terms of debate are too narrow and the spaces for debate bar access to all but a privileged few.

When produced as a space for the free flow of information (commodities), cyberspace promises the realization of this liberal utopian fantasy of a bulwark against the embodied power of the masses, against their ability to demonstrate (rather than debate) their needs in one decisive bursting en masse. For if cyberspace, in one respect, can break down (physical) barriers, allowing us to roam freely across an electronic frontier, it can also erect new (digital) barriers, both in terms of who gains access and of what can be accessed. The use of strong cryptography has been defended precisely on the grounds that a wall (of code) is needed to protect average law-abiding citizens from nefarious state surveillance practices. What my analysis in chapter 5 ultimately shows, however, is that the individuals who currently stand to gain the most from digital anonymity are those who may already occupy a position of privilege in a society that is being increasingly "frontierized." This is not an argument against strong cryptography, since subjugated groups can benefit from its use as well. Rather my point is that the terms of debate need to be broadened beyond an overarching concern with security (national or personal).

Safety is not an unqualified good. This is an enormously difficult statement to make in the current political climate, but all the more important to stress. While security matters, its focus is myopic and surprisingly undemocratic, perhaps deliberately so. Surveillance is not just a means for protecting populations; it is also a way of managing them. Privacy is not just about escaping repression; it is also a way of avoiding discovery, accountability, and responsibility. As blueprints for how cyberspace itself should be further developed, neither of these concerns offers satisfying prospects. The first works to make the body visible in order to dictate its needs and control its actions, in the process creating its own version of the visible body. The second works to hide the body, ostensibly to protect its needs but also to silence the needs of other bodies. Neither provides a space—literally—where diverse bodies (physical and otherwise) can come together as a public to debate and deliberate their own needs.

When produced as a virtual community where ordinary folks can get together, cyberspace approaches that ideal. And it does so, in particular, because it is produced self-consciously as one of the several social spaces we inhabit, making it an exploratory space that is allowed to intrude on our other social spaces even as our other social spaces (in the form of our "real-life" norms, expectations, and experiences) are allowed to intrude upon it. This is cyberspace as heterotopia: as an experience of spatial ordering itself that invites us to question, to explore, to doubt, and perhaps to live differently.

As a disembodied space for the liberal unencumbered self, however, cyberspace promises a utopian ecstasy (a "bodiless exultation") on which it ultimately cannot deliver. It fails to deliver because cyberspace is not a space we can inhabit completely (Gibson's fiction notwithstanding). It is, rather, a point of passage, an obligatory one, but a passage nonetheless. The celebration of the masses in the streets evinced in the univocal narrative of the dismantling of the Berlin Wall and the more subtle fears of the "return of the repressed" (Jürgen Habermas, cited in Benhabib 1997) embodied in *ein Volk* (one people) both betray an alternate ordering that confounds this ecstasy. They suggest how the embodied power of the masses can become one possible disruption of cyberspace itself as that "consensual hallucination" (Gibson 1984, 5) where the "hallucinogenic State" (Dominguez 1996), the information capitalist, and the liberal unencumbered self try but fail to forget these other bodies. That is to say, they fail as long as other social spaces continue to be produced by other bodies pressing their demands.

This is not a defense of so-called mob rule, but rather a condemnation of any "elite stance" that, as William Gibson puts it, evinces "a certain relaxed contempt for the flesh" (1984, 6). If leaving the body behind is what makes cyberspace seductive, this seduction may have its limits . . . and probably should.

Notes

Introduction

1. Most of the research materials for this study consist of documents that were at one time available on the World Wide Web (WWW) and may still be archived at the same location or somewhere else in cyberspace. I cite these materials by referencing the Web address, or Uniform Resource Locator (URL), where those files were stored the last time I accessed them. Given the dynamic nature of the Web, I also list the date I last visited those sites. When making a general reference to a site, I list the URL in a note. When referring to a specific electronic article, however, I have listed the URL as part of the fuller standard citation in the Works Cited list. Interested readers may be able to access referenced sites and WWW documents by typing the exact URL (including all punctuation marks and underscores) in the location window of their Web browser. If the document is no longer available at the address I have listed, it may be found by running a query (by document title, author, subject matter, and so forth) through one of several Web search engines, such as HotBot (http://www. hotbot.com) or Google (http://www.google.com).

As of this writing, information about the VHP was available on the National Library of Medicine (NLM) Web site at http://www.nlm.nih.gov/research/visible/ visible_human.html (retrieved 25 November 2001). I have drawn the preceding summary of the VHP from Rothman 1996 (179–95), Anthony 1996, and the National Library of Medicine 1997.

2. As is now well known, *discourse*—a concept Foucault himself promoted in his considerable body of work (see especially 1972 and 1981)—has become a central object of study in recent social theory. Foucault was interested in analyzing

the social conditions that make knowledge possible. Turning to an analysis of *enunciation* or language-in-use (what the Swiss structural linguist Ferdinand de Saussure called *parole*), Foucault theorized that one could discern a regularity in the relationships between the elements (statements, actions, subjects, objects, concepts, strategies) that make meaning possible (1972). It is this regularity—this quasi-structural system of relations—that he called *discourse.* Because Foucault related discourse to knowledge, his concept is often misrecognized as ideational, treated as a symbolic expression of thoughts that are first formulated in people's heads. This actually reverses the relationship he posited between discourse and thought. As I tried to suggest in my references above to synaptic connections, those connections are the effects of discourses rather than their origins. For Foucault, discourses are not quasi-intentional or instrumental ideologies constructed from some prior thought; rather, they are the regularity of relationships among signifiers and signifieds that are unconsciously produced in the course of (meaningful) social interaction. As subsequent theorists (e.g., Laclau and Mouffe 1987, 82–84) have argued, moreover, discursive formations include both linguistic and nonlinguistic practices. In this sense, too, the discursive is not the opposite of the material, but rather can and often does encompass material practices.

3. As some readers will have already guessed, my opening description of the dissection of Jernigan's body parodies Foucault's account of Damiens's torture in the first few pages of *Discipline and Punish* (3–6).

4. According to Foucault's translator Alan Sheridan (Foucault 1979, ix), the French verb *surveiller,* though closely related to the English noun *surveillance,* has no exact English counterpart. The English phrases *to monitor, to survey, to observe,* or even *to supervise* do come close, but they remain far more technical and/or neutral in connotation than the term *surveiller.* For this reason, Foucault himself, Sheridan continues, suggested that his seminal work on the prison *Surveiller et Punir* (published in 1975 by Editions Gallimard, Paris) be translated into English as *Discipline and Punish.* That Foucault regarded this as an appropriate translation suggests the close connection, in his work, between the concepts of surveillance and discipline.

5. The parallels between the VHP and Rembrandt's *The Anatomy Lesson of Dr. Nicolaas Tulp* deserve mention. As Francis Barker notes, the object of the public dissection immortalized by Rembrandt was also a recently executed criminal: in this case, a petty thief from Leiden named Aris Kint (1984, 73). She points out how the portrait registers a kind of "fusion of punishment and science" (73) as it inaugurates what was for its time a new, modern, bourgeois subjectivity that reinscribed the body in Cartesian terms, i.e., as objective matter separate from mind or soul and also, by extension, an appropriate object of knowledge

for medical analysis. Where Barker's study concerns this seventeenth-century construction of the body as material object, the VHP and cyberspace more generally invite us to consider what happens to the body, at the close of the twentieth century, when this fleshy object is made data. For a lengthier analysis of the digital body in relation to the VHP, see Waldby 1996b.

6. Apropos this, not only does the Visible Man remain anonymous at least within the scientific discourse of the NLM, but his female counterpart has been described even in the popular press only as "a 59-year-old Maryland woman who died in her sleep of a heart attack" and whose husband "offered her, *anonymously*, to science" (Laskas 1996, my emphasis). Her anonymity heightens the sense that she could be practically any woman.

7. For Waldby (1996a), the project haunts because it has an "aura of the uncanny" inasmuch as in these digital images of the Visible Human, "life and death exist in an ambiguous mixture."

8. Admittedly, my analysis also participates in this violence by describing it, but my interest is in opening up the space of the discourse, not the space of the corpse.

9. A pixel is a "picture element": the smallest unit on a computer screen created whenever a computer electronically excites phosphors on the video monitor to which it is attached (Cotton and Oliver 1994, 162). Relatively complex images emerge from mixing together pixels of different colors and shades, a digital form of pointillism.

10. Educational games such as *Where in the World Is Carmen Sandiego?* are a case in point, but I am also thinking about professional, computer-based training (CBT) software, such as the program one of my mother's doctors described to me in a conversation he and I had in 1998. He had just been to a medical convention and explained in detail how he had experimented with an interactive program that allowed users to simulate giving an injection deep into the cavities behind the kneecap. He relayed, with evident delight, that he got it right the very first time, but that when he failed his second attempt, the computer responded with the message "Ouch!"

11. The 1966 Hollywood film version included the rather memorable scene in which the villain is smothered by spongy, white, disease-attacking blood cells.

12. For James Der Derian, "the end game of simulation in work and war is to make the others' terror fun for us" (1994, 268). "Needless to say," he continues, "there is something wrong with this."

13. I am giving here a superficial reading of Arendt's notion of the "space of appearance" in the Athenian polis. As I argue in chapter 2, however, her "bodily politics" is more ambivalent about the body than this introductory gloss suggests.

14. "Walking in the City," of course, is the title to one of Michel de Certeau's studies in his work *The Practice of Everyday Life* (1988).

15. See, for example, Foucault's "Of Other Spaces" (1986).

16. Of course, the face can be digitally photographed and transmitted, simulating the interpersonal character of the face-to-face encounter. In a sense, then, technologies like video conferencing provide a different inflection of "face-to-face."

1. Theorizing Spaces

1. Although Foucault's writings, especially his work on the panopticon (1979), now provoke discussions about the spatial aspects of society, they were not initially, in my experience, read in those terms. I can think of two reasons why this might be so. First, despite Foucault's extensive use of spatial metaphors, his explicit discussions of space amounted to what Doreen Massey, with a little obvious contempt, refers to as "his occasional reflections on the importance of the spatial" (1994, 249). Second, where he mentions space, and even problematizes it, Foucault never really offers a thorough definition or elaboration of it. Perhaps this incompleteness, however—together, certainly, with his insightful spatial metaphors—has helped provoke the spatial turn in social theory, including a change in the way Foucault's own writings have been read. On his spatial metaphors, see Smith and Katz 1993 (71–74). For Foucault's own thoughts on the role of space and spatial metaphors in his work, see the interview "Questions on Geography" (1980, 63–77), which concludes with Foucault's own intriguing admission that "[g]eography must indeed necessarily lie at the heart of my concerns."

2. Other writers have made essentially the same point using the terms *real, material, actual,* or *geographic* space for physical space, and *imaginary, metaphorical, conceptual,* or *conceptualized* space for mental space. See, for example, the essays collected in Keith and Pile 1993.

3. Massey agrees that a better sense of the relationship between space and society followed from the introduction, in 1970s radical geography, of the notion that "space is a social construct," but she adds that the overriding emphasis on construction skewed analysis too much in favor of the social, treating space as no more than an outcome (1994, 254).

4. Initially, this was not an argument I found troubling. Part of the insight of poststructuralist theory has been precisely the sense that no necessary connection exists between signifier and signified. The objection that has been raised in relation to space, however, is that if the space in question involves physical phenomena, then some attention should be given to that physicality. Put anoth-

er way, the signifier, too, should be problematized. Space as construct, by contrast, tends to ignore the signifier as irrelevant to the construction of meaning.

5. This is not to suggest that geographers now want to erect some kind of *space-ism* that treats time as irrelevant; rather, they argue that both space and time are important. For her part, Massey proposes the concept of "space-time" as an object of study in social theory (1994, 249–72).

6. Kristin Ross makes essentially the same point when she notes that "[t]he difficulty [of reprioritizing space in social theory] is also one of vocabulary, for while words like 'historical' and 'political' convey a dynamic of intentionality, vitality, and human motivation, 'spatial,' on the other hand, connotes stasis, neutrality, and passivity" (cited in Massey 1994, 259).

7. Lefebvre's criticisms are of Foucault's arguments in *The Archaeology of Knowledge* (1972), originally published in French in 1969. Arguably, Foucault's subsequent work on the panopticon in his *Discipline and Punish* (1979)—the original French version of which came out a year after the publication, in 1974, of Lefebvre's *Production de l'espace* (see Lefebvre 1991)—is a bit more attentive to this issue of the space in question.

8. Lefebvre actually criticizes surrealism as a political practice, denying that symbolic disruptions of meaning could lead to transcendent revelations and hence to a project for social change (18–21), but he nonetheless considers it a practice that could "legitimately" (though reservedly) claim revolutionary intent (126). He seems to me, therefore, to refer implicitly to surrealism in his characterization of the spaces of representation.

9. This distinction between strategy as an act of dominance and tactic as a form of resistance is de Certeau's (1988, xix). It is important to note, however, how this distinction reproduces an order/resistance dichotomy as if dominant strategies simply involve the imposition of static orders, and acts of resistance are only ever about dynamic efforts to disrupt those orders. As I argue below, however, dominant spatial practices are more dynamic than fixed, and subversive spatial practices are also about fixing a different spatial order: both kinds of practices, in other words, propose (in necessarily incomplete ways) different spatial orderings. (My thanks to Kevin Hetherington for foregrounding these issues for me in relation to de Certeau's work.)

10. It is, of course, for this reason that software manufacturers have attempted to redefine themselves as service providers (rather than commodity producers) and, relatedly, to redefine their activity of selling software as a contractual licensing of its use (rather than a permanent transfer of its ownership). While they have been legally successful in these efforts, they have not been as culturally successful. Even self-styled upstanding, law-abiding citizens, who in every other

sense may respect property rights, have a difficult time understanding unentitled software copying as a kind of theft.

11. See, for example, Foucault 1972 and 1981. In discourse-analytic terms, an *articulation* implies both an act of enunciation and an act of association, as in the British vernacular phrase *an articulated lorry* (or truck) in reference to a cab that is linked to a trailer (Hall 1986, 53). This usage conveys the double sense that discursive statements (which may be spoken, written, or even inscribed in objects and practices) operate by making a number of provisional links or relationships between signifying elements. Hence, rather than a property inherent in those elements, meaning is an effect of the discursive relationships established among them in the process of speaking/linking, i.e., of articulating (Laclau and Mouffe 1985, 105).

12. I don't know if the use of the term *virtual* as a synonym for *unreal* is Foucault's usage or his English translator's. Since *virtual* has become a common synonym for anything that is computerized, however, the usage here confuses some of the issues I am trying to address. As will become clear in the following section, I use the term *virtual* in reference to computers to mean *the digital,* broadly speaking, but I do not mean by this something that is unreal.

13. I wish to thank Kevin Hetherington for sending me copies of his articles on heterotopia (1996a, 1996b) and especially an advance copy of his book (1997). His work has been the most useful in helping me develop a notion of heterotopia that is theoretically illuminating, especially in relation to a study of the spatiality of cyberspace. (Apropos, too, the sense of cyberspace as, in part, a global space for research—particularly when combined with the generous spirit of collegiality that represents the best of academia—it seems to me worth mentioning here that I came across a reference to Kevin's work on the Routledge Web site after doing a general Internet search on the term *heterotopia*. I then contacted him in the United Kingdom from my home in South Florida via e-mail.)

14. This is from James Harkness's introduction to the English translation of Foucault's essay *This Is Not a Pipe,* cited in Hetherington 1997 (43).

15. Hetherington maintains that "[t]his shift from modes of representing through resemblance to similitude is vital to the full understanding of the significance of heterotopia for Foucault" (1997, 43). I have cited this here because it is also important to my understanding of how cyberspace can be understood as a heterotopic space. As will become apparent in later chapters, the Internet is popularly constructed as a different kind of space when it is metaphorically characterized as an "Information Superhighway" or even an "Electronic Frontier." The play of difference is evident when the stress is put on *information* and on *electronic* (whose ambiguities I highlight in chapter 3). However, these meta-

phors quickly neutralize this difference through the implied resemblance to the more familiar spaces of *superhighway* and *frontier*. The immediately neutralized sense of otherness implied by these metaphors, however, is not the same as the claim I'm advancing when I argue that we should view cyberspace as a heterotopic space. These metaphors, as I will show in chapter 5, are part of a discursive effort to make cyberspace a less ambiguous space precisely by privileging a known spatiality: superhighways or frontiers. My position, by contrast, is that the ambiguity of this other space should be studied in terms of how it relates to the physical realm of face-to-face encounters, for it is through such processes of similitude/simulation (metonymy) that ordering becomes an issue and alternatives are proposed. In this respect, metaphorical efforts to neutralize the ambiguity of cyberspace may be seen as effects of the heterotopic confrontation between the physical and the virtual that computer simulation creates.

16. The sense that heterotopias have a certain shock value seems to me less applicable to what Foucault called "heterotopias of deviation," like the prison (1986, 25). After all, as Hetherington himself points out, part of what is involved in the panoptic process is an effort to remove the ambivalence of the (criminal) Other by naming and classifying it and therefore making it "Other but knowable" (1997, 60). Perhaps the shock, however, is registered in the criminal herself inasmuch as she is the one for whom the prison becomes an obligatory point of passage. That is, she is required to enter the prison and in that sense traverses two spaces, the carceral and the free, becoming subject to their alternate orderings. Hence, any analysis of heterotopia arguably requires some understanding of the agents for whom such spaces-between become obligatory points of passage.

17. Hetherington notes that both heterotopias and surrealism operate according to relations of similitude (1997, 43–46).

18. The notion of cyberspace as "mental geography" is derived by Michael Benedikt (1993, 2) from Gibson's *Neuromancer* (1984).

19. Similarly, Lefebvre maintains that "[t]he initial basis or foundation of social space is nature—natural or physical space. Upon this basis are superimposed—in ways that transform, supplant or even threaten to destroy it— successive stratified and tangled networks which, though always material in form, nevertheless have an existence beyond their materiality: paths, roads, railways, telephone links, and so on" (1991, 402–3). Cyberspace, I am arguing, falls into the second category, and, as such, one of the central issues of this study is how that more-than-material space may "transform, supplant or even threaten to destroy" the physical space that is one of its conditions of possibility.

20. Networking systems include local bulletin board services (BBSs), the hobbyist network of PCs called Fidonet, the old institutional network of IBM mainframes called Bitnet, the newsgroups that make up Usenet, and more

recently, the HyperText Transport Protocol (http://) sites composing the World Wide Web (WWW or Web), to name a few. When these typically open ("public") networks are linked together via gateways using Transmission Control Protocol/Internet Protocol (TCP/IP), they become part of the global network of networks known as the Internet. This is sometimes shortened to Net, although the Net or the Matrix may also refer more generally to all computer network systems, including commercial, subscriber systems like America Online (AOL), CompuServe, Prodigy, and so forth.

21. The wide variety of methods for CMC include electronic mail (e-mail), real-time chat mode, message posting on newsgroups and listservers, hyperlinking through Web browsers, data sharing through File Transfer Protocol (FTP), remote terminal manipulation via Telnet, multimedia transfers (including sound, animation, and video), and real-time video and audio computer conferencing. Some of these activities can also be conducted clandestinely through anonymous remailers and indiscriminately through automatic mailers. The latter is popular among businesses that, contrary to "netiquette," regard the Internet as a medium for free advertising and therefore *spam* newsgroups and personal e-mail addresses with their unsolicited ads (see Elmer-Dewitt 1994).

22. *Cyberpunk* initially referred to the subgenre of speculative fiction that includes Gibson's *Neuromancer* (which I discuss in chapter 3). That neologism is now used more generally to refer to most cyberspace enthusiasts, especially those who enjoy learning the intricacies of other people's programs and writing their own programs. In that sense, it has become somewhat synonymous with the term *hacker* (see chapter 4). The term *crackers,* finally, was actually invented by hackers themselves to distinguish between, on the one hand, their own benign practices of breaking into computer systems for the intellectual challenges they pose and, on the other hand, "cracking" into systems for malicious and/or illegal purposes, i.e., to steal or destroy data (*The Jargon File* 2000, "cracker"; see also Wilson 1994).

23. Steiner's cartoon was published in the 5 July 1993 issue of the *New Yorker* and is available online through the searchable database at http://www.cartoonbank.com (keywords: "internet dog"). It was retrieved on 18 November 2000.

24. I am grateful to Jennifer Milliken for drawing my attention to Schutz's work and offering many of the following points and references in my e-mail conversations with her.

25. In my view, the possibility exists here as well for modifying our typifications inasmuch as an unexpected counteraction may invite us to rethink our interpretation of the original action. And the obverse is also true: that having the

other present before us may not alter our typifications of her initial, catalytic actions ("If the problem is at work, why are you picking a fight with me?").

2. Democratic Utopias

1. *Government of the People* refers to the minimal conditions according to which a government can be said to be democratic, conveying the sense that democracy exists where at the very least a legitimate government administered by skilled elites is enabled (and can be changed) by the People as the "producers of governments" (Schumpeter 1976, 269). *Government for the People* conveys the more middling sense that political leaders and representatives express "the will of the People" in an institutional context within which additional mechanisms exist for citizens to communicate their concerns and interests to their representatives. Finally, *government by the People* denotes the maximal sense of a democratic government administered directly by assemblies of citizens.

2. For a classic statement of this issue, see Dahl and Tufte 1973.

3. Problems surfacing in the November 2000 U.S. presidential election have helped to raise questions about the continued legitimacy of the Electoral College, whose foundation is itself related to some outdated assumptions about space and democracy. According to historians, the Electoral College was meant to guard against a kind of regionalism: majoritarian rule by citizens of more populous states, who, lacking enough information about other candidates, would naturally select the better known candidates from their own state or region. Such concerns made more sense, of course, in the late 1700s, when transportation and communication across the geographically dispersed states of the Atlantic seaboard were slow and an individual's lot was almost entirely tied up with the socioeconomic vagaries of his immediate environment. These conditions no longer obtain, however, in an era characterized by the global space-economy of pan-capitalism and electronic media. In short, the challenges to the legitimacy of the Electoral College have helped to reveal that such solutions to space-related problems aren't permanent because the spaces themselves change.

4. The "problem of scale" actually refers to two separate issues: geographic size of territory (space) and numerical size of the citizenry (bodies). The two tend to be treated as one and the same problem partly on the fallible assertion that the bigger the space, the greater will be the number of bodies in it, an assertion tacitly based on the assumption that space is simply a static, physical container for bodies. It is that assumption that I challenge in this chapter. For an explicit discussion of this "problem," see Barber 1984 (245–51).

5. In fact, Madison and the other Federalists derived a great deal of rhetorical power in favor of the union by repeatedly associating the smaller state republics with the much demonized "pure Democracy," which Madison vividly

described as "spectacles of turbulence and contention . . . incompatible with personal security, or the rights of property . . . [and] as short in their lives, as they have been violent in their deaths" (1988a, 46).

6. Madison alludes to this distinction between a political core and an administrative periphery in *Federalist* No. 14, where he discusses remote states "which lie at the greatest distance from the heart of the union" (1988b, 65) and refers to the "center" of republics (both state and federal) as the site where elected representatives "meet . . . for the administration of public affairs" (64).

7. This point is difficult to make on the basis of *Federalist* No. 10, which treats citizenship as a universal category rather than a status restricted by sex, race, and property ownership. In keeping with the conventions of his time, however, Madison outlined typical franchise restrictions in some of his other writings (Held 1987, 63–64). That he considered property ownership a valid restriction, moreover, is consistent with the argument he does make in *Federalist* No. 10 that "the most common and durable source of factions, has been the various and unequal distribution of property" (1988a, 44). These points suggest that despite his focus on mitigating the effects of factions, Madison might have allowed for one mechanism for mitigating the cause of factions, namely, restricting citizenship to those who own property and who therefore have a greater stake in government as a means of protecting property rights. On the founders' narrow definition of "the People," see also McDonald 1985 (161–62).

8. Wright's piece was part of an issue of *Time* that included a look at how radio call-in shows may be contributing to "a new form of electronic populism and demagoguery" (Corliss 1995). The cover includes a photo of Rush Limbaugh smoking a large cigar, with a header asking "Is Rush Limbaugh Good for America?" For the range of reader responses to Wright's and Corliss's respective articles, see "Letters to the Editor: *Time*" 1995.

9. The quote is from American University political scientist James Thurber, cited in Wright. In general, I agree with this analysis but not with Wright's assessment. Powerful lobbies have enjoyed privileged access to Washington elites since long before the invention of faxes and e-mails. The new communication paths carved by information technologies through the Beltway buffer may actually help less powerful groups and individuals countervail that privileged access.

10. One of the remarkable ironies of Madison's legacy is that in *Federalist* No. 14, one of his rebuttals to the anti-Federalist claim that a republic needs to be kept small is that the republic cannot really get too large to govern since technological improvements in transportation and communication will make it possible for representatives to keep in touch with their constituencies: "[T]he intercourse throughout the union will be daily facilitated by new improvements" (1988b, 65). Of course, in the 1780s, this meant building new roads and inventing

better ways of navigating the natural waterways that connected the most remote states with "the heart of the union" (65). It is reasonable to assume, however, that even with these improvements, Madison understood that travel across the union (and hence communication, which at that time depended on physical transport) would take at least days to complete, a physical distance that provided the kind of buffer against factionalism that he sought. He could not have envisioned the ways that the invention of electronic technologies in the twentieth century have provided the means for permeating that buffer: indeed, for creating a new kind of political space. Even Madison's vision has become, in this sense, utopian to the extent that, according to Wright, *no place* exists where public-minded politicians (whoever they might be) can be completely isolated from the inducements of factions.

11. I may be forgiven for mixing vertical and horizontal metaphors if it is observed that the political space being mapped and remapped here (at least by SDS) was understood as, in a sense, conical, where the center of government is also the apex of power. This power, according to SDS and others among the New Left movement, however, was actually a centralization of political, military, and corporate forces, and hence was situated as much in Wall Street and Madison Avenue as in Washington, D.C., i.e., it had a few centers. On this issue, see "The Economy" section of "The Port Huron Statement" (SDS 1994, 338–45). See also Mills 1971.

12. On this distinction, see, for example, Mouffe 1995 (34–41). For an enlightening discussion of the Athenian and Roman ideals of citizenship underpinning, respectively, these communitarian and liberal conceptions of political agency, see Pocock 1995. Arendt, of course, would have resisted assimilating the Athenian ideal of citizenship to communitarianism. What she proffers, instead, as I show in the next section, is the sense of individuality-in-community, that our plurality is what we humans have in common, and it can surface only in the company of others (1958, 8).

13. This is not to suggest that SDS rejected the notion of large, administrative governments (nor even, for that matter, of institutions of representation). In fact, SDS aspired to mass-movement status through a national organizational framework and was partly reformist in nature, willing to work within existing representative institutions; it sought to do both, however, by linking together local publics of empowered citizens. By the same token, I do not mean to suggest that SDS was oppressively conformist; in fact, its politics were strongly motivated by anarchist tenets and a healthy respect for individual rights, but it nonetheless retained a community-building emphasis in its collectivist program and its efforts to practice a consensus politics.

14. Indeed, Arendt's major critique of society in *The Human Condition* is its

foundation in the "private" matters of "housekeeping"—brought "from the shadowy interior of the household into the light of the public sphere"—and its related inclination toward conformity in that "society always demands that its members act as though they were members of one enormous family which has only one opinion and one interest" (1958, 38, 39). See also d'Entrèves 1992 (151) and Disch 1996 (158–59).

15. The systematic exclusion of women in Athenian politics has incited a number of feminist attacks on Arendt and her philosophy for buying so thoroughly into a male-dominated standard of politics. Adrienne Rich and Mary O'Brien have been among her staunchest feminist critics (both cited in Dietz 1991, 232–33; and in Honig 1992, 232 n. 3). Among democratic theorists, Sheldon Wolin also takes Arendt to task for idealizing what he interprets as a performative politics of individual glorification: "a politics of actors rather than citizens, agonistic rather than participatory, encouraging qualities that would enable men to stand out rather than to take part of" (cited in Disch 1996, 21). For a convincing critique of this interpretation of Arendt's philosophy as agonistic, see Disch 1996 (73–90).

16. On this distinction between retrospective and prospective utopias, see Benhabib 1986 (42).

17. Her communications concept of power and her theory of the public realm certainly inform Habermas's work (see, especially, 1986). In addition, while some feminist scholars have been critical of Arendt, others have suggested ways in which her focus on collective action and plurality, her agonal politics, or her views on storytelling might inform a feminist politics (see, respectively, Dietz 1991; Honig 1992; and Disch 1996).

18. See, for example, her discussion of female and slave labor as concerned principally with bodily needs (1958, 72–73) and her explanation of the role that the institution of slavery served in antiquity (84). Dietz makes the same point regarding Arendt's uncritical observation of these exclusions (1991, 237).

19. Pitkin implies the same reading when she notes that Arendt sometimes describes the private realm as concerned more with a particular "attitude" or "outlook" than a particular class or gender (cited in Honig 1992, 221).

20. The importance of "relative economic and social equality as a foundation of political citizenship" is, according to Gibbons, one of the more salutary and underexplored characteristics of civic republicanism, one that should, in his view, inspire scholars in that tradition to develop a more thoroughgoing "political economy of citizenship" (1997, ¶21). The irony—perhaps the tragedy—of Arendt's theory is that by excluding substantive economic concerns from her notion of the political, she provides no mechanism for redressing the very asymmetries that she recognizes keep people from becoming most fully human.

21. For exceptions, see Cooper 1988 and Dietz 1994. Because they fail to explain what Arendt actually means by technology and to assess her critique in relation to her views about public space and the body, however, both authors tend to treat her criticisms of technology as essentially correct.

22. This reading of *Sputnik* in relation to the Archimedean perspective was suggested to me by comments that Lisa Disch made in an earlier draft of this chapter and is, in turn, informed by her careful analysis of Arendt's criticisms of Archimedean thinking. See especially chapters 2 and 3 of Disch 1996 (20–105). For Arendt's discussion of this in *The Human Condition,* see especially the section entitled "The Discovery of the Archimedean Point" (257–68).

23. The internal quotation is from E. A. Burtt, cited in Arendt 1958 (264–65).

24. With these words, Arendt constructs one of the earliest theoretical assessments of what can be read as *the Cyborg condition:* the condition of humans (permanently) altered by their associations with machines and transformed into cybernetic organisms. For a more positive spin on being cyborg, see Haraway 1989.

25. Neo-Luddites would vehemently disagree with this assertion, arguing that we can, in fact, choose not to use certain technologies; witness, for example, Kirkpatrick Sale's oft-repeated demonstration of smashing a computer with a sledgehammer to make the point that we can choose not to use computers (see Green 1996). I can (albeit, with considerable effort) respect that as a personal choice, but I doubt whether, in fact, this is a workable political choice. In the context of a society in which virtually every powerful entity (governmental, corporate, or individual) employs computer technologies to exercise its powers of surveillance and control, giving up those technologies would be utter folly, advocating by implication a quasi-separatist society (akin to Amish communities) that would leave the greater part of existing power relations intact. This point was brought home by Noah Green's commentary on Sale's sledgehammer routine: "Several swings and crashes later, one more kid in a Brooklyn public school was left without the tools she'll need to find a job when she graduates" (1996). It is unclear to me, moreover, whether opting out of computers is even a viable personal choice: if neo-Luddites like Sale use credit cards, for example, or depend in the least on government bureaucracies for obtaining certain benefits, then they indirectly employ the network databases that approve their credit purchases and track their social benefits.

26. As Richard Flacks, an early member of SDS, argues elsewhere, "the use of 'consensus'" by SDS was meant "to foster expression by the less-articulate" (1971, 28). This followed from the sense that to build consensus among a group of people, it was necessary first to elicit the plurality of opinions that existed among members of the group, including those typically silenced.

27. It is worth recalling here that this inner sameness is precisely the point of endeavors like the Visible Human Project (discussed in the introduction). From a medical standpoint, Jernigan is an acceptable stand-in for all humans because the life-sustaining functions of the vital organs are essentially the same for all humans, and he is an acceptable stand-in for all men because the reproductive functions of the male sex organs are essentially the same for all men. In this respect, Arendt is right to suggest that the reduction of humans to their bodies in a sense transforms us to mere objects that resemble one another, denying us the sort of distinctive political agency that for her is only possible when we speak and act. This sense of bodies as undistinguished objects underlies, as well, references to "mass society" and to "the masses" more generally; both reduce people to nothing more than an undifferentiated mass of bodies.

28. This is not to suggest that Arendt's philosophy is inappropriate to a feminist politics but that Dietz is perhaps wrong to accept the underlying premise that feminism needs a bodily politics. In my view, feminists have more in common with Arendt than we perhaps recognize. The feminist focus on the female body is primarily concerned with showing that women's reproductive capacities traditionally have been the basis for subjugating women and denying us the right to participate. In a sense, then, this focus recognizes that reducing women to no more than child-bearing bodies does violence to us, denying us the capacity to be fully human and political beings. This is precisely Arendt's point when she argues that the hierarchical order of the private realm is characterized by force and violence among unequals rather than by politics and power among equals. In fact, feminists and Arendt are insisting on the same point when they argue that a human being (regardless of her bodily attributes) should be recognized politically as a distinct "who" rather than treated violently as a given "what."

29. The space to which I am alluding here is not the same as the metaphorical or imaginary mental space that Arendt theorized in her later writings on judgment. Arendt postulates this "hypothetical public sphere" (Disch 1996, 165) in order to describe a form of "representative thinking" that takes a plurality of standpoints into account while at the same time rejecting the possibility of a universal, Archimedean standpoint from which one can judge. The plurality of standpoints at work in this public space, however, is produced in isolation by teaching "one's imagination to go visiting" other standpoints or positions and imagining "an *anticipated communication* with others" (Arendt, cited in Disch 1996, 157, emphasis added by Disch). By contrast, the bodiless public space I mean here is one produced in actual communication with remote others through a technological medium, like computer networking. It is not physical in the conventional sense of being a space in which human bodies move, but neither is it

merely a mental space produced by one's mind in isolation from others. In cyberspace, that is, I don't have to anticipate what others might say; I simply have to wait for a response. For a helpful discussion of Arendt's hypothetical public space, see Disch 1996, especially 141–71.

30. As Calhoun notes, Habermas's concept of civil society is richer than treatments of it that equate it to the private market: "Capitalist market economies formed the basis of this civil society, but it included a good deal more than that. It included institutions of sociability and discourse only loosely related to the economy" (1993, 7–8).

31. Although, as I noted in the previous section, the significance of the body, as such, is attenuated in the politics Arendt outlines.

32. Consequently, the notion of a public, political space under monarchies— i.e., the sovereign realm—was more often assimilated to corporal metaphors like the *body politic*. Such metaphors did not immediately disappear with the advent of constitutional monarchies and the introduction of republican institutions like parliament; they were instead modified into rather ambivalent metaphors like "the King's two bodies," where the King's "public" body was understood to encompass the king as the head of the body politic and parliament as the limbs. For the argument that it was the introduction of parliament that motivated interest in the two-bodies metaphor in Elizabethan England, see Kantorowicz 1985 (3). Elsewhere, however, I provide a gender explanation for why this metaphor became more salient under the reign of Queen Elizabeth I (Saco 1997).

33. The common people were typically excluded from such displays, although Habermas suggests that they became a kind of accidental audience of the courtly festivities taking place in the castle parks; representative publicity displayed itself "not for but 'before' the people" as a mass of onlookers "ever present in the streets" (1989, 8, 10).

34. As I read Habermas, civil society became depersonalized in at least three different senses. The court enclave from which it spawned had been partly aristocratic and hence achieved some of its recognition from the share of estate-based and inherited political authority that the nobles represented in themselves. This embodied, representative nobility in court society came to be replaced by the new, bourgeois man, who represented nothing in himself, but rather was simply "what he produced" (1989, 13). Hence, civil society came to be depersonalized, first, in the sense of displacing embodied noble authority with a kind of disembodied social status derived from commercial relations. Second, civil society, as I show in a moment, was seen as a set of forces outside the control of the privatized individual and hence was abstract and depersonalized in this second sense. Finally, as I note later, the authority of public opinion rested in large part on the ability of individuals to present their ideas as disinterested, public minded, and

in this sense impersonal. In short, civil society was depersonalized in terms, respectively, of its power base, its force, and its critical expression.

35. As Habermas suggests here, the democratic character of this space was ensured more by an ideal, liberal principle of equal access and participation—based on freedoms of assembly, association, and expression—than by its concrete actualization, since Habermas does acknowledge that women and propertyless males were often denied access to public spaces of debate.

36. Significantly, Hetherington inverts the causal connection Habermas imputes here, noting that the French Revolution was itself triggered in no small part by the conversations that developed in the putatively apolitical public sphere of arts and letters. His example is the heterotopic space of the Palais Royal, which, in addition to being a site of cultural debate, hedonistic pleasure, carnivalesque, and early commercial enterprise, became also a locus of seditious discourse, where Jacobins and freemasons "would meet and plot" (1997, 5). It was in the Café de Foy of the Palais Royal, too, that Camille Desmoulins, according to Hetherington, "clambered up onto a table and delivered the speech that was to lead to the storming of the Bastille, an event which has been seen as the spark for the French Revolution" (5).

37. The same point and citation from Habermas appear in Warner's excellent analysis, "The Mass Public and the Mass Subject" (1993). The following discussion of the public subject and the public body draws from that analysis. For a convincing discussion of how all modern cultural identities are mediated, see Tomlinson 1991.

38. To be sure, the rise of mass media is not the only causal factor Habermas points to in assessing what contributed to the demise of the bourgeois public sphere. In fact, he suggests that mass mediation of the social may itself have been an effect, a way for dominant classes to address more fundamental contributing factors. Chief among these was the opening up of the public sphere, in the nineteenth century, to increasing numbers of propertyless people—e.g., through electoral reform and expanded franchises—whose demands for social welfare helped to heighten immanent contradictions in the bourgeois public sphere between its putatively universal claims regarding civil liberties and its class-specific role of providing a buffer between the state and civil society. No longer capable of fulfilling its role of minimizing the state's intrusions into the economy, the bourgeois public sphere, according to Habermas, receded in importance, and the administration and manipulation of civil society, partly through the emergent mass media, increased in importance. In short, when the state penetrated more spheres of the private, the public itself became depoliticized: "[I]t simultaneously lost its political function, namely: that of subjecting the affairs that it had made public to the control of a critical public" (1989, 140).

39. Habermas's generalizations have given rise to questions—concretely empirical ones—about whether or not television and other broadcast media actually do diminish our ability and inclination to engage in rational-critical debate. These questions have been taken up in promising ways by recent media scholars analyzing general trends—many negative but some positive—regarding televisual modes of representation in relation to a viable, democratic public sphere (Dahlgren 1995) or, relatedly, analyzing the often active and countercultural modes of reception of various fan communities (Jenkins 1992). Their general conclusions are that mass-media audiences are not merely passive, uncritical consumers but actually retain some critical distance and engage in much more complex processes of negotiation, appropriation, and debate than Habermas suggests.

40. One can accept that this was Habermas's intention without therefore agreeing with him that such a sphere actually existed. On these issues, see Schudson 1993.

41. Madison, Hamilton, and Jay all signed their contributions to the *Federalist* papers under the collective persona of "Publius." And the anti-Federalists used pseudonyms such as "Cato," "Agrippa," and "Vox Populi" (voice of the people). Their use of pseudonyms was clearly influenced by this emergent public print discourse. Such pseudonyms were no doubt meant in part to encapsulate the central message of these tracts and also to authorize them by association with the traditions of thought (Roman-republican, Greek-skeptic, or anti-aristocratic) that they named (see McDonald 1985, 68). At the same time, however, they had the effect of distancing these political writings from their authors and thereby universalizing their message.

42. For a well-documented historical critique of the institutionalization of the ideal of objectivity in professional journalism, see Schudson 1978. See also Tuchman 1974 and Gans 1980. Collectively, such studies suggest that, despite intentions, journalistic practices—such as the tendency to regard government officials as the most reliable sources on key issues—have actually led to a rather skewed style of reporting. The ironic point to note here is that the resulting bias is itself an effect of how objectivity has been defined and structurally implemented.

43. My use of the masculine pronoun here is intentional since only the masculine subject, as constructed, can be truly universal. In a culture within which the most common counterpart to "women's issues" is not "men's issues" but rather "social issues," to write as a woman is necessarily to write from a partisan perspective.

44. The notion of "cyber café" is not something I've concocted but rather relates to actually existing sites, or rather to an overlay of physical and virtual sites

together. The term refers to physical coffee bars that have popped up in various countries throughout the world, including the United States, India, South Africa, the United Kingdom, Australia, Italy, South Korea, and many more. What makes these *cyber* cafés is that they include, as one of their selling points, computers with Internet hookups at several of their tables, offering patrons the opportunity to sip their cappuccinos while surfing the Net—i.e., to "Sip 'n' Surf" (see http://www.sipnsurf.com/ [visited 21 November 2000]). Complicating the physical/virtual distinction further is that cyber cafés in the physical sense almost always have a virtual counterpart on the Web. These Web sites typically offer Internet services and information and also chat room links that allow online visitors to engage each other in spontaneous discussion. Despite the marginally different services and linguistic cultures of such sites, the discursive connection between the place of the coffeehouse or café, on the one hand, and computer-mediated conversation, on the other, is apparent in the self-descriptions of many of these physical/virtual cafés. For a comprehensive list of cyber cafés, see the Internet Café Guide at http://www.netcafeguide.com/ indexa.html (visited 21 November 2000).

45. Struthers is the spokesperson for the Save the Children child-sponsorship program.

46. Shapiro, in this essay, again invokes Foucault's concept of heterotopia without explaining it, treating the term self-evidently as a reference to "spaces of otherness" (1997, ¶2, n. 3). Here, however, he seems more willing to apply that concept to actual sites rather than to a mode of critical reading that foregrounds the spatial strategies presupposed by a discourse (cf., Shapiro 1992).

3. Hardware and Software

1. In the computing industry, the abbreviation PC has two meanings. It can refer specifically to a subset of personal computers—first developed by IBM and later cloned by other manufacturers—that employed the DOS operating system invented at Microsoft and that now use Microsoft Windows or IBM's OS/2. This is meant to distinguish these personal computers from the MacIntosh computer developed by Apple and employing its proprietary operating system: hence the labels "Mac" or "PC" on software products to designate the operating systems with which they are compliant. In this study, by contrast, I use the abbreviation PC in its second, generic sense: as a reference to the "personal computer," which includes both IBM clones and Macs.

2. This distinction, too, between technology and culture is analytical rather than actual. As Escobar reminds us, "any technology represents a cultural invention" (1994, 211).

3. This characterization owes much to my reading of J. David Bolter's study

Turing's Man: Western Culture in the Computer Age. Published in 1984, the same year as Gibson's *Neuromancer* and while the Internet was still in its infancy, Bolter's work was completed too soon to take computer networking into account and before the term *cyberspace* became fashionable. Perhaps for that reason, however, he is able to give a better sense of the different kind of physicality underlying the momentous shift from atoms to bits: he does so by providing an excellent account of what he refers to simply and appropriately as "Electronic Space" (1984, 80–99).

4. These comparisons and the utopian message of technological progress they convey were epitomized in the mid-1990s in a project conducted by students of the Moore School of Electrical Engineering at the University of Pennsylvania, where the ENIAC was developed. In commemoration (backhanded compliment?) of the fiftieth anniversary of the ENIAC, they designed what they call the "ENIAC-on-a-chip," a hardware component that performs all the basic functions of its bulky namesake but on a microchip slightly smaller than an average-size human pinky nail (see Van der Spiegel 1997).

5. Obvious parallels exist between Bolter's description of electromagnetic forces *working on bodies at a distance* and the Archimedean epistemology and ontology that, as I showed in chapter 2, Arendt associates with space flight. These parallels imply a strong affinity between computer technologies and power-as-leverage. I address this issue in the next chapter.

6. In Telephone, one child (the sender) quickly whispers a message to another child (an analog of the sender), who then tries to whisper the entire message to another child, and so on, until the last child in the communication chain recites the message out loud, and all giggle at how much the final message has changed from the original.

7. Barlow's description is actually of the current cyberspace, which involves not simply the space of computing but of inter-networked systems and the personal computers that access and help compose those systems. The ability to create an undetermined number of perfect digital replicas, however, follows from the characteristics of bits more fundamentally and precedes networking and the PC. It is important to note, too, that the expansiveness of electronic space is not exactly limitless since, as I have said, it depends on hardware innovations and access. In fact, as J. David Bolter argues, "Lack of space is one of the two principal limitations of the electronic world. The other is computer time. Making intelligent use of the space at hand is a cardinal virtue in the craft of computer programming" (1984, 83). The challenge for both programmers and computer engineers has been how to cram more bits into less and less hardware space, and they have in fact been remarkably successful at churning out upgraded components that process more data in less time and on smaller chips,

thereby expanding the logical space of computer systems while shrinking their physical size.

8. Recalling the discussion in chapter 1, then, an analog is a metaphor that represents a privileged, preexisting referent, and a digital simulation is a metonym that employs similitude to create its own referent.

9. In the late 1980s and early 1990s, archivists of the Charles Babbage Institute (CBI) at the University of Minnesota conducted a series of interviews with members of IPTO and DARPA and their various projects, including the network project. These interviews resulted in a report on the history of DARPA/IPTO (Norberg and O'Neill 1992). Both the interviews and the report, available through CBI, inform the history I provide here. I'd like to thank the archivists at CBI, especially Kevin Corbitt, for providing me with these resources.

10. The researchers at DARPA/IPTO were not the only ones interested in developing better communications networks for command-and-control purposes. The U.S. Air Force had commissioned an earlier study from RAND that resulted in an eleven-volume report by Paul Baran on the concept of "distributed networks." The report was completed around 1962 and published and distributed by RAND in 1964 (see Baran 1964). Baran's early work, however, did not result in the creation of a prototype network. Part of the reason for this was lack of funding at RAND and skepticism on the part of AT&T technicians still mired in a circuit-switching mindset (Baran 1990b). Although much of the subsequent technology was developed independently of Baran's early work (see Kahn 1990), some of the researchers connected with DARPA's network project were familiar with and influenced by his concepts (see, especially, Uncapher 1989; and Kleinrock 1990). Furthermore, the network that was later implemented by IPTO and that evolved into the Internet was based on essentially the same structural design for a survivable network that Baran described in his early work. For these reasons, the following discussion draws heavily from Baran.

11. These protocols were developed by Vinton Cerf and Robert Kahn under the auspices of DARPA. Kahn at the time was a program manager for DARPA/IPTO (see Kahn 1990).

12. In his description of the 1962 ARPA conference that led to the network idea, Larry Roberts (the IPTO director, from 1969 to 1973, who launched the network project) notes: "I came to the conclusion that the next thing, really, was making all of this incompatible [research] work compatible with some sort of networking. In other words, we had all of these people *doing different things everywhere,* and they were all not sharing their research very well. . . . what I concluded was that we had to do something about communications, and that really, the idea of the *galactic network* that Lick [J. C. R. Licklider, the first director of IPTO, from 1962 to 1964, and again from 1974 to 1975] talked about . . . was

something that we had to start seriously thinking about" (1989, my emphasis). Roberts is popularly recognized as a pioneer of network communication (see Fjermedal 1995, 64).

13. As I have said, the distinction between bits and atoms is typically overstated (see, for example, Negroponte 1996). Nonetheless, one can reasonably argue, as I do here, that the redundancy and autonomy built into the networking infrastructure that evolved into the Internet do make the flow of bits in network space less susceptible to, as Luke puts it, "physiocentric space" (1997, ¶8), that is, less susceptible to at least minor changes in the material infrastructure, like physical damage to part of the network. Indeed, that was the point of these developments. That said, however, the Internet is not as "robust" from damage as early researchers had hoped. The weblike design and proliferation of nodes may allow the Internet to route around problems at particular geographic locations, but because bit space is both physical and logical, all computer space is potentially vulnerable to logical damage as well, i.e., from computer viruses. As I note briefly in the next chapter, considerable attention is now being turned to this type of vulnerability.

14. Once Internet access opened to a variety of individuals, many governments became anxious to regulate online activity, pointing to the dangers posed by terrorists, dissidents, hackers, and pedophiles. Hence, what was initially intended as a source of national security is now seen by some as a source of national insecurity (a potential threat). I discuss this paradox in more detail in Saco 1999.

15. For a good, nontechnical summary of these phases and how the current Internet works, see the online multimedia lecture by Charles Botsford (1999). Botsford repeatedly misstates the NSF as the "NFS" in the audio portion of the presentation and misidentifies Web creator Tim Berners-Lee as "Tim Beyers-Lee." These are minor errors, however, in what is otherwise a useful introduction for laypeople. A more detailed technical discussion of the Internet's architecture, infrastructure, and protocols is available in Rybaczyk 1998.

16. For a graphic representation of this, see the topology maps hosted by the "Atlas of Cyberspaces" project at http://www.cybergeography.org/atlas/topology.html (visited 18 October 2000).

17. "Public" IXs provide transit for any ISP willing to subscribe and pay for the exchange service. See, for example, the NAP product page for Pacific Bell at http://www.pacbell.com/Products_Services/Business/ProdInfo_1/1,1973,146-1-,00.html (visited 18 October 2000). A hyperlinked directory of public Internet exchanges can be found at http://www.ep.net/ (visited 30 November 2001).

18. Additional details about the peering connections analyzed in Gareiss

1999 are available in tables 1 and 2 of that study. Unfortunately, those tables are not properly linked off the main page. I found them, respectively, at http://www.eco-bay.com/Overview/Infos/Links/Tabelle1/body_tabelle1.html and http://www.eco-bay.com/Overview/Infos/Links/Tabelle2/body_tabelle2.html (both visited 9 October 2000).

19. An Asymmetric Digital Subscriber Line (ADSL) is a faster alternative to modem dial-up access for home users, delivering more Internet traffic over a large, unused portion of bandwidth on existing telephone lines. I describe ADSL in more detail in chapter 5.

20. A "hop" is an intermediate connection through which data is routed as it flows from one network device to another or as it travels through the Internet. Although tracerouting (a diagnostic utility) doesn't perfectly map the hops that a packet *will* take through the Internet (see Carl 1999), traceroute utilities do provide information about how packets are likely to travel from origin to destination. In this example, the packets took fewer hops because the same ISP was involved at both ends; in fact, since the packets began and ended on the same network, I wasn't technically *inter*-networking when I used my CyberGate dial-up account to access CyberGate's home page.

21. A significant issue in this respect is whether uploading something onto the Internet constitutes a sort of export. On this, see my discussion of the Zimmermann case in chapter 5.

22. Here I am paraphrasing computer historian Bob Cringely, author and host of the three-part PBS documentary *Triumph of the Nerds* (1996). The following discussion draws from Cringely's fascinating account of the invention of personal computing and the nerds it turned into billionaires.

23. Ownership figures, however, do not reflect actual usage. According to another report, the increase of computer use at work throughout the 1990s made home PC owners "technology-weary": as a result, between 1995 and 1999, the percentage of people who actually used their home computers fell from 90 percent to 53 percent (internet.com 1999b).

24. While average U.S. retail prices, in the mid-1990s, for basic desktop systems (including computer, monitor, printer, and modem) were in the $1,500 to $2,000 range—and high-end multimedia systems (with CD-ROMS and advanced video capabilities) sold in the $2,000 to $3,500 range—basic system prices dropped below the $1,000 mark by 2000, and below the $500 mark for those willing to sign up for three to four years of Internet service from providers such as MSN and CompuServe. Subscription rates for unlimited Internet access through a modem dial-up account currently average $20 per month. According to one forecast, however, Internet access will become, like call waiting, "a bonus feature provided by telephone companies" and may someday cost as little as

$2 per month (Simons 1997). Decreasing costs in Internet-ready PCs and appliances and in access subscription rates are contributing further to the growth of the Internet. By July 2000, according to one report (Charny 2000), more than half of the households in the United States (52 percent, or approximately 144 million people) had Internet access. Another study predicts that the global population of the Internet will reach "250 million in 2002, and 300 million by 2005" (internet.com 1999a), figures comparable to the size of the U.S. population, with an estimated 285,641,362 according to the U.S. Census Bureau's "Population Clock," at http://www.census.gov/main/www/popclock.html (visited 30 November 2001).

25. An Internet protocol (IP) address is a numerical address (more often a range of addresses) assigned to computers connected to the Internet. Site addresses are typically static, whereas users' addresses tend to be dynamically assigned by their ISPs and reassigned each time users log on. IP addresses under the current version-four system (IPv4) are composed of four groups of one to three numbers separated by periods, e.g., 64.58.76.229 (the IP address for the Yahoo site in November 2001). Most Internet users are unaware of IP addresses, however, because these are translated (by a user's Domain Name Server or DNS) to domain-name aliases, on the theory that a numerical address is harder to remember than www.yahoo.com. In addition to name recognition and recall, domain names make it possible for registrants to change ISPs and, by extension, IP addresses without having to change the domain names by which they are commonly known in the online world. That, too, is a consequence of the random access nature of computing: the fact that data can move to a new physical location (e.g., a different Web site) and still be accessible because it retains the same address label or the same domain name alias. The change occurs behind the scenes, as file allocation tables (FATs) on single computers or domain name tables on the Internet are updated to reflect, respectively, memory address or Internet address reassignments.

26. Many Web site owners (both individuals and companies) object to deep linking, arguing that they have important information, disclaimers, and occasionally also banner ads on their home pages. They may also object to others linking to their sites by "framing," making their sites appear from within another site's page frames. Browser frames allow site designers to partition the browser window into different segments or "frames," typically with a title banner in a top frame, a sidebar site index with hyperlinks along the left, and a main frame where the Web content for all activated links appears. There may also be a frame devoted to banner ads. For the most part, the title and index frames remain static, and all the dynamic surfing pops up in the large frame devoted to linked content. Because the content displayed in the main area is framed by titles and

indexes pertaining to the linking site, framing can give the false impression that all displayed content is owned and provided by the site whose name continues to be prominently displayed in one of these adjacent frames. Even the owners of personal Web pages, who may have no financial stakes in how their sites are accessed, may object to framing insofar as it confuses ownership and interferes with the aesthetic effects of their own Web page designs. For a summary discussion and case studies on the legal issues surrounding these various forms of linking, see Raysman and Brown 2000. For a spirited defense of deep linking as "an underlying principle of the World Wide Web," see Imboden 1999.

27. This experience obviously varies depending on system resources and the functions being performed. When resources are taxed, a computer user may become (almost painfully) aware of this processing, waiting up to several minutes for the results of her operation as the hard drive visibly (through its indicator light) and audibly (through its grinding) rearranges data. Slow access speeds (especially through modem dial-ups) and busy Web servers, moreover, can create a frustrating lag while surfing, a point caustically conveyed in references to the "World Wide Wait." The continuing drive toward speedier multimedia computers, a broader-bandwidth infrastructure (e.g., through fiber optics) and faster access (e.g., through a cable modem or a Digital Subscriber Line [DSL]) is helping to minimize these lags.

28. Although the PC has played an important role in providing individualized Internet access to home users, the development of low-end and low-cost "Internet appliances" (for example, cable-box type devices, like WebTV, that hook people's TV sets to the Internet) may, according to some analysts, rival the PC's role as the premiere Internet access device for individuals (Simons 1997; see also Oracle CEO Larry Ellison, interviewed on *Triumph of the Nerds* 1996). An extensive analysis of these alternatives is beyond the scope of this study. However, based on a brief review of one vendor's Web site (Network Computer, Inc.), this "hybrid" technology (TV and Internet) appears to be developing according to the paradigm at work in broadcast media, that is, as an easy-to-use device for information retrieval rather than as a medium for interactive communication with diverse others. This trend—while consistent with liberal-democratic assumptions—would undercut claims about the Internet as a space for participatory democratic communication, thus making this an important area for future research. See, for example, NCI's "Enhanced TV" Web pages, beginning at http://www.nc.com/etv/ntvindex.html (visited 7 January 1998).

29. Put another way, I think Stone assimilates Gibson's cyberspace to the Internet's cyberspace, or rather to what the Internet has come to mean for some (maybe many) computer users, apparently including Stone herself.

30. The short story first appeared in the July 1982 issue of *Omni* magazine.

An electronic reprint (Gibson 1982) is available online at the Cyberpunk Project site.

31. Reagan's free-enterprise ethic may have sparked Gibson's imagination, but ironically, it is Clinton's deregulatory, media-related policies, enacted in the Telecommunications Act of 1996, that may more directly help to bring Gibson's pessimistic cyberspace into being. On these issues, see, for example, Benton Foundation 1996. I return to this briefly in the conclusion, below, and in more detail in chapter 5.

32. Although I haven't seen any neuro-probes yet, the goal of virtual reality (VR) research is precisely to develop computer interfaces that provide this total immersion of the senses, a point implied succinctly by Negroponte when he notes, "The idea behind VR is to deliver a sense of 'being there'" (1996, 117). For a nontechnical explanation of developments in VR, see Hamit 1993. Woolley, by contrast, provides an intelligent (though occasionally overstated) criticism of "the excitable claims of virtual realists to have the power to create their own worlds" (1992, 60).

33. Although he does not cite McLuhan in this vein, William Mitchell, too, evokes this sense of the electronic extension of the human nervous system in his discussion of what he calls the *bodynet* (1995, 28–31). For a more explicit and theoretical application of McLuhan's ideas to cyberspace, see especially Woolley 1992 (123–35). Ron Deibert's work (1996, 1997) has been particularly suggestive in revising the "medium theory"of McLuhan and especially Harold Innis for the study of international relations in the context of a "Hypermedia Environment," suggesting more complex connections between communication, space, and identity in that, for medium theory, the media are not just channels for communications between environments, but instead epoch-changing technologies that constitute new environments all their own for new kinds of interactions and ways of being (Deibert 1996, 34). For an introduction to medium theory, see Meyrowitz 1994.

34. The site is located at http://www.eff.org/pub/Net_culture/Global_village/ (visited 29 January 1996).

35. That many of these hackers came from comfortable homes in the suburbs of Silicon Valley is a fact that seems to have been ignored in the creation of this mythos.

36. The displacement of public-access principles by profit-maximizing motives has been evident in other computer-related policy developments. See Miller 1996 (129–31) for a discussion of how public interest provisions were dropped from the Communications Act of 1994.

37. I discuss this further in chapter 5 in connection with the vision underlying the metaphor of the Information Superhighway.

4. Wetware

1. See Ross 1991 for a provocative critical account of the construction of computer virus scares and the related construction through vilification of hackers as a threat (a point to which I return in the second section below).

2. Donna Haraway's seminal article on "cyborgs" (1989 [1985]) fits in this category in a slightly tangential but significant way. Rather than conducting an empirical exploration into how computers are redefining us, Haraway asserts those redefinitions as her point of departure in what amounts to a memorable and often convincing polemic on feminist theorizing. Apropos this, she offers—explicitly as a "manifesto"—the biotechnical image of the cybernetic organism (part human, part machine) as a metaphor for the hybrid, postmodern identities of the high-tech, late twentieth century, arguing that the cyborg is the appropriate symbol for an anti-essentialist feminist politics in the context of integrated circuits. It is worth noting, however, that her provocative manifesto has become, in the words of Andrew Ross (in Penley and Ross 1991, 1), a "cult text," inspiring more than a few critical studies on the nexus between technology and culture (see, especially, Penley and Ross 1991; Stone 1996).

3. I mean this in two senses. First, online versions of the Jernigan story (discussed in the introduction) that attempt to rationalize the medical invasion of his body by reference to his being an executed killer exemplify how carceral discourses in general are projected into the electronic space of the Internet. But, second, more direct and, in a sense, contradictory examples of "wiring prisons" exist. Many corrections agencies and facilities, for instance, now have home pages on the World Wide Web; see, for example, the Federal Bureau of Prisons (at http://www.bop.gov/) and the Corrections Connection (at http://www.corrections.com/) (both visited 24 November 2000). Furthermore, although many states prohibit prison inmates from accessing the Internet directly, a number of prison-reform advocacy groups overseeing letter-writing programs between prisoners and others outside prison have begun acting as Internet intermediaries (e.g., Inmates Classified and Cyberspace Inmates, both cited in Hunter 1997). These third-party services post inmates' messages and home pages on the WWW and in turn deliver weekly hardcopy responses to inmates, thereby providing them with, as one commentator put it, "a space outside the cell" (Hunter 1997). This second and more literal wiring (connectivity) of prisons and prisoners to "a space outside" creates yet another heterotopic contradiction: this time by subtly challenging the whole notion of spatial confinement implied in the term and spatial practice of *incarceration*.

4. To be sure, compatibility problems have, in the past, made such conversions more difficult. The trend now, especially in business software, however, is

toward making programs interoperable across different versions of the same program, across different programs that perform the same function (e.g., different kinds of database programs), across different types of programs in the same environment (e.g., interoperability between an e-mail program and a word-processing program), and even across different platforms (i.e., operating systems). This trend makes data more universally accessible, despite differences in the types of computers and programs people are using. More to the point, interoperability is the principle governing software development (e.g., HTML, Java applets, and CGI forms for interactive database searches) on the World Wide Web, which is how most of us experience the Internet these days.

5. Lyon at least concedes that surveillance is "neither overwhelmingly negative in its effects nor incorrigibly evil in its character," and he considers, relatedly, that the metaphors of Big Brother and panopticon (and, implicitly, Super-panopticon) may be outdated (1994, 223, 78–79).

6. Nancy Fraser makes a similar point, arguing that Foucault's focus on institutional discourses ignores the involvement of noninstitutional actors, such as social movements, in politicizing issues; consequently, his account "misses the contestatory interplay among hegemonic and nonhegemonic" (1991, 186 n. 26). Relatedly, Katherine Hayles observes that "when actual situations involving embodied agents are considered, limits [to surveillance and control] appear that are obscured when the Panopticon is considered only as an abstract mechanism" (1992, 152).

7. The population census is a common site for such contestations, which can occasionally motivate a reevaluation of the categories themselves (see U.S. Census Bureau 1997a). These tactics are mentioned, as well, by Bill Tribe in the video *Urbicide: A Sarajevo Diary* (1993), documenting his return to the war-torn city, during a momentary cease-fire, to rescue his ex-wife and his son-in-law. Tribe notes that after ethnic conflicts had arisen but shortly before the siege of Sarajevo began, Bosnian citizens filling out a census survey replied to questions regarding their ethnicity with nonsensical responses like the ones in my example, pointedly refusing to contribute to the kind of divisiveness that led (their refusals notwithstanding) to their victimization. This suggests, of course, that such contestations may fail to make a difference, although I find their symbolic force very compelling in this context.

8. The hysteria surrounding computer virus scares, to which Morris's program has been articulated, is itself a discursive construct. In his analysis of its creation, Andrew Ross argues compellingly that the virus scare is a "profitable ideological moment" in the guise of a "'social menace,'" aimed at redefining intellectual property rights to reduce the effects of information technologies and the new forms of power they enable. It is in this context, he continues, that "a

deviant social class or group has been defined and categorized as 'enemies of the state' to help rationalize a general law-and-order clampdown on free and open information exchange" (1991, 112–13). In citing this, I don't mean to underestimate the damage to data and equipment that can be caused by computer viruses. However, reactions to the threat posed by hackers and viruses are out of proportion to the damage they actually cause. User errors, hardware problems, and programming flaws—such as those causing critical feedback loops that have brought down whole systems—occur with more frequency and generally result in greater financial loss.

9. Sterling 1993 (1–39) discusses one such incident: the January 1990 crash of AT&T's long-distance system. Even after the software glitch was discovered, officials continued to suspect that hackers had introduced a "logic bomb" into the system. This suspicion resulted in the May 1990 nationwide crackdown on electronic fraud called "Operation Sundevil" (Sterling 1993, 147–59). It involved the FBI, the U.S. Secret Service, and local police in several cities in a simultaneous, nationwide raid and seizure of the computers and files of several "known hackers." To the victims and many onlookers, the crackdown was a gross violation of several civil rights. This gave rise to the July 1990 formation of the Electronic Frontier Foundation (EFF), a group of computer professionals and hobbyists concerned with raising public awareness about civil liberties in cyberspace and with supporting litigation on behalf of victims and in the public interest (Barlow 1990; EFF 1990a and 1990b; see also Sterling 1993, 217–301). I discuss the EFF in more detail in the next chapter.

10. In contrast to standard e-mail programs, which automatically plug the sender's e-mail address into the message header, anonymous remailers, as the name implies, are programs (often installed at network sites designed specifically for this purpose) that resend e-mail messages through anonymous Internet addresses so that recipients cannot determine who sent the message (Dibbell 1993b). The legality of remailing systems has been contested in the United States and elsewhere (Froomkin 1995). Ambiguities surrounding changes in Finnish laws concerning e-mail privacy protection, for example, led to the demise of one of the first and most successful remailer sites (Schwartz 1996).

11. In Plato's *Republic*, Glaucon tells the story of a shepherd named Gyges who finds a gold ring of invisibility and begins doing unjust acts simply by virtue of the fact that he can now conceal his misdeeds. For Glaucon, the story proves that "a man is just, not willingly . . . but of necessity, for wherever any one thinks that he can safely be unjust, there he is unjust" (Plato 1973, 44). I am not the only writer to make what seemed to me at one time a novel connection between Plato's retelling of this myth and the implications of electronic anonymity; see also Schwartz 1996. Moreover, the sentiment this analogy expresses—

namely, that human beings are immoral by nature—has been applied to the Net even by computer civil libertarians like John Perry Barlow, who once remarked with slithering simplicity that "utterly unbridled liberty seems to favor the reptile in us" (1993b).

12. As Pasquale Pasquino reminds us, however, law enforcement agencies are only the most obvious of the multitude of social institutions, practices, and knowledges according to which a population is policed (1991, 116; see also Foucault 1991, 92).

13. I analyze the politics of encryption in more detail in the next chapter.

14. For more detailed descriptions of this underground, see, especially, Barlow 1990, Meyer and Thomas 1990, and Sterling 1993. That this underground community is male dominated is particularly well captured by Netta Gilboa (1996) in her contribution to an excellent collection of essays on gender in cyberspace (Cherny and Weise 1996).

15. For analyses of hacker nicknames and their significance, see especially Bechar-Israeli 1995 and Meyer and Thomas 1990.

16. Brand's credentials as an information source on both the '60s counterculture and the computer underground are impressive. He helped to found the *Whole Earth Catalog*, the *Whole Earth 'Lectronic Link* (aka "the WELL," one of the earliest and most famous computer conferencing services), and the now-annual Hackers Convention. He is listed as a "boardmember emeritus" of the EFF. He is also said to have written the first article on hackers, in 1973 (for *Rolling Stone*), and to have been the first author to use the term *personal computer* in print, in a 1974 publication entitled *Two Cybernetic Frontiers* (see EFF 1996a; Sterling 1993, 224–26). The WELL, as I show in the next section, provides much of the inspiration for Howard Rheingold's study, *The Virtual Community: Homesteading on the Electronic Frontier* (1993).

17. In fact, the growth of the Internet, according to one source, actually contributed in two significant ways to the demise of hacking as an elite practice: by providing a forum in which systems operators could warn each other about vulnerabilities in their systems that hackers could exploit and also by extending access to "formerly elite hangouts" (hacker bulletin boards and chat rooms) to "naive hacker-wannabes" (Roush 1995). Ironically then, despite the democratic impulses underlying the Hacker Ethic, "[t]he culture," as a disillusioned hacker using the alias "Asrock" put it, "began to die out when it got popular" (cited in Roush).

18. Still, it should be noted that data manipulation has also led to the development of search engines that have extended this paradigm of information retrieval to individuals as well, making the Internet more navigable. In fact, I have

been able to find the bulk of my research on the Internet itself, thanks to Web search engines like HotBot, Alta Vista, and Yahoo.

19. Subscriber networks are commercial, for-profit, proprietary networks that supply individual login accounts, often through local dial-up access numbers, primarily for the residential market. These accounts give individuals access to e-mail services, message forums, chat rooms, and various database services. Subscriber networks developed in the late 1970s—i.e., before the invention of Internet protocols—but many of them now also serve as Internet gateways for their customers. In general, the character of computer-mediated communication is the same on subscriber networks as on the Internet, with the important exceptions that commercial networks have always had advertisements on them, that they monitor and censor all of their message boards (principally for foul language), and that they occasionally drop subscribers for misconduct. Hence, online interactions tend to be more regulated and commodified on subscriber networks. See, on this, Rheingold's critique of Prodigy (1993, 276–79).

20. The acronym MUD stands variably for multi-user dimension, domain, or dungeon. The last of these is a reference to the nonelectronic, medieval role-playing game of Dungeons and Dragons (D&D), which has been the inspiration for some MUDs. Among the most significant derivatives of MUDs are "MUDs object-oriented" (MOOs), which allow users—in the form of their online avatar or persona—to perform actions (e.g., "move," "get," "look") on or in relation to a variety of objects, an interactive element that helps constitute the space of the MOO as a shared, social space, a multi-user space constituted as much by the actions of others as by one's own.

21. On the variety of practices and social experiences people can have in MUDs, see especially Turkle 1995, Reid 1995, and the "Textual Realities" essays, respectively, by Kendall, Fanderclai, and McRae (in Cherny and Weise 1996, 205–63).

22. See, especially, the essays collected in Jones 1995 and in Cherny and Weise 1996.

23. This is especially true of synchronous (real-time) exchanges, like Internet Relay Chat (IRC). Although participants can experience some lag time (waiting for their responses to post and sometimes finding that others' responses post before theirs so that the conversation itself is slightly out of sequence), the lag is sufficiently short for members to get a sense that others are present, sharing the same space and the same (near-) real-time. Similar feelings of presentness, however, can be experienced from the asynchronous mode of communication of the various message-posting services. That is, because other people's messages are accessible whenever we are present, those others appear to be immediately present with us. Mark Dery makes a similar point: "On-line conversations exhibit a

curious half-life; as the reader scrolls down-screen, scanning the lively back-and-forth of a discussion that may go back weeks, months, or even years, he experiences the puns, philippics, true confessions, rambling dissertations, and Generation X-er one-liners as if they were taking place in real time—which, for the reader watching them flow past on his screen, they are" (1993, 561). In this respect, cyberspace isn't only heterotopic (mixing up the here and there), but also in significant ways heterochronic, confusing past and present in one personally experienced duration of "connection time."

24. Advances in multimedia capabilities are making real-time video conferencing more widespread. As resources and bandwidths expand, therefore, the face of Internet exchanges may change, with projected video images of users becoming part of the customary way in which they interact with others online. As it is, many Web users post scanned photos of themselves on their home pages. But the bulk of social exchanges on the Internet, via chats, newsgroups, and e-mail listservers, is still predominantly textual and hence faceless. Furthermore, even with the projection of graphic representations of bodies into our online exchanges, the connection between those images and a particular user is based entirely on taking someone at her word since users can post essentially any picture as their own, and digital images can be manipulated and enhanced in a variety of undetectable ways, as my discussion of morphing, in the previous chapter, indicates.

25. Drawing from other, similar incidents, Spender's (1995) well-intentioned but often underinformed analysis of women and cyberspace comes to the same conclusions.

26. Though I agree that CMC raises a number of gender issues that need to be explored (and certainly more extensively than I can manage here), I find these arguments—that women are more prone than men to being duped or mistreated in cyberspace—more insulting than the kinds of identity "deceptions" that can occur online. Perhaps, however, I am exhibiting the sort of shift in reaction to this incident that Turkle has observed (1995, 230). Inasmuch as this was one of the first incidents of cross-dressing on a public network, early reactions tended to focus on the notion that a man had deceived several women by posing as a woman himself. "Today what disturbs us," Turkle explains, "is when the shifting norms of the virtual world bleed into real life" (i.e., in this case, that an online persona had been used to procure dates in the offline world). Turkle's point is overstated insofar as some observers are still bothered by the lie itself; I think she's generally correct, however, in suggesting that, over time, many of the men *and* women who habituate the Net have come to view gender switching as an ordinary and even normal part of online interactions. Of course, computer cross-dressing is not the only issue of relevance to women on the

Internet: for a particularly insightful and refreshingly inconclusive set of studies on gender and cyberspace, see Cherny and Weise 1996.

27. This is not to suggest that gender concerns are trivial—quite the contrary. Those issues, however, are sometimes raised in essentialist terms that affirm a unitary identity and a shared set of interests for all women by virtue of the fact that we all seem to have the same kind of sexed body. Stone raises more profound questions in the sense that she inquires into how bodies and identities become linked in the first place and how online practices often sever those links.

28. It bears emphasizing that this failure wasn't simply because Julie's friends felt betrayed by Lewin since, as I have said, he actually went online as himself before the Julie ruse was discovered. In fact, as Stone tells the story, Lewin had the Julie persona introduce the group "to her new friend, Sanford Lewin," whom Julie presented as "absolutely wonderful, charming, graceful, intelligent, and eminently worthy of their most affectionate attention" (1996, 77). The problem was that "Sanford's Sanford persona," as Stone puts it, couldn't live up to his own build and was nowhere near as interesting as his Julie persona.

29. The example of the turtles proverb is one that seems to make the rounds a lot in poststructuralist theory discussions. The argument is an anti-essentialist one, claiming that all social reality (including individual identity) is itself social constructs overlaid by other social constructs with no foundation that is simply given.

30. Here I am reading Butler through Hayles's distinction between *embodiment* and *body*. For Hayles, "Embodiment differs from the concept of the body in that the body is always normative relative to some set of criteria. . . . [It is] a normalized construct. . . . In contrast to the body, embodiment is contextual, enwebbed within the specifics of place, time, physiology and culture that together comprise enactment. Embodiment never coincides exactly with 'the body,' however that normalized concept is understood. Whereas the body is an idealized form that gestures toward a Platonic reality, embodiment is the specific instantiation generated from the noise of difference. *Relative to the body, embodiment is other and elsewhere, at once excessive and deficient in its infinite variations, particularities, and abnormalities*" (1992, 153–54, my emphasis). As for the connection between the two, Hayles argues that embodiment is the *"mechanism"* through which the discursive abstraction we call "the body" is made possible, involving incorporating practices that are not reducible to the inscribing practices by which the body is effected (1992, 156, Hayles's emphasis). This reading may not be wholly consistent with Butler's theory, though I think it actually clarifies her position inasmuch as it helps to explain how the performative repetition of a norm can fail to work (e.g., when the embodiment of the norm is excessive or deficient), which failure may, in turn, denaturalize that norm.

31. It is productive, and not simply limiting, in the sense that the different relationships culturally established between the body and the self are constitutive of several of our workaday identities, including gender, race, and even, as Stone insightfully points out, citizenship (1996, 40–41, 79), a point to which I return below.

32. This claim that a material substrate still matters typically becomes the basis for making materialist arguments against discursive ones (e.g., Ebert 1995). Ultimately, that seems to me a false distinction. However, I do agree, and have indeed been arguing, that Foucault, at least, focused his studies on practices of inscription to the exclusion of practices of incorporation.

33. I had to laugh when I originally typed this example. In the process of deliberately misspelling this phrase to make my point about how typos can disclose "the imperfect human," I tried typing *t-e-h*, but my word-processing program automatically corrected it to *t-h-e*. I'll let readers draw their own conclusions.

34. I don't mean to conflate the notions of nation and state here. My argument is about the constitution of citizenship in relation to the sovereign state; on the other hand, nationalist sentiments are often an integral component of that constitution as an identity, if not specifically as a legal status (see Leca 1992, 21–23).

35. In practice, the protection of national security interests can and often does entail sacrificing some bodies: primarily soldiers and also the nameless numbers of individuals cast out in strategic calculations as "collateral damage."

36. This is from the National Mail Voter Registration Form (http://www.fec.gov/votregis/pdf/nvra.pdf), an Adobe Acrobat file linked off the U.S. Federal Elections Commission's National Voter Registration Form page (http://www.fec.gov/votregis/vr.htm), retrieved on 24 November 2000.

37. U.S. citizens overseas can, of course, obtain an absentee ballot in lieu of voting in person, but even in this case, the Federal Post Card Application (FPCA) they have to complete requires overseas military personnel and civilians outside U.S. borders to locate themselves within a specific U.S. state by giving, respectively, their legal residence or their last stateside place of residence. See the *2000–2001 Voting Assistance Guide,* available as a set of Adobe Acrobat files from the Federal Voting Assistance Program Web site at http://www.fvap.ncr.gov/vagoo.html (visited 24 November 2000).

38. Note that I have been assuming that an embodied person *is* responsible for creating the virtual personae I talk about here. As it is, however, some of the things said and done by the characters in a MUD, for example, are actually spoofed (initiated, illicitly, by another online participant) and sometimes using an automated script, meaning that a program rather than a human typist is

more directly responsible for particular actions. As Lynn Cherny (1995) notes, locating agency is particularly difficult in the case of these scripted interactions. With technological capabilities expanding as rapidly as they are, moreover, programmers may soon (if they can't already) be able to devise sophisticated programs that entirely create their own richly textured, interactive personae. For reasons of length, however, I am bracketing from this analysis the additional issues raised by the possibility of artificial intelligence (AI) agents: put simply, there's no room for Max Headroom in this analysis.

39. The ideal of universal citizenship, which Young reveals to be a disembodied abstraction, is the product of a tradition of democratic theory (e.g., Beiner 1995) that attends to citizenship as political agency without considering how that identity is also about managing the population. Such theories, therefore, tend to ignore how it is that the citizen is made politically apprehensible through the mechanism of the locatable body. Even Young fails to raise these issues, focusing instead on how the ideal of universal citizenship, by its very abstractions, excludes women and minorities from what she conceives, exclusively, as an empowering identity.

5. Hacking Cyberspace

1. Both aspects of code work fall under the general term *cryptology,* the study of code (Bamford 1983, 49).

2. The National Institute of Standards and Technology (NIST) and the Automated Systems Division of the Department of Treasury were the two government escrow agencies named by the Clinton administration in its original Clipper proposal (U.S. Department of Justice 1994).

3. The comparative scarcity of nongovernmental advocates of Clipper helps to account for why I sometimes seem to construct the pro-Clipper stance, reductively, as the perspective of the state and its agencies. That the pro-Clipper camp seems more unified is perhaps also a function of the extent to which surveillance capabilities have become central features of government, administration, and enforcement practices.

4. Deriving from a synthesis of the terms *cipher* (code) and *cyberpunk* (the high-tech-rebel genre of speculative fiction popularized by William Gibson and others), *cypherpunk* connotes a sense of antiauthoritarianism through encryption. The term, according to Levy, refers less to a formal group than to an ethos: "Anyone who decides to spread personal crypto or its gospel is a traveler in the territory of Cypherpunk" (1993, 8). For a quasi-mission statement, see May 1992.

5. Barlow's lyrics (which include "The Music Never Stopped" and "Hell in a Bucket," among others) and his cyber-libertarian writings are archived at the

"John Perry Barlow Library" on EFF's site, at http://www.eff.org/~barlow/ library.html (last visited 25 July 2000).

6. Since export restrictions affect both software and hardware and in both computer and telephone products, opposition from the business community has actually included a broader coalition of about fifty software, computer, and telecommunications companies, among them Apple Computer, AT&T, Autodesk, Borland International, IBM, Lotus, Microsoft, Novell, Sun Microsystems, Sybase, and WordPerfect, some of which are also members of the lobby groups Software Publishers Association (SPA) and Business Software Alliance (BSA) (Dinsdale 1994; Maize 1995b). Despite its opposition, however, AT&T, according to one source, had already begun integrating the Clipper chip into its line of "secure" telephones by June 1994 (Levy 1994, 50).

7. *Wired* is described by *Newsweek* as the "*Rolling Stone* for the Computer Generation" (cited in White 1995, 23). The magazine has an online version (at http://www.wired.com/wired/) and an affiliated Internet-wide search engine called *HotBot* (at http://www.hotbot.com), both now part of the Lycos Network (last visited 31 August 2000). For the magazine's anti-Clipper views, see *Wired* 1993.

8. Screen resolution—an adjustable software setting limited to the amount of memory available on the video adapter card in a computer—is denoted in terms of the number of horizontal pixels by vertical pixels displayed on the monitor. A pixel, of course, is a dot of color, which, in the informational world of computers, is equivalent to a graphical datum. Read this way, screen resolutions determine how much graphical information is displayed on the monitor relative to its hardware dimensions. Monitor size and monitor resolution (in contrast to screen resolution) determine the absolute size and density of the image displayed. For example, on a computer that is set to a screen resolution of 640 x 480 pixels, an image of the same size would occupy the entire screen, and it would look smaller on a fourteen-inch monitor than on a seventeen-inch monitor. The same 640 x 480 image would occupy less than one-fourth of the screen area on a computer set to a screen resolution of 1280 x 1024 pixels. The standard for older color monitors and video adapter cards was a combination of a fourteen-inch monitor and a display set to 256 colors with a resolution of 640 x 480 pixels. Falling prices on computer equipment, however, are helping to make seventeen-inch color monitors a standard, with video cards capable of delivering a splash of over sixteen million colors with resolutions of 640 x 480, 800 x 600, 1024 x 768, 1280 x 1024, and even 1600 x 1200 for those who can tolerate slightly smaller print. According to several Web statistics based on browser and IP data collected from page hits (visits), the most common screen resolution, preferred by over 50 percent of Web users, is 800 x 600 pixels (see, for example,

internet.com 2000). These statistics, by the way, are simple to obtain. A short Java script embedded in the HTML code of a Web page can report this data back to any of a number of data-collecting sites that offer statistical services to Web designers. See, for example, http://www.TheCounter.com/ (visited 6 September 2000).

9. These dimensions refer to the welcome banner on the White House home page at http://www.whitehouse.gov/ (visited 31 August 2000).

10. A background graphic embedded in the page replicates itself as it blends into the image map, so the image appears, in fact, to occupy the entire screen space regardless of resolution. These graphics are part of the English language home page for the Vatican City, at http://www.vatican.va/phome_en.htm (visited 31 August 2000). The pages for the other languages employ similar graphics and are, therefore, just as impressive.

11. Less basic but increasingly common are the frames, CGI interactive forms, secured pages, and Java scripts that may also be designed into Web pages, particularly those for e-commerce sites.

12. This claim has been made, for example, by Apple cofounder Steve Jobs (cited in Schalit 1996). In Bob Cringely's history of personal computing, Jobs is portrayed as one of the visionaries who democratized computing by helping create some of the first successful and affordable desktop units (*Triumph of the Nerds* 1996). In a 1996 *Wired* interview, however, Jobs reveals a rather business-oriented notion of what counts as democracy in cyberspace. Question: "What about the Web as the great democratizer?" Answer: "If you look at things I've done in my life, they have an element of democratizing. The Web is an incredible democratizer. A small company can look as large as a big company and be as accessible as a big company on the Web. Big companies spend hundreds of millions of dollars building their distribution channels. And the Web is going to completely neutralize that advantage" (cited in Wolf 1996, 3).

13. The politics and semiotics of Internet domain names are, in fact, more varied and complex than this. U.S. government, educational, commercial, networking, and organizational sites, respectively, commonly have *.gov, *.edu, *.com, *.net, and *.org suffixes, while non-U.S. Web registrants use the two-letter codes assigned to their countries (for example, *.ca for Canada and *.jp for Japan). Although cyberspace "real estate" is virtually unlimited, popular domain name prefixes and suffixes are not. In fact, short, pithy, and recognizable secondary domain names (prefixes) in the popular *.com primary domain name area have been more or less exhausted by U.S. businesses. To help offset these limitations, seven new suffixes—.biz, .info, .name, .pro, .museum, .aero, and .coop—were approved in 2000 and are currently being implemented (Swartz 2000). These limitations, moreover, have already spawned a number of legal disputes, particularly over trademark infringements by "cybersquatters"

(individuals registering well-known trademarks as domain names in the hopes of selling the registered names back to the trademark owners for healthy sums). The desire to nab the choicest virtual real estate in the form of easy-to-remember Web addresses has also created a huge domain name market for those eager to "mine" the Internet by registering popular generic names: in fact, the idea that there's gold in them thar virtual hills is metaphorically exploited by one domain name market information site called the "Internet Goldrush," at http://www.igoldrush.com/ (visited 3 September 2000). On cybersquatting and domain name issues, see the documents collected in EFF's Internet address disputes archive at http://www.eff.org/pub/Intellectual_property/Internet_address_disputes/ (visited 24 September 2000). On domain name valuation, see Hayward 2000.

14. The EFF archives were not, of course, the only online sites from which I culled the sources I use in this analysis, but they do, nonetheless, offer a sizeable collection of documents and statements produced by both sides of the debate.

15. McConnell's testimony is part of the EFF Clipper archive and is available on the Web at http://www.eff.org/pub/Privacy/Clipper/mcconnell_nsa_clipper_050394.testimony (visited 24 September 2000).

16. The NSA home page is at http://www.nsa.gov (last visited 25 July 2000).

17. This claim and examples of the information collected by the NSA site are listed in a hyperlinked addendum to the privacy notice at http://www.nsa.gov/statistics.html (last visited 25 July 2000).

18. Feedback loops for broadcast communication are indirect in that they can't typically employ the same communications channels. The opportunities open to any viewer for giving a broadcaster feedback regarding a televised program, for example, are limited to making phone calls, sending e-mails, picketing, or voicing reactions through some other medium, one to which an average viewer has access. Televised rejoinders through a station's own public-access editorial slots don't really count inasmuch as viewers can only request air time for one of a very limited number of spots, and station personnel are the ones who ultimately decide which viewers will get those spots. Not surprisingly, many media corporations are now turning to the Web as a forum through which viewers can provide feedback on programming choices. In addition to developing Web sites with e-mail links for feedback purposes, some producers also occasionally lurk on fan newsgroups to find out what viewers think about their shows. The point here, however, is that they have had to turn to a two-way medium like the Internet for that feedback since their own broadcast medium hasn't facilitated this kind of communication.

19. In response to concerns about the use of institutional (especially university) accounts for posting pornographic materials to newsgroups, some institutional Web servers have begun prohibiting access to certain newsgroups (particularly those under the alt.sex hierarchy and alt.binaries newsgroups,

where binary graphics files can be posted). On the surface, this circumscribes
the kinds of activities in which users can engage. But this simply limits access
to particular forums; it does not circumscribe content overall. As long as users
have access to some newsgroups, they can post pretty much anything they want,
at least once. In fact, adult content has a funny way of appearing on a wide variety of newsgroup topics.

20. Commercial sites, too, and sites with unrelated content can be and often
are advertised on virtually any newsgroup, but those practices are frowned upon
and may be met with a number of e-mail replies complaining to the poster, provided that individual hasn't protected himself by using a phony e-mail address.

21. "Subcommander Marcos" is an alias for the leader of the Zapatista National Liberation Army (EZLN).

22. The U.S. site in question is at http://www.ezln.org. When I visited again
on 5 August 2000, the counter registered 902,948 hits, indicating that the popularity of the site had increased exponentially.

23. This section title is a pun on Barlow's "Decrypting the Puzzle Palace"
(1992), a reference to the NSA and the need to decipher its position on
cryptography.

24. The classic statement on these two notions of liberty is, of course, Berlin
1969. These distinctions relate, as well, to the traditional debate between liberalism and communitarianism that I outlined in chapter 2. Liberalism is marked
by an overriding concern with negative liberty (freedom from coercion) and
therefore stresses rights and security. Communitarianism privileges positive liberty (freedom to help determine the course of one's life), which stresses participation and obligations to the civic community.

25. Historically, national security concerns have overridden efforts to protect
the privacy of personal communications. Restrictions against wiretapping U.S.
citizens suspected of foreign espionage were virtually nonexistent before the
1978 passage of the Foreign Intelligence Surveillance Act. FISA helped establish
some protections—at least against unlawful surveillance of U.S. citizens *within*
U.S. borders—by requiring law enforcement and intelligence agencies, including
the NSA, to obtain wiretap warrants showing probable cause. However, FISA
also reinforced the understanding that surveillance in the name of national security is a special case requiring a separate and more discreet system. Under
FISA, the super-secret Foreign Intelligence Surveillance Court was established
to review warrant applications (Bamford 1983, 462–68). Between 1979 and 1994,
that court granted all of the 8,130 applications submitted to it (Brandt 1995).
Based on annual reports that the Office of Intelligence Policy and Review, a
branch of the Department of Justice, has posted online (at http://www.usdoj.gov/
04foia/readingrooms/oipr_records.htm [visited 2 December 2001]), the FISA

court received another 3,270 applications between 1996 and 1999, of which only one application, in 1997, was declined as pled and ultimately dropped by the department as a "moot" case (U.S. Department of Justice 1998). Ironically, Janet Reno's failure to pursue passage of the one denied application had some legislators calling for her resignation given that the warrant, according to another source (Bendavid 1999), involved the much publicized case of Dr. Wen Ho Lee, the physicist fired from the Los Alamos National Laboratories in March 1999 under suspicion of having leaked American nuclear weapons secrets to the Chinese government, and who was subsequently held in solitary confinement for 278 days without trial until his release in September 2000 (Drogin 2000; see also http://www.wenholee.org/ [visited 20 September 2000]). According to defenders of FISA, warrant applications consistently pass muster because they are carefully and meticulously prepared before they reach the court; to critics, however, the numbers indicate that even ostensibly impartial judges are seduced by the mystique surrounding national security and easily swayed by arguments cast in its terms (Bendavid 1999). The few provisions currently in place to protect American citizens from unconstitutional forms of surveillance may be further eroded by changes proposed to FISA in the wake of the September 11 terrorist attacks on the World Trade Center and the Pentagon (see Coyle 2001).

26. Of course, for Wright, this observation is not meant as a concession that the Internet really is democratic, but rather as evidence of the problems of hyperdemocracy, though he doesn't actually explain why the anti-Clipper petition was a problem.

27. In contrast to elected officials (who are arguably more vulnerable to adverse public opinion), law enforcement agents have been willing to argue that key-escrow should be mandatory and stronger alternatives outlawed (see, for example, FBI Director Freeh, cited in Meeks 1994).

28. While the recasting of citizens as "families" is typical of Republican discourse (such as the "Contract with America"), a nonpartisan broadening of this has been evident in law-and-order discourses. Even Clinton's 1995 United Nations speech (discussed below) employs a curiously Shakespearean family metaphor to frame the dangers of international crime: "a plague on everyone's house." (I'm grateful to Jennifer Milliken for bringing these points to my attention.)

29. This construction, of course, at once resonates with and negatively appropriates the computer counterculture's own self-understandings, as evinced, for example, by Stewart Brand's (1995) discussion of the hippie legacy underlying the hacker ethic (see chapter 4 of this volume).

30. Anarchism is a buzzword connoting lawlessness and chaos in some circles, and Baker (1994) was right, in part, to associate some Clipper opponents with this term. The Cypherpunks have, after all, posted a quasi-mission statement

entitled "The Crypto Anarchist Manifesto" (May 1992). But it should be noted, first, that not all Clipper opponents have been self-styled anarchists, and, second, even within the countercultural discourse of the Cypherpunks, the term has had other connotations that are obviously defensible from within a liberal framework, e.g., freedom from government. On the affinity between liberalism and anarchism, see Barber 1984 (6–11).

31. It is worth noting, however, that this statement conveys only an NSA concern with property, not privacy. In fact, nothing in the NSA statements that I have read—with the possible exception of the privacy notice on its Web site—suggests that the agency has a principled concern with individual privacy issues. Whenever privacy is mentioned, it is in the context of protecting the security and privacy of government computer systems (Conn, in Abernathy 1992; McConnell 1994). The NSA's comparative silence on individual privacy is perhaps not surprising given its reason-for-being as a spy agency.

32. These points, of course, apply to cyberspace as well. Gibson's work was to "cyberspace" what the Declaration of Independence was to "the United States of America": a performative that produced what it named (albeit, in Gibson's case, unintentionally and hence more directly in relation to the way it was taken up by his audience). Furthermore, as I argued in chapter 3, subsequent iterations have been quite different from Gibson's construct. On the relationship between performatives (illocutionary speech acts) and uptake, see Austin 1975 (116–17).

33. For an extended analysis of secrecy in freemason lodges that focuses on the alternative (heterotopic) form of sociality fostered there, see Hetherington 1997 (72–108).

34. On the Internet's contributions to transnational human rights activism, see Susan Brownmiller (in Long 1994, 56–58). On the benefits of countersurveillance measures to activists, see Banisar 1995.

35. In fact, several countries have been passing legislation to block Internet access to a variety of prohibited content. These include materials depicting or promoting child pornography, excessive violence, hate crimes, and a range of sex-related materials, which may include anything from graphic depictions of rape to nongraphic content that "advocates homosexuality or lesbianism" (see Singapore Broadcasting Authority 2000). In addition, several countries also have legislation that prohibits content illegally disclosing personal information, content that is defamatory, materials violating intellectual property rights, materials that disseminate fraudulent consumer information, materials deemed contrary to a nation's culture, and content involving a regulated industry (e.g., financial services and electronic casinos). For legislative summaries and an introduction to technical issues surrounding software filtering of prohibited content, see Internet Law and Policy Forum 1997. See also the "Content Regulation" updates

posted on the "Observatory of the Information Society" Web site of the United Nation's Educational, Scientific and Cultural Organization (UNESCO) at http://www.unesco.org/webworld/observatory/doc_cont_regulation/index.shtml (visited 29 August 2000).

36. The Freedom Forum describes itself as "a nonpartisan, international foundation dedicated to free press, free speech and free spirit" (Freedom Forum n.d.). Despite its lack of party affiliation, however, the foundation is backed by a major commercial interest in the media industry: it is supported by an endowment established by Frank E. Gannett, founder of the Gannett Co., Inc., one of the largest newspaper, information service, and media conglomerates in the United States.

37. That initiative began on 15 September 1993, with President Clinton's Executive Order No. 12864, establishing an Advisory Council (NIIAC) of government and industry leaders to devise a national strategy for building the Information Superhighway. See the Advisory Council's report entitled *A Nation of Opportunity: Realizing the Promise of the Information Superhighway* (NIIAC 1996). A "History of the Council and Executive Order" is included in the report as "Appendix A."

38. In fact, the NIIAC's report emphatically states that "[t]he Private Sector Must Be the Builder" of the Information Superhighway (see "Executive Summary, II. Recommendations, D. Key Roles," NIIAC 1996).

39. For other, more detailed analyses of these metaphors, see, for example, Miller 1996 (80–95), Adrian 1995, and Hunt and Doherty 1995.

40. The limited bandwidth capacity of UTP copper wire and the current impracticality of "pulling glass" (laying down fiber optic cables) between COs and terminal devices is a serious concern in Internet technology, particularly for companies interested in developing the Internet as a medium for delivering high-bandwidth content, like video-on-demand. For an overview of these issues, see Flournoy and Scott 1998.

41. A kilobit is a thousand bits. A megabit is a million bits.

42. Under "Benefits of the Information Superhighway," the NIIAC's report states explicitly, "The Information Superhighway is *more than the Internet.* It is a series of components, including the collection of public and private high-speed, interactive, narrow, and broadband networks that exist today and will emerge tomorrow" (1996, my emphasis).

43. See van Bakel 1996 for a brief overview of the bill and a detailed discussion of its passage and the EFF's role, which, according to the author, amounted to gaining minor concessions regarding privacy protection on the Internet and otherwise helping to put the seal of approval on an unpopular law.

44. Godwin (1995) credits John Perry Barlow for having coined the metaphor of the Electronic Frontier.

45. As I briefly noted in chapter 4, "Operation Sundevil" was a 1990 crackdown on the hacker threat that was spearheaded by the U.S. Secret Service and the Arizona attorney general's office. It involved a nationwide search and seizure of over forty computer systems, an estimated 23,000 floppies, and countless other materials belonging to people suspected of running underground BBSs trafficking in stolen credit card numbers and telephone codes (Sterling 1993 147–216). Sterling discusses the rise of the EFF and other groups in reaction to these hacker crackdowns (1993, 217–301). For a discussion of a similar hacker crackdown in Italy, see Ludlow 1994.

46. This emphasis on technical issues is problematic in other ways. As Stephen Doheny-Farina argues, the frontier metaphor actually masks our "domestication," our growing dependence on technology and on high-tech experts to guide us (lead us?) in its use: "[W]hat is silent in this image of emigration into the so-called Electronic Frontier is our utter surrender to technology maintained and controlled by others" (1994).

47. Schwichtenberg's comments are about the slick, postmodern television show of the 1980s, *Miami Vice*. She links this romantic ideal to what was then becoming a popular cultural standard for displaying the male body, i.e., as "the sensualization of movement" in films like *Saturday Night Fever*, with John Travolta strutting down the streets of New York (1986, 63 n. 8). My point, here, is that the Electronic Frontier metaphor evinces a similar fascination with this ideal. That this freedom of movement is related to dominant notions of masculinity is also relevant. Limitations of space, however, don't permit me to analyze all the ways in which cyberculture is also a gendered culture. On this issue, see, for example, Netta Gilboa's study of the hacker underground (1996), Keith White's comments on the "macho individualism" evident in *Wired* magazine's portrayal of the techno-rebel (1995, 24), and Paulina Borsook's lengthier memoirs of a Berkeley feminist working at *Wired*, which concludes with the memorable comment: "If one is not interested in participating in circle-jerk exercises and paying homage to the alpha male of the moment, what is there left to do at *Wired*?" (1996, 41). Finally, see also Laura Miller (1995) for the suggestive argument that the gender implications of the frontier metaphor—i.e., that women and children need protection there—may actually help to justify the Internet's future regulation, precisely for the sake of women and children.

48. In fact, encryption is already being used to enclose and restrict access to portions of the Internet being developed as "Virtual Private Networks" (VPN) for businesses. For a description of VPNs, see Hurwicz 1997.

49. This is the log line for a series of TV commercials and online ads for

Lotus Notes software that appeared in the late 1990s. In one of the televised installments, comic actor Denis Leary inquires of a teenage boy what he does online. The boy answers casually that he surfs, chats, and socializes with others. Leary interrupts the boy's reply and disdainfully orders him to go to bed. This exchange infantilizes precisely those information- and communications-oriented activities associated with the democratic potentials of the Internet. Having dismissed those concerns as trivial and immature, Leary then turns to the camera and, with direct audience address, tells us to "Work the Web."

50. The cover of the July 1994 issue of *Wired* depicts John Malone (who was at the time head of the cable TV megacorporation Tele-Communications, Inc.) with his face digitally reproduced over the body of Mel Gibson dressed as the Road Warrior. The caption reads "Infobahn Warrior." In the interview, Malone maintains that the regional Bells have grown too used to monopoly protections and therefore don't have the right kind of business culture for high-risk ventures like building the Superhighway: "I don't think their culture makes them very competitive, and that's their big vulnerability" (Kline 1994, 88). The obvious implication is that Malone has the right kind of competitive spirit to take on the task: he's an Infobahn Warrior.

51. This remarkable quote is from a 1987 speech by Chuck Hammill delivered at a libertarian conference on "The Future of Freedom." It was updated in December 1992 and reprinted as part of a January 1993 bulletin-board note about PGP (Zimmermann's strong encryption program) that was posted to the newsgroup soc.culture.hongkong. The post begins with a description of PGP and then introduces the speech as an explanation for "why you might consider using this program." That posting, with the full-text of Hammill's speech, is available online (in Whitaker 1993).

Conclusion

1. The ethnographically detailed empirical work of Sara Evans and Harry Boyte is exemplary in this respect (1986). Unfortunately, they tend still to conceptualize the "free spaces" where people "learn a new self-respect, a deeper and more assertive group identity, public skills, and values of cooperation and civic virtue" (17) in primarily face-to-face terms, admitting only in a footnote, where they cite Craig Calhoun, that "[t]his closeness [of community-building relations] seems to imply, *though not rigidly,* face-to-face contact, commonality of purpose, familiarity and dependability" (187n, my emphasis).

2. The sense that social spaces are produced and proliferate implies, too, a less unitary sense of cyberspace. In fact, notwithstanding my tendency to talk in terms of "the nature of cyberspace," what I tried to show, particularly in chapter 4, is that many different kinds of online practices are possible. What would need

to be done, in this respect, is to conduct analyses more detailed than I could manage here of the differences between, say, newsgroup posting, on the one hand, and mudding, on the other, and what different kinds of norms, identities, and social practices each of these modes of computer-mediated communication enable.

3. In the former category, I am thinking in particular about political figures such as Al Gore, Newt Gingrich, and Ross Perot, who, despite party differences, vaunt information technologies as civic-revitalizing supplements within a representative framework. Kirkpatrick Sale (1980) exemplifies the latter category inasmuch as his solution is to smash computers and return to pastoral communities built on a human scale. A less extreme form of the latter (gesturing toward a middle ground, though not quite) is exemplified by theorists like Benjamin Barber, who explore ways in which technologies might actually inform a more participatory democratic politics, but who always conclude that they can only supplement and should never replace the necessarily local foundations of civic virtue, a conclusion shared by Richard Sclove (1995) and James Brook and Ian Boal (1995).

4. For a discussion of these fundamental misconceptions and a more sophisticated understanding of the social origins and effects of technologies, see especially Sclove 1995 (10–24).

5. I am thinking, in particular, of the account van Bakel (1996) gives of the EFF's involvement, in Washington, in the formulation of the Digital Telephony Bill. Despite major concerns that the bill posed threats to civil liberties, the EFF was able to procure only minor privacy concessions. Van Bakel suggests that EFF organizers succumbed to the political bargaining process and compromised their principles.

6. The notion that technology can actually safeguard bodies seems patently false if one considers the deadly effects of mushroom clouds over Hiroshima, red-glaring rockets in the night skies of Baghdad, or even the comparatively less spectacular flash and fizzle of exhaust trailing what remained of the Challenger space shuttle. In fact, as Larabee (1994) shows in her powerful analysis of the NASA damage control that followed the Challenger explosion, the discursive construction of body-technology relationships as life-sustaining (let alone life-enhancing) is one that constantly has to be reproduced and often by concealing the machine-damaged body from public view. See also Disch's discussion (1996, ix–xvi) of the Smithsonian Institution's aborted plans, coinciding with the fiftieth anniversary of the Allied victory in World War II, for an Enola Gay exhibit, which featured the irreconcilable narratives of technology as at once enabling and deadly. In my terms, following Hetherington 1997, the original proposal to

exhibit the fuselage of the plane that dropped the atomic bomb on Hiroshima would have constituted the exhibit as a heterotopic space, juxtaposing, as Disch points out, a celebratory narrative of scientific progress jarringly against a critical narrative of mass destruction and the cold war uncertainties that followed the victory of the Allied powers.

Works Cited

Abernathy, Joe. 1992 (24 June). Comments on and reprint of the NSA's letter to J. Abernathy of the *Houston Chronicle* regarding request for interview. Retrieved 22 August 2000 from http://quark.cpsr.org/cpsr/privacy/crypto/tools/docs/nsa-letter.txt.

Adrian, Robert. 1995 (20 January). "Infobahn Blues." *CTheory.* Retrieved 22 August 2000 from http://www.ctheory.com/a-infobahn_blues.html.

Aleshire, Keith. 1994. "Big Government versus Your Privacy." *ComputerUser,* July, 32.

Anderson, Benedict. 1983. *Imagined Communities: Reflections on the Origin and Spread of Nationalism.* London: Verso.

Angel, Jonathan. 2000 (1 February). "Toll Lanes on the Information Superhighway." *Network Magazine.* Retrieved 6 October 2000 from http://www.networkmagazine.com/article/NMG20000517S0170 (1 of 7).

Anthony, Ted. 1996. "Dead Killer Becomes Online Body of Knowledge Technology." *Los Angeles Times,* 7 January, bulldog edition, A4.

Archibald, Dale. 1994. "Opinion—Telecommunications: The New Frontier." *Computer Buyer's Resource,* March, 5, 20.

Arendt, Hannah. 1958. *The Human Condition.* Chicago: University of Chicago Press.

Ark Interface. 1996. "Ark Interface Unveils a Virtual Community with Links to the World Wide Web." Press release. Retrieved 17 November 1997 from http://www.arkspace.com/proasis.html.

Austin, J. L. 1975. *How to Do Things with Words.* 2d ed. Edited by J. O. Urmson and Marina Sbisà. Cambridge: Harvard University Press.

"Author Won't Be Prosecuted." 1996 (11 January). The Associated Press Online

News Service. Retrieved 18 January 1996 from http://professional. infoseek.com/.

Baker, Stewart A. 1994. "Don't Worry, Be Happy: Why Clipper Is Good for You." Retrieved 22 August 2000 from http://www.wired.com/wired/archive/ 2.06/nsa.clipper.html (1 of 5). Originally published in *Wired* 2, no. 6.

Bamford, James. 1983. *The Puzzle Palace: A Report on America's Most Secret Agency.* New York: Penguin Books.

Banisar, David. 1995. "Bug Off! A Primer for Human Rights Groups on Wiretapping." Retrieved 22 August 2000 from http://www.privacy.org/pi/ reports/bug_off.html.

Baran, Paul. 1964. *On Distributed Communications, Vols. I–XI.* Santa Monica, Calif.: The RAND Corporation. Retrieved 22 August 2000 from http:// www.rand.org/publications/RM/baran.list.html.

———. 1990a. "Packet Switching." Attachment 3 of transcript of interview by Judy O'Neill, 5 March, in "Role of DARPA/IPTO in the Development of Computer Science Oral History Collection." Minneapolis: Charles Babbage Institute, University of Minnesota. Originally published in *Fundamentals of Digital Switching.* 2d ed. Edited by John C. McDonald. Plenum Publishing Corporation.

———. 1990b. Transcript of interview by Judy O'Neill, 5 March, in "Role of DARPA/IPTO in the Development of Computer Science Oral History Collection." Minneapolis: Charles Babbage Institute, University of Minnesota.

Barber, Benjamin R. 1984. *Strong Democracy: Participatory Politics for a New Age.* Berkeley and Los Angeles: University of California Press.

Barbrook, Richard. 1996 (15 May). "Global Algorithm 1.5: Hypermedia Freedom." *CTheory.* Retrieved 22 August 2000 from http://www.ctheory.com/ ga1.1-hyper_freedom.html.

Barbrook, Richard, and Andy Cameron. 1995. "The Californian Ideology." Retrieved 22 August 2000 from http://www.wmin.ac.uk/media/HRC/ci/ calif5.html.

Barker, Francis. 1984. *The Tremulous Private Body: Essays on Subjection.* London: Methuen.

Barlow, John Perry. 1990 (8 June). "Crime and Puzzlement." Retrieved 17 August 2000 from http://www.eff.org/pub/Misc/Publications/John_Perry_Barlow/ crime_and_puzzlement.1.

———. 1992. "Decrypting the Puzzle Palace." Retrieved 17 August 2000 from http://www.eff.org/pub/Misc/Publications/John_Perry_Barlow/ decrypting_puzzle.palace.

———. 1993a. "A Plain Text on Crypto Policy." Retrieved 17 August 2000 from

http://www.eff.org/pub/Misc/Publications/John_Perry_Barlow/
plain_text_on_crypto.txt.

———. 1993b. "Bill O' Rights Lite." Retrieved 17 August 2000 from http://www.
eff.org/pub/Misc/Publications/John_Perry_Barlow/bill_of_rights_lite.
article.

———. 1993c. "Selling Wine without Bottles: The Economy of Mind on the
Global Net." Retrieved 17 August 2000 from http://www.eff.org/pub/
Intellectual_property/idea_economy.article.

———. 1994a. "Jack In, Young Pioneer!" Retrieved 17 August 2000 from
http://www.eff.org/pub/Misc/Publications/John_Perry_Barlow/
jack_in_young_pioneer.article.

———. 1994b. "Jackboots on the Infobahn." *Wired* 2, no. 4: 40, 44, 46–48.

———. 1994c. "Stopping the Information Railroad." Retrieved 17 August 2000
from http://www.eff.org/pub/Misc/Publications/John_Perry_Barlow/
info_railroad_usenix_barlow_eff.speech.

———. 1995. "Is There a There There in Cyberspace." Retrieved 17 August 2000
from http://www.eff.org/pub/Publications/John_Perry_Barlow/HTML/
utne_community.html. Originally published in *Utne Reader* 68, March/
April, 53–56.

Barrett, Edward, ed. 1994. *Sociomedia: Multimedia, Hypermedia, and the Social
Construction of Knowledge.* Cambridge: MIT Press.

Bechar-Israeli, Haya. 1995. "From <Bonehead> to <cLoNehEAd>: Nicknames,
Play and Identity on Internet Relay Chat." *Journal of Computer-Mediated
Communication* 1, no. 2. Retrieved 17 August 2000 from http://jcmc.huji.
ac.il/vol1/issue2/bechar.html.

Beiner, Ronald, ed. 1995. *Theorizing Citizenship.* Albany: State University of New
York Press.

Bendavid, Naftali. 1999. "China Spy Probe Puts Spotlight on Hush-Hush Court."
Chicago Tribune, 27 May, News, 1.

Benedikt, Michael, ed. 1993. *Cyberspace: First Steps.* Cambridge: MIT Press.

Benhabib, Seyla. 1986. *Critique, Norm, and Utopia: A Study of the Foundations
of Critical Theory.* New York: Columbia University Press.

———. 1993. "Models of Public Space: Hannah Arendt, the Liberal Tradition,
and Jürgen Habermas." In *Habermas and the Public Sphere,* edited by Craig
Calhoun. Cambridge: MIT Press.

———. 1997. "In the Shadow of the Wall." *The Nation,* 29 December. Retrieved
17 August 2000 from http://www.thenation.com/issue/971229/1229benh.htm.

Benton Foundation. 1996. "Public Interest Issues in the Telecommunications Act
1996." *Technos Quarterly* 5, no. 3. Retrieved 24 August 2000 from http://
www.technos.net/journal/volume5/sb3vedro.htm.

Berlin, Eric. 1996. "CompuServe Bows to Germany." Retrieved 3 May 1996 from http://www.minfod.com/CurrentTrends/article2.html.

Berlin, Isaiah. 1969. *Four Essays on Liberty.* Oxford: Oxford University Press.

Berners-Lee, Tim. 1998. "The World Wide Web: A Very Short Personal History." Retrieved 5 August from http://www.w3.org/People/Berners-Lee/ShortHistory.html.

Bolter, J. David. 1984. *Turing's Man: Western Culture in the Computer Age.* Chapel Hill: University of North Carolina Press.

Bonchek, Mark S. 1995. "Grassroots in Cyberspace: Using Computer Networks to Facilitate Political Participation." Paper presented at the 53rd Annual Meeting of the Midwest Political Science Association, 6 April, Chicago, Ill. Retrieved 15 April 1998 from http://www.ai.mit.edu/people/msb/pubs/grassroots.html.

Borsook, Paulina. 1996. "The Memoirs of a Token: An Aging Berkeley Feminist Examines *Wired.*" In *Wired Women: Gender and New Realities in Cyberspace,* edited by Lynn Cherny and Elizabeth Reba Weise. Seattle: Seal Press.

Botsford, Charles C. 1999. "How the Internet Runs! A Free Lecture-Based Presentation on How the Networks of the World Interconnect to Create the Internet." Multimedia slideshow with Windows Media Player audio file. Retrieved 5 October 2000 from http://www.howtheinternetruns.com/ (1 of 41).

Bourdieu, Pierre. 1990. *The Logic of Practice.* Translated by Richard Nice. Stanford, Calif.: Stanford University Press.

Bowen, Charles. 1996. *Modem Nation: The Handbook of Grassroots American Activism Online.* New York: Times Books.

Brader, Mark. 1994. "XI—A Chronology of Digital Computing Machines (to 1952)." Retrieved 17 August 2000 from http://www.best.com/~wilson/faq/chrono.html.

Brand, Stewart. 1995. "We Owe It All to the Hippies." Retrieved 8 August 2000 from http://members.aye.net/~hippie/hippie/special_.htm. Originally published in *Time* 145, no. 12 (spring special issue): 54–56.

Brandt, Daniel. 1995. "Infowar and Disinformation: From the Pentagon to the Net." Retrieved 17 August 2000 from http://www-swiss.ai.mit.edu/6.805/articles/brandt-infowar.txt.

Branscomb, Anne Wells. 1994. "Jurisdictional Quandaries for Global Networks." In *Global Networks: Computers and International Communication,* edited by Linda M. Harasim. Cambridge: MIT Press.

Bromley, Hank. 1997. "Comments on sexism in network communications." Dissertation excerpt. Retrieved 7 April 1998 from http://www.gse.buffalo.edu/fas/bromley/gse500/readings/Women_CMC.htm.

Brook, James, and Iain A. Boal, eds. 1995. *Resisting the Virtual Life: The Culture and Politics of Information.* San Francisco: City Lights.

Browning, Graeme. 1996. *Electronic Democracy: Using the Internet to Influence American Politics.* Edited and with foreword by Daniel J. Weitzner. Wilton, Conn.: Pemberton Press.

Bukatman, Scott. 1993. *Terminal Identity: The Virtual Subject in Post-Modern Science Fiction.* Durham, N.C.: Duke University Press.

Bumgarner, Lee S. 1995. "The Great Renaming FAQ." Retrieved 22 August 2000 from http://www.vrx.net/usenet/history/rename.html.

Butler, Judith. 1990. *Gender Trouble: Feminism and the Subversion of Identity.* New York: Routledge.

————. 1993. *Bodies That Matter: On the Discursive Limits of "Sex."* New York: Routledge.

————. 1994. "Gender as Performance: An Interview with Judith Butler." By Peter Osborne and Lynne Segal. *Radical Philosophy* 67 (summer): 32–39.

Calhoun, Craig, ed. 1993. *Habermas and the Public Sphere.* Cambridge: MIT Press.

Carl, Jeffery. 1999. "The Imprecise Art of Tracerouting." *Boardwatch,* summer. Retrieved 6 October 2000 from http://www.ispworld.com/isp/traceroute_art.htm (1 of 5).

Case, Sue-Ellen. 1996. *The Domain-Matrix: Performing Lesbian at the End of Print Culture.* Bloomington: Indiana University Press.

Castells, Manuel. 1996. *The Rise of the Network Society, The Information Age: Economy, Society and Culture.* Vol. I. Cambridge, Mass.: Blackwell Publishers.

Center for Democracy and Technology. 2000. "An Overview of Clinton Administration Encryption Policy Initiatives." Retrieved 27 September 2000 from http://www.cdt.org/crypto/admin/initiatives.shtml.

"Center Stage." 1994 (26 May). Electronic transcript of "Center Stage" live chat with Stewart A. Baker. Retrieved 22 August 2000 from America Online, Inc. (AOL) (Keyword: Center Stage, AOL Live Transcripts, Archives, Transcripts 01/91 to 04/95, Filename: AUD0526.log).

Charny, Ben. 2000 (17 August). "More U.S. Households Online Than Not." *ZDNet News.* Retrieved 22 August 2000 from http://www.zdnet.com/zdnn/stories/news/0,4586,2616761,00.html.

Cherny, Lynn. 1995. "'Objectifying' the Body in the Discourse of an Object-Oriented MUD." *Works and Days* 25/26. Retrieved 24 August 2000 from http://www.iup.edu/~c271pdefault/cyberspaces/Cherney.html *[sic].*

Cherny, Lynn, and Elizabeth Reba Weise, eds. 1996. *Wired Women: Gender and New Realities in Cyberspace.* Seattle: Seal Press.

Cleaver, Harry. 1996a. "The 'Space' of Cyberspace: Body Politics, Frontiers and

Enclosures." Retrieved 22 August 2000 from http://www.lawyernet.com/ members/jimfesq/wca/1996/22/spaceofcyberspace.html.

———. 1996b. "Zapatistas in Cyberspace: A Guide to Analysis & Resources." Retrieved 22 August 2000 from http://www.eco.utexas.edu/Homepages/ Faculty/Cleaver/zapsincyber.html.

Clinton, William J. 1995. Remarks by the President to the U.N. General Assembly, 22 October, New York. Retrieved 22 August 2000 from http://www.pub. whitehouse.gov/uri-res/I2R?urn:pdi://oma.eop.gov.us/1995/10/23/3.text.1.

———. 1996. Remarks by the President in Signing Ceremony for the Tele-communications Act Conference Report, 8 February. Retrieved 8 August 2000 from http://www.pub.whitehouse.gov/uri-res/I2R?urn:pdi:// oma.eop.gov.us/1996/2/8/9.text.1.

———. 1997. Greek Independence Day: A National Day of Celebration of Greek and American Democracy. By the President of the United States of America: A Proclamation, 25 March. Retrieved 8 August 2000 from http:// www.pub.whitehouse.gov/uri-res/I2R?urn:pdi://oma.eop.gov.us/1997/ 3/25/5.text.1.

"Clipper II: Don't Trip over the Dogs and Ponies." 1995 (7 September). *VTW BillWatch* 17. Retrieved 20 January 1996 from http://www.isse.gmu.edu/ students/pfarrell/nist/vtwover.html.

Cohn, Carol. 1987. "Sex and Death in the Rational World of Defense Intellectu-als." *Signs* 12, no. 4: 687–718.

Constance, Paul. 1995 (25 August). "White House Retreats on Clipper Mandate." *Government Computer News.* Cahners Publishing Company. Retrieved 17 January 1996 from http://www.cahners.com/gcn/GCNNEWS/082195/ SI-PMO.HTM.

Cooke, Kevin, and Dan Lehrer. 1993. "The Internet: The Whole World Is Talking." *The Nation,* 12 July, 60–64.

Cooper, Barry. 1988. "Action into Nature: Hannah Arendt's Reflections on Technology." In *Democratic Theory and Technological Society,* edited by Richard B. Day, Ronald Beiner, and Joseph Masciulli. Armonk, N.Y.: M. E. Sharpe, Inc.

Corliss, Richard. 1995 (23 January). "Look Who's Talking: The Explosion of Radio Call-in Shows Has Created a New Form of Electronic Populism and Demagoguery." Retrieved 29 August 2000 from http://www.time.com/time/ magazine/archive/1995/950123/950123.cover.limbaugh.html. Originally pub-lished in *Time* 145, no. 4, 22ff.

Cotton, Bob, and Richard Oliver. 1994. *The Cyberspace Lexicon: An Illustrated Dictionary of Terms from Multimedia to Virtual Reality.* London: Phaidon Press Ltd.

Coyle, Marcia. 2001 (1 October). "September Attacks Prompt Sharp Debate on Scope of Surveillance Law." *Law.com*. Retrieved 24 November 2001 from http://www.law.com/cgi-bin/nwlink.cgi?ACG=ZZZ1NUCI6SC.

Dahl, Robert, and Edward R. Tufte. 1973. *Size and Democracy*. Stanford, Calif.: Stanford University Press.

Dahlgren, Peter. 1995. *Television and the Public Sphere: Citizenship, Democracy, and the Media*. London: Sage Publications.

Davies, Frank. 2001 (25 September). "Ashcroft: Terrorists Ahead Until New Laws Pass." *Miami Herald*. Retrieved 2 December 2001 from http://www.miami.com/herald/special/news/worldtrade/digdocs/091911.htm.

de Certeau, Michel. 1988. *The Practice of Everyday Life*. Translated by Steven Rendall. Berkeley and Los Angeles: University of California Press.

Deibert, Ronald J. 1996. "Typographica: The Medium and the Medieval-to-Modern Transformation." *Review of International Studies* 22: 29–56.

———. 1997. "World Order beyond Reality: Postmodern Identities in the Hypermedia Environment." Paper prepared for the Centre for International and Security Studies Fifth Annual Conference on "Culture, Identity and Global Security," 6–7 February, York University.

"The Denning-Barlow Clipper Chip Debate." 1994 (10 March). *Time Online* and *America Online*. Retrieved 22 August 2000 from http://www.eff.org/pub/Privacy/Clipper/barlow_v_denning.transcript.

Dennis, Everette E. 1994. "The Race for Content on the Information Super-highway: Self-Interest vs. the Public Interest." Address delivered at the Knight Center for Specialized Journalism, University of Maryland, 19 June. Retrieved 22 August 2000 from http://www.freedomforum.org/FreedomForum/resources/media_and_soc/tech_future/eedrace.html.

D'Entrèves, Maurizio Passerin. 1992. "Hannah Arendt and the Idea of Citizenship." In *Dimensions of Radical Democracy: Pluralism, Citizenship, Community*, edited by Chantal Mouffe. London: Verso.

Der Derian, James. 1994. "Lenin's War, Baudrillard's Games." In *Culture on the Brink: Ideologies of Technology*, edited by Gretchen Bender and Timothy Druckrey. Seattle: Bay Press.

Dery, Mark. 1993. "Flame Wars." *South Atlantic Quarterly* 92, no. 4: 559–68.

Dibbell, Julian. 1993a. "A Rape in Cyberspace." *Village Voice*, 21 December, 36–42.

———. 1993b. "Code Warriors: Battling for the Keys to Privacy in the Info Age." Retrieved 22 August 2000 from http://www.eff.org/pub/Privacy/Clipper/code_warriors.article. Originally published in *The Village Voice*, 3 August 1993.

Dietz, Mary G. 1991. "Hannah Arendt and Feminist Politics." In *Feminist*

Interpretations and Political Theory, edited by Mary Lyndon Shanley and Carole Pateman. University Park: The Pennsylvania State University Press.
————. 1994. "'The Slow Boring of Hard Boards': Methodical Thinking and the Work of Politics." *American Political Science Review* 88, no. 4: 873–86.

Dinsdale, Andrew P. 1994 (1 September). "Issue Management in a Networked World: The Case of 'Clipper.'" *Computer-Mediated Communication Magazine* 1, no. 5. Retrieved 22 August 2000 from http://sunsite.unc.edu/cmc/mag/1994/sep/issue.html.

Disch, Lisa Jane. 1996. *Hannah Arendt and the Limits of Philosophy.* Paperback edition with new preface. Ithaca, N.Y.: Cornell University Press.

Doheny-Farina, Stephen. 1994 (1 November). "Cybernauts in the Electronic Frontier: Pets on a Leash." *Computer-Mediated Communication Magazine* 1, no. 7. Retrieved 22 August 2000 from http://sunsite.unc.edu/cmc/mag/1994/nov/last.html.

Dominguez, Ricardo. 1996 (21 November). "Zapatistas: The Recombinant Movie." *CTheory.* Retrieved 22 August 2000 from http://www.ctheory.com/a41-zapatistas.html.

Drogin, Bob. 2000 (14 September). "Wen Ho Lee Freed; Judge Scolds U.S. Over Case Tactics." *Los Angeles Times.* Retrieved 8 September 2000 from http://www.latimes.com/news/nation/20000914/t000086722.html.

Druick, Zoe. 1995. "The Information Superhighway, or The Politics of a Metaphor." *Bad Subjects* 18. Retrieved 22 August 2000 from http://english-www.hss.cmu.edu/bs/18/Druck.html *[sic].*

Ebert, Teresa L. 1995. "(Untimely) Critiques of a *Red Feminism.*" In *Post-Ality: Marxism and Postmodernism,* edited by Mas'ud Zavarzadeh, Teresa L. Ebert, and Donald Morton. Washington, D.C.: Maisonneuve Press.

Electronic Frontier Foundation (EFF). 1990a. Mission Statement. Retrieved 22 August 2000 from http://www.eff.org/pub/Misc/Policies/.
————. 1990b. "New Foundation Established to Encourage Computer-Based Communications Policies." Retrieved 22 August 2000 from http://www.eff.org/pub/Misc/EFF/Historical/eff_founded.announce.
————. 1996a. "EFF Board, Staff & Volunteers—Biographical Information." Retrieved 22 August 2000 from http://www.eff.org/pub/EFF/bios.eff.
————. 1996b. "Your Constitutional Rights Have Been Sacrificed for Political Expediency: EFF Statement on 1996 Telecommunications Regulation Bill." Retrieved 22 August 2000 from http://www.eff.org/pub/Censorship/Exon_bill/cda_960201_eff.statement.

Elmer-Dewitt, Philip. 1994. "Battle for the Soul of the Internet." *Time* 144, no. 4, 25 July, 50–56.

Elshtain, Jean Bethke. 1982. "Democracy and the QUBE Tube." *The Nation,* 7–14 A ugust, 108–10.

Escobar, Arturo. 1994. "Welcome to Cyberia: Notes on the Anthropology of Cyberculture." *Current Anthropology* 35, no. 3: 211–31.

Espo, David. 2001 (2 October). "New Laws to Fight Terror Are Less Than the Attorney General Wants." *Associated Press.* Retrieved 24 November 2001 from http://www.lexisone.com/news/ap/ap_b100201a.html.

Evans, Sara M., and Harry C. Boyte. 1986. *Free Spaces: The Sources of Democratic Change in America.* New York: Harper & Row Publishers.

Fairclough, Norman. 1991. *Discourse and Social Change.* Cambridge: Polity Press.

Fjermedal, Grant. 1995. "The Tomorrow Makers." *NetGuide,* January, 55–67.

Flacks, Richard. 1971 (1966). "On the Uses of Participatory Democracy." In *Politics of the New Left,* edited by Matthew Stolz. Beverly Hills, Calif.: Glencoe Press.

Flournoy, Don M., and Thomas N. Scott. 1998. "The Last Mile: Where Tele-communications Traffic Slows to a Crawl." Ohio University, School of Telecommunications, ITS Project. Retrieved 27 September 2000 from http://www.tcomschool.ohiou.edu/its_pgs/lastmi.html.

Foucault, Michel. 1972. *The Archaeology of Knowledge and the Discourse on Language.* Translated by A. M. Sheridan Smith. New York: Pantheon Books.

———. 1973. *Madness and Civilization: A History of Insanity in the Age of Reason.* Translated by Richard Howard. New York: Vintage Books.

———. 1979. *Discipline and Punish: The Birth of the Prison.* Translated by Alan Sheridan. New York: Vintage Books.

———. 1980. *Power/Knowledge: Selected Interviews and Other Writings, 1972–1977.* Edited by Colin Gordon and translated by Colin Gordon, Leo Marshall, John Mepham, and Kate Soper. New York: Pantheon Books.

———. 1981. "The Order of Discourse." In *Untying the Text,* edited by Robert Young. London: Routledge & Kegan Paul.

———. 1984. "Space, Knowledge, and Power." Interview by Paul Rabinow. Translated by Christian Hubert. In *The Foucault Reader,* edited by Paul Rabinow. New York: Pantheon Books.

———. 1986. "Of Other Spaces." Translated by Jay Miskowiec. *Diacritics* (spring): 22–27.

———. 1991. "Governmentality." In *The Foucault Effect: Studies in Govern-mentality,* edited by Graham Burchell, Colin Gordon, and Peter Miller. Chicago: Chicago University Press.

———. 1994a. *The Birth of the Clinic: An Archaeology of Medical Perception.* Translated by A. M. Sheridan Smith. New York: Vintage Books.

————. 1994b. *The Order of Things: An Archaeology of the Human Sciences.* New York: Vintage Books.

Franklin, Curt. 2000 (7 August). "How a Digital Subscriber Line (DSL) Works." *How Stuff Works.* Retrieved 11 October 2000 from http://www.howstuffworks.com/dsl.htm (1 of 6).

Fraser, Nancy. 1991. *Unruly Practices: Power, Discourse and Gender in Contemporary Social Theory.* Minneapolis: University of Minnesota Press.

————. 1993. "Rethinking the Public Sphere: A Contribution to the Critique of Actually Existing Democracy." In *Habermas and the Public Sphere,* edited by Craig Calhoun. Cambridge: MIT Press.

Freedom Forum. (n.d.) "About *The Forum.*" Retrieved 24 August 2000 from http://www.freedomforum.org/FreedomForum/resources/general_pubs/fmagazine/archive/about.html.

————. 1994a. "The Digital Future Can Mean Great News for Newspapers, Journalists and News Consumers." *The Forum Magazine,* May. Retrieved 24 August 2000 from http://www.freedomforum.org/FreedomForum/resources/general_pubs/fmagazine/archive/may.html.

————. 1994b. "Information Superhighway: Begging for a Shorter Superhighway." *The Forum Magazine,* May. Retrieved 24 August 2000 from http://www.freedomforum.org/FreedomForum/resources/general_pubs/fmagazine/archive/may.begging.html.

Friedland, Lewis A. 1996. "Electronic Democracy and the New Citizenship." Retrieved 24 August 2000 from http://www.cpn.org/sections/new_citizenship/e-dem&new_citizenship1.html. Originally published in *Media, Culture & Society* 18: 185–212.

Friedrich, Otto. 1983. "Machine of the Year: The Computer Moves In." Retrieved 24 August 2000 from http://www.time.com/time/special/moy/1982.html. Originally published in *Time,* 3 January.

Froomkin, Michael. 1995. "Anonymity and Its Enmities." *The Journal of Online Law,* Article 4. Retrieved 24 August 2000 from http://www.wm.edu/law/publications/jol/froomkin.html.

Gans, Herbert J. 1980. *Deciding What's News: A Study of* CBS Evening News, NBC Nightly News, Newsweek, *and* Time. New York: Vintage Books.

Gareiss, Robin. 1999. "The Old Boys' Network." *Data Communications International,* October. Retrieved 9 October 2000 from http://www.eco-bay.com/Overview/Infos/body_infos.html (1 of 4).

Garfinkel, Simson. 1995 (10 April). "Learning Mitnick's Lesson." *Intelligent Agent.* Retrieved 24 August 2000 from http://hotwired.lycos.com/i-agent/95/15/index1a.html.

Garnham, Nicholas. 1993. "The Media and the Public Sphere." In *Habermas and the Public Sphere,* edited by Craig Calhoun. Cambridge: MIT Press.

Gibbons, Michael T. 1997. "Democracy's Deliberations." *Theory & Event* 1, no. 1. Retrieved 24 August 2000 from http://muse.jhu.edu/journals/theory_&_event/v001/1.1r_gibbons.html.

Gibson, William. 1982. "Burning Chrome." Retrieved 8 August 2000 from http://www.cyberpunkproject.org/lib/burning_chrome/.

———. 1984. *Neuromancer.* New York: Ace Books.

Gilboa, Netta (aka "grayarea"). 1996. "Elites, Lamers, Narcs and Whores: Exploring the Computer Underground." In *Wired Women: Gender and New Realities in Cyberspace,* edited by Lynn Cherny and Elizabeth Reba Weise. Seattle: Seal Press.

Godwin, Mike. 1993. "Law of the Net: Problems and Prospects." Retrieved 24 August 2000 from http://www.eff.org/pub/Publications/Mike_Godwin/law_of_the_net_godwin.article. Originally published in *Internet World,* Sept./Oct. 1993.

———. 1995. Foreword to *High Noon on the Electronic Frontier,* by Peter Ludlow. Retrieved 24 August 2000 from http://semlab2.sbs.sunysb.edu/Users/pludlow/foreword.txt.

Gore, Albert, Jr. 1994 (21 March). Remarks Prepared for Delivery by Vice President Al Gore, International Telecommunications Union. Retrieved 24 August 2000 from http://www.iitf.nist.gov/documents/speeches/032194_gore_giispeech.html.

Green, Noah. 1996. "A Smash." *Village Voice,* 20 February.

Habermas, Jürgen. 1971. *Towards a Rational Society.* London: Heinemann.

———. 1979. *Communication and the Evolution of Society.* Translated and with introduction by Thomas McCarthy. Boston: Beacon Press.

———. 1984. *The Theory of Communicative Action, Vol. 1: Reason and the Rationalization of Society.* Translated by Thomas McCarthy. Boston: Beacon Press.

———. 1986. "Hannah Arendt's Communications Concept of Power." In *Power,* edited by Steven Lukes. New York: New York University Press.

———. 1987. *The Theory of Communicative Action, Vol. 2: Lifeworld and System: A Critique of Functionalist Reason.* Translated by Thomas McCarthy. Boston: Beacon Press.

———. 1989. *The Structural Transformation of the Public Sphere: An Inquiry into a Category of Bourgeois Society.* Translated by Thomas Burger, with the assistance of Frederick Lawrence. Cambridge: MIT Press. Originally published as *Strukturwandel der Öffentlicheit,* Hermann Luchterhand Verlag, 1962.

———. 1993. "Further Reflections on the Public Sphere." Translated by Thomas Burger. In *Habermas and the Public Sphere,* edited by Craig Calhoun. Cambridge: MIT Press.

Hall, Stuart. 1986. "On Postmodernism and Articulation: An Interview with Stuart Hall." Edited by Lawrence Grossberg. *Journal of Communication Inquiry* 10, no. 2: 45–60.

Hamit, Francis. 1993. *Virtual Reality and the Exploration of Cyberspace.* Carmel, Ind.: Sams Publishing.

Haraway, Donna. 1989. "A Manifesto for Cyborgs: Science, Technology, and Socialist Feminism in the 1980s." In *Coming to Terms: Feminism, Theory, Politics,* edited by Elizabeth Weed. New York: Routledge.

Haring, Donald R. 1994. "Internetworking with Transmission Control Protocol/Internet Protocol." In *The Encyclopedia of Telecommunications,* edited by Fritz E. Froelich. Vol. 9. New York: Marcel Dekker, Inc.

Hayles, N. Katherine. 1992. "The Materiality of Informatics." Retrieved 24 August 2000 from http://www.press.jhu.edu/demo/configurations/1.1hayles.html. Originally published in *Configurations* 1, no. 1: 147–70.

———. 1993. "Virtual Bodies and Flickering Signifiers." Retrieved 24 August 2000 from http://englishwww.humnet.ucla.edu/Individuals/Hayles/Flick.html. Originally published in *October* 66 (fall): 69–91.

Hayward, Edwin. 2000. "A Long Hard Look at Domain Name Valuations." Retrieved 3 September 2000 from http://www.igoldrush.com/feata1.htm.

Heim, Michael. 1993. "The Erotic Ontology of Cyberspace." In *Cyberspace: First Steps,* edited by Michael Benedikt. Cambridge: MIT Press.

Held, David. 1987. *Models of Democracy.* Stanford, Calif.: Stanford University Press.

———. 1993. "Democracy: Past, Present, and Possible Futures." *Alternatives* 18: 259–71.

Herring, Susan C. 1993. "Gender and Democracy in Computer-Mediated Communication." *Electronic Journal of Communication* 3, no. 2. Retrieved 24 August 2000 from http://dc.smu.edu/dc/classroom/Gender.txt.

Hetherington, Kevin. 1996a. "Identity Formation, Space and Social Centrality." *Theory, Culture and Society* 13, no. 4: 33–52.

———. 1996b. "The Utopics of Social Ordering—Stonehenge as a Museum without Walls." In *Theorizing Museums: Representing Identity and Diversity in a Changing World,* edited by Sharon Macdonald and Gordon Fyfe. Oxford: Basil Blackwell.

———. 1997. *The Badlands of Modernity: Heterotopia and Social Ordering.* London: Routledge.

Hoffman, Russell D. 1996. "Interview with Author of *Pretty Good Privacy.*" Radio interview of Phil Zimmermann for *High Tech Today* (WALE), 2 February. Retrieved 24 August 2000 from http://www.animatedsoftware.com/ hightech/philspgp.htm.

Holland, John, Paula McMahon, Fred Schulte, and Jonathan King. 2001 (18 September). "Library Computers Targeted in Terrorism Investigation." *South Florida Sun-Sentinel.* Retrieved 2 December 2001 from http:// www.sun-sentinel.com/news/local/southflorida/sfl-culprits918. story?coll=sfla-home-headlines.

Honig, Bonnie. 1992. "Toward an Agonistic Feminism: Hannah Arendt and the Politics of Identity." In *Feminists Theorize the Political,* edited by Judith Butler and Joan W. Scott. New York: Routledge.

Hunt, Kevin and Mick Doherty. 1995 (1 January). "Of Ivory Towers and Info-bahns." *Computer-Mediated Communication Magazine* 2, no. 1. Retrieved 24 August 2000 from http://sunsite.unc.edu/cmc/mag/1995/jan/lastlink.html.

Hunter, Donna. 1997. "Convicted/Connected: Prisoners Online." *CNET TV.* Retrieved 11 October 2000 from http://coverage.cnet.com/Content/Tv/ Stories/prisoners_online.html.

Hurwicz, Mike. 1997. "A Virtual Private Affair." *Byte,* July. Retrieved 11 October 2000 from http://www.byte.com/art/9707/sec6/art3.htm.

Imboden, Durant. 1999. "In Defense of 'Deep Links.'" *Boardwatch,* March. Retrieved 1 August 2000 from http://boardwatch.internet.com/mag/99/mar/ bwm27.html.

"The International Traffic in Arms Regulations" (ITAR). 1992. *Code of Federal Regulations (CFR),* Title 22 (Foreign Relations), Chapter I (Department of State), Parts 120–30 (Subchapter M: International Traffic in Arms Regulations). Retrieved 24 August 2000 from http://www.epic.org/crypto/ export_controls/itar.html.

———. 1997. *Code of Federal Regulations (CFR),* Title 22 (Foreign Relations), Chapter I (Department of State), Parts 120–30 (Subchapter M: International Traffic in Arms Regulations). Retrieved 24 August 2000 from http://www.fas.org/spp/starwars/offdocs/itar/index.html (1 of 11).

Internet Law and Policy Forum. 1997. Preliminary report of the Internet Law and Policy Forum Working Group on Content Blocking. Retrieved 29 August 2000 from http://www.ilpf.org/work/content/content.htm (1 of 13).

internet.com. 1999a (1 June). "300 Million Online by 2005." *CyberAtlas: The Web Marketer's Guide to Online Facts.* Retrieved 22 August 2000 from http://cyberatlas.internet.com/big_picture/demographics/article/ 0,1323,5901_150071,00.html.

———. 1999b (21 June). "Home PC Usage Stagnates." *CyberAtlas: The Web Marketer's Guide to Online Facts.* Retrieved 22 August 2000 from

http://cyberatlas.internet.com/big_picture/demographics/article/
0,1323,5901_150021,00.html.

———. 1999c (23 March). "One-Quarter of U.S. Households Online."
CyberAtlas: The Web Marketer's Guide to Online Facts. Retrieved 22 August
2000 from http://cyberatlas.internet.com/big_picture/demographics/
article/0,1323,5901_150131,00.html.

———. 2000. Resolution statistics for August 2000 from TheCounter.com.
Retrieved 6 September 2000 from http://www.thecounter.com/stats/2000/
August/res.html.

Isin, Engin F. 1997. "Who Is the New Citizen? Towards a Genealogy." *Citizenship
Studies* 1, no. 1: 115–32.

The Jargon File. 2000 (31 January). Version 4.2.0. Online interactive lexicon.
Retrieved 24 August 2000 from http://www.science.uva.nl/~mes/jargon/.

Jenkins, Henry. 1992. *Textual Poachers: Television Fans and Participatory Culture.*
New York: Routledge.

Jennings, Karla. 1990. *The Devouring Fungus: Tales of the Computer Age.* New
York: W.W. Norton & Company.

Johnson, Brian D. 1995. "Mind Games with William Gibson." *Maclean's,* 5 June,
60. Retrieved 26 February 1998 from *CompuServe,* Magazine database,
Reference #: A17017439.

Jones, Steven G., ed. 1995. *CyberSociety: Computer-Mediated Communication and
Community.* Thousand Oaks, Calif.: Sage Publications.

Kahn, Robert E. 1990. Electronic transcript of interview by Judy O'Neill,
24 April. In "Role of DARPA/IPTO in the Development of Computer Science Oral History Collection." Minneapolis: Charles Babbage Institute.

Kane, Margaret. 1997 (14 August). "PC Prices: How Far, How Fast Will They
Fall?" *ZDNET News.* Retrieved 24 August 2000 from http://www.zdnet.com/
zdnn/content/zdnn/0814/zdnn0005.html.

Kantorowicz, Ernst H. 1985 (1957). *The King's Two Bodies: A Study in Mediaeval
Political Theology.* Princeton, N.J.: Princeton University Press.

Kapor, Mitchell. 1993. "Where Is the Digital Highway Really Heading? The
Case for a Jeffersonian Information Policy." Retrieved 17 August 2000
from http://www.eff.org/pub/Misc/Publications/Mitch_Kapor/
nii_kapor_eff_wired.article. Originally published in *Wired* 1, no. 3.

Kapor, Mitchell, and John Perry Barlow. 1990. "Across the Electronic Frontier."
Retrieved 17 August 2000 from http://www.eff.org/pub/Misc/Publications/
Mitch_Kapor/electronic_frontier.eff.

Keep Out. 1994. Vol. 1, no. 1, August/September. Retrieved 16 December 1994
from *CompuServe* (Go: NCSA, Infosecurity Forum, Library 3: News, Case
Studies, Filename: kpout1.zip).

Keith, Michael, and Steve Pile, eds. 1993. *Place and the Politics of Identity.* London: Routledge.

Kim, Albert. 1994. "The First Man into Cyberspace." *Entertainment Weekly,* no. 237–38, 26 August, 106.

Kleinrock, Leonard. 1990. Electronic transcript of interview by Judy O'Neill, 3 April. In "Role of DARPA/IPTO in the Development of Computer Science Oral History Collection." Minneapolis: Charles Babbage Institute.

Kline, David. 1994. "Infobahn Warrior." *Wired* 2, no. 7: 86–90, 130–31.

Krol, Ed. 1994. *The Whole Internet: User's Guide and Catalog,* 2d ed. Sebastopol, Calif.: O'Reilly & Associates, Inc.

Kroker, Arthur, and Michael A. Weinstein. 1994. *Data Trash: The Theory of the Virtual Class.* New York: St. Martin's Press.

Laclau, Ernesto, and Chantal Mouffe. 1985. *Hegemony and Socialist Strategy: Towards a Radical Democratic Politics.* London: Verso.

———. 1987. "Post-Marxism without Apologies." *New Left Review* 166: 79–106.

Landow, George P. 1992. *Hyper Text: The Convergence of Contemporary Critical Theory and Technology.* Baltimore: Johns Hopkins University Press.

Langfield, Martin. 1995 (13 December). "Mexico's Zapatista Rebels Ride the Internet." Reuters News Service. Retrieved 24 August 2000 from http://burn.ucsd.edu/archives/chiapas-l/1995.12/msg00068.html.

Larabee, Ann. 1994. "Remembering the Shuttle, Forgetting the Loom: Interpreting the Challenger Disaster." Retrieved 24 August 2000 from http://jefferson.village.virginia.edu/pmc/text-only/issue.594/larabee.594. Originally published in *Postmodern Culture* 4, no. 3, May 1994.

Laskas, Jeanne Marie. 1996. "Body of Knowledge." Retrieved 11 June 1997 from http://www.washingtonpost.com/wp-srv/WPlate/1996-06/09/009L-060996-idx.html. Originally published in *Washington Post,* 9 June, W05.

Leca, Jean. 1992. "Questions on Citizenship." In *Dimensions of Radical Democracy: Pluralism, Citizenship, Community,* edited by Chantal Mouffe. London: Verso.

Leeson, Lynn Hershman. 1996. "Sandy Stone Interview." In *Clicking In: Hot Links to a Digital Culture,* edited by Lynn Hershman Leeson. Seattle: Bay Press.

Lefebvre, Henri. 1991. *The Production of Space.* Translated by Donald Nicholson-Smith. Oxford: Blackwell Publishers.

"Letters to the Editor: *Time.*" 1995 (13 February). Retrieved 29 August 2000 from http://www.time.com/time/magazine/archive/1995/950213/950213.letters.html. Originally published *Time* 145, no. 7, 4.

Levy, Steven. 1993. "Crypto Rebels." Retrieved 22 August 2000 from http://

www.wired.com/wired/archive/1.02/crypto.rebels.html (1 of 14). Originally published in *Wired* 1, no. 2.

———. 1994. "The Battle of the Clipper Chip." *New York Times Magazine,* 12 June, 44–51, 60, 70.

Long, Marion. 1994. "We Are the World." *NetGuide,* December, 53–66.

Lubar, Steven. 1993. *Infoculture: The Smithsonian Book of Information Age Inventions.* Boston: Houghton Mifflin Company.

Lucyga, Dierk. 1996. "The CompuServe Incident: Chronicle of Events." Retrieved 27 May 1996 from http://www.uni-konstanz.de/~dierk/censorship/compuserve/chronik.html.

Ludlow, Peter. 1994. "Hardware 1: The Italian Hacker Crackdown." Appendix 2, in *High Noon on the Electronic Frontier: Conceptual Issues in Cyberspace.* Retrieved 13 April 1998 from http://semlab2.sbs.sunysb.edu/Users/pludlow/peter1.txt.

Luke, Timothy W. 1997. "Digital Beings and Virtual Times: The Politics of Cybersubjectivity." *Theory & Event* 1, no. 1. Retrieved 24 August 2000 from http://muse.jhu.edu/journals/theory_&_event/v001/1.1r_luke.html.

Lyon, David. 1994. *The Electronic Eye: The Rise of Surveillance Society.* Minneapolis: University of Minnesota Press.

Madison, James. 1988a. "The Federalist No. 10." In *The Federalist Papers by Alexander Hamilton, James Madison and John Jay,* edited by Garry Wills. New York: Bantam Books.

———. 1988b. "The Federalist No. 14." In *The Federalist Papers by Alexander Hamilton, James Madison and John Jay,* edited by Garry Wills. New York: Bantam Books.

Maize, Kennedy. 1995a (6 September). "Industry Slams Govt's Encryption Export Plan." *Newsbytes.* Reprinted in archived electronic post. Retrieved 24 August 2000 from http://www.interesting-people.org/archive/2279.html.

———. 1995b (14 August). "Lobbying Picks Up on Encryption Policy." *Newsbytes.* Retrieved 18 January 1996 from http://professional.infoseek.com/.

Markoff, John. 1993. "Electronics Plan Aims to Balance Government Access with Privacy." Reprinted in electronic collection of Clipper Chip articles compiled and distributed by Valerie Lambert. Retrieved 24 August 2000 from http://www.eff.org/pub/Privacy/Clipper/clipper.intro. Originally published in *New York Times,* 16 April 1993.

Masciulli, Joseph. 1988. "Rousseau Versus Instant Government: Democratic Participation in the Age of Telepolitics." In *Democratic Theory and Technological Society,* edited by Richard B. Day, Ronald Beiner, and Joseph Masciulli. Armonk, N.Y.: M. E. Sharpe, Inc.

Massey, Doreen. 1994. *Space, Place, and Gender.* Minneapolis: University of Minnesota Press.

Matzkin, Jonathan. 1996. "Civilizing the Electronic Frontier: CompuServe Turns to Technology." Retrieved 24 August 2000 from http://www.pcmag.com/special/reports/s960214d.htm. Originally published in *PC Magazine,* 14 February 1996.

May, Timothy C. 1992 (22 November). "The Crypto Anarchist Manifesto." Retrieved 24 August 2000 from http://www.activism.net/cypherpunk/crypto-anarchy.html.

McCandlish, Stanton. 1994 (21 July). Mailing list reprint, with commentary, of Vice President Gore's 20 July 1994 letter to Rep. Maria Cantwell regarding the Clipper Chip. Retrieved 22 August 2000 from http://www.eff.org/pub/Privacy/Key_escrow/Clipper/gore_clipper_retreat_cantwell_072094.letter.

McConnell, John M. 1994 (8 July). Letter to Senator Ernest P. Hollings requesting funds for Clipper policy implementation. Reprinted in *EFFector Online 7,* no. 12. Retrieved 24 August 2000 from http://www.eff.org/pub/Publications/EFF_newsletters/EFFector/HTML/effect07.12.html.

McDonald, Forrest. 1985. *Novus Ordo Seclorum: The Intellectual Origins of the Constitution.* Lawrence: University Press of Kansas.

McKenzie, Alexander A., and David C. Walden. 1991. "ARPANET, the Defense Data Network, and Internet." In *The Encyclopedia of Telecommunications,* edited by Fritz E. Froelich. Vol. 1. New York: Marcel Dekker, Inc.

McLuhan, Marshall. 1964. *Understanding Media: The Extensions of Man.* New York: McGraw-Hill.

McRae, Shannon. 1996. "Coming Apart at the Seams: Sex, Text and the Virtual Body." In *Wired Women: Gender and New Realities in Cyberspace,* edited by Lynn Cherny and Elizabeth Reba Weise. Seattle: Seal Press.

Meeks, Brock. 1994 (20 October). "Jacking in from the 'Sooner or Later' Port." *CyberWire Dispatch.* Retrieved 24 August 2000 from http://www.cyberwerks.com/cyberwire/cwd/cwd.94.10.20.html.

Meyer, Gordon, and Jim Thomas. 1990. "The Baudy World of the Byte Bandit: A Postmodernist Interpretation of the Computer Underground." Retrieved 24 August 2000 from http://wiretap.spies.com/Gopher/Library/Cyber/meyer.cu.

Meyrowitz, Joshua. 1994. "Medium Theory." In *Communication Theory Today,* edited by David Crowley and David Mitchell. Stanford, Calif.: Stanford University Press.

Miller, James. 1994. *'Democracy is in the Streets': From Port Huron to the Siege of Chicago.* Cambridge: Harvard University Press.

Miller, Laura. 1995. "Women and Children First: Gender and the Settling of the

Electronic Frontier." In *Resisting the Virtual Life: The Culture and Politics of Information,* edited by James Brook and Iain A. Boal. San Francisco: City Lights.

Miller, Steven E. 1996. *Civilizing Cyberspace: Policy, Power, and the Information Superhighway.* New York: ACM Press.

Mills, C. Wright. 1971. "The Structure of Power in American Society." In *Politics of the New Left,* edited by Matthew Stolz. Beverly Hills, Calif.: Glencoe Press.

Mitchell, William J. 1995. *City of Bits: Space, Place, and the Infobahn.* Cambridge: MIT Press.

Moruzzi, Norma. 1990. "The Social Question, the Mask, and Masquerade." In "Speaking through the Mask: The Construction of the Body in the Political Thought of Hannah Arendt." Ph.D. diss., Johns Hopkins University.

Mouffe, Chantal. 1991. "Democratic Citizenship and the Political Community." In *Community at Loose Ends,* edited by The Miami (Ohio) Theory Collective. Minneapolis: University of Minnesota Press.

——. 1995. "Democratic Politics and the Question of Identity." In *The Identity in Question,* edited by John Rajchman. New York: Routledge.

——, ed. 1992. *Dimensions of Radical Democracy: Pluralism, Citizenship, Community.* London: Verso.

Munro, Neil. 1994 (24 November). "Of Taxes, Taps, and 'Total Encryption.'" *Washington Technology Online.* Retrieved 24 August 2000 from http://www.wtonline.com/archive/1994_NOVEMBER_24/gen_news/gen_news1.html.

Nadelmann, Ethan. 1993. *Cops across Borders: The Internationalization of U.S. Criminal Law Enforcement.* University Park: Pennsylvania State University.

National Information Infrastructure Advisory Committee (NIIAC). 1996. "A Nation of Opportunity: A Final Report of the United States Advisory Council on the National Information Infrastructure." Retrieved 24 August 2000 from http://www.benton.org/Library/KickStart/nation.home.html (1 of 11).

The National Library of Medicine (NLM). 1997. "*Fact Sheet:* The Visible Human Project." Retrieved 24 August 2000 from http://www.nlm.nih.gov/pubs/factsheets/visible_human.html.

Negroponte, Nicholas. 1996. *Being Digital.* New York: Vintage Books.

Negt, Oskar, and Alexander Kluge. 1993. *Public Sphere and Experience: Toward an Analysis of the Bourgeois and Proletarian Public Sphere.* Foreword by Miriam Hansen. Translated by Peter Labanyi, Jamie Owen Daniel, and Assenka Oksiloff. Minneapolis: University of Minnesota Press.

Norberg, Arthur L., and Judy E. O'Neill. 1992. "A History of the Information Processing Techniques Office of the Defense Advanced Research Projects

Agency." With contributions by Kerry J. Freedman. Minneapolis: Charles Babbage Institute.

Oguibe, Olu. 1996. "Forsaken Geographies: Cyberspace and the New World 'Other.'" Paper for the Fifth International Cyberspace Conference, Madrid. Retrieved 24 August 2000 from http://english-server.hss.cmu.edu/internet/oguibe/.

Oldenburg, Ray. 1989. *The Great Good Place.* New York: Paragon House.

Olsen, Stefanie. 2001 (26 October). "Critics: Patriot Act Puts Privacy at Risk." *ZDNet News.* Retrieved 30 October 2001 from http://www.zdnet.com/zdnn/stories/news/0,4586,5098862,00.html.

"Open Sesame." 1994. *The MacNeil/Lehrer Newshour,* 7 April. Public Broadcasting System. Transcribed by Marc Hedlund. Retrieved 24 August 2000 from http://www.eff.org/pub/Privacy/Key_escrow/Clipper/macneil-lehrer_crypto.transcript.

Pasquino, Pasquale. 1991. "Theatrum politicum: The Genealogy of Capital—Police and the State of Prosperity." In *The Foucault Effect: Studies in Governmentality,* edited by Graham Burchell, Colin Gordon, and Peter Miller. Chicago: University of Chicago Press.

Penley, Constance, and Andrew Ross, eds. 1991. *Technoculture.* Minneapolis: University of Minnesota Press.

Petrey, Sandy. 1990. *Speech Acts and Literary Theory.* New York: Routledge.

Pike, John. 1997. "CyberStats—1996: How Many People Are Online." Retrieved 22 August 2000 from http://www.fas.org/cp/netstats1996.html.

Piller, Charles, and Dave Wilson. 2001 (19 September). "The Terrorists Are Winning the Cyber War." *Los Angeles Times.* Retrieved 2 December 2001 from http://www.latimes.com/news/nationworld/nation/la-091901techspy.story.

"Planet Oasis Fact Sheet." 1997. Retrieved 17 November 1997 from http://www.arkspace.com/pofacts.html.

Plato. 1973. *The Republic and Other Works.* Translated by B. Jowett. Garden City, N.Y.: Anchor Books.

Pocock, J. G. A. 1995. "The Ideal of Citizenship since Classical Times." In *Theorizing Citizenship,* edited by Ronald Beiner. Albany: State University of New York Press.

Poster, Mark. 1990. *The Mode of Information: Poststructuralism and Social Context.* Chicago: University of Chicago Press.

Privacy International. 1995. Summary of "Big Brother Incorporated: A Report on the International Trade in Surveillance Technology and its Links to the Arms Industry." Retrieved 24 August 2000 from http://www.privacy.org/pi/reports/big_bro/intro.html.

Public Broadcasting System (PBS). 1996. "InterNetworking." Summary of the

20 May installment of the televised series *Life on the Internet*. Retrieved
20 June 1996 from http://www.pbs.org/internet/newsgroups/story.html.

Public Culture. 1994. Special Issue: The Black Public Sphere. Vol. 7, no. 1 (fall).

Putnam, Robert D. 1995. "Bowling Alone: America's Declining Social Capital."
Retrieved 24 August 2000 from http://calliope.jhu.edu/demo/
journal_of_democracy/v006/putnam.html. Originally published
in *Journal of Democracy* 6, no. 1: 65–78.

Quittner, Joshua. 1997. "Divorce Internet Style." *Time* 149, no. 15, 14 April, 72.

RAND. 1996. "Strategic War . . . in Cyberspace." Retrieved 24 August 2000 from
http://www.rand.org/publications/RB/RB7106/RB7106.html.

Raysman, Richard, and Peter Brown. 2000. "Recent Linking Issues." Retrieved
1 August 2000 from http://www.brownraysman.com/publications/
techlaw/nylj0200.htm. Originally published in *New York Law Journal,*
8 February.

Reid, Elizabeth. 1995. "Virtual Worlds: Culture and Imagination." In *CyberSociety:
Computer-Mediated Communication and Community,* edited by Steven G.
Jones. Thousand Oaks, Calif.: Sage Publications.

Rheingold, Howard. 1993. *The Virtual Community: Homesteading on the Electronic Frontier.* Reading, Mass.: Addison-Wesley Publishing Company.

————. 1995. "Communication Is Political." Tomorrow (online column),
21 August. Retrieved 24 August 2000 from http://www.well.com/user/hlr/
tomorrow/compol.html.

Roberts, Lawrence G. 1989. Electronic transcript of interview by Arthur L.
Norberg, 4 April. In "Role of DARPA/IPTO in the Development of
Computer Science Oral History Collection." Minneapolis: Charles Babbage
Institute.

Rodger, Will. 1996 (18 May). "White House Reviving Clipper Wiretap Plan."
Inter@ctive Week. Retrieved 24 August 2000 from http://www.zdnet.com/
intweek/daily/960518y.html.

Rose, Lance. 1993. "Electric Word: Just When You Thought It Was Safe to Encrypt
Again." *Wired* 1, no. 6: 25.

Ross, Andrew. 1991. "Hacking Away at the Counterculture." In *Technoculture,*
edited by Constance Penley and Andrew Ross. Minneapolis: University of
Minnesota Press.

Rothman, David H. 1996. *NetWorld! What People Are Really Doing on the
Internet, and What It Means to You.* Rocklin, Calif.: Prima Publishing.

Roush, Wade. 1995. "Hackers: Taking a Byte out of Computer Crime." *Technology
Review,* April. Retrieved 24 August 2000 from http://www.techreview.com/
articles/apr95/Roush.html.

Ryan, Mary P. 1993. "Gender and Public Access: Women's Politics in Nineteenth-

Century America." In *Habermas and the Public Sphere,* edited by Craig Calhoun. Cambridge: MIT Press.

Rybaczyk, Peter. 1998. *Novell's Internet Plumbing Handbook.* San Jose, Calif.: Novell Press.

Saco, Diana. 1997. "Gendering Sovereignty: Marriage and International Relations in Elizabethan Times." *European Journal of International Relations* 3, no. 3: 291–318.

———. 1999. "Colonizing Cyberspace: 'National Security' and the Internet." In *Cultures of Insecurity: States, Communities, and the Production of Danger,* edited by Jutta Weldes, Mark Laffey, Hugh Gusterson, and Raymond Duvall. Minneapolis: University of Minnesota Press.

Sale, Kirkpatrick. 1980. *Human Scale.* New York: Perigee Book.

Sandel, Michael, ed. 1984. *Liberalism and Its Critics.* Oxford: Basil Blackwell.

Sawicki, Jana. 1991. *Disciplining Foucault: Feminism, Power, and the Body.* New York: Routledge.

Saxonhouse, Arlene. 1991. "Aristotle: Defective Males, Hierarchy, and the Limits of Politics." In *Feminist Interpretations and Political Theory,* edited by Mary Lyndon Shanley and Carole Pateman. University Park: Pennsylvania State University Press.

Schalit, Joel. 1996. "The Information Super Yahweh." *Bad Subjects* 24. Retrieved 24 August 2000 from http://english-www.hss.cmu.edu/bs/24/schalit.html.

Schatzki, Theodore R., and Wolfgang Natter, eds. 1996. *The Social and Political Body.* New York: Guilford Press.

Schofield, John. 1994. "Pretty Good Phil: The Story of Philip Zimmermann, Author of Pretty Good Privacy." *Keep Out* 1, no. 1 (August/September). Retrieved 16 December 1994 from *CompuServe* (Go: NCSA, Infosecurity Forum, Library 3: News, Case Studies, Filename: kpout1.zip).

Schudson, Michael. 1978. *Discovering News: A Social History of American Newspapers.* New York: Basic Books.

———. 1993. "Was There Ever a Public Sphere? If So, When? Reflections on the American Case." In *Habermas and the Public Sphere,* edited by Craig Calhoun. Cambridge: MIT Press.

Schumpeter, Joseph. 1976. *Capitalism, Socialism and Democracy.* London: Allen and Unwin.

Schutz, Alfred. 1967. *The Phenomenology of the Social World.* Translated by George Walsh and Frederick Lehnert. Introduction by George Walsh. Evanston, Ill.: Northwestern University Press.

Schutz, Alfred, and Thomas Luckmann. 1973. *The Structures of the Life-World.* Evanston, Ill.: Northwestern University Press.

————. 1989. *The Structures of the Life-World.* Vol. II. Evanston, Ill.: North-western University Press.

Schwartau, Winn. 1994. *Information Warfare: Chaos on the Electronic Super-highway.* New York: Thunder's Mouth Press.

Schwartz, John. 1995. "Privacy Program: An On-Line Weapon? Inventor May Face Indictment for Encryption Software Sent Abroad." *Washington Post,* 3 April, final edition: A1.

————. 1996. "Networkings: With E-Mail Privacy in Jeopardy, 'Remailer' Closes up Shop." *Washington Post,* 16 September, final edition, F19.

Schwichtenberg, Cathy. 1986. "Sensual Surfaces and Stylistic Excess: The Pleasure and Politics of *Miami Vice.*" *Journal of Communication Inquiry* 10, no. 3: 45–65.

Sclove, Richard E. 1995. *Democracy and Technology.* New York: Guilford Press.

Scott, Joan W. 1992. "'Experience.'" In *Feminists Theorize the Political,* edited by Judith Butler and Joan W. Scott. New York: Routledge.

Shapiro, Michael J. 1992. *Reading the Postmodern Polity: Political Theory as Textual Practice.* Minneapolis: University of Minnesota Press.

————. 1994. "Moral Geographies and the Ethics of Post-Sovereignty." *Public Culture* 6, no. 3: 479–502.

————. 1997. "Bowling Blind: Post Liberal Civil Society and the Worlds of Neo-Tocquevillean Social Theory." *Theory & Event* 1, no. 1. Retrieved 24 August 2000 from http://muse.jhu.edu/journals/theory_&_event/v001/1.1shapiro.html.

Shulman, George. 1983. "The Pastoral Idyll of *democracy.*" *democracy* 3, no. 4: 43–54.

Simons, David. 1997 (7 January). "Internet 'Appliances' on Upswing, IDC Says." *New York Times Syndicate.* Retrieved 7 January 1998 from http://nytsyn.com/live/Hard/007_010797_132237_29097.html.

Singapore Broadcasting Authority. 2000. "The Singapore Broadcasting Authority Act (Chapter 297): Internet Code of Practice." Retrieved 29 August 2000 from http://www.sba.gov.sg/work/sba/internet.nsf/pages/code.

Smith, Neil and Cindi Katz. 1993. "Grounding Metaphor: Towards a Spatialized Politics." In *Place and the Politics of Identity,* edited by Michael Keith and Steve Pile. London: Routledge.

Soja, Edward W. 1989. *Postmodern Geographies: The Reassertion of Space in Critical Social Theory.* London: Verso.

————. 1993. "Postmodern Geographies and the Critique of Historicism." In *Postmodern Contentions: Epochs, Politics, Space,* edited by John Paul Jones III, Wolfgang Natter, and Theodore R. Schatzki. New York: Guilford Press.

Spelman, Elizabeth. 1982. "Woman as Body: Ancient and Contemporary Views." *Feminist Studies* 8, no. 1: 109–31.

Spender, Dale. 1980. *Man Made Language.* London: Routledge.

———. 1995. *Nattering on the Net: Women, Power and Cyberspace.* North Melbourne: Spinifex Press.

Sterling, Bruce. 1993. *The Hacker Crackdown: Law and Disorder on the Electronic Frontier.* New York: Bantam.

———. 1994. "So, People, We Have a Fight on our Hands." *Wired* 2, no. 7: 71–74.

Stone, Allucquère Rosanne. 1993. "Will the Real Body Please Stand Up?: Boundary Stories about Virtual Cultures." In *Cyberspace: First Steps,* edited by Michael Benedikt. Cambridge: MIT Press.

———. 1996. *The War of Desire and Technology at the Close of the Mechanical Age.* Cambridge: MIT Press.

Stranahan, Paul. 1996. "Telecommunications Act of 1996." *Jones Telecommunications & Multimedia Encyclopedia.* Retrieved 24 August 2000 from http://www.digitalcentury.com/encyclo/update/telcom1.html.

Students for a Democratic Society (SDS). 1994. "The Port Huron Statement." Appendix in James Miller, *"Democracy is in the Streets": From Port Huron to the Siege of Chicago.* Cambridge: Harvard University Press. Also available online at http://hs1.hst.msu.edu/~hst306/documents/huron.html (retrieved 17 August 2000).

"Subcommander Marcos." 1992. *"Chiapas: el Sureste en dos vientos, una tormenta y una profecía."* Retrieved 5 August 2000 from http://spin.com.mx/~floresu/FZLN/archivo/ezln/1994/chiapas.htm. English translation: "Chiapas: The Southeast in Two Winds, A Storm and a Prophecy." Retrieved 5 August 2000 from http://www.ezln.org/SE-in-two-winds.html.

Sullivan, Erin. 1996. "Regulation of Internet Access in China." Retrieved 3 May 1996 from http://www.ta.doc.gov/aptp/china/NETREG.HTM.

Swartz, Jon. 2000 (17 November). "New Domain Name Suffixes Approved." *USA Today.* Retrieved 1 December 2001 from http://www.usatoday.com/life/cyber/tech/cti815.htm.

Swett, Charles. 1995. "Strategic Assessment: The Internet." Paper prepared for the Office of the Assistant Secretary of Defense for Special Operations and Low-Intensity Conflict (Policy Planning). Retrieved 24 August 2000 from http://www.fas.org/cp/swett.html.

Terzian, Philip. 1996. "Through the Global Sewer." *Washington Times,* 21 February, final edition, A19.

Thompson, John B. 1990. *Ideology and Modern Culture.* Stanford, Calif.: Stanford University Press.

Tomlinson, John. 1991. *Cultural Imperialism: A Critical Introduction.* Baltimore: Johns Hopkins University Press.

Triumph of the Nerds. 1996. PBS. WPBT, Miami. 12 June. Transcript retrieved 24 August 2000 from http://www.pbs.org/nerds/transcript.html (1 of 4).

Tuchman, Gaye, ed. 1974. *The TV Establishment: Programming for Power and Profit.* Englewood Cliffs, N.J.: Prentice-Hall.

Turkle, Sherry. 1984. *The Second Self: Computers and the Human Spirit.* New York: Simon & Schuster.

———. 1995. *Life on the Screen: Identity in the Age of the Internet.* New York: Simon & Schuster.

Turner, Bryan S. 1984. *The Body and Society: Explorations in Social Theory.* Oxford: Basil Blackwell.

———. 1992. "Outline of a Theory of Citizenship." In *Dimensions of Radical Democracy: Pluralism, Citizenship, Community,* edited by Chantal Mouffe. London: Verso.

———. 1997. "Citizenship Studies: A General Theory." *Citizenship Studies* 1, no. 1: 5–18.

Twomey, Patrick. 1996 (20 March). "Regulating the Internet: Scene Setting." *Student Human Rights Law Centre Newsletter* 1, no. 2. Retrieved 24 August 2000 from http://www.nott.ac.uk/~llzweb/hrlc/hrnews/march96/reg.htm.

Ubois, Jeff. 1995. "Ruling Class." Interview with Tony Rutkowski. *Internet World,* January, 60–65.

Ullman, Ellen. 1996. "Come In, CQ: The Body on the Wire." In *Wired Women: Gender and New Realities in Cyberspace,* edited by Lynn Cherny and Elizabeth Reba Weise. Seattle: Seal Press.

Uncapher, Keith. 1989. Electronic transcript of interview by Arthur L. Norberg, 10 July. In "Role of DARPA/IPTO in the Development of Computer Science Oral History Collection." Minneapolis: Charles Babbage Institute.

U.S. Census Bureau. 1997a. "Results of the 1996 Race and Ethnic Targeted Test." Retrieved 24 August 2000 from http://www.census.gov/population/www/documentation/twps0018/section-1.html.

———. 1997b. "Table 1. Households with Computers and Year of Purchase, by Presence of Children, Family Income, Education, and Age of Householder: October 1997." Retrieved 22 August 2000 from http://www.census.gov/population/socdemo/computer/report97/tab01.txt.

U.S. Department of Justice. 1994. "Attorney General Makes Key Escrow Encryption Announcements." February 4. Retrieved 29 August 2000 from http://www.eff.org/pub/Privacy/Key_escrow/Clipper/reno_key_escrow.announce.

———. 1996. Electronic transcript of press release from the office of Michael J. Yamaguchi, U.S. Attorney for the Northern District of California, announcing decision to decline prosecution in 1991 Usenet distribution of Phil Zimmermann's PGP encryption program. Retrieved 31 August 2000 from http://www.eff.org/pub/Legal/Cases/PGP_Zimmermann/usatty_pgp_011196. announce.

———. 1998 (29 April). 1997 Annual Foreign Intelligence Surveillance Act Report to Congress. Retrieved 2 December 2001 from http://www.usdoj.gov/04foia/readingrooms/97fisa_ltr.htm.

U.S. Department of State. 1996. Amendments to the International Traffic in Arms Regulations, 30 December. 61 Federal Register 251, 61 FR 68633. Retrieved 27 September 2000 from http://www.cdt.org/crypto/clipper311/961230_itar.txt.

U.S. Senate. 1996. *Telecommunications Act of 1996.* 104th Cong., 2d sess. Retrieved 29 August 2000 from ftp://ftp.loc.gov/pub/thomas/c104/s652.enr.txt

van Bakel, Rogier. 1996. "How Good People Helped Make a Bad Law." Retrieved 22 August 2000 from http://www.wired.com/wired/archive/4.02/digitel.html (1 of 10). Originally published in *Wired* 4, no. 2.

Van der Spiegel, Jan. 1997. "ENIAC-on-a-Chip." Retrieved 29 August 2000 from http://www.ee.upenn.edu/~jan/eniacproj.html.

Wakeman, Nick. 2001 (21 September). "IT Infrastructure Is Key to Homeland Defense." *Washington Technology.* Retrieved 19 November 2001 from http://www.washtech.com/news/govtit/12654-1.html.

Waldby, Catherine. 1996a. "Revenants: The Visible Human Project and the Digital Uncanny." Retrieved 29 August 2000 from http://wwwmcc.murdoch.edu.au/ReadingRoom/VID/Uncanny.html. Also published in *Body & Society* 3, no. 1 (March 1997): 1–16.

———. 1996b. "The Visible Human Project: Data into Flesh, Flesh into Data." Retrieved 29 August 2000 from http://wwwmcc.murdoch.edu.au/ReadingRoom/VID/wildbiol1.html.

Waller, Douglas. 1995. "Onward Cyber Soldiers." *Time* 146, no. 8, 21 August, 38–44.

Wark, McKenzie. 1993. "Lost in Space: Into the Digital Image Labyrinth." *Continuum: The Australian Journal of Media & Culture* 7, no. 1. Special Issue: Dependency/Space/Policy, edited by Brian Shoesmith and Ian Angus. Retrieved 29 August 2000 from http://wwwmcc.murdoch.edu.au/ReadingRoom/7.1/Wark.html.

Warner, Michael. 1993. "The Mass Public and the Mass Subject." In *Habermas and the Public Sphere,* edited by Craig Calhoun. Cambridge: MIT Press.

Weatherford, Jack. 1997. *The History of Money: From Sandstone to Cyberspace.* New York: Three Rivers Press.

Weik, Martin H. 1961. "The ENIAC Story." *Ordnance: The Journal of the American Ordnance Association* (January–February). Retrieved 29 August 2000 from http://ftp.arl.mil/~mike/comphist/eniac-story.html.

"What You Can Do." 1994. *Wired* 2, no. 4: 48–49.

Whitaker, Russell Earl. 1993. "Fight Communists with Cryptography." Includes "From Crossbows to Cryptography: Thwarting the State via Technology," speech by Chuck Hammill. Retrieved 29 August 2000 from http://www.eff.org/pub/Crypto/Crypto_misc/crossbows_to_cryptography.paper.

White, Keith. 1995. "The Killer App: *Wired* Magazine, Voice of the Corporate Revolution." *The Baffler* 6: 23–28.

White, Richard. 1994 (17 March). "An Invitation to a Debate: Encryption on the Electronic Frontier." Retrieved 3 April 1995 from *CompuServe* (Go: NCSA, Infosecurity, Forum, Library 6: Encryption, Filename: encryp).

White House. 1994a. "Fact Sheet: Public Encryption Management." 4 February. Retrieved 29 August 2000 from http://www.eff.org/pub/Privacy/Clipper/wh_clipper.factsheet.

———. 1994b. Statement of the press secretary announcing adoption of the Clipper standard, 4 February. Retrieved 29 August 2000 from http://www.eff.org/pub/Privacy/Clipper/wh_press_secy.statement.

———. 1996a. "Text of President Clinton's Executive Order Implementing Clipper 3.1.1," with related documents. Retrieved 27 September 2000 from http://www.cdt.org/crypto/clipper311/clipper311exo.html.

———. 1996b. "Vice President Announces Special Envoy for Cryptography." Retrieved 27 September 2000 from http://www.cdt.org/crypto/clipper311/961115_WH_pr.html.

Wilson, David L. 1994. "'Crackers': A Serious Threat." *The Chronicle of Higher Education,* 17 August: A23–24.

Winegrad, Dilys, and Atsushi Akera. 1996. "ENIAC at Fifty: A Short History of the Second American Revolution." Retrieved 29 August 2000 from http://www.upenn.edu/almanac/v42/n18/eniac.html. Originally published in *Almanac: The University of Pennsylvania's Journal of Record, Opinion and News* 42, no. 18 (30 January).

Wired. 1993. "Electronic Privacy—A Call to Action." Retrieved 31 August 2000 from http://www.eff.org/pub/Privacy/Clipper/wired_clipper.alert.

Wolf, Gary. 1996. "Steve Jobs: The Next Insanely Great Thing." Retrieved 29 August 2000 from http://www.wired.com/wired/archive/4.02/jobs.html (1 of 8). Originally published in *Wired* 4, no. 2.

Woolley, Benjamin. 1992. *Virtual Worlds: A Journey in Hype and Hyperreality.* Oxford: Blackwell Publishers.

Wright, Robert. 1995. "Hyperdemocracy! Washington Isn't Dangerously Dis-

connected from the People; the Trouble May Be It's Too Plugged In."
Retrieved 29 August 2000 from http://www.time.com/time/magazine/
archive/1995/950123/950123.cover.html. Originally published in *Time* 145,
no. 4, 23 January, 14ff.

Young, Iris Marion. 1995. "Polity and Group Difference: A Critique of the Ideal of
Universal Citizenship." In *Theorizing Citizenship,* edited by Ronald Beiner.
Albany: State University of New York Press.

Zakon, Robert H. (aka "Hobbes"). 2000 (1 July). "Hobbes' Internet Timeline
v5.1." Retrieved 29 August 2000 from http://www.isoc.org/zakon/Internet/
History/HIT.html.

Zimmermann, Philip. 1994a. Foreword to *Protect Your Privacy: The PGP User's
Guide,* by William Stallings. Reprinted in *Computer Underground Digest* 6,
no. 100 (27 November). Retrieved 29 August 2000 from http://
venus.soci.niu.edu/~cudigest/CUDS6/cud6.100.

———. 1994b (11 October). "PGP User's Guide, Volume I: Essential Topics."
2.6.2 Retrieved 29 August 2000 from ftp://ftp.pgpi.org/pub/pgp/2.x/doc/
pgpdoc1.txt.

Index

absolute space (Newtonian), 3, 6–7, 10, 11

accountability, 143, 156; in cyberspace, 128, 167; privacy and, 210; spatial, 134

ADSL (Asymmetric Digital Subscriber Lines): mass media aspects of, 184–85

agora: "electronic," xiv–xv; as ideal space of participatory democracy, xxiv

alias. *See* pseudonymity

analog/digital distinction: described, 84–85; relative to metaphor/metonymy, 232n.8

Anderson, Benedict, 108, 126

anonymity: of body as object, xx, 215n.6, 226n.27; countersurveillance and, 119, 171; ethics of, 117, 240–41n.11; as liberal privilege, 210; of monetary transactions, 193. *See also* pseudonymity

anonymous remailers, 117, 220n.21, 240n.10

apparatuses of security, 113, 141

apprehensible: defined, 136–37

Archimedean perspective (Arendt), 51–52; computers and, 114, 231n.5

Arendt, Hannah, xxvi, 36, 139, 165, 224n.15, 226n.28; body politics of, 47, 48–49, 55–60; on physical space, 54; quote of, 50, 53, 54, 55, 59; on speech and action, 47, 49, 69; technological determinism of, 60, 225n.24; on technology, 50, 52

ARPAnet, 89, 91

articulation, discursive, 11–13; of "the body," 57, 132, 135; defined, 218n.11; of spatial elements, 12

as-if simultaneity (Schutz), 32

Asymmetric Digital Subscriber Lines. *See* ADSL

Athenian democracy, xiii–xv; exclusions of, 47–48, 205–6, 224n.15

Bamford, James, 110

Baran, Paul, 88, 93, 232n.10

Barber, Benjamin, 36, 200, 256n.3; on electronic communications, 43–44

Barlow, John Perry, 147; on anarchy

National Security Agency (NSA), 110,
252n.31; role in U.S. encryption
debate, 166, 172; Web site of,
151–52
Negroponte, Nicholas, 84
neo-Luddite, xv, 225n.25
network space, 78; as here/there mix,
94. *See also* computer network
Neuromancer (Gibson): quote from,
xxii

obligatory point of passage (Latour):
heterotopia as, 21, 219n.16; survey
form as, 115–16, 239n.7
"Of Other Spaces" (Foucault): quote
from, 14–15
Oguibe, Olu, xxiii–xxiv, 26
"Operation Sundevil," 187, 240n.9,
254n.45
ordering: process of, 19; spatial, 18,
217n.9
Order of Things, The (Foucault), 12;
quote from, 16, 19
other spaces. *See* heterotopia

panopticon, 239n.5, 239n.6; described, xviii; Super-, 111, 114–15;
and wiring prisons, 111, 238n.3
performativity (Butler), 131; of
"cyberspace," 252n.32; embodiment and, 244n.30; of "United
States," 168–69; virtual, 137
personal computer (PC): embodied
experience of, 98, 132–33; history
of, 95–96; and institutional/
individual mix, 99; as security apparatus, 113. *See also* computers
personal security, 142; democracy as
threat to, 195–96, 221–22n.5; en-

cryption and, 159; in liberal state
discourses, 180; negative liberty of,
160
PGP. *See* Pretty Good Privacy
*Phenomenology of the Social World,
The* (Schutz): quote from, 30–31
physical: defined, 24
physiocentrism (Luke), 109; defined,
83
policing, by states, 133–34, 161;
Internet's challenge of, 167, 176;
privacy concerns and, 170; redefined, 163, 169
polis, 47; Arendt's description of,
54–55, 59; size of, 52
politics of concealment, 139, 174–75,
193, 206; by hackers, 123
"Port Huron Statement, The." *See*
Students for a Democratic Society
Poster, Mark: on computer as identity
referent, 120; on "participatory
surveillance," 112; on reductivism
of data, 113; on Superpanopticon,
111, 114–15
postmodernity, 18
power: as leverage, 51–52, 114; disciplinary, 112, 208
presence: metaphysics of, 135; virtual,
129, 149
Pretty Good Privacy (PGP), 144, 159.
See also Zimmermann, Philip
privacy, 210; as liberal edge against
democracy, 195–96; statements on
the Internet, 151; in U.S. encryption policy, 157–61, 170–73, 192,
203
private "peering" agreements
(Internet), 93
"problem of scale, the": defined,

Diana Saco is an interdisciplinary cultural, political, and international relations theorist. She has published in *European Journal of International Relations, Millennium,* and in edited volumes of both media and security studies. Her exploration of online fandoms led to her interest in cyberspace as a democratic space for culture-debating publics. Now based in Florida, she works as a computer network administrator for a Fort Lauderdale law firm and continues her study of the Internet as fan fiction writer and as independent researcher of politics and culture in the digital age.